J.K. LASSER'S™

1001 DEDUCTIONS
AND TAX BREAKS
2026

J.K. LASSER'S™

1001 DEBUCTIONS AND TAX BREAKS 2026

Your Complete Guide to Everything Deductible

Barbara Weltman

WILEY

Library of Congress Cataloging-in-Publication Data is Available:

ISBN 9781394358700 (Paperback)
ISBN 9781394358724 (ePDF)
ISBN 9781394358717 (ePUB)

Cover Design: Wiley
SKY10128869_101725

Contents

Introduction

The word "taxes" makes most people groan. There are good reasons for this response: First of all, the cost of paying your taxes annually can be a financial burden. You may feel taken to the cleaners every time you view your paycheck *after* withholding for federal income taxes (not to mention state income taxes as well as Social Security and Medicare taxes). And taxes are time consuming—to gather information, meet with a tax professional if you use one, or prepare and submit your own returns.

Second, it can cost you money to get your taxes done. The IRS says that about 55% of taxpayers use paid preparers for their returns. Of course, because more than 90% of individual income tax returns are completed by computer (through a paid preparer, with software, or through FreeFile or Direct File), knowing the places where deductions and credits are entered on the return is not critical to you; it's effectively done automatically.

Third, the tax law is very complicated and changing all the time. The One Big Beautiful Bill Act (OBBBA), enacted in 2025, made many changes, some of which apply for 2025 and some begin in 2026 or later. And some legislation from earlier years takes effect in 2025.

Fourth, you have to know what the tax rules are and can't claim ignorance to avoid taxes and penalties. Even if you use a tax professional or tax preparation software to prepare your return, you remain responsible for your taxes. The Tax Court has noted that using software is not an automatic excuse to avoid underpayment penalties.

How can you combat the feeling of dread when it comes to taxes? It helps to know that the tax law is peppered with many, many tax breaks to which you may be entitled. These breaks allow you to *not* report certain economic benefits you enjoy or to subtract certain expenses from your income or even directly from your tax bill. As the famous jurist Judge Learned Hand once stated (in the 1934 case of *Helvering v. Gregory* in the Court of Appeals for the Second Circuit):

> **Anyone may arrange his affairs so that his taxes shall be as low as possible; he is not bound to choose that pattern which best pays the Treasury. There is not even a patriotic duty to increase one's taxes. Over and over again the Courts have said that there is nothing sinister in so arranging affairs as to keep taxes as low as possible. Everyone does it, rich and poor alike, and all do right, for nobody owes any public duty to pay more than the law demands.**

So get your tax affairs in order and legally reduce what you pay each year to Uncle Sam!

In getting a handle on how to do this by taking advantage of every tax break you may be entitled to without running afoul of the Internal Revenue Service (IRS), there are some simple rules to keep in mind. They include:

- You must report all of your income unless a specific law allows you to exclude or exempt it (so that it is never taxed) or defer it (so that it is taxed at a later time).

- You can claim deductions only when and to the extent the law allows. Deductions are referred to as a "matter of legislative grace"; Congress doesn't have to create them and does so only for some purpose (for example, to encourage economic activity or to balance some perceived inequity in the tax law).

- Tax credits are worth more than tax deductions. A credit reduces your tax payment on a dollar-for-dollar basis; a $1,000 credit saves you $1,000 in taxes. A deduction is worth only as much as the top tax bracket you are in. Suppose you are in the 24% tax bracket, which means this is the highest rate you pay on at least some of your income. If you have a $1,000 deduction, it is worth $240 (24% of $1,000) because it saves you $240 in taxes you would otherwise have to pay.

- In a number of cases, different deduction rules apply to the alternative minimum tax (AMT), a shadow tax system that ensures you pay at least some tax if your regular income tax is lower than it would have been without certain deductions.

Whether you prepare your return by hand, use computer software or an online solution, or rely on a professional, this book is designed to tell you how to get every tax edge you're entitled to. Knowing what to look out for will help you plan ahead and organize your activities in such a way that you'll share less of your hard-earned money with the government.

Tax-Favored Items

There are 5 types of tax-advantaged items receiving preferential or favorable treatment under the tax law:

1. *Tax-free income*—income you can receive without any current or future tax concerns. Tax-free income may be in the form of exclusions or exemptions from tax. In many cases, tax-free items do not even have to be reported in any way on your return.

2. *Capital gains*—profits on the sale or exchange of property held for more than one year (long-term). Long-term capital gains are subject to lower tax rates than the rates on other income, such as salary and interest income, and may even be tax free in some cases. Ordinary dividends on stocks and capital gain distributions from stock mutual funds are taxed at the same low rates as long-term capital gains.

3. *Tax-deferred income*—income that isn't currently taxed. Since the income builds up without any reduction for current tax, you may accumulate more over time. But at some point the income becomes taxable.

4. *Deductions*—items you can subtract from your income to reduce the amount of income subject to tax. There are 2 classes of deductions: those "above the line," which are subtracted directly from gross income, and those "below the line," which can be claimed only if you itemize deductions instead of claiming the standard deduction (explained later). And there are some deductions subtracted from adjusted gross income that may be claimed whether or not you itemize other personal deductions.

5. *Credits*—items you can use to offset your tax on a dollar-for-dollar basis. There are 2 types of tax credits: one that can be used only to offset tax liability (called a "nonrefundable" credit) and one that can be claimed even if it exceeds tax liability and you receive a refund (called a "refundable" credit). Usually you must complete a special tax form for each credit you claim. For 2025, the premium tax credit can be enjoyed on an advanced basis by using it to reduce health insurance premiums for coverage through a government marketplace. And credits for new or used electric vehicles acquired by September 30, 2025, could have been sold to the dealer, enabling the buyer to get the benefit of the credit up front.

This book focuses on different types of tax-favored items: exclusions (tax-free income), above-the-line deductions that don't require itemizing, itemized deductions, tax credits, and other benefits, such as subtractions that reduce income. At the end of this Introduction you'll see symbols used to easily identify the type of benefit being explained.

Limits on Qualifying for Tax-Favored Items

In many cases, eligibility for tax benefits or the extent to which they may be claimed depends on adjusted gross income (AGI) or modified adjusted gross income (MAGI).

Adjusted gross income is gross income (all the income you are required to report) minus certain deductions (called "adjustments to gross income" on Schedule 1 of Form 1040 or 1040-SR). Adjustments or subtractions you can make to your gross income to arrive at your adjusted gross income are limited in 2025 to the following items:

- Alimony payments for pre-2019 divorces and separation agreements
- Archer Medical Savings Accounts (MSAs) (for accounts set up prior to 2008)
- Attorneys' fees and costs for certain discrimination claims or IRS whistle-blower claims
- Business expenses of self-employed individuals
- Capital loss deductions of up to $3,000
- Educator expenses up to $300
- Fee-basis government officials' expenses
- Foreign housing expenses
- Forfeiture-of-interest penalties because of early withdrawals from certificates of deposit (CDs)
- Health Savings Account (HSA) contributions
- Individual Retirement Account (IRA) deductions
- Jury duty pay turned over to your employer
- Legal fees for unlawful discrimination claims
- Moving expenses of members of the military
- Net operating losses (NOLs)
- Olympic and Paralympic medals and prize money that are nontaxable
- One-half of self-employment tax
- Performing artist's qualifying expenses
- Qualified retirement plan contributions for self-employed individuals

- Rent and royalty expenses
- Repayment of supplemental unemployment benefits required because of the receipt of trade readjustment allowances
- Self-employed health insurance deduction
- Simplified employee pension (SEP) or savings incentive match plan for employees (SIMPLE) contributions for self-employed individuals
- Student loan interest deduction up to $2,500
- Travel expenses to attend National Guard or military reserve meetings more than 100 miles from home

Figuring AGI may sound complicated, but in reality it's merely a number taken from a line on your tax return. For example, AGI is the figure you enter on line 11a of the 2025 Form 1040 or 1040-SR.

AGI does not take into account the 4 new deductions for 2025 (figured on Schedule 1-A):

- Deduction for interest on car loans up to $10,000
- No-tax-on-tips deduction up to $25,000
- Overtime pay deduction up to $12,500 ($25,000 for joint filers)
- Senior bonus deduction up to $6,000

These deductions, along with the standard deduction or itemized deductions and the qualified business income deduction (below) are subtracted from AGI to arrive at taxable income.

Modified adjusted gross income is AGI increased by certain items that are excludable from income and/or certain adjustments to gross income. *Which* items are added back varies for different tax breaks. For example, the MAGI limit on eligibility to claim the student loan interest deduction is AGI (disregarding the student loan interest deduction) increased by the exclusion for foreign earned income and certain other foreign income or expenses. All of these items are explained in this book.

Household income is a term in tax law used to determine eligibility for the premium tax credit to help pay for health coverage purchased through a government marketplace. Household income is explained further in this book in connection with these tax rules.

Qualified business income. If you are an owner in a pass-through entity—a sole proprietorship, limited liability company, partners, or S corporation—you may be eligible for a qualified business income (QBI) deduction. QBI for purposes of this personal deduction is explained further in Chapter 14.

Taxable income. This is the amount of income remaining after subtracting deductions. Taxable income is the amount on which taxes are figured. Taxable income is also the threshold used for determining the QBI deduction explained in Chapter 14.

Alternative minimum taxable income (AMTI) is the income on which the alternative minimum tax is figured. It is essentially taxable income increased by tax preferences and increased or decreased by certain adjustment items. The AMT and the exemption subtracted from AMTI is explained in Chapter 15.

Standard Deduction versus Itemized Deductions

Every taxpayer, other than a dependent of another taxpayer, is entitled to the basic standard deduction if they choose not to itemize personal deductions. This is a subtraction from your income, and the amount you claim is based on your filing status. Table I.1 shows the standard deduction amounts for 2025. Almost 90% of all filers used the standard deduction.

Additional standard deduction amounts. In addition to the basic standard deduction, certain taxpayers can increase these amounts. An additional standard deduction amount applies to those age 65 and older and for blindness. For 2025, the basic additional amount is $2,000 for individuals who are not married and are not a surviving spouse and $1,600 for those who are married or a surviving spouse.

Example

In 2025, you are single, age 68, and *not* blind. Your modified adjusted gross income is $70,000. Your standard deduction is $17,750 ($15,750 + $2,000).

Instead of claiming the standard deduction and any additional standard deduction amount if applicable, you can opt to list certain deductions separately (i.e., *itemize* them). While only about 10% of individuals itemize, this

TABLE I.1 Standard Deduction Amounts for 2025

Filing Status	Standard Deduction
Married filing jointly	$ 31,500
Head of household	23,675
Single (unmarried)	15,750
Surviving spouse	31,500
Married filing separately	15,750

still means millions of individual taxpayers don't use the standard deduction and need to know about itemized deductions. Itemized deductions include:

- Medical expenses
- Taxes
- Interest payments
- Gifts to charity
- Casualty and theft losses of personal-use property in federally-declared disaster areas
- Casualty and theft losses related to income-producing property
- Gambling losses
- Estate tax payments on income in respect of decedents

Generally, claim the standard deduction when it is greater than the total of your itemized deductions. But it may save overall taxes to itemize, even when total deductions are less than the standard deduction, if you are subject to the alternative minimum tax (AMT). *The reason:* The standard deduction cannot be used to reduce income subject to the AMT, but certain itemized deductions can.

Looking Ahead

Starting 2026, individuals in the top tax bracket of 37% face an additional reduction of their total itemized deductions. Each dollar of itemized deduction is allowed at a maximum of 35%, not the 37% tax rate. Technically, this means reducing itemized deductions by 2/37 of the lesser of total itemized deductions or the amount by which taxable income exceeds the 37% bracket threshold.

If a married couple files separate returns and one spouse itemizes deductions, the other must also itemize and cannot claim a standard deduction.

Planning pointer: Because you may not know until it comes time to file your return whether it pays to itemize or claim the standard deduction, it's advisable to retain receipts and other required documentation for itemized expenses . . . just in case.

Impact of Deductions on Your Chances of Being Audited

Did you know that the IRS collects statistics from taxpayers to create profiles of average deductions? If you claim more than the average for your income range, the IRS's computer *may* select your return for further examination. But audit rates have been low for several years. And given the departure of many IRS employees as a result of DOGE, it doesn't look like audit rates will spike any time soon.

Tax experts agree that you should claim every deduction you are entitled to. Just make sure to have the necessary proof of your eligibility and other records you are required to keep in case your return is examined.

How to Use This Book

This book is tied to Form 1040, *U.S. Income Tax Return for Individuals*. It can also be used for Form 1040-SR, *Income Tax Return for Seniors;* a form specifically for seniors age 65 and older.

The chapters in this book are organized by subject matter so you can browse through them to find the subjects that apply to you or those in which you have an interest.

Each tax benefit is denoted by an icon to help you spot the type of benefit involved:

 Exclusion

 Above-the-line deduction

 Itemized deduction (a deduction taken *after* figuring adjusted gross income)

 Credit

 Other benefit (e.g., tax deferral or a subtraction other than an above-the-line or itemized deduction that reduces income)

There are references to free IRS publications on a variety of tax topics that you can download from the IRS website (www.irs.gov) or obtain free of charge by calling 800-829-1040.

You'll also see key dates for various actions, such as filing returns, contributing to retirement plans, and reporting foreign financial accounts to the U.S. Treasury. For example, the deadline for filing 2025 federal income tax returns is April 15, 2026.

In the appendices, you'll find a listing of items that can be adjusted each year to reflect cost-of-living changes so you can plan ahead, as well as a checklist of items that are tax free, and a checklist of items that are not deductible.

Throughout the book you will see alerts to possible changes to come. Remember: the tax law is continually changing. For a *free* update on tax developments, look for the Supplement to this book in February 2026, by going to www.jklasser .com, as well as to my website, www.BigIdeasForSmallBusiness.com.

You and Your Family

The nature of families is changing, and taxes have specific rules for them. Do the old clichés still ring true? Can two still live as cheaply as one? Are things really cheaper by the dozen? For tax purposes, there may be a penalty or bonus for being married versus single, depending on the income of each spouse and the particular tax break involved. And there are certain tax breaks for having a family.

This chapter explains family-related tax benefits, such as tax credits related to your children, and the consequences of marital dissolutions. For more information on these topics, see IRS Publication 501, *Dependents, Standard Deduction, and Filing Information*; IRS Publication 503, *Child and Dependent Care Expenses*; IRS Publication 504, *Divorced or Separated Individuals*; and IRS Publication 596, *Earned Income Credit*.

Marital Status

Whether you are married or single has a significant impact on your taxes. In some cases, being married results in a "marriage bonus," which means effectively averaging taxes when one spouse works and the other does not or has only modest income. In other cases, being married results in a "marriage penalty," which means that two working spouses earning about the same likely will pay higher total tax than if they were single. For some tax rules, a married couple has the identical tax break as a single individual, such as the $3,000 capital loss deduction against ordinary income, the adoption credit limit ($17,280 in 2025), and the $40,000 limit on itemizing state and local taxes, which is a distinct disadvantage for those who are married. For some tax rules, a married couple has double the tax break for singles, such as the ordinary loss deduction for so-called Section 1244 stock, so marital status makes no difference here.

There are a number of filing statuses that determine eligibility for various tax breaks:

- Married filing jointly (MFJ)
- Married filing separately (MFS)
- Head of household (HOH)
- Single
- Qualifying surviving spouse with a dependent child (QSS)

You need to know which term applies to you. The terms are not further defined here and often cause confusion, so check IRS Publication 501 if you are unsure. Under federal tax law, the terms "husband," "wife," and "spouse" are gender neutral. The term "husband and wife" means two individuals lawfully married to each other. Those in a civil union or domestic partnership are not married for federal income tax purposes.

Bonus Deduction for Seniors

If you are age 65 or older, you may can claim a special deduction of up to $6,000. The deduction can be taken whether or not you itemize other deductions.

Income limit. The deduction applies only if modified adjusted gross income does not exceed a set amount: $75,000 for singles and $150,000 for joint filers. The $6,000 extra additional standard deduction amount phases out for singles with MAGI over $75,000 and is fully phased out at $175,000. For joint filers, the phase-out range is $150,000 to $250,000. The $6,000 deduction is reduced by 6% for each one dollar over the initial threshold.

Example

You are single, age 68, with modified adjusted gross income of $85,000 ($10,000 over the initial MAGI threshold). The $6,000 deduction is reduced by $600 (6% of $10,000), so the bonus deduction is $5,400.

Where to Claim the Deduction

The deduction is claimed on Schedule 1-A of Form 1040 or 1040-SR.

Dependents

While the exemption for dependents has been eliminated, the concept continues to apply for various purposes. For example, for purposes of a child tax credit that may be claimed for a qualifying child or a dependent who is not a qualifying child, the concept of dependents continues to apply. The definition of dependent varies for certain purposes and is explained in each relevant tax break in this book. For example, the amount of income for a qualifying relative taken into account in determining a dependent for purposes of head of household status and some other tax breaks in 2025 is $5,200.

Qualifying Child

The following is a brief explanation of a qualifying child and a qualifying relative (someone who is not a qualifying child):

A qualifying child must meet all of the following conditions:

- *Relationship test:* The child must be your son or daughter (natural, adopted, step, and in some cases foster) or a descendant of your sibling (e.g., niece or nephew).
- *Age test:* The child must be younger than you and either younger than 19 years old, be a "student" younger than 24 years old as of the end of the calendar year, or any age but permanently and totally disabled.
- *Residency test:* The child must live with you in the United States for more than half the year (special rules for noncustodial parents are explained later).
- *Joint return test:* The child cannot file a joint return unless doing so only to claim a tax refund.
- *Support test:* The child does not provide more than half of his or her own support.

Multiple people claiming the child as a dependent. Where one parent has physical custody of the child, he or she can waive treating the child as a dependent to permit the noncustodial parent to do so. The waiver (annually or permanently) is made on Form 8332, *Release/Revocation of Release of Claim to Exemption for Child by Custodial Parent*. The form applies to some benefits (e.g., child tax credit) but not for other benefits (e.g., earned income tax credit, dependent care credit, head of household status).

Where 2 people are eligible to treat the child as a dependent, a "tie breaker rule" comes into play. Generally, the person with greater physical custody (determined by counting the nights that the child spends with each person) is determinative. When there's an even split, other rules are used to decide which person can treat the child as a dependent.

Qualifying Relative

This is a person who is not a qualifying child and who meets all of the following conditions:

- *Relationship test.* The person must be either related to you in a stated way (e.g., a child too old to be a qualifying child, grandchild, parent, certain in-laws, aunt, uncle, niece, or nephew) or a member of your household.
- *Support test.* You must provide more than half of the person's support for the year.
- *Gross income test.* The person must have a gross income below a set amount ($5,200 in 2025).

Child Tax Credit

The U.S. Department of Agriculture estimates that it costs a middle-class family over $233,610 to raise a child born in 2015 to age 18 (there are no newer statistics), but if you factor in inflation, the cost becomes nearly $309,180 today). In recognition of this cost, the tax law allows you to claim a tax credit.

Benefit ⊕

You may claim a tax credit of up to $2,200 for each qualifying child under the age of 17. You may claim a $500 credit for a qualifying dependent (a person who is not a qualifying child). If the credit for a qualifying child that you are entitled to claim is more than your tax liability, you may be entitled to a refund under certain conditions.

Generally, the credit up to $1,700 per qualifying child is refundable for 2025. This refundable credit usually is allowed to the extent of 15% of earned income over $2,500.

If you have 3 or more children for whom you are claiming the credit, you are entitled to an additional child tax credit. In reality, the additional child tax credit is merely a larger refund of the credit you are ordinarily entitled to. There are 2 ways to figure your refundable amount (the additional child tax credit) and you can opt for the method that results in the larger refund:

1. 15% of earned income over $2,500 up to the lesser of this calculation or the unused child tax credit of $1,700 per qualifying child
2. Excess of your Social Security and Medicare taxes (plus the so-called employer share of self-employment taxes, if any) over your earned income credit for the year (the earned income credit is explained in the next main section)

Conditions

To claim the child tax credit, you must meet 3 conditions:

1. You must have a qualifying child or a qualifying dependent.
2. Your income must be below a set amount.
3. You must include a Social Security number for each qualifying child as well as one for yourself.

QUALIFYING CHILD

You can claim the $2,200 credit only for a "qualifying child." There are 5 tests for a qualifying child and you must meet all of them. Here are the 5 requirements for a qualifying child:

1. *Age test.* The child must be under age 17 by the end of the year. This age limit applies even if a child is disabled (but an older child may be a qualifying dependent for purposes of a $500 credit, as explained later).
2. *Residence test.* The child must have the same principal residence as you for more than half the tax year. There are some exceptions in certain cases for a child of divorced or separated parents, a kidnapped child, temporary absences, and for a child who is born or dies during the year.
3. *Support test.* The child does not provide more than half of his or her support.
4. *Social Security number.* No refundable or nonrefundable credit can be issued unless the child has a Social Security number. The Social Security number must be issued on or before the due date of your return. A Social Security card that is labeled "not valid for employment" (i.e., it is only good for purposes of receiving federal benefits, such as Medicaid) is not treated as a valid Social Security number for purposes of the child tax credit. You must also have a Social Security number. If you file jointly, one spouse must have a Social Security number.
5. *Nationality.* The child must be a U.S. citizen or national, or a resident of the U.S. The person can't be a resident of Canada or Mexico.

QUALIFYING DEPENDENT

You can claim the $500 nonrefundable child tax credit for a qualifying dependent, provided you have a Social Security number of that person. A "qualifying dependent" is a person who is not a qualifying child and who is viewed as a dependent. More specifically, a dependent is a qualifying relative. There are 5 tests for being a qualifying relative, all of which must be met:

1. *Relationship test.* The person must be your child (including adopted or step); your grandchild or great-grandchild; in-law (son, daughter, father, mother, brother, or sister); parent or stepparent; sibling (including step and half); and aunt, uncle, niece, or nephew if related by blood.

2. *Gross income test.* For 2025, this means having gross income exceeding $5,200.

3. *Support test.* You must provide more than half of the person's support for the year.

4. *Qualifying child test.* The person cannot be a qualifying child for you or any other taxpayer.

5. *Residency test.* The qualifying dependent must be a U.S. citizen, national, or residence of the United States. The person can't be a resident of Canada or Mexico.

MAGI LIMIT

You must have modified adjusted gross income (MAGI) below a set amount. The credit you are otherwise entitled to claim is reduced or eliminated if your MAGI exceeds a set amount. MAGI for purposes of the child tax credit means AGI increased by the foreign earned income exclusion, the foreign housing exclusion or deduction, or the possession exclusion for American Samoa residents.

The credit amount is reduced by $50 for each $1,000 of MAGI or a fraction thereof over the MAGI limit for your filing status. The phaseout begins if MAGI exceeds the limits found in Table 1.1.

Example

In 2025, you are a head of household with 2 qualifying children. You are single and your MAGI is $210,000. Your credit amount of $4,000 ($2,000 × 2) is reduced by $500 ($210,000 − $200,000 = $10,000 excess MAGI ÷ [$1,000 × $50]). Your credit is $3,900 ($4,400 − $500).

TABLE 1.1 Phaseout of Child Tax Credit over MAGI Limits in 2025

Filing Status	MAGI Limit
Married filing jointly	$400,000
Other filing status	200,000

REFUNDABLE CREDIT

If the credit you are entitled to claim is more than your tax liability, you can receive the excess amount as a "refund." It's called the additional child tax credit (ACTC), even though it's only a portion of the regular child tax credit. The refund is limited to 15% of your taxable earned income (such as wages, salary, tips, commissions, bonuses, and net earnings from self-employment) over $2,500, for a maximum refundable amount of $1,700.

Planning Tips

The child tax credit and the credit for other dependents should be factored into income tax withholding from paychecks to enjoy the tax savings throughout the year. If you know you will become entitled to claim the credit (e.g., you expect the birth of a child), you may wish to adjust your withholding so that you don't have too much income tax withheld from your paycheck. Increase your withholding so that less income tax is withheld from your pay by filing a new Form W-4, *Employee's Withholding Certificate*, with your employer. There is a Tax Withholding Estimator at https://www.irs.gov/individuals/tax-withholding-estimator to help you complete Form W-4.

If you can't claim a credit for a qualifying child because the child doesn't have a valid Social Security number, you may be able to claim the credit for a qualifying dependent. For example, if there is another taxpayer identification number (e.g., Adoption Taxpayer Identification Number, or ATIN), you may be eligible for the $500 credit.

In figuring estimated taxes for 2026, keep in mind that the credit limit is increased for inflation. Check the Supplement for details.

Pitfalls

If you claim the foreign earned income exclusion to exclude income earned abroad up to the annual dollar limit ($130,000 in 2025), you cannot receive the refundable additional child tax credit.

For 2025 returns filed in 2026, the IRS is not permitted to issue tax refunds for the refundable child tax credit before mid-February 2026. As a result, refunds usually aren't received until the third or fourth week in February, even for returns submitted in January 2026.

Where to Claim the Credit

On page 1 of Form 1040 or 1040-SR, enter dependents for whom you are claiming a child tax credit or credit for other dependents, along with their Social Security numbers and relationship to you. The additional child tax credit is figured on Schedule 8812 of Form 1040 or 1040-SR. The nonrefundable child tax credit or the credit for other dependents is entered on line 19 of the return. The additional child tax credit is entered on line 28 of the return.

Earned Income Credit

Low-income taxpayers are encouraged to work and are rewarded for doing so by means of a special tax credit, called the earned income credit. The earned income credit is the second-largest program, after Medicaid, that provides assistance to low-income people. The amount of the credit varies with income, filing status, and the number of dependents, if any. The credit may be viewed as a "negative income tax" because it can be paid to taxpayers even if it exceeds their tax liability.

Benefit ✚

If you are a working taxpayer with low or moderate income, you may qualify for a special tax credit of up to $8,046 in 2025. The amount of the credit depends on several factors, including your adjusted gross income, earned income, and the number of qualifying children. Table 1.2 shows the maximum credit you may claim based on the number of your qualifying children, if any.

The credit is "refundable" because it can be received in excess of the tax owed.

Looking Ahead

Beginning in 2026 there is an extra earned income credit for Purple Heart recipients who lose Social Security disability benefits upon returning to work. The extra credit is equal to the amount of lost benefits for one year. It's a one-time benefit.

Starting in 2028, there is a new pre-certification process for each qualifying child in order to claim the credit. This will have to be done before the credit is claimed on the tax return. The IRS is going to set up a monitoring system to ensure that duplicate credit claims aren't being made (that 2 or more taxpayers aren't claiming a credit with respect to the same child).

TABLE 1.2 Maximum Earned Income Credit for 2025

Number of Qualifying Children	Maximum Earned Income Credit
No qualifying child	$ 639
1 qualifying child	4,328
2 qualifying children	7,152
3 or more qualifying children	8,046

Conditions

To be eligible for the credit, you must have earned income from being an employee or a self-employed individual. The amount of the credit you are entitled to claim depends on several factors.

QUALIFYING CHILDREN

You may claim the credit even if you have no qualifying child. But you are entitled to a larger credit if you have one qualifying child and a still larger credit for 2 or more qualifying children.

To be a qualifying child, the child must:

- Be a qualifying child as defined earlier in the chapter under the child tax credit
- Live in your U.S. household for more than half the year
- Qualify as your dependent if the child is married at the end of the year
- Be a U.S. citizen or resident (or a nonresident who is married to a U.S. citizen and elects to have all worldwide income subject to U.S. tax)

If you do not have a qualifying child, you must be at least age 25 but under age 65.

EARNED INCOME

Earned income includes wages, salary, tips, commissions, jury duty pay, union strike benefits, certain disability pensions, U.S. military basic quarters and subsistence allowances, and net earnings from self-employment (profit from your self-employment activities). Military personnel can elect to treat tax-free combat pay as earned income for purposes of the earned income credit.

Nontaxable employee compensation, such as tax-free fringe benefits or salary deferrals—for example, contributions to company 401(k) plans—is not treated as earned income.

Earned income does not include pensions and retirement plan distributions, long-term disability and military disability pensions, welfare, Social Security benefits (for retirement or disability), and unemployment benefits.

To qualify for the maximum credit, you must have earned income at or above a set amount. Table 1.3 shows the earned income you need to obtain the top credit (depending on the number of your qualifying children, if any).

ADJUSTED GROSS INCOME

If your adjusted gross income is too high, the credit is reduced or eliminated. Table 1.4 shows the AGI phaseout range for the earned income credit. This depends not only on the number of qualifying children, if any, but also on your filing status, as shown in the table.

JOINT RETURN

If you are married, you usually must file a joint return with your spouse in order to claim an earned income credit. This requirement is waived if your spouse did not live in your household for the last 6 months of the year or you have a decree, instrument, or written agreement of separation and did not live with a spouse by the end of the year. In this case, assuming you paid the household expenses in which a qualifying child lived for the full year, you qualify as single for purposes of the earned income credit (using "other taxpayers" limits on AGI).

Example

You are married and file a joint return. You and your spouse have 1 qualifying child. In 2025, if your AGI is less than $30,470, your earned income credit is *not* subject to any phaseout. If your AGI is $57,554 or higher, you cannot claim *any* earned income credit; it is completely phased out. If your AGI is between these amounts (within the phaseout range), you may claim a reduced credit.

TABLE 1.3 Earned Income Needed for Top Credit in 2025

Number of Qualifying Children	Earned Income Needed for Top Credit
No qualifying child	$ 8,490
1 qualifying child	12,730
2 or more qualifying children	17,880

TABLE 1.4 AGI Phaseout Range for the Earned Income Credit in 2025

Number of Qualifying Children	Married Filing Jointly	Other Taxpayers
No qualifying child	$17,730–26,214	$10,620–19,104
1 qualifying child	$30,470–57,554	$23,250–50,434
2 qualifying children	$30,470–64,430	$23,350–57,310
3 or more qualifying children	$30,470–68,675	$23,350–61,555

CHILDLESS INDIVIDUALS

The minimum age for claiming the earned income credit usually is 19. The minimum age for a full-time student is 24; it's 18 for a former foster child or homeless youth. The maximum age is 65.

If you have a qualifying child who lacks a Social Security number, you may claim the earned income tax credit as if you were childless.

Planning Tips

The credit is based on a set percentage of earned income. The good news is that you don't have to compute the credit. You merely look at an IRS Earned Income Credit Table, which accompanies the instructions for your return. If your return is prepared by computer, the computation is automatic based on the information—your filing status, AGI, earned income, number, if any, of qualifying children—you input.

You can have the IRS figure your credit for you (you don't even have to look it up in the table). To do this, just complete your return up to the earned income credit line and put "EIC" on the dotted line next to it. If you have a qualifying child, complete and attach Schedule EIC to the return. Also attach Form 8862, *Information to Claim Earned Income Credit after Disallowance*, if you are required to do so as explained next.

If your child does not qualify as your dependent because of the tie-breaker rule (discussed earlier in this chapter), you may claim the earned income credit with no qualifying child. For example, a grandmother has a home in which her daughter and the baby (granddaughter) live. Under the tie-breaker rule, while the baby could be a qualifying child of the grandmother and mother, she is the daughter's qualifying child. The grandmother can claim the earned income tax credit with no qualifying child, assuming all other requirements for the credit are met. Alternatively, if the daughter foregoes the dependency exemption, the grandmother can claim the grandchild as her dependent and the earned income tax credit, assuming that her AGI exceeds the daughter's AGI. In this instance, the daughter could claim the earned income tax credit with no qualifying child, assuming all other requirements for the credit are met.

Pitfalls

You lose eligibility for the credit if you have unearned income over $11,950 in 2025 from dividends, interest (both taxable and tax free), net rent or royalty income, net capital gains, or net passive income that is not self-employment income.

You lose out on the opportunity to claim the credit in future years if you negligently or fraudulently claim it on your return. (If you use a paid preparer, he or she is required to perform to diligence before allowing you to claim the earned income credit.) You are banned for 2 years from claiming the earned income credit if your claim was reckless or in disregard of the tax rules. You lose out for 10 years if your claim was fraudulent. If you become ineligible because of negligence or fraud, the IRS issues a deficiency notice. You may counter the IRS's charge by filing Form 8862, *Information to Claim Earned Income Credit after Disallowance*, to show you are eligible. If the IRS accepts your position and recertifies eligibility, you don't have to file this form again (unless you again become ineligible).

For 2025 returns filed in 2026, the IRS is not permitted to issue tax refunds for the refundable earned income tax credit before February 15, 2026. As a result, refunds usually aren't received until the third or fourth week in February, even for returns filed in January 2026.

Where to Claim the Earned Income Credit

You claim the earned income credit on line 27 of Form 1040 or 1040-SR.

Dependent Care Expenses

Many taxpayers must pay for the care of a child in order to work. According to the World Population Review, the cost of childcare in 2025 for an infant or toddler in the U.S. is nearly $15,000 at a center. The tax law provides a limited tax credit for such costs, technically called the child and dependent care credit, but more commonly referred to as the dependent care credit. The amount of the credit you may claim depends on your income. It may be as much as 35% of eligible expenses. Or, if your employer helps with childcare costs, you may exclude the payments from your income.

Benefit

If you hire someone to care for your children or other dependents to enable you to work or you incur other dependent care expenses, you may be eligible for a tax credit of up to $2,100. More specifically, this credit is a percentage of eligible dependent care expenses (explained later). The credit percentage for 2025 ranges from a low of 20% to a high of 35%. The maximum amount of expenses that can be taken into account in figuring the credit is $3,000 for one qualifying dependent and $6,000 for 2 or more qualifying dependents.

If your employer pays for your dependent care expenses, you may be able to exclude this benefit from income up to $5,000.

Looking Ahead

Starting in 2026, the dependent care credit is greatly enhanced. The credit rate is up to 50%. And the adjusted gross income phase-out threshold increases to $75,000 for singles and $150,000 for joint filers. But even for those fully phased out, there is still a minimum credit of 20% applicable to the expense caps (unchanged) of $3,000 for one qualifying individual or $6,000 for 2 or more qualifying individuals.

The exclusion for employer-provided dependent care assistance increases to $7,500.

Conditions for the Tax Credit

There are a number of conditions for claiming the dependent care credit; you must satisfy all 6 of them to claim the credit:

1. Incur the expenses to earn income.
2. Pay expenses on behalf of a qualifying dependent.
3. Pay over half the household expenses.
4. File a joint return if you are married.
5. Have qualifying expenses in excess of employer reimbursements.
6. Report information about the child care provider.

INCUR THE EXPENSES TO EARN INCOME

The purpose of the dependent care credit is to enable you to work. This generally means that if you are married, you both must work, either full time or part time.

A spouse who is incapacitated or a full-time student is not required to work in order to claim the credit; he or she is treated as having earned income of $250 per month if there is one qualifying dependent or $500 per month if there are 2 or more qualifying dependents.

Example

You are a single mother and a full-time student with 1 child. You are treated as having earned income of $3,000 for the year ($250 × 12). You can use this income in figuring your credit, even though you didn't actually receive this income.

PAY EXPENSES ON BEHALF OF A QUALIFYING DEPENDENT

This is for your child under the age of 13, your incapacitated dependent of any age, or your spouse who is incapacitated.

If your child has his or her 13th birthday during the year, you can take into account expenses incurred up to this birthday.

Only certain types of child care expenses can be taken into account in figuring the credit. Qualifying expenses can be incurred in your home or outside the home (using a day care center). You cannot include amounts paid to you, your child who is under age 19 at the end of the year, your spouse, or any other person you can claim as a dependent.

EXAMPLES OF QUALIFYING EXPENSES

- Babysitter
- Day camp, including a specialty camp such as one for soccer or computers
- Day care center
- Housekeeper (the portion of compensation allocated to dependent care)
- Nursery school
- Private school (The costs for first grade and higher do not qualify unless the child is handicapped, provided the child spends at least 8 hours per day in your home.)
- Transportation, if supervised (so that it is part of care), such as to a day camp or after-school program not on school premises, but not the cost of personally driving a dependent to and from a dependent care center

You do not have to find the least expensive means of providing dependent care. For example, just because your child's grandparent lives in your home doesn't mean you must rely on the grandparent for childcare; you can pay an unrelated person to babysit in your home or take your child to a daycare facility.

The expenses you incur for dependent care must be greater than any amount you exclude as employer-provided dependent care.

PAY OVER HALF THE HOUSEHOLD EXPENSES

You (and your spouse) must pay more than half of the maintenance expenses of the household.

FILE A JOINT RETURN IF MARRIED

Generally, to claim the credit you *must* file a joint return if eligible to do so. But you can claim the credit even though you are still married if you live apart from your spouse for over half the year, you pay over half the household expenses for the full year, and your spouse is not a member of your household for the last 6 months of the year. In this case, you qualify to file as unmarried (single).

REPORT INFORMATION ABOUT THE DEPENDENT CARE PROVIDER

You must list the name, address, and employer identification number (or Social Security number) of the person you pay for dependent care. No employer identification number is required if payment is made to a tax-exempt charity providing the care.

If the person has not completed Form W-4, *Employee's Withholding Allowance Certificate*, as your household employee, you can obtain the necessary information by asking the provider to complete Form W-10, *Dependent Care Provider's Identification and Certification*, or by looking at a driver's license or other government-issued photo ID, business letterhead, or invoice. This may seem like a lot of bother and formality for a babysitter, but if you want to claim the credit, you must comply with this information-reporting requirement.

HOW TO FIGURE YOUR CREDIT PERCENTAGE BASED ON AGI

The amount of the credit you claim for 2025, if any, depends on your AGI. Fortunately, no matter how large your AGI, you are entitled to a minimum credit of 20% of eligible expenses. Table 1.5 shows you the maximum credit you may claim based on your AGI and number of dependents.

TABLE 1.5 Dependent Care Credit Limits in 2025

AGI	Credit Percentage	1 Dependent	2 or More Dependents
$15,000 or less	35%	$1,050	$2,100
$15,001–17,000	34	1,020	2,040
$17,001–19,000	33	990	1,980
$19,001–21,000	32	960	1,920
$21,001–23,000	31	930	1,860
$23,001–25,000	30	900	1,800
$25,001–27,000	29	870	1,740
$27,001–29,000	28	840	1,680
$29,001–31,000	27	810	1,620
$31,001–33,000	26	780	1,560
$33,001–35,000	25	750	1,500
$35,001–37,000	24	720	1,420
$37,001–39,000	23	690	1,380
$39,001–41,000	22	660	1,320
$41,001–43,000	21	630	1,260
$43,001 and over	20	600	1,200

You have 1 qualifying child and adjusted gross income of $40,000. Your credit is 22% of your dependent care expenses up to $3,000, for a credit of $660.

Conditions for the Exclusion

Benefits must be provided by your employer under a written dependent care plan that does not discriminate in favor of owners or highly compensated employees (for example, top executives cannot obtain greater benefits than you). The dollar limit in 2025 on this benefit is $5,000 (or $2,500 if you are married and file separately).

The same limits apply to a flexible spending arrangement (FSA), which is an employer plan to which you contribute a portion of your pay to be used for dependent care expenses. This salary reduction amount is *not* currently taxable to you; it becomes tax-free income that you withdraw from the FSA to cover eligible expenses.

Planning Tips

If you have the option of making salary reduction contributions to your company's flexible spending arrangement (FSA) for dependent care expenses, decide carefully on how much to contribute each month. Married couples filing jointly in 2025 are limited to the same amount in total as singles ($5,000). You can use the funds in the FSA only for dependent care expenses; you cannot, for example, use any of the funds for your medical expenses or other costs. Any funds not used up by the end of the year (or within the first 2½ months of the next year if your employer has a grace period) are forfeited; they do not carry over.

The IRS has not ruled clearly about whether virtual daycare expenses qualify for the credit. But if it can be shown that the cost was incurred to enable a parent to work and the virtual daycare—not the parent—is providing care, then it seems the expenses could be taken into account.

Pitfalls

If in the same month you and your spouse both did not work and were either full-time students or not physically or mentally capable of caring for yourselves, only one of you can be treated as having earned income ($250 or $500 as explained earlier in this chapter) in that month.

If you qualify to receive an exclusion for an employer's plan, you must reduce the amount of eligible expenses used in figuring the credit by the amount of the exclusion.

> **Example**
>
> You have 1 child and receive reimbursement from your employer's plan for 2025 of $2,500. In figuring your tax credit (assuming you are eligible for the maximum credit), you can use only $500 of eligible expenses ($3,000 − $2,500). In essence, if your exclusion in 2025 is $3,000 for 1 child or $6,000 if you have 2 or more children, you cannot claim any tax credit.

If you participate in a dependent care FSA, distributions from the plan are treated as employer reimbursements. Like excludable benefits, distributions from FSAs reduce the amount of expenses you can use to figure the credit.

Check with the administrator of the dependent care FSA you participate in to learn about possible carryovers or using up contributions after the year is over.

If you pay someone to care for your dependent in your home, you are the worker's employer. You are responsible for employment taxes. For more information about these employment taxes, see IRS Publication 926, *Household Employer's Tax Guide*, at www.irs.gov.

Where to Claim the Tax Credit or Exclusion

You figure the credit and the exclusion on Form 2441, *Dependent Care Expenses*. The amount of the credit is entered on Schedule 3 of Form 1040 or 1040-SR.

Report taxable dependent care benefits from Form 2441 on line 1e of Form 1040 or 1040-SR.

If you owe employment taxes for a dependent care worker, you must file Form 1040 or 1040-SR and complete Schedule H, *Household Employment Taxes*, which is attached to the return. You include employment taxes you owe on Schedule 2 of Form 1040 or 1040-SR.

Adoption Costs

One out of every 25 families in the United States has an adopted child. Each year, more than 150,000 children are adopted in the United States, with costs for a private adoption in 2025 as much as $60,000 or more. Taxpayers who adopt a child may qualify for a tax credit, a portion of which is refundable. The amount of the credit may or may not fully offset actual costs for the adoption. If an employer pays for adoption costs, a worker may be able to exclude this fringe benefit from income up to a set dollar limit. And, there's a waiver of the 10% early distribution penalty for withdrawals from retirement plans up to $5,000 to pay adoption expenses (but the distribution itself is taxable).

Benefits

If you adopt a child, you may be eligible to claim a tax credit for the expenses you incur. The maximum credit is $17,280 per child in 2025. The same dollar limit applies whether you are single or married. The credit is 100% of eligible adoption expenses up to this dollar limit. If you adopt a child that the state has determined as having special needs (e.g., a medical condition), the credit is $17,280 without regard to your actual adoption expenses. For 2025, $5,000 of the credit is refundable, which means you can receive it even if it's more than your tax bill. The credit, including one for a special needs child, is subject to income limits.

Example

In 2025, your income is $100,000; you pay $9,000 in attorney's and adoption agency fees to adopt a child who is not a special needs child (the adoption becomes final in 2025). You can claim a tax credit of $9,000 (100% of your eligible costs that do not exceed $17,280). If the child adopted is a special needs child, then the credit is $17,280, even though this is greater than the amount of actual adoption expenses. Of the allowable credit, $5,000 is refundable.

If your employer pays or reimburses you for adoption expenses, you may exclude this benefit from your income; it is tax free to you if you meet eligibility conditions. The exclusion has the same dollar limit and income limits as the credit.

If a tax-exempt organization makes a payment to help pay adoption costs, the payment is not taxable. The payment is viewed as a gift to the recipient.

If you take withdrawals from your 401(k) plan to pay for adoption expenses, you are not subject to the 10% early distribution penalty even though you're under age 59 ½. The penalty waiver only applies to distributions up to $5,000 for the adoption of an individual (other than a child of the taxpayer's spouse) who is under age 18 or who has a physical or mental incapacity making the person incapable of self-support. The distribution is taxable, but can be recontributed within 3 years to a retirement plan so that you can recoup any taxes paid on the distribution by filing an amended return.

Conditions

To claim the adoption credit or exclusion, 2 key conditions apply:

1. You must pay qualified adoption expenses.
2. Your modified adjusted gross income cannot exceed a set amount.

There is an additional condition for married persons; they must file jointly unless they are legally separated or live apart for the last 6 months of the year. This requirement applies even if only one spouse is adopting a child.

The determination of whether a child is a special needs child must be made by the state or an Indian tribal government; a taxpayer cannot make this call on his or her own.

QUALIFIED ADOPTION EXPENSES

Qualified expenses include any reasonable and necessary expenses related to the adoption. These include:

- Adoption agency fees
- Attorney's fees
- Court costs
- Travel expenses while away from home (including meals and lodging)

NONQUALIFIED EXPENSES

Not all adoption-related expenses can be taken into account. Expenses related to the following are nonqualified:

- Adopting your spouse's child
- Expenses paid using funds received from a government program
- Expenses that violate the law
- Surrogate parenting arrangement

MODIFIED ADJUSTED GROSS INCOME LIMIT

To be eligible for the full credit or the exclusion, your modified adjusted gross income (MAGI) in 2025 cannot exceed the amount listed in Table 1.6.

Example

You adopt a child in 2025 and your MAGI is $275,000. You can only claim a partial credit (assuming the child is not a special needs child) because your MAGI exceeds the threshold of $259,190 but not the limit of $299,190.

TABLE 1.6 MAGI Phaseout Range for the Adoption Credit in 2025

Credit Amount	MAGI
Full credit	Not more than $259,190
Partial credit	Over $259,190 but under $299,190
No credit	$299,190 or more

Modified adjusted gross income for this purpose is AGI increased by the foreign earned income exclusion; the foreign housing exclusion or deduction; and the exclusion for income from Guam, American Samoa, Northern Mariana Islands, or Puerto Rico.

Planning Tips

The amount of the adoption credit cannot be more than your tax liability for the year. Tax liability for this purpose means your regular tax, plus your tentative alternative minimum tax (without regard to the foreign tax credit), dependent care credit, credit for the elderly or disabled, either education credit, child tax credit, or mortgage interest credit.

If the credit exceeds your tax liability, you can carry the excess credit forward for up to 5 years beyond the year in which the credit arose.

If your employer has an adoption assistance program but you aren't entitled to some or all of the exclusion (e.g., your MAGI is too high or your expenses exceeded the dollar limit), plan to pay tax on the amount your employer pays or reimburses you. The employer is *not* required to withhold income tax on these payments. Employer-paid expenses are reported on your Form W-2.

There are no income limits for using the penalty waiver for distributions from qualified retirement plans to pay adoption expenses.

Obtain a taxpayer identification number for the child if he/she does not have one. Use Form W-7A, *Application for Taxpayer Identification Number For Pending Adoption*, to obtain a temporary tax ID for a child in a domestic adoption who does not have or is unable to obtain his or her own Social Security number.

Pitfall

The year for which you are entitled to claim the credit depends on the type of child you are adopting.

CHILD WHO IS A U.S. CITIZEN OR RESIDENT

If you adopt or are adopting a child who is a U.S. citizen or resident, use Table 1.7 to see the year for which to claim the credit for payments you make.

TABLE 1.7 Year to Claim the Credit for Adoption of a U.S. Citizen or Resident Child

When You Pay Expenses	When You Claim Credit
Any year before year the adoption becomes final (or falls through)	Year after year of payment
Year adoption becomes final (or falls through)	Year adoption becomes final (or falls through)
Any year after year adoption becomes final (or falls through)	Year of payment

FOREIGN CHILD

You can take the credit only if the adoption becomes final. Use Table 1.8 to see the year in which to claim the credit.

Example

In 2024, you start the adoption process, hiring a lawyer and paying a retainer of $3,000. In 2024, the lawyer helps you work with an authorized adoption agency to which you pay a fee of $10,000 to adopt your daughter, a U.S. resident. The child is placed with you at that time. In 2025, you pay the lawyer an additional $5,000 and the adoption becomes final in this year. You may *not* claim any credit in 2024. In 2025, you may claim a credit up to $17,280, comprised of $13,000 [retainer and adoption fee] paid in 2024 and $4,280 of the $5,000 additional attorney's fee paid in 2025. The excess expenses of $720 [$5,000 − $4,280]) are not carried over and cannot be used in the future.

Where to Claim the Adoption Credit, Exclusion, or Penalty Waiver

You figure the adoption credit on Form 8839, *Qualified Adoption Expenses*, which is attached to your return. The amount of the credit is entered on Schedule 3 of Form 1040 or 1040-SR. The refundable part of the adoption credit is entered on line 30 of Form 1040 or 1040-SR (it's taken from line 8 of Form 8839).

To claim the credit, you must retain certain documents; they do not have to be attached to the return.

- For U.S. adoptions, attach a copy of the adoption order or decree.
- For adoptions finalized abroad, include the child's Hague Adoption Certificate, an IH-3 visa, or a foreign adoption decree translated into English. If the child's country of origin is not a party to the Hague Convention, then attach a copy of the translated decree or an IR-2 or IR-3 visa.
- If you adopt a special needs child, also attach the state determination of the child's special needs status certificate so you can claim the full $17,280, regardless of the adoption costs you paid.

If your employer paid or reimbursed you for qualified expenses, you must also complete Form 8839 to figure excludable benefits. Taxable benefits are reported on line 1f of Form 1040 or 1040-SR.

TABLE 1.8 Year to Claim the Credit for Adoption of a Foreign Child

When You Pay Expenses	When You Claim Credit
Any year before year adoption becomes final	Year adoption becomes final
Year adoption becomes final	Year adoption becomes final
Any year after year adoption becomes final	Year of payment

Distributions from qualified retirement plans for adoption expenses are reported to you on Form 1099-R and entered on line 5a of Form 1040 or 1040-SR; if the total distribution is for adoption expenses up to the dollar limit, enter zero on line 5b. You must also file Form 5329 to claim the penalty exception If you timely recontribute the distribution for adoption expenses, file Form 1040-X for the year of the distribution to claim a tax refund.

Foster Care

Taxpayers who care for children in foster care and receive funds for expenses may not be taxed on those funds. Instead, they may be able to exclude the payments they receive from income.

Benefit

Exclusion for foster care payments. If you receive foster care payments to care for a child placed with you by a state or local agency or a tax-exempt foster care placement agency, you are not taxed on those payments. They are fully excludable; there is no dollar limit.

Qualified payments include payments for the provision of foster care. They also include difficulty-of-care payments to account for the additional care required for a child with physical, mental, or emotional handicaps. Payments under a state Medicaid Home and Community-Based Services Waiver (Medicaid waiver) program are treated as difficulty-of-care payments.

The exclusion for foster care payments is limited to payments received for 5 qualifying individuals who are over age 18. The exclusion for difficulty-of-care payments is limited to payments received for 10 qualifying individuals who are over age 18. There are no limits on the number of children age 18 or under for whom the exclusion may be claimed.

Deduction for out-of-pocket costs. See Chapter 6.

Condition

Foster care payments include only those made by a state or local government or qualified foster care placement agency for the care of a qualified foster child or a difficulty-of-care payment. Also, you and the foster child must live in the same home.

Planning Tips

If you are a foster care parent dealing with a private agency, make sure the placement entitles you to exclude payments received for the care of the child. Some other tax breaks may be claimed with respect to a foster child, such as the earned income credit. Check the other tax breaks throughout this chapter.

Pitfalls

Payments received from private agencies that are not tax-exempt entities, even though licensed by the state, are not excludable from income.

Payments made to a child's biological parent cannot be excluded, even if labeled "foster care payment" because such parent is never a foster parent.

Where to Claim the Exclusion

Foster care payments are not reported on the return if they are excludable. If you care for more than the allowable number of children over age 18, you must include the payments in income. Report this as "other income" on Schedule 1 of Form 1040 or 1040-SR.

Child Support

Divorced or separated parents may be ordered by a court to make support payments for a child of the marriage. Even an unwed parent may be instructed to support his or her child. The recipient of child support payments, typically the parent with whom the child resides, is not taxed on these payments. The parent making the payments cannot deduct them, but paying child support may entitle the parent to other tax write-offs discussed throughout this chapter.

Benefit ⊗

Child support payments are not taxable to the child, nor to the parent who receives them on behalf of the child. There is no dollar limit to this benefit. It does not matter whether child support payments are made pursuant to a divorce decree or separation agreement made before 2019 or after 2018 (when the rules for alimony payments were changed).

Conditions

Payments for child support should be fixed. If they are set by a decree of divorce or separate maintenance or a separation agreement, they are considered to be fixed.

In addition, if payments made to a parent will be reduced or terminated upon a contingency related to the child, then those payments are treated as being fixed for child support. Contingencies for this purpose include:

- Reaching the age of majority (generally age 18 or 21, depending on the law in your state)
- Leaving school
- Marrying
- Entering military service
- Moving out of the custodial parent's home
- Starting to work and/or attaining a set income level

Planning Tip

If a parent is required to pay both alimony and child support under a pre-2019 divorce decree and makes a single payment that is less than the total amount due, the first dollars are considered tax-free child support. This is relevant if the alimony is pursuant to a divorce decree or separation agreement executed before 2019 under which alimony payments are deductible.

Example

Ed owes his former spouse $1,000 each month to cover alimony of $600 and child support of $400. Assume they were divorced before 2019. In March 2025, Ed pays only $500. Of this amount, $400 is treated as child support; $100 is treated as alimony.

Pitfalls

The parent who makes child support payments cannot deduct them. They are not considered to be part of deductible alimony payments where applicable (explained in the next section).

If a reduction in child support payments to a parent is not specifically tied to the child's age of majority but is scheduled to occur within 6 months before or after such date, the reduction is treated as if it was tied to the child. This means that the amount subject to reduction is viewed as child support and not as deductible alimony if a pre-2019 divorce decree or separation agreement is involved. The same rule applies if you are making payments on behalf of more than one child and there are at least 2 reductions, each of which is within a year of a child's reaching the age of majority.

If you receive interest on past due child support, the interest is taxable. It is not treated as tax-free child support.

If you are due a refund of federal income tax because you overpaid it through withholding or estimated taxes, you won't receive it if you are delinquent on your child support payments. The IRS is authorized to divert your refund to the parent owed the child support payments as long as the state provides notice to you and a procedure you can follow to contest this action.

Where to Claim the Exclusion

Child support payments received are not reported on the return.

Alimony

Taxpayers who are required by a court to make payments to a spouse or former spouse can deduct such payments if the divorce or separation agreement was executed before January 1, 2019. The payments may be called alimony, support, or spousal maintenance, depending on state law (called "alimony" here for convenience). The tax law, in most cases, imposes symmetry on the treatment of alimony so that the government effectively comes out even, as explained below.

Benefit

If you have a divorce or separation agreement executed before 2019, and you make payments to a spouse or former spouse for alimony, support, or spousal maintenance, you can deduct the payments if certain conditions are met. There is no dollar limit on this deduction. The deduction is claimed as an adjustment to gross income; you do not have to itemize your other deductions to write off alimony payments you make. There is no income limit on you for this deduction. But if you make payments pursuant to a divorce or separation agreement executed after December 31, 2018, you cannot deduct your payments.

Conditions

There are 4 conditions that must be met for payments made under a pre-2019 divorce decree or separation agreement to a spouse or former spouse to be considered alimony:

1. Amounts must be paid pursuant to a legal requirement, such as a court decree.
2. Payments must be made in cash.
3. You must live apart from your spouse or former spouse.
4. Your responsibility to make payments must terminate on the death of your spouse or former spouse.

Typically, alimony is deductible by the payer is taxable to the recipient—the government effectively nets no additional tax revenue from the arrangement. But this symmetry is not required. If you meet all of the conditions, you can deduct your alimony payments even if your former spouse is not required to pay tax on them (for example, your former spouse lives abroad where alimony is exempt income).

PAYABLE UNDER A COURT DECREE

You can't deduct alimony under a pre-2019 divorce decree or separation agreement if you voluntarily make payments. You must either be ordered to do so under a decree of divorce, legal separation, or support or agree to make payments under a written separation agreement.

If the marriage is annulled and you are ordered to make payments, they can be treated as alimony if the other conditions are satisfied.

CASH PAYMENTS

You can deduct only payments under a pre-2019 divorce decree or separation agreement made in cash, not property. But you don't necessarily have to make these payments directly *to* your spouse or former spouse. Payments made *on behalf of* your spouse or former spouse qualify for the deduction if required by the divorce decree or separation agreement. For example, if you are ordered to pay your former spouse's rent with a check directly to the landlord, you can treat the payment as alimony if the other conditions are met.

If you continue to own the home in which your former spouse resides (i.e., own it by yourself or jointly with your former spouse) and you pay the mortgage and other expenses, only some of these expenses qualify as deductible alimony—even if you are required to make the payments under the terms of a divorce decree or separation agreement. If you own the home, you benefit from the payment of the mortgage, real estate taxes, and other maintenance on the property and cannot deduct these payments. If you own the home jointly, only one-half of your payments can be treated as alimony because only one-half benefits your spouse or former spouse. (Of course, you can deduct mortgage interest and real estate taxes as itemized deductions as explained in Chapter 4.)

LIVING APART

To deduct payments under a pre-2019 divorce decree or separation agreement, you and your spouse or former spouse must not live in the same household. This means separate residences; merely having separate bedrooms in the same home is not good enough for payments to be treated as alimony.

Payments made while you are preparing to leave can be deducted. There is a one-month limit so that only payments made within one month prior to your departure can be treated as alimony. If it takes you longer to move out, your earlier payments are not deductible.

PAYMENT RESPONSIBILITY ENDS ON DEATH

Your responsibility to make payments to your spouse or former spouse must end if that person dies in order for payments under a pre-2019 divorce decree or separation agreement to be deductible alimony. If your obligation to make payments continues beyond the recipient's death (for example, you must continue to pay until total payments reach a set amount), you cannot treat *any* of the payments as alimony (even those made before death).

Generally, the divorce decree should state that your obligation to make payments ends on the recipient's death. But this isn't necessary as long as this condition is part of the law in your state.

The fact that your estate continues to be liable for payments after your death does not prevent you from treating your payments as alimony.

Planning Tips

If you have a pre-2019 divorce decree or separation agreement, don't make voluntary payments if you want to deduct them. If you want to ensure that increased payments qualify as deductible alimony, you need to amend the court order or separation agreement to incorporate the change. If a pre-2019 divorce decree or separation agreement is changed or amended, the old alimony rules continue to apply unless the revised document specifically says that the new rules (i.e., that payments are not deductible by the spouse who pays or taxable to the spouse who receives) should apply.

The Tax Court made it clear that paying health insurance premiums for an ex-spouse through a cafeteria plan may qualify as deductible alimony, even though the payments are made on a pre-tax basis (a double tax benefit for the paying spouse).

Pitfalls

Payments made to someone who was never legally your spouse cannot be treated as alimony. For example, if you make payments to a domestic partner, you cannot deduct them even though they otherwise have all the earmarks of alimony. This does not apply to annulments.

Property settlements are not deductible.

Where to Claim the Deduction

The amount of deductible alimony payments is entered on Schedule 1 of Form 1040 or 1040-SR. There is no separate form or schedule to complete when deducting alimony. But you *must* include the recipient's Social Security number on your return (to allow the IRS to cross-check whether the recipient reported the alimony as income) and the date of the divorce or separation agreement (to allow the IRS to see whether alimony is deductible).

ABLE Accounts

If you have a child who became disabled before age 26 or meets certain eligibility conditions, there is a special savings account that generally does not adversely impact eligibility for means-tested government programs (e.g., Medicaid). The account can be used on a tax-free basis for various disability-related expenses (including funeral and burial costs). See details in Chapter 2.

Looking Ahead

Starting in 2026, eligibility for ABLE accounts is increased to age 46. This means that veterans and others with the onset of a disability before age 46 will qualify for ABLE accounts.

Trump Accounts

If you have a child born between January 1, 2025, and December 31, 2028, the federal government will open an investment account. This will be automatic; no action will be required by you. Trump Accounts are discussed in Chapter 8.

Medical Expenses

The cost of medical care is expensive and rising at faster than the overall rate of inflation. Even if you have medical coverage, there are co-pays and deductibles, as well as the cost of noncovered expenses that can mount up. Fortunately, the tax law provides you with some relief for the high cost of medical care by allowing you to treat your medical expenses in special tax-advantaged ways, as explained in this chapter. For example, you may have tax-free benefits from employer-provided medical plans.

To learn more about medical and dental expenses, see IRS Publication 502, *Medical and Dental Expenses*, IRS Publication 969, *Health Savings Accounts and Other Tax-Favored Health Plans*, and IRS Publication 974, *Premium Tax Credit*. A discussion of employer-paid sick leave is in Chapter 13.

Individual Mandate

Back in 2010, the Affordable Care Act (ACA) created an individual health coverage mandate that required individuals to have minimum essential health coverage or pay a penalty, but the penalty was repealed and does not apply after 2018. While there is no federal individual mandate, there may be state-level mandates. Of course, most people want health coverage and the tax-advantaged ways to do this are covered in this chapter.

Employer-Provided Health Insurance

Employers with 50 or more full-time and full-time equivalent employees are required to offer affordable health coverage for their staff and dependents or pay a penalty. Most of these employers offer health coverage. What's more, many employers that are not required to provide coverage do so anyway. This means that many employees enjoy coverage through their employers at no cost to them; others pay a portion of coverage and the employers pay the rest. The value of employer-paid coverage is tax free, regardless of amount.

Benefit

The value or amount that an employer pays for premiums to cover you, your spouse, your dependent, and a child under the age of 27 is not taxable. There is no dollar limit on the amount of coverage you can receive on a tax-free basis.

Conditions

There are none; as long as you are an employee, your company-paid coverage is tax free to you. This is so even though the amount of this employee benefit is reported on your Form W-2.

Planning Tips

If both you and your spouse work and each is entitled to health coverage, compare the medical plans and choose the one that offers the better coverage. If you must contribute toward your coverage, but your spouse does not and can include you, it may be preferable to decline your employer's coverage so you can use your spouse's plan.

If you do not have a group health plan at work but your employer reimburses you for the premiums of individual coverage, the reimbursement may be tax free; see the discussion on *Health Reimbursement Arrangements* later in this chapter.

Pitfalls

While employer-paid coverage for spouses is tax free, this treatment does not apply to domestic partners. Employees are taxed on employer-paid coverage for their domestic partners.

If you are 65 and older and covered by an employer plan of a company with fewer than 20 employees, Medicare is your primary payer. Be sure to apply for Medicare within 3 months before and 3 months after you turn age 65 (7-month enrollment period) so that you have the right coverage.

Where to Report the Benefit

You do not have to report this tax-free fringe benefit. Even if your employer reports the value of the coverage on your W-2 form, this does not change the tax-free treatment of the benefit to you.

Premium Tax Credit

If you do not have coverage through an employer, Medicare, Medicaid, or certain other program but think you may have trouble paying for private insurance, you may be eligible for a tax credit to help pay for coverage if you purchase it through a government health insurance Marketplace (also known as the Exchange). There is the federal Marketplace and state-run marketplaces in 19 states and the District of Columbia. The credit is refundable (it can exceed the amount of taxes owed) and can even be applied toward premiums throughout the year.

Benefit ✚

If you have low or moderate income, you may qualify for the premium tax credit. It is an advanceable, refundable tax credit for eligible people who purchase coverage through a government health insurance Marketplace. The credit amount varies with household income for eligible taxpayers.

You can choose to have the credit paid in advance to your insurance company you've chosen from the Marketplace, or you can claim all of the credit when you file your tax return for the year. If you choose to have the credit paid in advance, you will have to reconcile on your tax return the amount paid in advance with the actual credit to which you are entitled.

Looking Ahead

Starting in 2026, there are a number of changes for the premium tax credit:

- No premium tax credit is available if household income exceeds 400% of the federal poverty line, or FPL.
- No advance credit will be paid for provisional eligibility. Individuals will pay the full (unsubsidized) premium for coverage through the Marketplace until eligibility is officially confirmed.
- There's no cap on excess repayment liability. Those receiving excess advance premium tax credits must repay the full amount.
- Those with income less than 100% of the FPL who do not qualify for Medicaid cannot claim the premium tax credit.
- No credit will be allowed for anyone who uses a mid-year Special Enrollment Period due to changes in income or life changes.

Starting in 2027, the credit is limited to U.S. citizens and residents, as well as those with certain refugee status. And those enrolled in coverage through the Marketplace who are receiving the advance premium tax credit will have to provide updated household income information each year.

Conditions

To qualify for the credit, all of the following conditions apply:

- You must obtain coverage through a government health insurance Marketplace, such as HealthCare.gov.
- You must apply for the credit at the time you purchase your coverage by estimating household income, unless you are waiting until you file your return to claim the credit.
- If your employer offers coverage, it is not *affordable* to you.
- You are not eligible for a government program (e.g., Medicare, Medicaid, CHIP, or TRICARE).
- If you are married, you must file jointly, unless you are a domestic abuse victim and file separately.
- You are not someone else's dependent.

COVERAGE THROUGH AN EXCHANGE

Only coverage purchased through a government Marketplace ("exchange") can entitle you to the credit. If you buy identical coverage directly from the insurer, you do not qualify for the credit; you didn't get it through a government Marketplace. It is not necessary that you obtained the coverage online; you may have submitted paper returns or obtained coverage by telephone.

APPLY FOR THE CREDIT

The federal government does not automatically give you the credit. You must prove eligibility for the credit, either at the time you purchase your health coverage from an exchange or when you file your return.

HOUSEHOLD INCOME LIMITS

The credit amounts for individuals and families depends on having household income between 100% and 400% of the federal poverty line for their family size. But for 2025, those with household income above 400% of the federal poverty line qualify for the same credit amount as those at 400%.

Household income has a special meaning for purposes of the premium assistance credit. It is modified adjusted gross income (MAGI) of everyone in your household (you, your spouse, and anyone claimed as a dependent who is required to file a tax return). MAGI for this purpose is adjusted gross income plus any excluded foreign income, nontaxable Social Security benefits (including tier 1 Railroad Retirement benefits) (including benefits attributable to prior years received as part of a lump sum in the current year), and tax-exempt interest. It does *not* include Supplemental Security Income (SSI).

Eligibility for the credit depends on your household income relative to the federal poverty line, although those with household income above 400% of the federal poverty line may still claim a credit for 2025. The 2025 credit is based on poverty amounts listed in Table 2.1. The amount of the credit depends on your household income as a percentage of the federal poverty line. Table 2.2 lists the percentage of household income you are required to pay of the premiums for coverage obtained from the government Marketplace in 2025. This is referred to as your *expected contribution*. The percentage applicable to you is applied toward the second-lowest cost of a silver plan (or if there is only one silver plan available to you, then the cost of this silver plan); this is your tax credit.

Example

In 2025, a single individual (the only person in the household) has household income of $35,000. He is eligible for the premium tax credit (see Table 2.1). Because his household income is at least 200% but less than 250% (Table 2.2), his applicable percentage is 4.00%. Assuming the cost of the second-lowest silver plan available to him is $5,000 for the year, he's expected to contribute $1,400 (4% of $35,000). His credit amount is $3,600 ($5,000 – $1,400).

TABLE 2.1 2025 Poverty Amounts in the Contiguous States and D.C.*

Household Size	Household Income
One individual	$15,060 (100%) up to $60,240 (400%)
Family of 2	$20,440 (100%) up to $81,760 (400%)
Family of 3	$25,820 (100%) up to $103,280 (400%)
Family of 4	$31,200 (100%) up to $124,800 (400%)
Family of 5	$36,580 (100%) up to $146,320 (400%)
Family of 6	$41,960 (100%) up to $167,840 (400%)
Family of 7	$47,340 (100%) up to $191,840 (400%)
Family of 8	$52,720 (100%) up to $210,880 (400%)
Family of more than 8	Add $5,380 for each additional person

*The guidelines are higher in Alaska and Hawaii; see https://aspe.hhs.gov/poverty-guidelines.

TABLE 2.2 Household Income Percentage Limit

Household Income Percentage of Federal Poverty Line	Initial Percentage	Final Percentage
Less than 150%	0.00%	0.00%
At least 150% but less than 200%	0.00%	2.00%
At least 200% but less than 250%	2.00%	4.00%
At least 250% but less than 300%	4.00%	6.00%
At least 300% but less than 400%	6.00%	8.50%
At least 400%	8.50%	8.50%

UNAFFORDABLE EMPLOYER COVERAGE

Even if your employer offers coverage, you may still be eligible for the premium tax credit. The employer's coverage in 2025 is deemed "unaffordable" if premiums for self-only coverage (even if you have family coverage) exceed 9.02% of your household income (see the definition of household income under *household income limits* earlier). (In 2026, the "unaffordable" percentage will be 9.96%.) If your employer offers multiple health coverage options, the affordability test applies to the lowest-cost option available to you that also satisfies the minimum value requirement (i.e., the plan covers at least 60% of the expected total allowed costs for covered services). If your employer offers any wellness programs, the affordability test is based on the premium you would pay if you received the maximum discount for any tobacco cessation programs, and did not receive any other discounts based on wellness programs.

You cannot claim the credit if you enroll in an employer plan, even if it is unaffordable. If you receive reimbursement from your employer for individually-obtained coverage under a QSEHRA (discussed later in this chapter), there is a coordination of the reimbursement with the credit, so you can't receive a double benefit.

INFORMATION RETURNS

There are 3 information returns that contain information about your health coverage.

1. Form 1095-A, *Health Insurance Marketplace Statement*. This is issued by the government Marketplace to anyone who obtained coverage through it (whether through the federal or state exchange).

2. Form 1095-B, *Health Coverage*. If you request it, this form is issued by an insurance company for private coverage or a small business (fewer than 50 employees) that has a self-insured plan, such as a Health Reimbursement Arrangement. As a practical matter, most small businesses do not have self-insured plans, so if you buy coverage individually (not through an exchange) or have employer coverage in a group health plan from a small business, you won't receive the Form 1095-B.

3. Form 1095-C, *Employer-Provided Health Insurance Offer and Coverage*. If you request it, this form is issued by a large employer (50 or more employees); it describes the coverage you have (or don't have).

The form(s) you receive are not attached to your return; retain the form(s) with your tax papers for the year. Only Form 1095-A is relevant to the premium tax credit because the credit applies only to coverage obtained through the Marketplace. Employers give you notice that Form 1095-B and 1095-C won't be furnished unless you request them.

Planning Tips

If you are 26 or younger, you may obtain coverage through an employer plan of your parent.

If you got married during the year, file a joint return, and one or both of you have received the premium tax credit on an advance basis, there is an alternative way to compute the allowable credit amount given that household income has changed. Under the alternative computation (called the "year of marriage rule") you may reduce the amount of excess credit, if any, that must be repaid. The computation is complex, but it's illustrated in examples in Reg. §1.36B-4(b)(5) and in IRS Publication 974.

Plan now for coverage for 2026. Use your 2025 income, increases in the poverty amounts, and an increase in the percentage used to determine whether coverage is unaffordable to make projections for credit eligibility. Under federal law, like the federal Marketplace, state Marketplaces must have open enrollment from November 1 through January 15.

TABLE 2.3 Maximum Repayment Amount for 2025 Premium Tax Credit Advance

MAGI as % of FPL	Single Taxpayers (other than surviving spouses and heads of household)	Other Taxpayers
Less than 200%	$375	$750
200%–299%	$975	$1,950
300%–399%	$1,625	$3,250

Pitfalls

As mentioned earlier, you cannot claim the credit if you buy coverage directly from the insurer. This is so even if the coverage is identical to what is sold through the government Marketplace.

If there is a change during the year in your marital status, number of dependents, or household income that may work to increase or decrease the initial credit amount used on an advanced basis to pay insurance premiums, you'll have to reconcile this when you file your 2025 income tax return. For 2025, there are limits on what you may be required to repay of the advance premium tax credit (the "subsidy"). This cap is based on modified adjusted gross income (MAGI) as a percentage of the federal poverty level (FPL) (Table 2.1 on page 34). Table 2.3 shows the limits on the maximum repayment amount.

Where to Claim the Credit

Figure the credit on Form 8962, *Premium Tax Credit*. If you claimed the credit on an advanced basis when you signed up for coverage through the Marketplace, now determine whether the allowable credit is *more* or *less* than the amounts advanced during the year. Report the excess advanced premium tax credit repayment on Schedule 2 of Form 1040 or 1040-SR. Report the net premium tax credit on Schedule 3 of Form 1040 or 1040-SR.

Itemized Medical Expenses

Medical care for most Americans today is very costly. Even those with insurance still pay out-of-pocket for many things, including copayments, noncovered procedures, and, often, the insurance premiums themselves. The tax law recognizes that medical costs, even though they are personal expenses, should be deductible if they exceed a set percentage of your income.

Benefit

If you itemize deductions instead of claiming the standard deduction, you can write off medical expenses that are not covered by insurance, employer payments, or government programs to the extent they exceed 7.5% of adjusted gross income.

Example

Your adjusted gross income is $100,000 and you itemize deductions. You have $12,000 of medical costs that are not covered by insurance. You can deduct $4,500—the first 7.5% ($7,500) is nondeductible.

There is no dollar limit on what you can deduct for medical expenses once you pass the AGI threshold.

A separate deduction for health insurance for self-employed individuals is discussed later in this chapter; this cost is not dependent on itemizing.

Conditions

To be treated as qualified medical expenses, payments must be for the diagnosis, cure, mitigation, treatment, or prevention of disease, or any treatment that affects a part or function of your body. And they can't be nonqualified expenses explained later.

Deductible expenses include those paid not only for yourself but also for a spouse and any qualifying dependent (a qualifying child or qualifying relative, as explained in Chapter 1).

Example

In 2025, you provide more than half of your mother's support, including the payment of all her medical expenses. Her gross income is $12,000, which is more than the $5,200 limit for a dependent. But you can include your payment of her medical expenses with yours when figuring your medical expense deduction.

Examples of Deductible Medical Expenses

PROFESSIONAL SERVICES

- Annual physical
- Chiropodist
- Chiropractor
- Christian Science practitioner
- Conciege services (called direct primary care arrangements)
- Dermatologist
- Dentist
- Full body electronic scans
- Gynecologist
- Neurologist
- Nurse, including board, wages, and employment taxes on wages
- Nurse's aide for an elderly person in need of supervision and assistance
- Obstetrician
- Ophthalmologist
- Optician
- Optometrist
- Osteopath
- Pediatrician
- Physician
- Physiotherapist
- Plastic surgeon for medically necessary surgery
- Podiatrist
- Practical nurse
- Psychiatrist
- Psychoanalyst
- Psychologist
- Registered nurse
- Surgeon
- Telehealth services

DENTAL SERVICES

- Artificial teeth
- Cleaning teeth
- Dental x-rays
- Extracting teeth
- Filling teeth
- Gum treatment
- Oral surgery
- Orthodontia

EQUIPMENT AND SUPPLIES

- Abdominal supports
- Arches
- Artificial eyes and limbs
- Autoette
- Back supports
- Blood sugar test kit
- Braces
- Braille books and magazines
- Condoms
- Contact lenses
- Crutches, canes, and walkers
- Elastic hosiery
- Eyeglasses
- Hearing aids and their batteries
- Heating devices
- Home exercise equipment for doctor-prescribed weight loss
- Home pregnancy test
- Invalid chair
- Iron lung
- Lactation equipment and supplies
- Mattress to alleviate arthritic condition
- Orthotics and orthopedic shoes (but only the excess over the cost of regular shoes)

- Oxygen or oxygen equipment to relieve breathing problems caused by a medical condition
- Personal protection equipment (PPE) for preventing the spread of disease
- Protheses
- Reclining chair if prescribed by a doctor
- Repair of special telephone equipment for someone who is hearing impaired
- Sacroiliac belt
- Seeing Eye dog and its maintenance
- Splints
- Telephone-teletype costs and television adapter for closed-caption service for someone who is hearing impaired
- Television adapter to display the audio part of programs as subtitles for the hearing impaired
- Truss
- Wheelchair
- Whirlpool baths prescribed by a doctor
- Wig advised by a doctor as essential to the mental health of a person who lost all hair from disease

HOME IMPROVEMENTS

- Air conditioner where necessary for relief from an allergy or for relieving difficulty in breathing
- Cost of installing stair-seat elevator for a person with a heart condition
- Fluoridation unit
- Lead-based paint removal to prevent a child with lead poisoning from eating the paint (but not the cost of repainting the scraped area)
- Ramps for wheelchair access
- Swimming pool (the portion of the cost that does not increase the home's value)

INSURANCE

- Blue Cross Blue Shield
- Contact lens replacement insurance

- Health insurance premiums you pay to cover hospital, surgical, and other medical expenses (Health insurance paid by your employer is not deductible by you, but you aren't taxed on this benefit.)
- Long-term care insurance to the extent permitted for your age (explained later in this chapter)
- Medicare premiums
- Medigap (supplemental Medicare insurance)
- Membership in a medical service cooperative
- Student health fee

MEDICINE AND DRUGS

- Birth control pills
- Insulin
- Prescription drugs
- Viagra if medically prescribed

TESTS

- 23andMe DNA testing (the portion of the cost related to medical information)
- Blood tests
- Cardiograms
- COVID-19 home testing
- Full body electronic scans
- Metabolism tests
- Spinal fluid tests
- Sputum tests
- Stool examinations
- Urine analyses
- X-ray examinations

TREATMENTS AND PROGRAMS

- Abortion
- Alcoholism inpatient treatment at a therapeutic center
- Acupuncture
- Blood transfusion
- Breast reconstructive surgery following a mastectomy

- Childbirth classes for expectant mothers
- Childbirth delivery
- Clarinet lessons advised by a dentist for the treatment of tooth defects
- Convalescent home—for medical treatment only
- Diathermy
- Drug treatment center—inpatient care costs
- Egg donor fees (including legal fees for preparation of a contract between the taxpayer and the donor)
- Electroshock therapy
- Fertility treatments, including in vitro fertilization and surgery to reverse prior sterilization
- Health institute fees for exercises, rubdowns, and so on that are prescribed by a doctor as treatments necessary to alleviate a physical or mental defect or illness
- Hearing services
- Hospitalization
- Hydrotherapy
- Kidney donor's or possible donor's expenses
- Laser eye surgery or keratotomy
- Lifetime care (see "Continuing Care Facilities and Nursing Homes" section later in this chapter)
- Long-term care costs for someone who is chronically or terminally ill
- Navajo healing ceremony ("sings")
- Organ transplant (including the costs of a donor or prospective donor)
- Prenatal and postnatal visits
- Psychotherapy
- Radium therapy
- Remedial reading for someone with dyslexia
- Sex reassignment surgery for someone with gender identity disorder (GID)
- Special school for a mentally or physically impaired person if the main reason for attendance is to use its resources for relieving the disability
- Sterilization
- Stop-smoking programs

- Surgery to remove loose skin following 100-pound weight loss
- Tutoring for severe learning disabilities
- Umbilical cord blood banking services if needed to treat an existing or imminently probable disease
- Vaccines
- Vasectomy
- Weight-loss program to treat obesity, high blood pressure, or other condition

TRAVEL

- Ambulance hire
- Autoette (auto device for handicapped person)
- Bus fare to see doctors, obtain treatment (including attendance at AA meetings), or pick up prescriptions
- Cab fare and ridesharing to see doctors, obtain treatment (including attendance at AA meetings), or pick up prescriptions
- Car use to see doctors, obtain treatment (including attendance at AA meetings), or pick up prescriptions at 21¢ per mile for travel in 2025
- Conference expenses (travel costs and admission fees) for medical conferences on an illness or condition suffered by you, your spouse, or dependent
- Lodging to receive outpatient care at a licensed hospital, clinic, or hospital-
equivalent facility, up to $50 per night ($100 per night if you accompany a sick child)
- Train fare to see doctors, obtain treatment (including attendance at AA meetings), or pick up prescriptions

Planning Tips

Payments by credit card are deductible in the year of the charge (not in the year of paying the credit card bill), so year-end charges for unreimbursed expenses (such as prescription sunglasses) are deductible in the year of the purchase.

If you don't expect your medical expenses to be sufficient to exceed the AGI floor this year, hold off on elective procedures until next year. Then you can effectively bunch expenses (this year's and next year's) into one year to exceed the AGI floor.

Pitfalls

Not every expense of a medical nature is deductible. Here is a listing of instances where no deduction was allowed by the IRS:

- Antiseptic diaper services
- Bottled water purchased to avoid the city's fluoridated water
- Breast augmentation surgery for a male who undergoes sex reassignment surgery
- Burial, cremation, and funeral costs
- Child care so a parent can see a doctor
- Cosmetic surgery *unless* it is medically necessary (For example, a nose job to improve appearance is not a qualified medical expense, but one done following a car accident to repair a nose broken in the accident is a qualified expense.)
- Dancing lessons
- Ear/body piercing
- Hair transplant
- Health club and gym memberships for maintaining general good health or appearance
- Illegal drugs and controlled substances (e.g., laetrile) in violation of federal law
- In vitro fertilization costs incurred to enable a healthy man to have a woman carry his child
- Marijuana, even if prescribed by a doctor in a state permitting the prescription (it is a controlled substance under federal law, but this could change, so check the Supplement)
- Marriage counseling fees
- Massages recommended by a doctor to relieve stress
- Maternity clothes
- Menstrual supplies (e.g., tampons) (but these costs can be reimbursed by HSAs, FSAs, etc. explained later in this chapter)
- Nicotine patches and gums
- Nutritional supplements, including vitamins, and herbal supplements
- Organ donations (e.g., a kidney)
- Over-the-counter medicines without a doctor's prescription (although they can be reimbursed through HSAs, FSAs, and other plans discussed later in this chapter)

- Premiums on policies guaranteeing a specified income each week in the event of hospitalization
- Prescription drugs purchased abroad, such as from Canada (although there is an FSA exception in certain situations)
- Special foods or beverage substitutes (in lieu of what is normally consumed)
- Surrogacy expenses (products and services involving assisted reproductive technologies not being performed on the taxpayer, such as egg donor costs, egg retrieval, sperm freezing, IVF medical costs, legal and agency fees for the surrogacy, childbirth expenses related to the surrogate pregnancy, and surrogate medical insurance related to the pregnancy)
- Swimming lessons
- Tattooing
- Teeth-whitening treatment
- Toothpaste
- Umbilical cord blood banking services to treat a disease that might possibly develop in the future
- Veterinary fees (other than for service animals)
- Weight-loss program to improve general good health or appearance

When figuring the deductible portion of home improvements made for medical reasons, such as a swimming pool used to alleviate a medical condition, only the portion of the cost that does not increase the home's value is deductible. As a practical matter, the cost of making improvements to accommodate a disability, such as installing ramps or widening doors, usually doesn't add any value to the home and is fully deductible.

Medical expenses are also deductible for purposes of the alternative minimum tax (AMT) to the same extent as for the regular tax.

Where to Claim the Deduction

Itemized medical expenses are reported in the first part of Schedule A of Form 1040 or 1040-SR. The total of all itemized deductions is then entered on line 12e of Form 1040 or 1040-SR.

RECORDKEEPING

Retain all canceled checks, doctors' statements, receipts, and other evidence of medical expenses you paid. If you are deducting car mileage for medical-related travel, keep a detailed record of the date and distance of each trip in a diary, logbook, or other record keeper.

Self-Employed Health Insurance Deduction

Self-employed individuals (including those owning more than 2% S corporation stock who are not self-employed) cannot deduct their health insurance costs from their business income. This means that health insurance costs do not reduce net earnings from self-employment. But these individuals are permitted to deduct premiums as an adjustment to gross income (an "above-the-line deduction") even if they do not itemize other deductions.

Benefit

Self-employed individuals and shareholders owning more than 2% of S corporations can deduct all of their health insurance directly from gross income. The write-off can be taken even if other deductions are not itemized.

This deduction includes not only payments for basic medical insurance but also long-term care insurance. There is no dollar limit on this deduction.

Conditions

To qualify for this write-off, you and your spouse may not have any employer-subsidized coverage. This condition applies on a month-by-month basis.

> **Example**
>
> If you are eligible through your spouse for employer-subsidized coverage in January and opt to pay your own coverage that month, you do not qualify for the deduction. But if, in February, you are self-employed and no longer qualify under your spouse's employer's plan, you can deduct your premium starting this month.

Also, the deduction cannot exceed the net earnings from the business in which the medical insurance plan is established. These earnings may not be aggregated with earnings from other businesses. For S corporation shareholders, the deduction cannot be more than wages from the corporation (if this was the business in which the insurance plan was established).

Planning Tips

You can claim the deduction whether you buy the insurance through the business or individually, as long as you meet the conditions explained earlier. If you are an employee of an S corporation owned by your parent and are covered by a company health plan, you are treated the same as your parent: the premiums are taxable income to you, but you can deduct 100% of the premiums as an adjustment to gross income. In effect, you're treated like a self-employed person even though you are an employee of the corporation.

Premiums for Medicare Part B coverage for a self-employed individual can qualify for the above-the-line deduction. So, too, do premiums for long-term care insurance to the extent listed in Table 2.4. But COBRA coverage does not qualify as eligible coverage for purposes of this above-the-line deduction because the insurance isn't under the self-employed's business (it's a former employer's plan).

If you are paying for your medical insurance, you may wish to combine this with a Health Savings Account (explained later in this chapter).

Pitfalls

The deduction does not offset business expenses. In the case of S corporation shareholders owning more than 2% of the corporation, the shareholder can deduct his or her premiums from gross income only if the corporation pays the premiums or reimburses the shareholder for the premiums *and* includes the premiums as wages on the shareholder's Form W-2.

The self-employed health insurance deduction is a reduction to qualified business income for purposes of the qualified business income deduction (see Chapter 14).

Where to Claim the Deduction

Figure the deduction on Form 7206, *Self-Employed Health Insurance Deduction*. The self-employed health insurance deduction is then reported on Schedule 1 of Form 1040 or 1040-SR (whether or not you itemize other medical expenses).

Long-Term Care Coverage

Individuals who are suffering from chronic conditions such as Alzheimer's disease or are merely elderly and incapable of self-care (such as feeding and bathing themselves) require long-term care, either in their own homes or in nursing homes or other facilities. According to a SeniorLiving.org, the average annual cost in 2025 of a nursing home stay in a private room is now $131,583 ($114,665 for a semiprivate room); it is $427,464 for a private room in Alaska. What's more, the cost of in-home care and adult daycare are also very high. These costs generally are *not* covered by Medicare or supplemental Medicare insurance. Only special insurance, called long-term care insurance, pays for long-term care. The tax law allows a portion of this special medical insurance to be deductible.

Benefit

You can deduct a portion of long-term care insurance premiums as a qualified medical expense (based on your age).

TABLE 2.4 Deductible Long-Term Care Premiums for 2025

Age by Year-End	Deduction Limit
Age 40 or younger	$ 480
Age 41–50	900
Age 51–60	1,800
Age 61–70	4,810
Age 71 or older	6,020

Benefits received under a long-term care policy generally are treated as tax-free income (the benefits are an exclusion from income).

Conditions

Since there are 2 benefits—a deduction for the payment of long-term care insurance premiums and an exclusion from income for benefits received under the policy—different conditions apply for each.

CONDITIONS FOR THE DEDUCTION

You can deduct only a portion of premiums based on your age. For 2025, the federal deduction is limited to the amounts shown in Table 2.4.

The premium limit is on a per-person basis.

Example

Both you and your spouse carry long-term care insurance. You are age 68 and your spouse is age 59. Your annual premium is $5,000 and your spouse's premium is $3,500. You can treat $6,610 ($4,810 for you and $1,800 for your spouse) of your total $8,500 premiums as a deductible medical expense if the sum of your medical expenses exceeds 7.5% of your AGI.

CONDITIONS FOR THE EXCLUSION

The exclusion from income for benefits received under the policy applies only to qualified long-term care services provided to a person who is chronically ill and that are necessary for medical or personal care and are provided under a plan of care prescribed by a licensed health care practitioner. You are chronically ill if a licensed health care practitioner certifies that within the past 12 months you meet *either* of these conditions:

- You are unable for at least 90 days to perform at least 2 activities of daily living without substantial assistance, due to loss of functional capacity. Activities of daily living include eating, toileting, transferring, bathing, dressing, and continence.

- You require substantial supervision for your safety due to severe cognitive impairment.

If the policy pays your long-term care expenses, you can exclude these payments.

Benefits paid under an indemnity-type contract are fully excludable to the extent they cover long-term care expenses. If you receive benefits under a per diem contract, there is a per-day dollar limit on what you can exclude. For 2025, the exclusion is $420 per day, even if your actual expenses are less.

Planning Tips

Since the average annual cost of a nursing home is very steep and can be expected to escalate in coming years, you might want to carry long-term care coverage to pay some or all of this cost if it arises. The younger you are when you purchase the policy, the smaller your annual premiums will be (they are fixed at the time of purchase although they may increase thereafter). Also, advanced age, a pre-existing condition, or some impairment may make it difficult if not impossible to obtain coverage.

Long-term care insurance may be available as an employee fringe benefit under your company's cafeteria plan. If you opt for this coverage, you are not taxed on this benefit.

If you add a long-term care rider to a life insurance or annuity contract, the premiums are not deductible when payments for long-term care are a charge against the cash surrender value of the life insurance policy. If there isn't such a charge, then the premiums for the long-term care portion are deductible subject to the limitations discussed earlier.

Many states allow more generous deductions or credits, even if you receive no benefit at the federal level. In New York, for example, there is a 20% tax credit, with no age or dollar limitation.

And some states have long-term care insurance partnerships, which are programs that encourage individuals to buy long-term care insurance while offering special state benefits. These benefits allow you to keep certain assets while qualifying for Medicaid for long-term care once you exhaust your insurance coverage. You can find a list of states offering these partnerships from the American Association for Long-Term Care (www.aaltci.org/long-term-care-insurance/learning-center/long-term-care-insurance-partnership-plans.php).

Commercial annuities can offer a long-term care rider. Such annuities usually cost from 35% to 50% more than stand-alone annuities.

The portion of the premiums allocable to long-term care coverage is deductible up to the limits described in this chapter, but only if the policy meets the tax law definition of qualified long-term care insurance contract. If you have such a policy or are considering one, ask the insurance company about this condition to nail down a deduction.

Pitfall

Since long-term care insurance usually pays a fixed dollar amount and, hopefully, you won't need long-term care for many years to come, it can be difficult to know how much insurance to carry. Consider including a cost-of-living rider to adjust your dollar coverage for inflation.

Where to Claim the Deduction and/or Exclusion

The deduction for long-term care insurance premiums is treated like other deductible medical expenses. Generally, they are included with your other itemized medical expenses (up to your allowable dollar limit for your age). If you are self-employed, you can include this amount with your other medical insurance claimed as part of the self-employed health insurance deduction, which is an adjustment to gross income.

Long-term care benefits are reported on Form 1099-LTC, *Long-Term Care and Accelerated Death Benefits*. If you receive benefits under a long-term care policy that are fully excludable, you do not have to report anything on your return. But if you are limited in what you can exclude (as explained earlier), excess benefits are reported as "other income" on Schedule 1 of Form 1040 or 1040-SR.

Flexible Spending Accounts for Health Care

Companies are increasingly forced to make employees pay for some or all of their medical expenses. But they can assist them by creating special arrangements, called flexible spending accounts (health FSAs), that enable employees to pay for some medical expenses on a pretax basis. This means employees can dedicate some of their wages to special accounts used for medical expenses. Amounts put into these accounts are not currently taxed. The maximum amount you can contribute to a health FSA in 2025 is $3,300. The limit for 2026 will be adjusted for inflation; check the Supplement for an update.

Benefit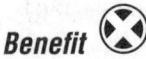

Businesses can set up flexible spending accounts (FSAs) to allow employees to pay for expenses not covered by insurance on a pretax basis. Before the start of the year employees agree to a salary reduction amount as their contribution to the FSA. These amounts are not treated as taxable compensation and are not subject to Social Security and Medicare (FICA) taxes. Employees then use these amounts any time during the year to pay for qualified medical costs, including health insurance premiums or other expenses not covered by insurance, such as orthodontia and prescription eyeglasses.

For purposes of health FSAs, reimbursable medical expenses include prescription medications and insulin, as well as over-the-counter medications (no prescription is necessary), condoms and over-the-counter birth control, personal protective equipment (PPE) to prevent the spread of COVID-19 and home test kits, menstrual products, and glucose monitors.

Conditions

The plan can set the limits on how much you can commit to the FSA each year up to the dollar limit allowed for the year (e.g., $3,300 for 2025). It may be fixed as a percentage of your compensation (e.g., up to 6%). Ask your plan administrator for details on your contribution limits and the deadline for signing up each year. Just because you were in the FSA this year does not automatically cover you for next year; you may be required to complete the same paperwork all over again.

Planning Tips

You can tap into your annual contribution at any time during the year, even before you have fully paid into the FSA.

> **Example**
>
> In December 2024 you agree to contribute $1,800 for 2025, which is $150 each month, to your company's FSA. In February 2025, when you have contributed only $300, you pay a dental bill of $1,500 that is not covered by insurance. You submit the paid bill to your plan administrator and receive the full reimbursement of $1,500.

Your employer can adopt an approved grace period for using up prior year contributions. The grace period cannot extend past March 15 of the following year.

Instead of a grace period, the plan may allow for a carryover of unused amounts to the following year. The carryover of unused amounts from 2025 is capped at $660.

At an employee's request, an employer can transfer funds in an FSA to an employee's Health Savings Account (HSA). The limit on the transfer is the lesser of the account balance on the date of transfer or on September 21, 2006. This is a one-time opportunity.

Reservists called to active duty can take penalty-free withdrawals from their FSAs for any purpose (not just medical).

Pitfalls

FSAs operate on a use-it-or-lose-it basis subject to the grace period or limited carryover discussed earlier. If you contribute more than your covered medical expenses for the year and cannot use it up in the contribution year or grace period (if applicable) and cannot take advantage of the carryover, you can't get the money back. Don't agree to a salary reduction amount in excess of what you reasonably expect to use for medical expenses. You can only make a prospective change in your salary reduction amount during the year if there's a qualifying event, such as marriage, divorce, death of a spouse, or birth or adoption of a child.

FSAs cannot pay for any expenses that would not qualify as a deductible medical expense (other than for over-the-counter medications and menstrual products). For example, FSAs cannot be used to pay for cosmetic surgery unless it is medically necessary—for example, to correct a birth defect, or for a breast pump, which is helpful to a nursing mother but does not treat or mitigate a medical condition.

If you leave the job before using up your FSA contributions for the year, you usually have to spend the unused amount within a time fixed by the plan (usually by the end of the month in which the employment ends). And, if you opt for COBRA (see later in this chapter), then FSA funds can continue to be used through the end of the year and through the grace period if applicable; no additional contributions can be made to the FSA after termination of employment.

Where to Claim the Benefit

Since this benefit is an exclusion from income, you do not have to report anything on your return. Compensation reported on your Form W-2 is reduced to the extent of your FSA contributions. FSA salary reduction contributions are not reported on Form W-2.

You are required to account to the FSA administrator in order to receive payments from the plan. For example, you may be asked to submit a paid bill for prescription sunglasses in order to receive reimbursement from the FSA, and the bill must be submitted within a certain period after incurring the expense. Talk to your plan administrator for rules on how to obtain reimbursements from the plan.

Health Reimbursement Arrangements

Companies are continually looking for ways to reduce their health care costs for employees. Health reimbursement arrangements allow employers to reimburse employees for certain medical costs if the arrangements conform to certain requirements.

Individual Coverage HRAs

Your employer may choose to reimburse you for your individually-obtained health coverage under an individual coverage health reimbursement arrangement (ICHRA). You don't contribute to this arrangement, although your employer can set up a salary reduction arrangement for you to pay premiums in excess of the reimbursements. An ICHRA is available only if your employer does not have traditional group health coverage. The reimbursement amount is fixed by your employer. Again, use the reimbursements to pay some or all of the premiums on health coverage you buy privately (on or off the government marketplace) or for Medicare. Depending upon the terms of your employer's plan, reimbursements can also be used to pay unreimbursed medical costs. These include amounts listed as itemized medical expenses earlier in this chapter. You are not taxed on the reimbursements.

Planning Pointers

You must substantiate your premium payments as required by your employer. This may include signing a statement attesting to coverage or providing other proof of coverage.

You are permitted once a year to opt out of the ICHRA if you find that the coverage isn't affordable. You can then obtain coverage through a Marketplace and use the premium tax credit (discussed earlier in this chapter) for premium payments.

Pitfall

You can be reimbursed only for eligible medical expenses (i.e., those that would be deductible by itemizers), assuming the plan allows for reimbursements of expenses other than insurance premiums. You cannot, for example, be reimbursed for vitamins and other health supplements.

Where to Claim the Benefit

Since this benefit is an exclusion from income, you do not have to report anything on your return.

Excepted Benefit HRAs

This option, called an excepted benefit health reimbursement arrangement (EBHRA), is a supplement to an employer's group health coverage to pay for co-payments, deductibles, other amounts not covered by insurance, and excepted benefits (e.g., dental and vision care). The dollar limit is fixed by the government annually and is $2,150 in 2025.

Looking Ahead

The 2026 limit on reimbursements under an EBHRA will be $2,200.

Planning Pointers

You must substantiate your payments as required by your employer. This may include signing a statement attesting to coverage or providing other proof of coverage.

Unused amounts may be carried forward to the next plan year.

Pitfall

Reimbursements cannot be used to pay health insurance premiums other than premiums for COBRA, short-term limited duration insurance, and dental and vision care.

Where to Claim the Benefit

Since this benefit is an exclusion from income, you do not have to report anything on your return.

QSEHRAs

Small businesses can offer Qualified Small Employer Health Reimbursement Arrangements (QSEHRAs), which are plans that enable employers to reimburse employees for their individually obtained health coverage on a tax-free basis. This benefit is paid entirely by employers; no employee salary reduction contributions are made. It is an alternative to the Individual Coverage HRA discussed earlier in this chapter.

Benefit ⊗

The value of the reimbursement received from your employer is not includible in gross income. This is so even though it may be reported on your Form W-2.

Conditions

There are several conditions for the exclusion to apply:

- Your employer must be a "small employer" (fewer than 50 full time/full-time equivalent employees) and not have any other group health plan.
- You must submit proof to your employer that you obtained health coverage.
- The amount of the annual reimbursement for 2025 is capped at $6,350 for self-only coverage or $12,800 for family coverage.

Planning Tip

While the Tax Code does not specify that reimbursement can cover an employee's cost under a spouse's plan through the spouse's employer, the IRS suggested in informal advice in 2015 that this could be possible. More IRS guidance is needed on this point.

Pitfalls

You cannot claim a premium tax credit for your coverage paid with QSEHRA reimbursements, even though your income is low enough that you'd otherwise qualify for it. If you claim the credit, the QSEHRA benefit is reduced dollar for dollar.

If you don't have coverage for the full year, the dollar limit for reimbursement is prorated. For example, if you have family coverage from July through December 2025, your exclusion is limited to $6,400 (half of the $12,800 annual limit).

Benefits under a QSEHRA do not have to be given to an employee who has not completed 90 days of service, is under age 25, or is a part-time or seasonal employee. If you are in any of these categories, check with your employer about reimbursements for your premiums.

Where to Claim the Benefit

Since this benefit is an exclusion from income, you do not have to report anything on your return.

Health Savings Accounts

Individuals who are covered by health insurance policies with high deductibles may be eligible to contribute money to a special savings account, called a Health Savings Account (HSA). HSAs have become a way to obtain needed health coverage now on an affordable basis. In 2024 (the most recent year for statistics), there were over 61 million people who had HSAs. HSAs can be obtained individually or through an employer if such a benefit is offered. Many employers are offering these accounts along with high-deductible health insurance (defined later), either as an employee's health care choice or the only option available.

Benefit

If you have a "high-deductible" health insurance policy (defined in the "Conditions" section), you can contribute to a special savings account. HSAs provide triple tax benefits:

1. Contributions within set limits are deductible as an adjustment to gross income (you do not have to itemize deductions to claim this benefit). See

TABLE 2.5 Health Savings Account Contribution Limits for 2025

Your Age	Self-Only Plan	Family Plan
Under age 55	$4,300	$8,550
55 or older	$5,300	$9,500*

*If both spouses are age 55 or older and contribute to add an additional $1,000, they must have separate HSAs.

Table 2.5 for 2025 limits. The limits for those under age 55 can be indexed for inflation (the limits for 2026 are in the *Planning Tips*); the additional contribution limit for those age 55 and older remains at $1,000.

2. Interest or other earnings in the account are tax deferred.

3. Withdrawals used to pay medical costs are tax free.

Conditions

To contribute to an HSA, you must meet 2 conditions:

1. You are not covered by Medicare.

2. You are covered by a high-deductible health plan (HDHP). Healthcare.gov has a filter to help you identify high-deductible health plan options on the government Marketplace.

MEDICARE

HSAs are designed to cover individuals who do not qualify for Medicare. Therefore, you are ineligible to make contributions to an HSA once you are enrolled in Medicare. Since determination of eligibility is made month by month, you may be qualified for a deduction for the portion of the year before you are covered by Medicare.

QUALIFYING HIGH-DEDUCTIBLE HEALTH INSURANCE

You must have a high-deductible health plan (HDHP) for at least all of December in 2025. This can be an insurance policy that you have obtained personally or coverage provided by your employer. The determination of whether you have such coverage is made on the first day of the month.

A high-deductible policy is one that falls within certain limits. (See Table 2.6.) An HDHP can pay for telehealth services and certain preventive care (listed below) without failing to be an HDHP.

TABLE 2.6 2025 High-Deductible Policy Limits

	Self-Only Coverage	Family Coverage
Annual deductible at least	$1,650	$3,300
Limit on out-of-pocket expenses	$8,300	$16,600

Looking Ahead

Starting in 2026, bronze and catastrophic plans purchased on a government marketplace are treated as HDHPs.

You cannot have any other health coverage, other than accident insurance, dental care, disability coverage, disease-specific coverage (such as cancer insurance), long-term care, vision care, and workers' compensation. But having a direct primary care membership not exceeding $150 per month for an individual or $300 per month for family coverage is not treated as other health coverage if you are enrolled in an HDHP.

The IRS has identified certain procedures and other expenses that can be covered by an HDHP *without* a deductible:

PREVENTIVE CARE PAYABLE BY HDHPS FOR THOSE DIAGNOSED WITH SPECIFIED CONDITIONS

- Angiotensin converting enzyme (ACE) inhibitors for congestive heart failure, diabetes, and/or coronary artery disease
- Anti-resorptive therapy for osteoporosis and/or osteopenia
- Beta-blockers for congestive heart failure and/or coronary artery disease
- Blood pressure monitor for hypertension
- Continuous glucose monitors
- Inhaled corticosteroids for asthma
- Insulin and other glucose-lowering agents for diabetes
- Retinopathy screening for diabetes
- Peak flow meter for asthma
- Glucose monitors and test strips for diabetes
- Hemoglobin AIc testing for diabetes
- International normalized ratio (INR) testing for liver disease and/or bleeding disorders
- Low-density lipoprotein (LDL) testing for heart disease

- Selective serotonin reuptake inhibitors (SSRIs) for depression
- Statins for heart disease and/or diabetes

OTHER ITEMS PAYABLE BY HDHPS WITHOUT A DEDUCTIBLE

- All types of breast screening for individuals who have not been diagnosed with breast cancer
- Blood glucose monitors and test strips
- Certain insulin products without regard to whether the insulin product is prescribed to treat an individual diagnosed with diabetes or prescribed for the purpose of preventing the exacerbation of diabetes or the development of a secondary condition
- Condoms
- Over-the-counter birth control
- Telehealth services

Tax-Free Withdrawals

Only account distributions used to pay qualified medical expenses are tax free. This does not include health insurance premiums other than for coverage listed below.

GENERAL EXPENSES

- Any expense that could be claimed as an itemized medical deduction (see the section earlier in this chapter)
- Child and adult immunizations
- COBRA premiums
- Health insurance premiums if unemployed
- Menstrual products
- Obesity weight-loss programs
- Over-the-counter medications (no prescription is necessary)
- Periodic health evaluations, such as annual physicals
- Personal protective equipment preventing the spread of COVID-19 (e.g., masks, hand sanitizer, sanitizing wipes)
- Premiums for long-term care insurance
- Routine prenatal and well-child care
- Screening services, such as those listed
- Sunscreen and lip balm with an SPF of 30 or more
- Tobacco cessation programs
- Vaporizers

Examples of Screening Services Treated as Medical Expenses for HSAs

CANCER SCREENING

- Breast cancer (e.g., mammogram)
- Cervical cancer (e.g., Pap smear)
- Colorectal cancer
- Oral cancer
- Ovarian cancer
- Prostate cancer (e.g., prostate-specific antigen [PSA] test)
- Skin cancer
- Testicular cancer
- Thyroid cancer

HEART AND VASCULAR DISEASES SCREENING

- Abdominal aortic aneurysm
- Carotid artery stenosis
- Coronary heart disease
- Hemoglobinopathies
- Hypertension
- Lip disorders

INFECTIOUS DISEASES SCREENING

- Bacteriuria
- Chlamydial infection
- COVID-19
- Gonorrhea
- Hepatitis B virus infection
- Hepatitis C
- Human immunodeficiency virus (HIV) infection
- Syphilis
- Tuberculosis infection

MENTAL HEALTH CONDITIONS AND SUBSTANCE ABUSE SCREENING

- Dementia
- Depression
- Drug abuse

- Family violence
- Problem drinking
- Suicide risk

METABOLIC, NUTRITIONAL, AND ENDOCRINE CONDITIONS SCREENING

- Anemia, iron deficiency
- Dental and periodontal disease
- Diabetes mellitus
- Obesity in adults
- Thyroid disease

MUSCULOSKELETAL DISORDERS SCREENING

- Osteoporosis

OBSTETRIC AND GYNECOLOGIC CONDITIONS SCREENING

- Bacterial vaginosis in pregnancy
- Gestational diabetes mellitus
- Home uterine activity monitoring
- Neural tube defects
- Preeclampsia
- Rh incompatibility
- Rubella
- Ultrasonography in pregnancy

PEDIATRIC CONDITIONS SCREENING

- Child developmental delay
- Congenital hypothyroidism
- Lead levels in childhood and pregnancy
- Phenylketonuria
- Scoliosis, adolescent idiopathic

VISION AND HEARING DISORDERS SCREENING

- Glaucoma
- Hearing impairment in older adults
- Newborn hearing

Planning Tips

It is up to you to keep track of medical costs so that you can prove withdrawals from your HSA were used to pay qualified expenses. The financial institution with which you have your account won't ask you for any substantiation on your part. Neither will your employer if the account is set up through your company.

HSAs can be funded by a one-time transfer by an employer from a flexible spending account (FSA) or by a health reimbursement arrangement (HRA), to an employee's HSA or an IRA rollover. Transfers from FSAs and HRAs are limited (as explained earlier in this chapter). Rollovers from IRAs are not currently taxed.

Deductible contributions to HSAs can be made up to the due date of the return (without regard to extensions). So, a contribution for 2025 can be made up to April 15, 2026. HSAs can be funded by means of a direct deposit of a tax refund; you must complete Form 8888 for this purpose. Be sure to designate whether the refund is being used to fund a 2025 or 2026 contribution, assuming eligibility for both years.

Example

If you expect a refund for 2025 taxes and plan to contribute to an HSA for 2025, file your return early enough so that the IRS has time to process it and transfer your refund directly to the HSA (you must provide account information to make the transfer possible). Alternatively, use a 2025 refund to make a contribution to an HSA for 2026 if eligible to do so for that year.

Funds in the HSA can be used for retirement savings. Since there is no tax on earnings when the account is building up, the healthier you stay (and the less you need to use account funds for medical bills), the more you'll have in retirement to use for any purpose. While the withdrawals for nonmedical purposes will be taxed, there is no penalty on any withdrawals once you reach age 65. Recognize the implications for taxation on the account when an owner dies. It can be rolled over tax free to a spouse who can then use the account in the same manner as an owner. But if there's a different beneficiary, the funds become immediately taxable to that beneficiary. If circumstances permit, it's better to drain the account for the owner's medical expenses before death.

Looking Ahead

For 2026, the contribution limits for HSAs are $4,400 for self-only coverage and $8,750 for family coverage. Those age 55 or older can add another $1,000. The parameters for a high deductible health plan in 2026 are a minimum deductible of $1,700 and maximum out-of-pocket limit of $8,500 for self-only coverage ($3,400 and $17,000 respectively for family coverage).

Pitfalls

If you take withdrawals to pay nonmedical expenses, the distribution is taxed as ordinary income, regardless of your age or the investments in the HSA. In addition, if you are under age 65, you are also subject to a 20% penalty (unless you are disabled). Taxable income treatment and the 20% penalty applies if the IRS levies on the HSA to cover back taxes, even though the withdrawal is involuntary. There is no 20% penalty on distributions because of the account owner's death.

If you have a separate prescription drugs benefit plan that has no deductible (only copayments for each prescription), you cannot be an eligible individual for HSA purposes.

If you receive a retroactive lump sum from Social Security because you begin taking benefits after your full retirement age, keep in mind that you'll also be automatically enrolled in Medicare retroactively. This means that any contributions made to your HSA during that retroactive period are "excess contributions" (contributions for the portion of the year prior to the Medicare coverage are permissible). Excess contributions are subject to a 6% excise tax until the excess amount, plus earnings on it, are withdrawn from the account.

If you inherit an HSA and are not a surviving spouse of the account owner, you must take a complete distribution of the account and include all of the funds in your income. Check to see if you qualify for a deduction for federal estate tax on the HSA (see Chapter 15).

If, for any reason, you file an amended return to claim a tax refund, you cannot have the refund deposited directly into your HSA as you can with a refund from an original return. You'll need to receive a paper check from the government (there are no direct deposits for refunds from amended returns) and then make your HSA contribution.

Where to Claim the Benefits

The deduction is figured on Form 8889, *Health Savings Accounts (HSAs)*. The deduction is then claimed on Schedule 1 of Form 1040 or 1040-SR.

An employer does not report HSA contributions—by the employer or employee—on Form W-2. If your employer contributes to an HSA on your behalf, this is a tax-free fringe benefit; no reporting is required.

Withdrawals are reported to you (and the IRS) on Form 1099-SA, *Distributions from an HSA, Archer MSA, or Medicare Advantage MSA*. Funds withdrawn for anything other than medical expenses are taxable as ordinary income. Report the income on Schedule 1 of Form 1040 or 1040-SR as other income. If you owe a 20% penalty on withdrawals for nonmedical purposes before age 65, you report the penalty on Schedule 2 of Form 1040 or 1040-SR.

Archer Medical Savings Accounts

Self-employed individuals and small employers had been able to set up Archer Medical Savings Accounts (MSAs) to save money for their health insurance costs by combining a "high-deductible" medical insurance policy with this special savings plan. The opportunity to set up new MSAs expired at the end of 2007, so contributions for 2025 can be made only to MSAs set up before 2008. (As far as I could determine, there are fewer than 150,000 individuals now covered by Archer MSAs.). If they have a policy that falls within parameters set by the tax law, then they (or their employees) can contribute a fixed amount to an IRA-like account. Contributions are deductible, earnings are not currently subject to tax, and withdrawals for medical purposes are tax free (i.e., contributions and earnings on contributions used to pay medical costs are never taxed). Archer MSAs are an alternative to HSAs for eligible taxpayers, although HSAs usually are more favorable and have largely replaced the use of Archer MSAs.

Benefit

If you are self-employed or an employee of a small employer with a "high-deductible" health insurance policy (defined in "Conditions" section), you can contribute to a special savings account that can be tapped to cover unreimbursed medical expenses. There are several benefits to Archer MSAs:

- Contributions within set limits are deductible (or tax free if made by your employer).
- Interest or other earnings in the account are tax deferred.
- Withdrawals used to cover medical expenses are tax free.

Conditions

You must be self-employed or an employee of a "small employer" covered by a "high-deductible" health insurance policy. A small employer is an employer who had on average 50 or fewer employees during either of the 2 preceding calendar years. As long as the Archer MSA was in place before 2008 the employer can continue to have an Archer MSA and be treated as a small employer as long as it had no more than 200 employees each year after 1996.

TABLE 2.7 2025 Limits on Deductibles and Out-of-Pocket Expenses

Type of Coverage	Minimum Annual Deductible	Maximum Annual Deductible	Maximum Annual Out-of-Pocket Expenses
Individual (self-only policy)	$2,850	$4,300	$5,700
Family	$5,700	$8,550	$10,500

A high-deductible policy is one that falls within certain limits on deductibles and out-of-pocket expenses required to be paid (other than premiums) before the policy kicks in. (See Table 2.7.)

Example

In 2025, you are self-employed and have a self-only health insurance policy with an annual deductible of $3,000 and a limit on out-of-pocket expenses of $5,200. You had set up an MSA in 2006 and have been funding it annually. Assuming you meet other conditions, you have a high-deductible plan and can fund your Archer MSA in 2025.

You (or your spouse) cannot have any other health plan that is not a high-deductible plan. But coverage under certain other health plans will not prevent you from being able to fund an Archer MSA. Other coverage you may have *in addition* to a high-deductible plan includes insurance covering accidents, disability, dental care, vision care, long-term care, benefits related to workers' compensation, a specific illness or disease, or a fixed amount per day or other period of hospitalization.

Assuming you meet the conditions for claiming a deduction, the amount of the deduction is limited to 65% of your annual insurance deductible for self-only coverage or 75% of your annual insurance deductible for family coverage.

Example

In 2025, you are self-employed and have a health insurance policy for family coverage with a $6,800 annual insurance deductible (which is more than the minimum deductible of $5,700 but less than the maximum deductible of $8,550 in 2025). In 2025, you can contribute $5,100 to an Archer MSA ($6,800 × 75%) (assuming the account was set up prior to 2008 and the out-of-pocket expense limit does not exceed $10,500 in 2025).

If you have coverage for only part of the year, you must prorate the deduction.

Example

Same facts as in the preceding example but you end coverage on June 30, 2025, and maintain it for the balance of the year. You can contribute $2,550 to an Archer MSA ($6,800 × 75% ÷ 12 months × 6 months).

Contributions for 2025 must be made no later than April 15, 2026.

Planning Tips

You can roll over funds in an Archer MSA tax free to a Health Savings Account. This may be advisable because of the extensive availability of financial institutions offering HSAs compared with limited Archer MSA options.

Assuming eligibility, you can fund an Archer MSA for 2025 or 2026 via a direct deposit of your 2025 tax refund. Just provide the IRS with the account information on Form 8888 and your refund will be transferred directly to your account.

As in the case of HSAs, you can use an Archer MSA to provide retirement income. Money can be withdrawn for any purpose penalty-free after you attain age 65.

Pitfalls

If you are self-employed, you cannot contribute more than your net earnings from self-employment. If you have a loss year, you cannot fund an Archer MSA.

Example

You are 65 years old and, because you have stayed healthy, the funds in your account have accumulated to $10,000. You can withdraw this money to take a vacation. While you'll owe income tax on the withdrawal because you are not using the funds for medical reasons, you are not subject to the 20% penalty (explained next).

If you withdraw funds from an Archer MSA for other than medical expenses before attaining age 65, the funds are subject to a 20% penalty unless you are disabled (or die).

WHEN YOU DIE

If you have an Archer MSA, you can name your spouse as the beneficiary of the account. Your spouse becomes the owner of the account when you die. If you designate any other person as your beneficiary, the account ceases to be an Archer MSA on your death and the funds remaining in the account are taxable to the beneficiary as income. If there is no designated beneficiary, the balance of your account is included as income on your final tax return.

Where to Claim the Benefits

The deduction is figured on Form 8853, *Archer MSAs and Long-Term Care Insurance Contracts*. The deduction is then claimed on Schedule 1 of Form 1040 or 1040-SR.

If your employer contributes to an Archer Medical Savings Account on your behalf, this is a tax-free fringe benefit; no reporting is required. The contribution is not reported on Form W-2.

REPORTING INCOME

Withdrawals are reported to you (and the IRS) on Form 1099-SA, *Distributions from an HSA, Archer MSA, or Medicare Advantage MSA*. Funds withdrawn for anything other than medical expenses are taxable as ordinary income. Report the income on Schedule 1 of Form 1040 or 1040-SR as other income.

If you owe a 20% penalty on withdrawals for nonmedical purposes before age 65, you report the penalty on Schedule 2 of Form 1040 or 1040-SR.

ABLE Accounts

Federal law enables states to create special accounts called Achieving a Better Life Experience (ABLE) accounts, which are designed to ease the financial burden of families with disabled children. At present, ABLE accounts are live in 46 states and the District of Columbia, but those in the 4 states without ABLE accounts can open an account in another state that allows nonresidents to do so. These accounts generally do not adversely impact eligibility for means-tested government programs (e.g., Medicaid can continue regardless of the amount of assets in the account).

Benefit ⊗

Contributions to an ABLE account are not tax deductible. But earnings grow on a tax-deferred basis and withdrawals for qualified disability purposes are tax free.

The maximum contribution amount in 2025 is $19,000 per beneficiary. The contribution limit can be increased under certain circumstances if it's made by the designated beneficiary. Contributions can also be made by rolling over funds from a 529 plan, subject to the annual contribution limit.

Conditions

The beneficiary of the ABLE account must be either:

- Receiving Social Security disability payments on account of blindness or a disability that occurred before age 26
- Certified by a doctor that he or she is blind or disabled due to an impairment that began before age 26 and that is expected to result in death or last (or has lasted) for at least 12 months

Looking Ahead

Starting in 2026, the age for an ABLE account rises to 46. It's estimated that an additional 6 million Americans, including 1 million veterans, will then have access to ABLE accounts.

The beneficiary can have only one ABLE account at a time.

Distributions from an ABLE account are excludable from income only if used for qualified disability expenses, which include:

- Assistive technology
- Education
- Employment training
- Funeral and burial expenses
- Health
- Housing
- Personal support services
- Prevention and wellness
- Transportation

Planning Tips

Investment choices can be changed up to 2 times per year. And contributions may entitle the beneficiary to claim the retirement savers credit (see Chapter 5).

A family that has been thinking of setting up a supplemental needs trust for a disabled child should consider whether an ABLE account can meet the family's objectives. Discuss the situation with a knowledgeable attorney.

ABLE account programs are active in all but a handful of states. Check the map at the ABLE National Resource Center at www.ablenrc.org/state-review

for information on your state. You do not have to open an account in your state; there is no residency requirement for having an ABLE account.

Pitfalls

While assets in an ABLE account do not prevent eligibility for Supplemental Support Income (SSI), once the account balance reaches $100,000, SSI benefits are suspended (but not terminated).

A distribution is comprised of a return of contributions (which are not taxed) and a receipt of earnings (which are taxed). This is figured on a pro rata basis. In addition, there is a 10% penalty on the taxable amount of the distribution (regardless of the beneficiary's age).

Where to Claim the Benefit

You do not report contributions you make to an ABLE account on your return (remember, they are not deductible).

COBRA Coverage

The Consolidated Omnibus Budget Reconciliation Act of 1986, or COBRA for short, imposed a new requirement on certain employers who maintain health insurance coverage for workers: allow workers who leave the job to continue their company coverage for a period of time (at the workers' expense). The opportunity to continue under the company's health plan means that terminated workers and other eligible people can pay for medical insurance at group rates.

Benefits

Under federal law, if you work for a company that regularly employs 20 or more workers and has group health insurance, you are entitled to continue under the employer's group plan even if you leave employment (voluntarily or are laid off for any reason other than gross misconduct) or your hours are reduced below the level entitling you to employer-paid coverage. This is referred to as COBRA continuation coverage, or simply COBRA. Your state may have its own "mini-COBRA" law, so, even if the employer has fewer than 20 employees, state law may extend COBRA rights to employees and former employees.

Being eligible for and electing COBRA coverage gives you 2 key benefits:

1. Health insurance at an affordable group rate (but see Planning Tips).
2. A deduction for premium payments if you itemize your medical expenses.

You can continue COBRA coverage for up to 18 months or until you become eligible under a new employer's plan, you qualify for Medicare, or you fail to make your COBRA payments (there is usually a 30-day grace period). The coverage period can be extended to 29 months if you become disabled within the first 60 days of COBRA coverage. Your family can retain COBRA coverage for up to 36 months if their eligibility results from your death.

You usually must pay the full cost of coverage, plus up to 2% as an administrative fee (payment of 102% of the premiums). But you enjoy the group term rates, which may be less than what you could purchase on your own. Your payment of premiums under COBRA is a deductible medical expense (explained earlier).

Conditions for Coverage

If your employer is subject to COBRA, you must notify the employer about a qualifying event and opt for coverage within 60 days of that event (no extensions are granted). A qualifying event includes:

- You terminate employment (voluntarily or involuntarily, as long as you are not terminated for fraud or other gross misconduct).
- Your parent has health insurance through his or her employer and you attain the age at which you no longer qualify (generally through age 26).
- Your spouse has health coverage through his or her employer and you divorce your spouse.

SECOND COBRA ELECTION PERIOD

This second time to opt for COBRA applies only if you were receiving trade adjustment allowance (TAA) benefits (or would be but for the requirement that you first exhaust unemployment benefits), you lost health coverage because of termination of employment that resulted in TAA eligibility, and you did not elect COBRA during the regular COBRA election period.

Planning Tips

Before opting for COBRA, see if there are less costly health insurance options. For example, if your spouse is working, his or her employer may offer less expensive health coverage. You may be able to buy coverage through a professional or trade association or through the government Marketplace that is less expensive than COBRA.

If you obtain COBRA coverage with the federal subsidy, even if the subsidy is taxable to you, there is still a cost savings.

Pitfalls

COBRA may not be less costly than coverage you could obtain on an individual basis through the government insurance Marketplace. You may even qualify for help paying premiums through an advance of the premium tax credit explained earlier in this chapter.

You can reduce your current level of coverage under COBRA, but you can't increase it. For example, if you had dental coverage but now wish to eliminate it (and the expense) under COBRA, you can do so. But if you didn't have dental coverage, you can't add it under COBRA.

COBRA does not apply to long-term care insurance. You may be able to pick up the long-term care policy individually when you leave employment, but your employer is not required to offer you this coverage through COBRA.

If you leave employment and are at least 65 years old, Medicare is your primary carrier so apply for coverage. This is so even if you opt for COBRA coverage for medical costs not covered by Medicare. Medicare is usually the primary coverage; COBRA is secondary.

Where to Claim the Deduction

COBRA payments are treated as a deductible medical expense (see earlier in this chapter).

Medicare

In 1965, Congress introduced a federally sponsored health insurance program as part of the Social Security Act. This program, called Medicare, is designed primarily to provide those age 65 and older with affordable comprehensive health coverage. Today, the program has grown to afford seniors various types of coverage options, from fee-based services to managed care programs. More than 67 million Americans are now covered by Medicare.

Benefit

If you are age 65 or older, are under age 65 and disabled for at least 2 years, or have end-stage renal disease, you are entitled to participate in Medicare. Your monthly premiums (whether paid directly by you or withheld from your Social Security benefits check), as well as your copayments and deductibles under Medicare, are qualified medical expenses that are deductible to the extent your total exceeds 7.5% of adjusted gross income (see the general rules on deducting medical expenses, including medical insurance, discussed earlier in this chapter). You are not taxed on the benefits you receive through Medicare. If you are self-employed, you can treat your Medicare premiums as self-employed coverage. This is 100% deductible as an adjustment to gross income; no itemizing is required.

If your Medicare premiums are being withheld from Social Security benefits, the amount of your annual Medicare premiums is reported to you in the description of the amount in box 3 of Form SSA-1099, *Social Security Benefit Statement*.

Part A, which covers hospitalization, is free (those who did not work a sufficient number of quarters can pay for this coverage). Part B, which covers doctors' charges and certain other expenses, requires you to pay a monthly premium. The premium is subtracted from your Social Security benefits if you are collecting benefits. Both Part A and Part B have certain copayments or deductibles for your covered medical expenses.

There is a Medicare prescription drug plan called Part D. For 2025, there is an annual deductible of $590 ("deductible period"). Then you pay 25% of prescription drug costs ("initial coverage period"); this period is capped at $2,000. Then you reach the period of catastrophic coverage where you pay nothing for covered medications for the rest of the year.

Part C, called Medicare Advantage, includes both Part B and Part D coverage. More than half of all Medicare beneficiaries have Part C coverage.

Extra Help program. Certain low-income beneficiaries qualify for additional assistance to pay for prescription drugs in what is called the Extra Help program. To be eligible for partial Extra Help in 2025, beneficiaries enrolled in Medicare Part D must have an annual income in 2025 below $23,712 if single or $31,968 if married and not be eligible for any other prescription drug coverage (including outpatient prescription drug coverage through Medicare managed care plans). Income does not include earned income tax credit payments. Beneficiaries cannot have savings and resources (excluding a home, car, personal possessions, and a burial plot) exceeding $17,600 if single or $35,130 if married and living together for Extra Help in paying for prescription drugs. More modest income and asset limits apply for full Extra Help. Details on the Medicare drug program can be found at www.medicare.gov or through the Medicare Rights Center at https://bit.ly/2NxzsZq.

Conditions

To be eligible for free coverage under Part A, you (or your spouse) must have at least 40 quarters of Medicare-covered employment. If you don't have the necessary number of quarters, you can pay for this coverage.

Part B is available to just about anyone age 65 or older (there are no minimum work requirements). The same is true for Part C.

Part D is available to all Medicare beneficiaries.

Planning Tips

Medicare coverage generally isn't automatic; you must apply for it if you haven't yet applied for Social Security benefits. You should contact your local Social Security office to apply for Medicare 3 months before the date you reach your full retirement age so that coverage can start on time.

If you have been collecting Social Security benefits before your full retirement age (e.g., starting at age 62), you do not have to apply when you near age 65; enrollment in Medicare Part A (hospitalization insurance) in this case is automatic and free; but you must then decide whether to also elect Medicare Part B (health insurance). Alternatively, you can enroll in Medicare Advantage (Part C), which provides the same coverage as Parts A and B (and in most cases Part D as well).

If you opt for traditional fee-for-service Medicare (rather than some managed care program within Medicare), you may want to purchase supplemental Medicare insurance ("Medigap" coverage). Medigap premiums are deductible as a qualified medical expense (explained earlier in this chapter).

Pitfalls

If you claim the standard deduction (including the additional amount for being age 65 or older), you cannot deduct your Medicare payments since you do not itemize deductions.

If your modified adjusted gross income in 2023 was above a certain amount for your filing status, you are subject to surcharges on your 2025 Medicare premiums. For example, the "standard" premium for Part B coverage in 2025, the premium paid by most beneficiaries, is $185.00 per month. Tables 2.8 and 2.9 (one for Part B and one for Part D) show the 2025 surcharges and total premiums for higher-income taxpayers, which are based on modified adjusted gross income (MAGI) in 2023.

TABLE 2.8 Part B Premiums for 2025

2023 MAGI for Joint Filers	2023 MAGI for Other Filers*	Total Monthly Part B Premium for 2025
Up to $212,000	Up to $106,000	$185.00
$212,001 to $266,000	$106,001 to $133,000	$259.00
$266,001 to $334,000	$133,001 to $167,000	$370.00
$334,001 to $400,000	$167,001 to $200,000	$480.90
$400,001 to $749,999	$200,001 to $499,999	$591.90
$750,000 or greater	$500,000 or greater	$628.90

*Married persons filing separately who did not live apart for the entire year are subject to a monthly premium for 2025 of $409.90 if 2023 MAGI was over $106,000 but under $394,000, or $628.90 if 2023 MAGI was $394,000 or more.

TABLE 2.9 Part D Premiums for 2025

2023 MAGI for Joint Filers	2023 for Other Filers*	Total Monthly Part D Premiums for 2025
Up to $212,000	Up to $106,000	Plan premium (no surcharge)
$212,001 to $266,000	$106,001 to $133,000	$13.70 + plan premium
$266,001 to $334,000	$133,001 to $167,000	$35.30 + plan premium
$334,001 to $400,000	$167,001 to $200,000	$57.00 + plan premium
$400,001 to $749,999	$200,001 to $499,999	$78.60 + plan premium
$750,000 and higher	$500,000 and higher	$85.80 + plan premium

*Married persons filing separately who did not live apart for the entire year are subject to a monthly premium for 2023 of $78.60 if 2023 MAGI was over $106,000 but under $394,000, or $85.80 if 2022 MAGI was $394,000 or more.

The Medicare surcharges for 2026, based on MAGI for 2024, will be included in the Supplement.

If you wait too long to apply for Medicare Part B, your monthly premium will be increased. To obtain the lowest possible premium, you *must* apply either within a 7-month window extending from 3 months before to 4 months after your 65th birthday, or, if still employed and covered at work where employer coverage is your primary coverage (there are more than 20 employees at the company), within 8 months after that ends.

If you did not sign up for Medicare Part D but were eligible to do so, and you do not have other "creditable coverage" (e.g., employer or other coverage that is at least as good as Medicare), you are penalized 1% per month for each month you delay.

Example

If you wait 15 months to sign up beyond the deadline, you pay 15% of the premium as a penalty when you enroll. If the premium is normally $40 per month, you'd pay $46 per month ($40 plus 15% penalty). The penalty percentage continues for the rest of your life.

When figuring the tax on Social Security benefits, you use gross benefits (the amount reported in box 5 of Form SSA-1099) even though benefits you received are reduced by Medicare premiums.

Where to Claim the Deduction

You deduct premiums as well as your copayments and deductibles as itemized medical expenses (see earlier in this chapter). You must complete Schedule A and attach it to Form 1040 or 1040-SR.

Continuing Care Facilities and Nursing Homes

Elderly and infirm individuals may require round-the-clock care because of their age or condition. Comprehensive programs in special living arrangements are now used to care for these individuals. A portion of the cost may qualify as a deductible medical expense for those who itemize. Unless the cost is covered by long-term care insurance, it is likely that annual costs are high enough to warrant itemizing personal deductions and claiming a write-off for the cost of this care.

Benefit

Advanced age and/or chronic illness may require ongoing daily treatment. Payments for nursing homes, convalescent homes, and sanitariums may be treated as deductible medical expenses. The deduction generally is not limited to the portion covering medical care; it also includes lodging and meals if confinement is primarily for the purpose of medical treatment.

If the main reason for admission is not medical care, you can still treat the portion of monthly fees allocable to medical care as a deductible medical expense. Typically, this applies to fees to continuing care facilities—the portion of the fees for medical care is deductible but the portion covering lodging and meals is not.

Conditions

Admission to the facility must be *primarily* for medical treatment to deduct all charges and fees. You can prove this by showing that:

- Entry was on or at the direction of a doctor.
- Attendance or treatment at the facility has a direct therapeutic effect on the condition suffered by the patient.
- Attendance at the facility is for the treatment of a specific ailment and not merely for general good health.

Planning Tip

Generally, prepayments for future care are not currently deductible medical expenses. You can claim a current deduction if you can show there is a current obligation to pay and you can establish the portion of the prepayment allocated to medical care.

Example

You and your spouse enter a retirement home that requires the payment of an entrance fee of $50,000, plus monthly payments of $1,000, to cover your accommodations, meals, and medical care for life. The home estimates for you that 10% of the entrance fee and 15% of the monthly fee are used for medical care. If you leave the home, you are entitled to a refund of a portion of the founder's fee. On these facts, you can treat 10% of the entrance fee and 15% of the monthly fee paid in the year as deductible medical expenses.

Pitfall

If you claim the standard deduction (including the additional amount for being age 65 or older), you cannot deduct your payments for continuing care facilities or nursing homes since you do not itemize deductions. As a practical matter, if you are a resident in such a facility for a full year and you don't have long-term care insurance, the cost will generally result in a large enough medical deduction to warrant itemizing your deductions in lieu of claiming the standard deduction, even with the additional amount for age.

Where to Claim the Benefit

See itemized medical expenses earlier in this chapter.

Accelerated Death Benefits

Whoever thought that life insurance could be beneficial to the person insured? Today, policies intended to provide death benefits to heirs may be used for lifetime assistance to the insured under special circumstances. The proceeds receive the same tax-free treatment as death proceeds in certain circumstances.

Benefit ⊗

If you own a life insurance policy with cash value and become terminally or chronically ill, you may be able to tap into that cash value on a tax-free basis to pay medical and other personal expenses.

There are 2 ways in which to use a life insurance policy to provide you with current cash on a tax-free basis:

1. Tap into the policy's cash surrender value under an accelerated death benefit clause if the policy contains such an option.
2. Sell the policy to a viatical settlement company (a company in the business of buying policies under these conditions).

Conditions

You must be terminally or chronically ill to qualify for the exclusion. You are considered to be terminally ill if a physician certifies that you suffer from an illness or physical condition that is reasonably expected to result in death within 24 months of the date of certification.

You are considered to be chronically ill if a licensed health care practitioner certifies that within the past 12 months you meet *either* of these conditions:

- You are unable for at least 90 days to perform at least 2 activities of daily living without substantial assistance, due to loss of functional capacity. Activities of daily living include eating, toileting, transferring, bathing, dressing, and continence.
- You require substantial supervision for your safety due to severe cognitive impairment.

LIMITS FOR THE CHRONICALLY ILL

While *all* payments received by someone who is terminally ill are fully excludable (whether or not such amounts are used for medical care), limits apply to those who are chronically but not terminally ill. The same limits for benefits received under a long-term care policy apply for this purpose. If accelerated death benefits are not more than the daily dollar limit ($420 in 2025) and do not exceed actual long-term care costs, they are fully excludable. But any excess amounts are taxable.

Planning Tip

To the extent you use accelerated death benefits for medical expenses, you reap a double tax benefit: The funds are tax-free income to you, and you can treat the payments you make as deductible medical expenses if you itemize your deductions.

Pitfall

To the extent you use your life insurance policy while you are alive, there is that much less for your beneficiaries after your death. If you have other options to cover your expenses, you might weigh your current needs against your beneficiaries' needs after your death in deciding whether to use accelerated death benefits.

Where to Claim the Benefit

Benefits are reported to you on Form 1099-LTC, *Long-Term Care and Accelerated Death Benefits*. If benefits are fully excludable, they are not reported. If a chronically ill person receives benefits in excess of the limit ($420 per day in

2025), such amounts are reported as other income on Schedule 1 of Form 1040 or 1040-SR.

Decedent's Final Illness

There are no special deductions for someone who dies. But the tax law provides opportunities on the timing of deductions for the deceased. Those handling the affairs of a person who has died can choose how to claim medical deductions for optimum tax savings.

Benefit

Payments of medical expenses for a deceased spouse or dependent can be deducted as a medical expense in the year they are paid, even if this is before or after the person's death.

A decedent's personal representative (executor, administrator, etc.) has a choice of how to treat medical expenses—as an itemized deduction on the decedent's final income tax return (to the extent provided) or as a deduction on the estate tax return. Of course, if the decedent's estate is too small to require the filing of an estate tax return, there is no real choice; the expenses should automatically be treated as a deduction on the decedent's income tax return. But no deduction can be claimed unless there is itemizing on the decedent's final income tax return.

If the personal representative of a decedent's estate pays medical expenses within one year of death, an election can be made to treat the expenses as if they were paid by the decedent in the year the services were provided rather than the year in which they were paid. This may entitle the personal representative to file an amended return for the decedent for a prior year.

Example

In 2024, the decedent received treatment for a condition that eventually resulted in her death on May 1, 2025. At the time of death, payment for this treatment was outstanding. Assuming her personal representative pays any of her unreimbursed cost in February 2025, the personal representative may file an amended return for the decedent for 2024 to include the payment along with the decedent's other deductible medical expenses.

Condition

The decision on when and where to claim the decedent's medical expenses is made by the personal representative—the executor, administrator, or other person empowered by a court to act for the estate. This person can override a decision by a surviving spouse.

Planning Tip

Generally, if the decedent leaves an estate large enough to be subject to estate tax, it usually is preferable to claim the deduction on the estate tax return because the estate tax rate is 40%. What's more, *all* of the medical expenses can be deducted on the estate tax return; there is no AGI floor for this purpose. Of course, given the federal estate tax exemption of $13.99 million per person in 2025, most people who die in 2025 will not have any federal estate tax, so the costs of a final illness will probably be deducted on the final income tax return.

Pitfall

If the personal representative opts to deduct medical expenses on the decedent's income tax return, the portion that is not deductible because of the applicable percentage of AGI cannot be claimed on the estate tax return.

EXAMPLES OF NONDEDUCTIBLE EXPENSES FOR A DECEDENT

- Burial fees
- Cremation costs
- Funeral expenses
- Perpetual care for a grave or mausoleum

Where to Claim the Benefit

If the personal representative opts to deduct eligible medical expenses on the decedent's income tax return, a statement must be attached to the return agreeing *not* to claim the expenses as a deduction on the decedent's estate tax return.

Medical Insurance Rebates

Insurance companies must spend a set portion of premiums (called a medical loss ratio) on health services. If they fail to do so by overspending on salaries and other administrative costs, they are required to rebate premiums in the form of cash or premium reductions to policyholders. The payouts usually are issued by September 30, 2025, for rebates on coverage in 2024. Private insurers were expected to pay out about $1.1 billion to consumers in 2025 as rebates on their 2024 coverage. Not everyone receives a rebate, but if you do, it may be tax free or taxable to you.

Benefit ⬤

If you claimed the standard deduction, any rebate is fully tax free. If you itemized deductions, the rebate is taxable to you according to the tax benefit rule (the same rule for tax refunds applies to medical insurance rebates so you can use Worksheet 16.1 to figure your taxable amount). Similarly, if you are self-employed and claimed a deduction for premiums from gross income, the rebate is taxable.

If, under an employer plan, you paid premiums through a salary reduction contribution using pretax dollars, the rebate is treated as additional compensation to you in 2025. If you used after-tax dollars, the rebate is taxed according to the tax benefit rule.

Where to Report the Rebate

If you determine that the 2024 rebate received in 2025 is taxable, do *not* amend your 2024 return. Instead report the taxable portion as "other income" on Schedule 1 of your 2025 Form 1040 or 1040-SR.

Forgiveness of Medical Debt

In 2024, Connecticut became the first state to cancel medical debt for eligible residents. A number of other states and local governments have efforts underway or help with cancellation of medical debt.

The state contracted with a non-profit organization to buy the debt. For federal tax purposes, income from the cancellation of debt forgiven by a non-profit organization is not taxable; it's treated as a gift from the organization.

Some other locations, such as New Orleans, New York City, and Pittsburgh, have or are considering similar programs. If the debt is simply forgiven by the government, it is taxable; if it's forgiven by a non-profit organization, as is the case in Connecticut, it is a tax-free gift.

Education Costs

No one doubts the importance of education—for ourselves, our children, and our grandchildren—but obtaining it can be pricey. According to MEFA.org, the average cost in the U.S. for college tuition, fees, food, and housing for the 2025–2026 school year is $60,358 at a 4-year private school, $25,668 for a 4-year in-state school, and $45,413 for a 4-year out-of-state school. And don't forget other costs, such as books and supplies, transportation, etc. Fortunately, the tax law provides many incentives to help you save for education and to pay for it on a tax-advantaged basis.

This chapter explains the tax deductions, credits, and other breaks you can claim with respect to education costs. For more information, see IRS Publication 970, *Tax Benefits for Education*.

FAFSA Submissions

If you want to apply for federal financial aid for yourself or your child, you must complete the Free Application for Federal Student Aid (FAFSA). The information on the application is based on your federal income tax return.

Submission of the 2025–2026 FSFSA is July 1, 2025, through June 30, 2026. New on this FAFSA form is the Who's My FAFSA Parent? wizard, which is an online tool to help dependent children identify which parent(s) will be a required contributor on their FAFSA form. There is also a new page that confirms if their information was successfully matched with IRS records to request federal tax information to help complete the financial sections.

The information on the application can be based on the *prior*-prior year's information (2 years prior), instead of the prior year's information. This allows tax information from the prior-prior year to be readily available.

Example

The FAFSA form for aid in the 2025–2026 school year was based on your 2023 federal income tax return. Information on your 2025 federal income tax return won't come into play until the 2027–2028 FAFSA form.

You can retrieve your tax return information from the IRS electronically through Fafsa.ed.gov if you e-filed your tax return. While this option has been available for a while, the new submission deadline makes it easier for you as well as more students and their parents to use the option.

Employer-Paid Education Assistance

Companies want an educated workforce. Some are willing to underwrite the cost of additional education for their employees. The tax law not only allows companies to deduct the costs they pay on behalf of workers for higher education, but also workers can enjoy this fringe benefit tax free up to a set dollar amount each year. Education assistance includes payments toward employees' student loans.

Benefit ⊗

If your employer pays or reimburses you for the cost of higher education under an educational assistance program (undergraduate or graduate level), you are not taxed on payments up to $5,250 in 2025. If the courses are job-related, there is no dollar limit to the exclusion from income for this employer-paid fringe benefit. This fringe benefit is not subject to Social Security and Medicare (FICA) taxes.

If you work for an educational institution and receive tuition reductions, such benefit may be excludable (see Conditions, next).

If in 2025 your employer pays your student loan debt directly or reimburses you for it, you aren't taxed on up to $5,250.

Looking Ahead

Starting in 2026, the $5,250 will be adjusted for inflation. Check the Supplement for the 2026 dollar limit.

Conditions

Different conditions apply to employer-paid education under an education assistance plan and tuition reduction if you work for a college or university.

EMPLOYER-PAID EDUCATION

Employer-paid education must be furnished under an employer's written education assistance plan that does not discriminate in favor of owners or highly paid employees.

The courses do *not* have to be job-related to qualify for the limited exclusion of $5,250 in 2025. For example, if you are currently a programmer and your employer pays for accounting courses, you can still exclude the benefit.

There is no dollar limit on the amount you can exclude from income if you meet the following 3 conditions:

1. The courses relate to your current job.
2. The courses do not qualify you for a new profession.
3. You have already met the job's minimum education standards.

For example, if you are a programmer who takes more programming courses, the value of this employer-paid benefit is fully excludable.

TUITION REDUCTION

If you work for an educational institution, you are not taxed on tuition reductions for you, your spouse, and your dependents (as well as widows or widowers of deceased or former employees) if:

- The courses are undergraduate courses. If you are a graduate student who is a teaching or research assistant, you aren't taxed on tuition reduction as long as it is in addition to regular pay for your teaching or research activities.

- The benefit is *not* payment for teaching or other services. If you receive a scholarship under the National Health Services Corps Scholarship Program or the Armed Forces Health Professionals Scholarship Program, you can exclude any reduction despite your service requirements.

If you are eligible for tuition reduction, the benefit is not limited to courses taken at the school in which you work. You can exclude from your income the value of courses you take at any school covered by a tuition reduction agreement (area colleges and universities typically have reciprocal class agreements).

STUDENT LOAN REPAYMENT

Your employer's payment of up to $5,250 toward your student loan debt obtained to pay tuition and other expenses that would be tax free if the employer had originally paid them in 2025 (as explained earlier) is not taxable. The payment may be made by the employer directly to the lender or as a reimbursement to you for your payments. Such student loan assistance can be done annually.

Planning Tip

If you are seeking a job and plan to pursue college or graduate courses while working or have student loan debt to repay, look for a company with an educational assistance plan. The value of this benefit can be substantial to you if you use it fully and should be factored into the compensation package being offered for the position.

Example

You are in the 24% tax bracket and in 2025 your employer pays for courses totaling $5,000. If you had to pay for these courses yourself, you would need to earn an additional $6,200 in income to have the funds to pay for the courses yourself.

Pitfalls

Generally, you must attain a certain course grade for your employer to pay for the education. Make sure you understand what you must do to obtain reimbursement or have your course fully paid by your employer.

An educational assistance program can only cover your qualified expenses. It cannot provide reimbursement for a spouse or dependent.

You cannot use any benefit received under an employer's plan as the basis for claiming a second tax benefit. For example, if your employer pays $2,000 for a course you take, you cannot claim an education credit for this amount. Or if your employer pays for a student loan, you cannot deduct interest paid on that loan (explained later in this chapter).

Where to Claim the Exclusion

If employer-provided education assistance is excludable from income, it is not reported on your return. You may find the amount of employer-paid education benefits reported on your Form W-2 for information purposes only; it is not added to your compensation.

Scholarships, Fellowships, and Grants

According to some estimates there are about 1.7 million scholarships available each year. About one-third of undergraduates receive Pell Grants, the largest federal scholarship program. Scholarships are available through government programs, nonprofit organizations, and corporations that support education. Grants are made on the basis of need, scholastics, or special talents (such as athletics or music). The tax law enables you to receive this money on a tax-free basis under certain circumstances.

Benefit

If you are enrolled in a degree program at a school and receive a scholarship, fellowship, or grant, you can exclude the portion of the grant for tuition, course-related fees, books, supplies, and equipment. There is no dollar limit on this exclusion.

If you receive a Fulbright award, it is fully taxable (unless you can claim the foreign earned income exclusion explained in Chapter 13).

Condition

For tax-free treatment to apply, the grant must be for study in a degree program. A degree program includes:

- Primary and secondary school
- College or university degree programs

- Full-time or part-time scholarships for study at a school that provides an education program acceptable for full-time credit toward a degree or offers a program of training to prepare students for employment in a recognized occupation

Planning Tips

For education planning purposes, obtaining a scholarship, fellowship, or grant is the best way to finance learning. The award doesn't cost you anything and doesn't have to be repaid. Explore carefully any grants to which you, a spouse, or a dependent may be entitled.

Stipends and non-tuition fellowship payments for graduate and postdoctoral students, which are not treated as taxable compensation, can be treated as such for purposes of making IRA contributions.

Pitfalls

Scholarship amounts for room, board, and incidental expenses are taxable.

If you are an undergraduate athlete who receives a stipend based on a share of licensing revenue, you are taxed on the stipend because it is compensation for the use of your name, image, and likeness. The school says whether you are an employee or independent contractor, which determines how to handle taxes on the stipend.

If you are a graduate student who receives payment (a stipend) for teaching, doing research, or providing other services as a condition of the grant, you are taxed on the payment. Such amount is reported on Form W-2 and is subject to income tax withholding.

Generally, no exclusion can be claimed if receipt of a federal grant is conditioned on your performing services in the future. For example, if you receive a scholarship that requires you to teach for at least 3 years as a condition of the grant, you cannot exclude this grant from your income.

Where to Claim the Exclusion

If the grant is excludable from income, you do not have to report it on your return.

If the grant is partially taxable (for example, you are not a degree candidate and so are taxed on the portion of the grant for housing), you report this as other income on Schedule 1 of Form 1040 or 1040-SR. If you are a graduate student receiving a stipend for services, such amounts are reported as wages directly on Form 1040 or 1040-SR.

American Opportunity Credit

The tax law allows you to claim a limited tax credit, called the American opportunity credit, when you pay for higher education. The credit applies whether you pay out-of-pocket from savings or borrow the money. You may claim the credit each year you qualify for it.

Benefit

If you meet certain conditions and do not claim the lifetime learning credit discussed later, you can claim the American opportunity credit for higher education costs of up to $2,500 per student (100% of the first $2,000 of costs, plus 25% of the next $2,000 of costs). For example, if you have twins who are freshmen in college, you can qualify for a credit of up to $5,000.

In 2025, 40% of the credit is refundable in most situations (it can be repaid to you even though it is more than your tax liability).

Conditions

To claim the American opportunity credit, you must meet all 5 of these conditions:

1. Payments relate to the first 4 years of higher education.
2. Payments are made on behalf of an eligible student.
3. Payments are made to an eligible institution.
4. Payments cover qualified higher education costs.
5. Your modified adjusted gross income (MAGI) is not above a set limit.

Looking Ahead

Starting in 2026, having a valid Social Security number is another condition for claiming the American opportunity credit.

FIRST 4 YEARS OF HIGHER EDUCATION

The credit applies for only the first 4 years of college or other postsecondary school. If a student takes 5 or more years to earn a college degree, the American opportunity credit applies only for study during the first 4 years of higher education.

Example

Your child started college in September 2023. Assuming you qualify, you can claim an American opportunity credit for tuition in 2025 because your child is still within the 4-year limit.

ELIGIBLE STUDENT

The credit may be claimed for you, your spouse, or your dependent. The student must be enrolled for at least one academic period (a semester, trimester, or quarter) during the year.

No credit may be claimed if the student has a federal or state felony drug conviction on his or her record.

ELIGIBLE EDUCATIONAL INSTITUTION

Only payments to an eligible institution entitle you to claim the credit. This includes any accredited public, nonprofit, or proprietary postsecondary institution eligible to participate in the student aid programs administered by the U.S. Department of Education. Enrollment in a foreign educational institution probably will not entitle you to claim this tax credit. Ask your school if it is eligible, or check www.studentaid.ed.gov.

Enrollment must lead to a degree, certificate, or other recognized educational credential.

QUALIFIED HIGHER EDUCATION COSTS

Qualified expenses include *only* tuition, related fees, and books, supplies, and required equipment. Related fees can include, for example, a student activity fee paid to the institution if it is required for all students and no portion of it covers personal expenses. Hobby or sports courses and noncredit courses do not qualify for the credit *unless* they are part of the student's degree program.

The following costs do *not* qualify for the credit:

- Any expenses paid with tax-free educational assistance
- Room and board (even if they are required to be paid to the institution as a condition of enrollment)
- Medical expenses
- Transportation
- Insurance
- Personal living expenses

The cost of a computer may qualify for the credit if it is needed for attendance at the school. Otherwise, it is viewed as a personal expense for which the credit cannot be taken.

As a practical matter, the institution furnishes the student with an information return showing qualified tuition and related expenses paid for the year. The return, Form 1098-T, *Tuition Payments Statement*, for 2025 is issued by January 31, 2026, and usually you need to have received the form in order to claim the credit.

Prepayment. If you prepay before the end of 2025 expenses for an academic period that begins within the first 3 months of 2026, you can include this amount when figuring your 2025 credit. You cannot choose to take the credit for the prepayment in 2026.

Example

In December 2025 you pay tuition for your child for the semester beginning February 2026. You can include the tuition payment as part of qualified expenses in figuring your 2025 credit.

MAGI LIMIT

The ability to claim the credit depends on your modified adjusted gross income (MAGI). MAGI for this purpose is adjusted gross income increased by the foreign earned income exclusion and other foreign items.

If your MAGI is below a phaseout range, then the full credit can be claimed; a partial credit is allowed for those with MAGI within the range. No credit can be claimed if MAGI exceeds the range. Table 3.1 shows the phaseout ranges for 2025, which are not adjusted annually for inflation.

Example

In 2025, you are single, with MAGI of $85,000. Your top credit is limited to $1,250 (one-half of the maximum credit of $2,500), since you are midway in the MAGI phaseout range. If your MAGI is $75,000, you can claim a credit up to $2,500; if your MAGI is over $100,000, you cannot claim any credit.

TABLE 3.1 2025 MAGI Phaseout Range for Education Credits

Filing Status	MAGI
Married filing jointly	$160,000–180,000
Other filing status*	$ 80,000–90,000

*No credit may be claimed by married persons filing separately.

Planning Tips

You can claim the credit even though eligible expenses are paid with the proceeds of a loan. You can also claim the credit if eligible expenses are paid by someone other than you, your spouse, or your dependent, such as the student's grandparent. The payment is treated as having been made by the student, and as your dependent, this entitles you to claim the credit if you are otherwise eligible to do so.

As the parent, if you pay the expenses but your MAGI is too high to permit you to claim the credit, you can waive your right to do so. This will allow your child to claim the credit on his or her own return (assuming the child has tax liability and can benefit from the credit). Your child can claim the credit even though you pay the expenses.

Pitfalls

The credit must be coordinated with other education tax benefits you may be qualified to use. You can claim the credit in the same year in which you receive distributions from a Coverdell education savings account (ESA) or 529 plan. But the expenses on which you base the credit cannot be the same expenses used to figure the tax-free portion of the distributions.

> **Example**
>
> Your child's college tuition bill for the year is $15,000. You pay $5,000 of this amount from a 529 plan. For purposes of figuring the credit, you can take only $10,000 of eligible expenses into account ($5,000 is used as a tax-free distribution from the 529 plan).

If you claim a credit and in a later year (after you have filed the return and claimed the credit) receive a refund of an amount that was used to figure the credit, you must recapture some or all of the credit. This means you must repay some or all of the credit. You treat the recaptured amount as additional tax liability for the year of recapture. Do not amend the return on which the credit was claimed.

> **Example**
>
> In 2025, you take an American opportunity credit of $2,500 based on $4,000 of tuition costs. In 2026, your child receives a grant reimbursing him for tuition of $1,000. You must recapture $250 (25% of $1,000). You report this recapture as "other income" on your 2026 return.

You cannot claim the credit for expenses that are paid by tax-free scholarships, fellowships, grants, veterans' educational assistance, or employer-provided educational assistance. You cannot claim the credit for expenses of apprenticeship programs; they are not viewed as academic (but see Lifetime Learning Credit).

Where to Claim the Credit

The American opportunity credit is figured on Form 8863, *Education Credits*. The refundable portion of the credit is then entered on line 29 of Form 1040 or 1040-SR. The nonrefundable portion of the credit is entered on Schedule 3 of Form 1040 or 1040-SR.

Lifetime Learning Credit

The tax law allows you to claim a limited tax credit, called the lifetime learning credit, when you pay for higher education and do not claim the American opportunity credit. The credit applies whether you pay out-of-pocket from savings or borrow the money. You may claim the credit each year you qualify for it.

Benefit

If certain conditions are met, you can claim a credit of up to $2,000 on your return for the payment of qualified higher education costs for you, your spouse, or your dependent. In contrast to the American opportunity credit, which is a per student credit, the lifetime learning credit is per taxpayer. So if you have 3 children in college, your lifetime learning credit for the year is limited to $2,000 (assuming you qualify to claim it).

Unlike the American opportunity credit, which applies only for the first 4 years of higher education, the lifetime learning credit can be claimed for any higher education, including graduate-level courses and certain apprenticeship programs.

Conditions

Most of the conditions for the lifetime learning credit are the same as those for the American opportunity credit detailed earlier, unless otherwise noted here. The same planning tips and pitfalls also apply.

The ability to claim the lifetime learning credit depends on your modified adjusted gross income (MAGI). The limits for this credit are the same as the limit applicable to the American opportunity credit. If your MAGI is below a phaseout range, then the full credit can be claimed; a partial credit is allowed for those with MAGI within the phaseout range. No credit can be claimed if your MAGI exceeds the range. Table 3.1 earlier in this chapter shows the phaseout ranges.

Looking Ahead

Starting in 2026, having a valid Social Security number is another condition for claiming the lifetime learning credit.

ELIGIBLE STUDENT

There is no ban on claiming the lifetime learning credit for a student who has a felony drug conviction on his or her record, as there was for claiming the American opportunity credit.

HIGHER EDUCATION

Unlike the American opportunity credit, which can be claimed only for courses leading to a degree, the lifetime learning credit can be claimed for one or more courses at an eligible educational institution that are part of a postsecondary degree program or part of a nondegree program taken to acquire or improve job skills. In other words, the student does not need to be pursuing a degree or other recognized educational credential.

There is no limit on the number of years for which the lifetime learning credit may be claimed.

Planning Tip

Since the lifetime learning credit cannot be claimed for a student for whom an American opportunity credit is claimed, decide which credit produces the greater tax savings. Usually, this is the American opportunity credit because there is a higher credit limit ($2,500 versus a $2,000 limit for the lifetime learning credit). Once a student is beyond 4 years of college, then there is no choice; only the lifetime learning credit can be claimed.

Pitfalls

The same pitfalls applicable to the American opportunity credit apply to the lifetime learning credit. This means you usually must receive Form 1098-T before claiming the credit.

Where to Claim the Credit

The lifetime learning credit is figured on Form 8863, *Education Credits*. The credit is then entered on Schedule 3 of Form 1040 or 1040-SR.

Work-Related Education

Americans are always trying to better themselves. If you are self-employed, you may be eligible to deduct your education costs. Employees cannot deduct their education costs.

Benefit

If you pay for education related to your current line of work, you may be able to deduct your expenses.

If you qualify for the deduction by meeting all of the conditions, you claim the deduction as a business expense if you are self-employed. There is no dollar limit on this deduction.

Conditions

To deduct education expenses, you must meet all 5 of these conditions:

1. You are self-employed.
2. You already meet the minimum job requirements for your work (as set by your employer or state law).
3. The courses maintain or improve your skills or you are required by your employer or by law to take the course to keep your current salary or position.
4. The courses do not lead to a new line of work.
5. You pay for eligible education expenses.

SELF-EMPLOYED

You cannot deduct the cost of courses taken before you start to work.

Working for only a short period of time before beginning an MBA program may not establish you in a trade or business. For example, the Tax Court denied a deduction for the costs of an MBA to an individual who graduated from college in 2007 and started the MBA program in 2009 after holding only short-term positions, none of which required or even related to an MBA.

MINIMUM JOB REQUIREMENTS

You must meet the minimum work requirements based on a review of the laws and the regulations of your state and the standards of your profession or business.

If work requirements change after you start your trade or business, any courses you take to meet the new standards are deductible.

Example

You graduated from college with a degree in physical therapy and set up your own practice. Then state law is changed to require physical therapists to complete at least one year of graduate school to retain certification, you can deduct the cost of the additional year of schooling because you had already met your initial minimum job requirements.

MAINTAIN OR IMPROVE SKILLS REQUIRED BY LAW

General education courses are not deductible. The courses must be designed to keep you up to date and qualified.

Courses that give you a specialty *within* your current line of work are deductible.

EXAMPLES OF DEDUCTIBLE COURSES

- Accounting manager who obtains an MBA.
- Attorney in practice who takes LLM courses to obtain a master's degree in taxation.
- Continuing education courses by professionals.
- Dentist who takes courses in orthodontics. This postgraduate schooling improves professional skills as a dentist.
- Practicing psychiatrist who takes courses at an accredited psychoanalytic institution.
- Psychiatrist who takes personal therapy sessions.

NOT A NEW LINE OF WORK

If the courses enable you to follow a new line of work, they are not deductible.

EXAMPLES OF NONDEDUCTIBLE COURSES

- Software engineer who obtained an executive MBA.
- Law school (even by someone who intends to continue in his or her original line of work, such as accounting).
- Nurse who takes courses that qualify him or her to become a physician's assistant.
- NASA engineer who obtained a pilot's license (even though this helped with his engineering activities).

ELIGIBLE EDUCATION EXPENSES

If you qualify for the deduction, it is not limited to the cost of tuition and fees as is the case with many other types of education tax breaks. The deduction applies not only to the cost of courses but also to:

- Books and supplies.
- Local transportation expenses to and from the course, including bus, subway, rideshare and taxi fares, or train fares. If you use your car, you can deduct mileage at the rate of 70¢ per mile for 2025, plus parking and tolls.
- Lodging, meals, and transportation. If you attend courses out of town, you can deduct away-from-home expenses. The deduction for meals is limited to 50% of actual cost.

Planning Tip

When taking continuing education courses or seminars for your work as a self-employed individual, be sure to retain proof of attendance and the costs involved.

Pitfall

You cannot claim both a deduction for education costs and a personal tax credit (American opportunity credit or lifetime learning credit) for the same expenses.

Where to Claim the Deduction

As a self-employed person, you deduct the expenses directly as a business expense on Schedule C of Form 1040 or 1040-SR. Partners and those in a multi-member LLC who are not reimbursed by the business for their education costs can deduct them on Schedule E.

Student Loan Interest

Millions of students must borrow money to pay for their education. Repayment of student loans runs between 5 and 25 years. Some may have loans forgiven. If not, the tax law allows interest on student loans to be deductible each year within limits.

Benefit ⬆

If you pay interest on student loans, you may be able to deduct up to $2,500 of interest as an adjustment to gross income (if your actual interest payment is more than $2,500, your deduction is limited to that amount). There is no limit on the number of years you can claim this deduction; as long as you continue to pay off the loan, you can deduct your interest if eligible to do so.

If the loan is canceled, you may qualify for tax-free treatment on the debt forgiveness (explained later in this chapter).

If your employer pays your student loan (interest and principal) up to $5,250 under an educational assistance plan, you are not taxed on this benefit (explained earlier in this chapter).

Conditions

There are a couple of conditions for claiming a deduction for student loan interest as an adjustment to gross income. You must meet both:

1. The loan must be a qualified loan.
2. Your modified adjusted gross income cannot exceed a set limit (there is a partial deduction allowed if MAGI falls within a phaseout range).

LOAN QUALIFICATIONS

To be treated as a student loan for which interest is deductible, the loan must have been taken out solely to pay qualified education expenses. Qualified education expenses relate to a qualified educational institution (virtually all accredited public, nonpublic, and proprietary postsecondary institutions are eligible educational institutions). Qualified education expenses include:

- Tuition and fees
- Room and board
- Books, supplies, and equipment
- Other necessary expenses (including transportation to and from school)

You cannot deduct interest on a loan from a related person or made under a qualified employer plan. Related persons include:

- Spouses
- Siblings and half-siblings
- Parents
- Grandparents
- Children
- Grandchildren
- Certain corporations, partnerships, trusts, and exempt organizations

The loan must be for you, your spouse, or your dependent (in the year you take out the loan). The loan must be taken for an eligible student, who is enrolled at least half-time in a degree program.

You must be legally obligated to make payments on the loan. For example, if your child took out the loan and you are now helping her make the payments, you cannot deduct the interest because you are not the borrower (you are not legally responsible for the loan). Your child can deduct the interest even if you make the payments as long as your child is not your dependent.

If the loan is a revolving line of credit (e.g., credit card debt), interest qualifies as student loan interest only if funds on the line are used solely to pay qualified education expenses.

MAGI LIMITS

You can claim the full deduction if your modified adjusted gross income is below the phaseout range. A partial deduction is permitted if your MAGI is within the phaseout range. No deduction can be claimed if your MAGI exceeds the phaseout range, which is adjusted annually for inflation. Table 3.2 shows the 2025 phaseout ranges for claiming the student interest deduction.

TABLE 3.2 2025 Phaseout Ranges for Student Interest Deduction

Filing Status*	MAGI
Unmarried (single), head of household, and surviving widow(er)	$ 85,000–100,000
Married filing jointly	$170,000–200,000

*You cannot claim the deduction if you are married filing separately.

Example

You are single and graduated from college in May 2025. You start to pay back your loans, paying interest in 2025 of $800. You can deduct this amount in full if your MAGI is under $85,000. If you landed your dream job and earned $100,000 or more in just the 7 months remaining in 2025, you cannot deduct any of your student loan interest because your MAGI is above the limit for your filing status.

Planning Tips

If a student has taken the loan and a parent, grandparent, or anyone else pays the debt, the student is treated as having made the payment and can take the student loan interest deduction, provided the student is not a dependent and has MAGI below the threshold amount. In some instances, the cancellation of student loans can be tax free (usually the cancellation of a debt is taxable). This is explained later in this chapter.

If your employer reimburses you for student loan debt under an educational assistance plan (explained earlier in this chapter), this is a tax-free fringe benefit. But you may not deduct the interest that is part of the repayment.

Cancellation of student loan debt is discussed later in this chapter.

Pitfall

If your employer helps to pay your student loan debt and this does not fall under an educational assistance plan, this is taxable compensation to you.

Where to Claim the Deduction

The deduction is claimed on Schedule 1 of Form 1040 or 1040-SR. No special form or schedule is required.

Savings Bonds for Education

The first savings bonds, series A, were issued in 1935 at 75% of face value in denominations of $25 to $1,000, paying 2.9% accrued interest, and were sold through the U.S. Post Office. Since then savings bonds have become a permanent investment vehicle. Today, savings bonds can be purchased only online through TreasuryDirect.gov. Sales of savings bonds have dropped dramatically since the Treasury eliminated over-the-counter sales at banks. If you hold savings bonds and decide to cash them in to pay for higher education costs, you may be eligible to receive the interest tax free.

Benefit ⊗

If you redeem U.S. savings bonds to pay for qualified higher education costs or to contribute to a 529 plan or Coverdell education savings account, you are not taxed on the interest as long as your modified adjusted gross income (MAGI) is below a set amount. There is no dollar limit to this benefit; if you qualify you can exclude from income all of the interest received on the redemption of the bonds.

Conditions

Assuming you have not been reporting interest on the savings bonds annually but deferring it, you can claim the exclusion if you meet all 4 of these conditions:

1. Eligible bonds.
2. Eligible taxpayer.
3. MAGI limit.
4. Qualified use of redemption proceeds.

ELIGIBLE BONDS

The exclusion applies only to series EE bonds and I bonds.

ELIGIBLE TAXPAYER

You must be the purchaser of the bond and hold it in your name or the joint name of you and your spouse. You must have been at least 24 years old when you purchased the bonds.

No exclusion can be claimed for interest on bonds held in the child's name or in the joint name of you and your child.

If you are married, you must file jointly to claim the exclusion.

MAGI LIMIT

To claim a full or partial exclusion you cannot have modified adjusted gross income (MAGI) over a fixed dollar limit (which is adjusted annually for inflation). MAGI for this purpose means AGI increased by the redeemed interest, the deduction for student loan interest, foreign earned income exclusion and other foreign items, and the exclusion for employer-paid adoption.

Table 3.3 shows the phaseout range for 2025. If your MAGI is below the start of the phaseout range, you can claim a full exclusion. If your MAGI is over the phaseout range, no exclusion can be claimed, even if all of the other conditions are met. If your MAGI is within the phaseout range, you can claim a partial exclusion.

Example

In 2025, you are married filing jointly with MAGI of $145,000. You redeem bonds with interest of $5,000, and you use all of the redemption proceeds for qualified higher education expenses. You can exclude $5,000 interest because your MAGI is in the middle of the phaseout range. If MAGI is $164,240–the midpoint in the phase-out range–you can exclude one-half, or $2,500, of the interest.

TABLE 3.3 2025 Phaseout Ranges for Savings Bond Interest Exclusion

Filing Status*	MAGI
Unmarried (single) and head of household	$99,500–114,500
Married filing jointly and surviving widow(er)	$149,250–179,250

*No exclusion can be claimed if you're married and file separately.

QUALIFIED USE OF REDEMPTION PROCEEDS

The proceeds must be used only for a qualified purpose:

- Paying higher education costs, which is limited to tuition and fees for a college, university, or vocational school that meets federal financial aid standards. The higher education expenses can be for you, your spouse, or a dependent.
- Funding a 529 plan or a Coverdell education savings account.

If the proceeds from the redemption exceed the amount used for a qualified purpose, you can exclude a portion of the interest based on the ratio of expenses (or funding) to the redemption amount.

Example

In 2025, you redeem bonds worth $10,000, using $5,000 to pay your child's qualified higher education costs. Interest on the bonds is $3,000. Since half of the proceeds were used for qualified expenses, half of the interest, or $1,500, is eligible for the exclusion (assuming the other conditions are met).

Planning Tips

If you are holding EE or I savings bonds and want to know how much they are worth today, you can check their redemption values of paper bonds using the Paper Savings Bond Calculator at www.savingsbonds.gov.

The U.S. Treasury has changed the way in which interest on Series EE bonds is computed. Rather than adjusting the interest semiannually, these bonds now pay a fixed rate until redemption or maturity. As a result, Series I bonds may be a better option because their interest rate still adjusts semiannually for inflation.

Interest on savings bonds is *never* subject to state income tax (such interest is always exempt).

Pitfalls

You cannot use this exclusion to pay college expenses for your grandchild *unless* the grandchild is your dependent in the year in which the bonds are redeemed.

You cannot claim the exclusion if you are married and file a separate return from your spouse.

Where to Claim the Exclusion

If you claim the exclusion, you must complete Form 8815, *Exclusion of Interest from Series EE and I Bonds Issued after 1989*, and attach it to your return.

Coverdell Education Savings Accounts

Is the high cost of a prep school or college in your child, niece or nephew, or grandchild's future? If you decide to help save for this expense, consider doing so using a tax-advantaged savings account, called a Coverdell education savings account (ESA), designed for this purpose.

Benefit

You may be able to contribute up to $2,000 annually to a savings account for each beneficiary. The account is called a Coverdell education savings account (ESA). The account can have multiple contributors, but no more than $2,000 can be placed in a beneficiary's account for any one year. The contribution is not deductible.

Earnings on contributions accumulate tax deferred. If withdrawals from the account are used to pay qualified education expenses, the earnings become tax free.

Conditions

There are a couple of conditions for funding a Coverdell ESAs as well as for taking tax-free distributions.

1. For purposes of contributions, they can be made only on behalf of an eligible beneficiary (defined next) by a contributor whose modified adjusted gross income does not exceed set limits. Contributions must be made in cash, not property.
2. For purposes of tax-free distributions, funds must be used only for eligible expenses.

ELIGIBLE BENEFICIARY

Generally, a beneficiary is a person who is under the age of 18 at the time the contribution is made. So, if a beneficiary attains the age of 18 on July 1, 2025, contributions can be made through June 30, 2025.

A beneficiary can also be a special needs person over the age of 18. A special needs beneficiary is one who requires additional time to complete his or her education because of a physical, mental, or emotional condition. This would include, for example, a person with a learning disability.

MAGI FOR CONTRIBUTORS

There is no familial requirement for contributors. Anyone can make a Coverdell ESA contribution on behalf of an eligible beneficiary, as long as the contributor meets MAGI limits. Contributions can even be made by the beneficiary.

In order to contribute the full $2,000 to a Coverdell ESA, your modified adjusted gross income cannot be more than a set limit. MAGI for this purpose means adjusted gross income increased by the foreign earned income exclusion, the foreign housing exclusion or deduction, the exclusion for income from American Samoa, or the exclusion for income from Puerto Rico.

A reduced contribution limit applies if your MAGI falls within a phaseout range. No contribution can be made if your MAGI exceeds the phaseout range, which is not adjusted annually for inflation. The MAGI phaseout range for Coverdell ESA contributors may be found in Table 3.4; they are not adjusted annually for inflation.

Example

In 2025, you are a single parent with MAGI of $80,000. You can make a $2,000 contribution on behalf of your 12-year-old child. But if your MAGI is between $95,000 and $110,000, only part of the $2,000 may be contributed (you figure the limit using a worksheet provided in IRS Publication 970).

CASH CONTRIBUTIONS

Contributions must be made in cash; you cannot contribute property to a Coverdell ESA. If you own stocks or mutual funds, you must sell the property and invest the proceeds. You may incur a capital gain on the sale of property.

ELIGIBLE EXPENSES

Coverdell ESAs can be used for education in grades K–12 and/or for higher education without any dollar limit. Primary and secondary school can be public, private, or religious school.

The range of eligible expenses for which tax-free withdrawals can be made is quite broad. Just about anything related to education is a qualified expense.

EXAMPLES OF ELIGIBLE ELEMENTARY AND SECONDARY SCHOOL EXPENSES

- Academic tutoring
- Books
- Computer and peripheral equipment; software only if it is predominantly educational in nature

TABLE 3.4 MAGI Phaseout Ranges for Coverdell ESA Contributors

Filing Status	MAGI Phaseout Range
Married filing jointly	$190,000–220,000
Other taxpayers	$ 95,000–110,000

- Extended day programs required or provided by the school
- Internet access
- Special services for a special needs beneficiary
- Supplies
- Transportation
- Uniforms

EXAMPLES OF ELIGIBLE HIGHER EDUCATION EXPENSES

- Books, supplies, and equipment
- Room and board
- Tuition and fees

Planning Tips

You can open a Coverdell ESA at any bank or other financial institution that has received IRS approval to offer Coverdell ESAs. You can then select the investments you prefer, from certificates of deposit to stocks and mutual funds (to the extent available from the institution you select).

Just like IRA contributions, contributions to Coverdell ESAs can be made up to the due date of the return for the year to which they relate. Obtaining a filing extension does not extend the deadline for making contributions.

Example

Contributions for 2025 may be made only up to April 15, 2026, even if the contributor and/or the beneficiary has obtained a 6-month filing extension.

You can turn taxable custodial accounts under the Uniform Gifts to Minors Act (UGMA) or the Uniform Transfers to Minors Act (UTMA) into tax-free Coverdell ESAs using the funds in the custodial account for contributions. But only cash contributions are permitted to a Coverdell ESA, so investments in the custodial accounts must first be sold so that the proceeds can be contributed.

> ### Example
>
> Junior has $5,000 in an UTMA account that owns shares in a mutual fund, the earnings from which are reported annually as taxable income to Junior. The custodian of the account can opt to sell $2,000 from the mutual fund in the custodial account each year and contribute the proceeds to a Coverdell ESA of which Junior is the designated beneficiary (assuming he meets the age and MAGI limits). The account can own shares in the same mutual fund, but now the earnings become tax deferred and, if funds are withdrawn for qualified expenses, they become tax free.

You can change accounts from one financial institution to another by means of a tax-free rollover. You may not be satisfied with the service or investment options you have at one financial institution and can switch by means of a rollover to another financial institution.

You can move money in a Coverdell ESA between certain beneficiaries on a tax-free basis. The amount withdrawn from a Coverdell ESA can be rolled over to the same or a new designated beneficiary who is a member of the original beneficiary's family (listed in the next section). The rollover must be completed within 60 days. There are no tax consequences to naming a new designated beneficiary (as long as such beneficiary is permissible).

If you are beneficiary of the account and get married and then divorced before age 30, funds awarded by a divorce decree or separation agreement to the spouse do not trigger a taxable transaction to either party as long as the transfer of funds is through a direct rollover or a retitling of the account.

You can fund contributions to a Coverdell ESA by means of a direct deposit of a tax refund. For example, say you are owed a refund on your 2025 return. Use the refund to contribute to a Coverdell ESA (assuming you meet eligibility requirements) by filing the return early enough for the IRS to process it and electronically transfer the refund to the Coverdell ESA by the due date of the 2025 return, for a 2025 contribution (you can also use the 2025 tax refund to make a 2026 contribution if your income allows it and the beneficiary will not have aged out of eligibility).

Anyone who receives a military death gratuity or payment under the Servicemen's Group Life Insurance (SGLI) program can contribute this amount to a Coverdell ESA; the usual contribution limit and MAGI limit do not apply in this case.

Pitfalls

While distributions can be used to pay for primary and secondary school expenses, they cannot be used for home schooling.

If you contribute more than $2,000 on behalf of a beneficiary within one year, the excess amount is subject to a 6% excise tax (this is a penalty). The penalty is paid by the beneficiary (not the contributor). But the penalty can be avoided by withdrawing the excess contribution, plus any earnings on the contribution, before the beginning of the 6th month following the year of the contribution (e.g., by June 1, 2026 [May 31 is Sunday] for 2025 contributions).

Example

In 2025, Aunt Mary contributes $2,000 to a Coverdell ESA for Amy. Unaware of Aunt Mary's contribution, Uncle Ed also contributes $2,000 to a Coverdell ESA for Amy in 2025. Amy can avoid the 6% excise tax on the excess $2,000 contribution by withdrawing it, plus any earnings, by June 1, 2026 (May 31 is on a Sunday). Whether she chooses to give it back to Aunt Mary or Uncle Ed or split it between them is up to Amy.

The 6% excise tax continues to apply each year in which excess contributions (and earnings on excess contributions) remain in the Coverdell ESA.

Taxable distributions, which are withdrawals made to pay for noneligible expenses, are not only taxed as ordinary income but are subject to a 10% additional tax unless a penalty exception applies. Exceptions to the 10% penalty are:

- Distributions are made to a beneficiary or to the estate of a designated beneficiary on or after the death of a designated beneficiary.
- Distributions are made because the designated beneficiary is disabled.
- Distributions are made because the designated beneficiary received a tax-free grant or educational assistance allowance that equals or exceeds the distribution.
- Distributions are taxable only because the qualified expenses are reduced by expenses taken into account in figuring an education credit.

Withdrawals from a Coverdell ESA can be made in the same year in which an education credit is claimed. But the same expenses cannot be used for both benefits.

Withdrawals from both a Coverdell ESA and a 529 plan are permitted in the same year. But if total withdrawals exceed qualified higher education expenses, the expenses must be allocated between the Coverdell ESA and 529 plan to figure the taxable portion of the withdrawals. Generally, the allocation is based on the ratio of the Coverdell ESA withdrawals to the total withdrawals.

> **Example**
>
> In 2025, Henry begins college and withdraws $800 from a Coverdell ESA and $3,200 from a 529 plan to pay $3,000 of eligible expenses. Of the $800 withdrawn, $600 is tax free: $800 Coverdell ESA withdrawal ÷ $4,000 total withdrawals = 0.2; 0.2 × $3,000 qualified expenses = $600.

Funds remaining in the account become taxable to the beneficiary within 30 days of attaining age 30 (or within 30 days of death if the beneficiary dies before age 30). The 30-year age limit does not apply to a special needs beneficiary (defined earlier).

Tax on the earnings in the account can be avoided if the balance in the account is transferred to another eligible beneficiary within 60 days of a beneficiary attaining age 30 (or death if earlier). An eligible beneficiary for this purpose includes members of the beneficiary's family:

- Spouse
- Child or stepchild
- Grandchild
- Brother, sister, half-brother, or half-sister
- Niece or nephew
- Parent or stepparent
- Grandparent
- In-laws and the spouses of any of the listed relatives

Where to Claim the Exclusion

Contributions to a Coverdell education savings account are not reported on the return of the contributor or the beneficiary. Similarly, withdrawals that are not taxable are not reported on any return.

If contributions are subject to the 6% excise tax, the beneficiary figures the excise tax in Part V of Form 5329, *Additional Taxes on Qualified Plans (Including IRAs) and Other Tax-Favored Accounts*, and reports it on Schedule 2 of Form 1040 or 1040-SR.

If withdrawals from a Coverdell ESA are taxable, they are reported on the beneficiary's return as "other income" on Schedule 1 of Form 1040 or 1040-SR. If they are also subject to the 10% additional tax, this amount is figured in Part II of Form 5329, *Additional Taxes on Qualified Plans (Including IRAs) and Other Tax-Favored Accounts*.

Qualified Tuition Programs (529 Plans)

You can help save for the higher education expenses of your child or grandchild using a tax-advantaged account called a 529 plan. The 529 plan is a qualified tuition program offering federal (and in some cases state) tax incentives for savings.

Benefit ⊗

There are 2 types of qualified tuition programs (QTPs): a prepayment plan under which payments are guaranteed to cover (or partially cover) tuition, regardless of tuition increases, and a savings-type plan in which the funds you will have available to pay for education depend on the investment performance of your account. From a tax perspective, both types of plans are governed by the same tax rules under Section 529 of the Internal Revenue Code (hence the name "529 plans"), and both types of plans have the same benefits and conditions.

While contributions to qualified tuition programs do not generate a federal income tax deduction or credit, the long-term benefits are considerable:

- Earnings within the plan are tax deferred.
- If funds in the plan are used to pay qualified education costs, they are tax free (the earnings on the contributions are never taxed in this case).
- Unused amounts can be transferred tax free to another beneficiary if the original beneficiary does not go to college or otherwise need the funds.
- Long-term 529 plans can be transferred to the beneficiary's Roth IRA (limits apply).

There may be state income tax deductions or credits for the contributions to qualified tuition programs as well. For example, if you are a resident in New York, you can deduct contributions to the New York 529 College Savings Program up to $5,000 ($10,000 for married couples filing jointly) on your New York state income tax return each year that contributions are made. Vermont residents can take a 10% tax credit on up to $2,500, for a maximum credit of $250 per beneficiary ($500 per beneficiary for a married couple).

Conditions

Most conditions and requirements are fixed by each state's own 529 plan. For tax purposes, there are a couple of key conditions to obtaining all of the benefits under a qualified tuition program:

1. Contributions can be made only to qualified tuition programs. There are no federal tax limits on annual or total contributions to a 529 plan. These limits are fixed by each state's unique program (e.g., New Hampshire's plan

has a $569,123 cap per beneficiary in 2025 and no contributions can be made once the plan reaches this cap).

2. Distributions can be withdrawn only for qualified expenses.

QUALIFIED TUITION PROGRAMS

Contributions can be made only to state plans and IRS-approved private college/ university plans. A personally devised plan, even one that mimics the investment strategies of the state plans, does not entitle you to these benefits.

At present, all states offer savings-type plans and 9 states plus D.C. have prepaid tuition plans.

QUALIFIED EXPENSES

For distributions from qualified tuition programs to be tax free, they must be used only to pay for qualified expenses.

Higher education expenses. For higher education purposes, these include tuition, fees, books, supplies, computers and technology (e.g., internet access), and room and board (if the student is enrolled at least half time). For distributions after July 4, 2025, qualified expenses also include continuing education costs tied to recognized credential programs. There is no set dollar limit on these expenses, including room and board. Any reasonable amount for room and board (including expenses of off-campus housing) can qualify.

Qualified expenses also include costs associated with registered apprenticeships, even though these are not considered "higher education." And qualified expenses include student loan repayments up to a set limit. This is $10,000 in a lifetime for the beneficiary and the same for each of the beneficiary's siblings (sisters, brothers, stepsisters, and stepbrothers).

Expenses for K-12. For 2025, funds in 529 plans can be used for tuition at private or religious primary and secondary schools (grades K–12) up to $10,000 annually. The dollar limit applies per student, so if a student is a beneficiary of more than one 529 plan, only $10,000 can be used annually for the student without any federal income tax on the distribution.

For distributions after July 4, 2025, qualified expenses for K-12 also include curriculum materials, books or other instructional materials, online instruction, tutoring by a licensed instructor, exam fees (e.g., SAT and ACT), dual enrollment, and educational therapy for students with a disability.

Looking Ahead

Starting in 2026, the K-12 tax-free withdrawal limit doubles to $20,000 per student. In addition to private, public, and religious school, withdrawals can be made for home schooling expenses.

LONG-TERM 529 PLANS

If you have a "long-term" 529 plan that still has money it, you can transfer funds *tax free* to the beneficiary's Roth IRA. But a parent's 529 plan for a child can't be rolled over to a parent's Roth IRA. The 529 plan must have been open for at least 15 years and the funds used for the transfer to the Roth IRA must have been in the 529 plan for at least 5 years. This means the rollover option can't be used if contributions to the 529 plan were made within the last 5 years.

The maximum annual rollover to a Roth IRA is limited to the annual IRA contribution limit, which is $7,000 for 2025. The lifetime limit on such rollovers is $35,000. The rollover must be a trustee-to-trustee transfer.

The beneficiary must have earned income at least equal to the rollover amount. And the amount rolled over reduces what the beneficiary can contribute to the Roth IRA for the year.

Example

A grandparent has a 529 plan for a grandchild who is now out of college and working. Assuming the plan is a long-term 529 plan and the grandparent makes a trustee-to-trustee rollover of $5,000 to the grandchild in 2025, the grandchild's Roth IRA contribution limit for 2025 is $2,000 ($7,000 − $5,000).

Planning Tips

The terms and conditions of qualified tuition programs vary considerably from state to state. You can learn about the investment options, fees, and other rules on state 529 plans at www.savingforcollege.com. For details on the private 529 plan created by a consortium of private colleges and universities (nearly 300 schools participate), go to www.collegewell.com.

If you plan for your child to attend your alma mater on a legacy basis, ask the school whether it offers or plans to offer a tuition prepayment plan.

For purposes of the federal financial aid formula, funds in 529 plans are not considered to be the assets of the student. Also, distributions from grandparent-owned 529 plans no longer have any impact on a student's financial aid.

Qualified tuition programs can be used effectively for estate planning purposes. For example, a wealthy grandparent can reduce the size of his or her estate while funding an education savings plan for a grandchild with little or no gift tax cost. If you plan to make sizable contributions in one year, you can elect to treat the contributions as made equally over 5 years. This will entitle you to apply the annual gift tax exclusion, which is $19,000 in 2025 ($38,000 for married persons making joint gifts), 5 times to avoid or reduce gift tax.

> **Example**
>
> In 2025, when the annual gift tax exclusion is $19,000 per beneficiary, you contribute $90,000 (or $180,000 per couple) to a state savings plan for your grandchild. Since you can treat the $95,000 as having been made ratably over 5 years, there is no taxable gift in this transfer. The transfer is fully offset by the annual gift tax exclusion ($19,000 × 5).

If the contribution exceeds this limit, the excess amount is treated as a gift in the year the contribution is made.

Amounts in a 529 plan can be transferred to a new beneficiary or rolled over tax free within 60 days of a distribution. There is a limit of one transfer or rollover per year. But a beneficiary can be changed without making a transfer or rollover; the new name is substituted for the old one on the same account. This option applies only if the new beneficiary is a member of the old beneficiary's family, which includes:

- Child or grandchild
- Stepson or stepdaughter
- Sibling or stepsibling
- Parent or grandparent
- Stepparent
- Aunt or uncle
- Niece or nephew
- Son-in-law, daughter-in-law, father-in-law, mother-in-law, brother-in-law, or sister-in-law
- The spouse of any relative on this list
- First cousin

In the case of a savings-type 529 plan, if the account declines in value from the amount contributed, the loss may be recognized when all of the funds in the account are distributed. The IRS says that the loss is treated as a miscellaneous itemized deduction which is not deductible. Some tax experts believe that the loss is simply claimed as an ordinary loss. This theory has yet to be tested in court.

You can change investment selections once a year, and whenever there is a change in beneficiary.

Amounts in a 529 plan can be rolled over tax free to an ABLE account if the ABLE account beneficiary or this designated beneficiary's family member is the beneficiary of the 529 plan. Any amount rolled over counts toward the overall limit on annual contributions to an ABLE account. Because such rollover is counted, it probably isn't a good idea to do it and instead fund the ABLE account; this maximizes the overall savings for the beneficiary.

Funds within 529 plans offer asset protection in case of bankruptcy. Contributions to the plan made at least one year but less than 2 years before filing for bankruptcy are protected up to $5,000. Contributions made 2 years or more before filing for bankruptcy are fully protected (no dollar limit applies). All contributions made within one year of filing for bankruptcy are at risk.

Pitfalls

If funds are withdrawn from a 529 plan and *not* used for qualified education expenses, earnings on the distribution are taxable. For example, if part of a distribution is used for spending money or travel expenses, the earnings on this portion of the distribution are taxable.

Example

If $25,000 is withdrawn and $20,000 is used for qualified expenses while $5,000 is used for spending and travel money, earnings on the $5,000 portion of the distribution are taxable.

In addition, the portion of the distribution representing earnings on contributions is subject to a 10% penalty. But both the tax and the penalty on a refund made by the institution (e.g., because the student receives a scholarship) can be avoided by redepositing the funds in the 529 plan within 60 days of receipt.

Withdrawals from a 529 plan can be made in the same year in which an education credit is claimed, but the same expenses cannot be used for both benefits.

If withdrawals are made from a 529 plan and Coverdell ESA in the same year and the total withdrawal exceeds qualified education expenses, a portion of the withdrawal is taxable. How to figure the taxable portion was explained earlier in the Coverdell Education Savings Accounts section, under "Pitfalls."

Where to Claim the Exclusion

Contributions to qualified tuition programs are not reported on the return of the contributor or the beneficiary.

Distributions from qualified tuition programs are not reported if they are tax free. To figure the tax-free portion of distributions, you can use a worksheet for this purpose in IRS Publication 970. For any year in which distributions are made, the 529 plan must send you (and the IRS) an information return, Form

1099-Q, *Qualified Tuition Program*. For distributions in 2025, the form must be issued no later than February 2, 2026 (January 31, 2026, is a Saturday).

ABLE Accounts

If you have a disabled child or are under age 26 (beginning in 2026 it's age 46) and meet certain eligibility conditions, you can have a special savings account that generally does not adversely impact eligibility for means-tested government programs (e.g., Medicaid). The ABLE account is similar to a 529 savings plan (discussed earlier in this chapter), but differs in several ways. An ABLE account can be used on a tax-free basis for education and job training, as well as other qualified disability expenses. And funds can be transferred up to a limited amount from a 529 plan to an ABLE account on a tax-free basis, as explained earlier in this chapter. See details in Chapter 2.

Seminars

You've seen the ads: Attend a seminar to learn all about this subject or that. While some seminars are free of charge, others can cost hundreds or even thousands of dollars. From a tax standpoint, the cost of seminars is deductible only under limited circumstances.

Benefit ⊜

Work-related seminars for self-employed individuals may be deducted if the conditions for work-related education discussed earlier in this chapter are met.

No deduction can be claimed for seminars on self-improvement that are not work-related. No deduction can be claimed for investment seminars.

Where on the Return to Claim the Deduction

See work-related education for self-employed individuals discussed earlier in this chapter.

Educational Travel

Saint Augustine said, "The world is a book, and those who do not travel read only a page." Taxwise, the cost of travel usually is a nondeductible personal expense. But there are exceptions for which the cost of travel may be deductible.

Benefit ⬚

They say travel is broadening (a century ago, wealthy young men and women used to "take the grand tour" as a coming-of-age lesson). From a tax perspective, a deduction for educational travel is extremely limited. As a general rule, no deduction can be claimed for educational travel. But this ban does not apply to overseas courses and lectures, the cost of which may qualify for a work-related education deduction for a self-employed individual.

Conditions

To be deductible as work-related education, travel must meet all of the conditions discussed earlier in this chapter.

Planning Tip

Overseas courses need not be taken for credit to qualify for a deduction. For example, an English teacher who took a course on Greek myths in Greece taught by university professors was allowed a deduction for her travel expenses and course registration fees even though she did not take the courses for credit (this case arose when employees were able to deduct education costs as miscellaneous itemized deductions.).

Pitfall

No deduction can be claimed for travel that is merely beneficial. For example, an architect who travels to Europe to view cathedrals there cannot deduct the cost of the trip as an education expense.

Where to Claim the Deduction

See work-related education for self-employed individuals discussed earlier in this chapter.

Cancellation of Student Loans

It's been estimated that outstanding student loan debt totals more than $1.77 trillion. If you are facing mountains of debt from student loans, you may be able to not only have your loans canceled, but have them canceled without any tax cost to you.

Benefit ⊗

Normally, the cancellation of a loan results in taxable income to the borrower. But under certain conditions, the cancellation of a student loan can be tax free. There is no dollar limit to this benefit.

Conditions

There are 3 different ways in which the cancellation of your student loan debt is not treated as income.

1. ***Public Service Loan Forgiveness (PSLF) programs.*** You can exclude the debt forgiveness on your student loan from income if you are required to work for a set period of time in a certain profession (e.g., nursing, medicine, law, or education) for any of a broad class of employers. The loan must have been made by a qualified lender, which includes:
   - The government (federal, state, or local government or an agency of the government)
   - A tax-exempt public benefit corporation
   - An educational institution if the loan is made under an agreement with the government or a tax-exempt public benefit corporation or under a program designed to encourage students to serve in occupations or areas with unmet needs

2. ***Relief on account of death or disability.*** There is no income from the cancellation of this debt on account of the death or total and permanent disability of the student. Loans eligible for this tax-free discharge are those made by a qualified lender listed above as well as a private education loan (Section 140(7) of the Consumer Protection Act).

3. ***General relief through 2025.*** The exclusion also applies to the discharge of student loans after December 31, 2020, and before January 1, 2026, for most student loans for higher education, including government loans, loans by eligible education institutions, and private education loans subject to the Truth in Lending Act. The IRS advised lenders not to issue Form 1099-C, *Cancellation of Debt.*

Planning Tip

Because tax-free treatment of forgiveness of student loans is very limited, those with existing debt should look for ways to modify favorably the terms of repayment. Law changes have made this more challenging. Still, look for income-driven repayment (IDR) options.

Pitfall

Don't assume that filing for bankruptcy will erase your student loan debt. A discharge for student loan debt in bankruptcy may be allowed for undue hardship. And an appellate court also allowed a discharge under a new interpretation of the bankruptcy law.

Where to Claim the Benefit

If the loan forgiveness is tax free, you do not report anything on your return. If cancellation of your student loan is not tax free, report it as other income on Schedule 1 of Form 1040 or 1040-SR. Generally, debt forgiveness that is not tax free is reported to you (and to the IRS) on Form 1099-C, *Cancellation of Debt.*

Penalty-Free Withdrawals from IRAs

Distributions can be taken from an IRA before age 59 ½ if the funds are used to pay qualified higher education costs for yourself, your spouse, or dependent. The Tax Court has said that funds used to buy a computer are *not* a qualified expense where its use is not required for any course and access to computer-posted course syllabi can be done through school computers in the library.

Withdrawals can be taken penalty free only in the year in which you pay the expenses.

Government Reimbursements

If you have a disabled child who cannot receive adequate education in your school district and you are reimbursed by your school district for the costs of special education, you are *not* taxed on this reimbursement. Since federal law requires schools to provide special education, you are treated as if you incur the costs on behalf of the school district.

Internships and Apprenticeships

The Inflation Reduction Act of 2022 imposed prevailing wage and apprenticeship requirements on businesses that want to claim certain enhanced tax breaks. If you're paid while learning on the job, your wages are includible in gross income, but the value of your training is not taxable. The U.S. Department of Labor estimates that the value of training through a registered apprenticeship program is $40,000 to $150,000.

As mentioned earlier in this chapter, distributions from 529 plans can be taken tax free to cover the costs of registered apprenticeship programs.

Your Home

Home ownership is part of the American dream and an important way to build wealth. High interest rates have made home ownership challenging for many at this time. Still, home ownership is prevalent. According to the U.S. Census Bureau, 65% of Americans owned their own homes in the second quarter of 2025. There are many reasons that we want to own rather than rent a home—for example, as a way to build up equity. And with full-time and hybrid remote work arrangements, having a good place to do it means being a homeowner for many individuals. There are also sound tax reasons favoring home ownership. Certain expenses of home ownership are deductible. And when you sell your home, some or all of your profit may be tax free. If you had problems with your mortgage or lost your home to foreclosure, there may be special tax breaks for you.

This chapter explains the tax breaks you can claim with respect to your home. Disaster losses that can befall your home, and the deductions you can claim for them, are explained in Chapter 12. The home office deduction for using a portion of your home for business is explained in Chapter 14.

For more information, see *Selling Your Home*; IRS Publication 530, *Tax Information for First-Time Homeowners*; IRS Publication 936, *Home Mortgage Interest Deduction*; and IRS Publication 4681, *Canceled Debts, Foreclosures, Repossessions, and Abandonments*.

Mortgages

Mortgages are a way to leverage yourself into home ownership: The bank or other lender (called the mortgagee) lends you the funds needed to buy your home over and above your out-of-pocket investment. You become the mortgagor and each month repay a portion of the principal (the money you borrowed), plus interest. While your repayment of principal is *never* deductible, you may be able to deduct your interest payments.

Benefit

Interest on your home mortgage may be fully deductible as an itemized deduction. There is no dollar limit on the amount of interest you can deduct annually, but there are limits on the size of the mortgage on which the interest is claimed. The mortgage interest rule applies to both fixed and adjustable rate mortgages.

The amount of acquisition indebtedness on which interest is deductible depends on when the loan was obtained:

- For loans obtained before October 14, 1987: No loan limit. As a practical matter, most of these old mortgages have been fully repaid by now.
- For loans obtained after October 13, 1987, and before December 16, 2017: $1 million.
- For loans obtained after December 15, 2017: $750,000.

The limits apply to your main home and one other residence. If unmarried co-owners jointly own a home, each can use the applicable limit on acquisition indebtedness. For example, if a brother and sister bought a home together on May 1, 2017, with a $2 million mortgage, each can deduct interest on their share of the $1 million of the loan limit. In effect, the limit applies per residence.

A special limitation applies to distressed homeowners, as explained later.

Conditions

For interest to be fully deductible, you must meet 4 conditions:

1. Acquisition indebtedness (which is usually a mortgage used to buy or build your home) cannot exceed the limits explained earlier.
2. The debt must be secured by the residence.
3. You deduct interest on no more than 2 residences.
4. You are personally obligated for repayment of the debt.

ACQUISITION INDEBTEDNESS

Acquisition indebtedness is usually a mortgage obtained to buy, build, or substantially improve a home (subject to the 2-residence limit). If you use the funds to construct your home, only interest paid during the 24-month period starting with the month in which construction begins is deductible. Interest paid before or after this 24-month period is not acquisition indebtedness; it is treated as nondeductible personal interest.

> ### Example
>
> In May 2025, you buy land to build your dream home and obtain a construction loan in June. Construction begins in September 2025, and the home is completed in June 2026. On your 2025 return, you may deduct interest on the loan starting with interest in September 2025, the month in which construction began. Since the home is completed within 24 months, interest for January 2026 through the end of construction is deductible on your 2025 return.

If a loan is taken out within 90 days after construction is completed, it may still qualify in full as acquisition indebtedness. It qualifies as acquisition indebtedness to the extent of construction expenses incurred within the last 24 months before the completion of the home, plus expenses through the date of the loan.

Same as the preceding example, except that in July 2025 you refinance the loan. Since the loan is obtained within 90 days after building completion, it qualifies as acquisition indebtedness, and interest is deductible.

How much renovation is required to be considered a substantial improvement to the home? There is no clear rule. Generally, if you add a room, convert an attic, garage, or basement to living space, or renovate a kitchen, you can safely treat interest on the loan as acquisition indebtedness. Just about any type of capital improvement that adds to the basis of your home constitutes a substantial improvement; a repair is not a capital improvement, and a loan to make repairs is not acquisition indebtedness.

What is a "home"? A home for this purpose isn't limited to a single-family dwelling. It also includes a condominium or cooperative unit, houseboat, mobile home, or house trailer as long as it has sleeping, cooking, and toilet facilities.

DEBT SECURED BY THE HOME

The loan must be secured by your main or second home in order for interest on the loan to be deductible. "Secured" means that the loan is recorded in your city, town, or county recording office or the loan satisfies similar requirements under your state's law that gives the lender the right to foreclose against your home if you fail to repay the loan.

TWO-RESIDENCE LIMIT

A deduction for mortgage interest is limited to 2 residences: your main home and a second residence. If you have more than 2 homes, you can select which of the additional homes to designate as your second residence for interest deduction purposes. Obviously, it pays to designate the home with the larger interest payments (assuming the total amount of debt on the 2 homes does not exceed your applicable dollar limit discussed later). You can change your designation from year to year.

If a married couple files jointly, they can designate a second residence as a home even if it is owned or used by one of them. But if they file separately, each spouse generally may deduct interest on debt secured by one home unless they agree in writing to allow one spouse to deduct interest on the main home plus a second residence.

If you rent out your home for fewer than 15 days, this has no affect on your mortgage interest deduction. If you rent out a home during the year but use it for personal (nonrental) purposes for more than 14 days or 10% of the rental days, you can still treat the home as a personal residence for which the interest is deductible. In counting rental days, include any days that the home is held for rental. In counting personal days, include any days your home is used by close family members.

Example

In addition to your main home, you own a beachfront condominium that you rent out through a rental agency 2 weeks each year at the start of the summer season. You spend the balance of the summer at your unit, so your personal use is sufficient for your home to be treated as a personal residence despite the rental. You can designate your condo as your second residence and deduct interest on the mortgage on the condo.

PERSONAL LIABILITY

To deduct interest on a home mortgage you must be personally obligated for its repayment. If, for example, you are financially unable to obtain a mortgage so your parents help you out by obtaining the loan, you cannot deduct mortgage interest (even if you pay the lender directly rather than repaying your parents).

One case did allow a homeowner to deduct interest on a loan obtained by a brother because the homeowner had a poor credit rating, but the facts in the case were unique; the homeowner was contractually obligated to his brother to pay off the mortgage.

DOLLAR LIMIT

The amount treated as acquisition indebtedness on which interest can be deductible is the total amount of such debt on your principal residence and designated second home. As explained earlier in this chapter, the time the mortgage is taken determines the dollar limit of the loan on which interest is deductible.

For loans obtained before October 14, 1987, there is no loan limit; most of these loans have already been fully repaid. For loans obtained after October 13, 1987, and before December 16, 2017, the dollar limit is $1 million. And for loans obtained after December 15, 2017, the dollar limit is $750,000.

Example

In January 2025, you take out a $500,000 mortgage to purchase a main home. The loan is secured by the main home. In February 2025 you take out a $250,000 loan to purchase a vacation home. The loan is secured by the vacation home. Because the total amount of both mortgages does not exceed $750,000, all of the interest paid on both mortgages is deductible. But if you took out a $250,000 home equity loan on the main home to purchase the vacation home, then the interest on the home equity loan (explained later in this chapter) would not be deductible.

If the total amount of acquisition indebtedness exceeds the applicable dollar limit, then only a percentage of the interest is deductible based on this formula:

$$\frac{\text{Applicable dollar limit}}{\text{Total acquisition indebtedness}} \times \text{Interest payment}$$

Example

In January 2025, you take out a $500,000 mortgage to purchase a main home. The loan is secured by the main home. In February 2025, you take out a $500,000 loan to purchase a vacation home; the loan is secured by the vacation home. Total interest paid in 2025 is $60,000. Because the total amount of both mortgages exceeds $750,000, your deductible interest is: $45,000 ($750,000/$1,000,000 x $60,000).

DISTRESSED HOMEOWNERS

A distressed homeowner is someone who is at risk of foreclosure because of delinquent mortgage payments. Such a homeowner may obtain help in making mortgage payments. The IRS has created a safe harbor for determining the amount of mortgage interest a distressed homeowner can claim. The safe harbor runs through 2025. More specifically, such a homeowner may deduct the lesser of:

- Actual home mortgage interest payments to the mortgage servicer or the state housing finance agency (HFA)
- Amounts shown on Form 1098 for mortgage interest received, real property taxes, and mortgage insurance premiums (if otherwise deductible by the homeowner). States may issue Form 1098-MA, *Mortgage Assistance Payments*, in lieu of Form 1098. HAF payments may include amounts for real estate taxes and utilities. Under the safe harbor, HAF payments may be allocated to utilities before being allocated to mortgage and/or property tax payments.

Planning Tips

Think hard about the type and amount of mortgage you want to take out when you buy your home. Once you have purchased your home, additional financing generally doesn't qualify as acquisition indebtedness.

If you refinance home acquisition debt, the refinanced amount is treated as home acquisition debt, but only up to the amount of the balance of the old mortgage principal just before the refinancing. If you take out equity by refinancing for a higher amount than the outstanding balance and don't use the funds to substantially improve the home securing the debt, then only interest on the refinanced amount is deductible.

Example

Your home today is worth $500,000 and the remaining balance of your old mortgage is $200,000. If you refinance for $350,000 and use $50,000 of the proceeds to buy a personal car, take a vacation, and pay off some credit card debt and $100,000 to make substantial improvements. You can deduct interest on only $300,000 ($200,000 of acquisition indebtedness and $100,000 of home equity debt used to make substantial improvements).

When you sell your home, look at the settlement papers to determine the interest charged up to the date of sale so that you don't overlook any interest deduction you may be entitled to claim.

Looking Ahead

Starting in 2026, mortgage insurance premiums to purchase a residence are treated as acquisition indebtedness. But adjusted gross income limits apply to the deduction for mortgage insurance premiums.

Pitfalls

You cannot deduct your interest if you claim the standard deduction; you must itemize deductions to claim this benefit.

In 2025, you cannot deduct mortgage insurance premiums as interest. This option expired at the end of 2021 and does not begin again until 2026.

You cannot deduct mortgage fees that you paid to obtain the loan, such as the cost of an appraisal, a credit report, or loan assumption fees. But points paid to obtain the mortgage may be deductible, as discussed later.

You cannot deduct interest on mortgage assistance payments made on your behalf under Section 234 of the National Housing Act. And you must reduce mortgage interest by any mortgage interest tax credit (explained later in this chapter).

The IRS has a good idea about what your initial mortgage was because the outstanding mortgage balance at the start of the year and the loan origination date are reported by the lender to the IRS and you on Form 1098.

A married person filing separately has an interest deduction limit on borrowing up to one-half the applicable dollar limit for acquisition indebtedness (e.g., $500,000 for pre-December 16, 2017, mortgages; $375,000 for post-December 15, 2017, mortgages), even if the other spouse does not claim *any* mortgage interest deduction.

Where to Claim the Deduction

You deduct home mortgage interest on Schedule A of Form 1040 or 1040-SR. The amount of mortgage interest is reported annually to you by the lender on Form 1098, *Mortgage Interest Statement*, or for distressed homeowners, Form 1098-MA, *Mortgage Assistance Payments*.

Mortgage Interest Tax Credit

The government's policy is to encourage home ownership. To help low-income people become homeowners, the government offers certain assistance, including the opportunity to claim a tax credit for mortgage interest.

Benefit ⊕

Even better than deducting your mortgage interest, you may be eligible for a tax credit of up to $2,000 of home mortgage interest paid through mortgage interest certificates. These certificates are issued to certain homeowners as a means of encouraging home ownership. The credit may be claimed regardless of whether you itemize your personal deductions or claim the standard deduction.

If you received a mortgage credit certificate from your state or local government in connection with the purchase or renovation of your main home, you may be entitled to claim a tax credit with respect to your mortgage interest. The amount of the credit is the percentage shown on your mortgage credit certificate multiplied by the lesser of:

- Interest you paid during the year on your actual loan amount
- Interest you paid on the loan amount shown on your mortgage credit certificate

The credit cannot be more than $2,000 if the percentage shown on your mortgage credit certificate is 20% or more.

You must reduce your deduction for home mortgage interest by the amount of any credit you claim.

Conditions

You can claim this tax credit only if you meet 2 conditions:

1. You have received a mortgage credit certificate from your state or local government ("qualified mortgage credit certificate").
2. Your home meets certain requirements ("qualified home").

QUALIFIED MORTGAGE CREDIT CERTIFICATE

Qualified mortgage interest certificates are issued by a state or local government or agency under a qualified mortgage credit certificate program designed to help low- and moderate-income people become homeowners. You qualify for the credit only if you receive a qualified mortgage credit certificate (MCC). Certificates issued by the Federal Housing Administration, the Department of Veterans Affairs, and the Farmers Home Administration as well as Homestead Staff Exemption Certificates do not qualify.

QUALIFIED HOME

The home must be your main home. The value of your home cannot exceed a certain value:

- A value of 90% of the average area purchase price
- A value of 110% of the average area purchase price in certain targeted areas

Planning Tips

If you are thinking about buying a home but do not know if you can afford the payments, you may be able to swing a deal if you qualify for this type of government assistance. For information about special financing programs, visit the National Council of State Housing Agencies (NCSHA) at https://www.ncsha.org/resource/mortgage-credit-certificate-program-qa/.

If you qualify for the credit and it exceeds your tax liability without regard to other tax credits, you do not lose the credit. Instead, you can carry the excess amount forward to be used in a future year if you are also eligible for the credit in that year.

If you refinance your mortgage, you do not lose your eligibility to claim the credit if your certificate is reissued and the reissued certificate meets 5 conditions:

1. It must be issued to the original holder of the existing certificate for the same property.

2. It must entirely replace the existing certificate (you cannot retain any portion of the outstanding balance of the existing certificate).

3. The certified indebtedness on the reissued certificate cannot be more than the outstanding balance on the existing certificate.

4. The credit rate of the reissued certificate cannot be more than the credit rate of the existing certificate.

5. The reissued certificate cannot result in a larger amount of interest than is otherwise allowable under the existing certificate for any year.

Pitfalls

You must reduce your deduction for home mortgage interest by the amount of the credit.

If you own your home jointly with a person who is not your spouse, you must divide the credit between the two of you according to your respective ownership interests. If you each own a 50% interest in the home, then you are each entitled to one-half of the credit.

If you buy a home using a mortgage credit certificate and sell it within 9 years, you may have to repay some of the credit.

Where to Claim the Credit

You figure the credit on Form 8396, *Mortgage Interest Certificate*, and enter the amount of the credit on Schedule 3 of Form 1040 or 1040-SR.

If you are subject to recapture of the credit because you sold your home within 9 years of using the mortgage credit certificate, you must complete Form 8828, *Recapture of Federal Mortgage Subsidy*. You report the recaptured amount on Schedule 2 of Form 1040 or 1040-SR.

Home Equity Loans

Equity is the amount of money you would receive, over and above any outstanding mortgage, if you were to sell your home today. Equity is built up in 2 ways: by paying down a mortgage on the home and by appreciation in property values. As your equity increases, you may be able to tap into it *without* selling the home by refinancing (as discussed earlier) or by using a home equity loan. This loan may be the only loan on the property or it may be a second or even third loan in addition to any other home mortgage.

The deduction is allowed for interest on a home equity loan is allowed only if the funds are used to buy, build, or substantially improve your main home or second home and the loan is secured by the home. It is subject to the overall limit on acquisition indebtedness discussed earlier in this chapter.

> ## Example
>
> In May 2025, you took out a home equity loan to pay off credit card debt and take a vacation. No interest on this loan is deductible in 2025. But if you used the funds to add a room to your main home and the total amount of your mortgage plus home equity loan does not exceed $750,000 (the applicable limit for loans made after December 15, 2017), then all the interest is deductible.

Points

"Points" are additional charges for acquiring a loan. Each point is 1% of the loan amount. In general, the more points you pay, the lower your interest rate on the loan. Points generally are deductible; the only question is *when* they can be deducted.

Benefit

When you take out a mortgage, you may pay points to the lender. Points paid to obtain a home mortgage are deductible as part of your itemized interest deduction. In some cases points are deductible in full in the year in which they are paid while in other cases they must be amortized (deducted ratably) over the term of the loan.

Conditions

First determine whether the payment qualifies as "points" (defined next). Then see if the points can be deducted in full in the year of payment or must be deducted over the term of the mortgage.

IMMEDIATE DEDUCTIBILITY

If the loan is taken to buy, build, or substantially improve your main home, you may deduct the points in the year of payment if you meet the following conditions:

- Points are charged for interest and not for services performed by the lender. The designation of the payment, as points, loan origination fees, or otherwise, is not controlling of the tax treatment; it is the purpose for which the money is charged that governs whether you can treat points as interest.
- The loan is secured by your main home. If the loan relates to a second home, you cannot fully deduct the points in the year of payment.

- The charging of points is an established business practice in the geographical area in which you are located.
- The amount of points is computed as a percentage of the loan and specifically earmarked on the loan closing statement as points, loan origination fees, or loan discount.
- You pay the points directly to the lender. Points withheld from the loan proceeds used to buy your main home are treated as having been paid directly to the lender. Points withheld from loan proceeds used to substantially improve your main home are not immediately deductible; you must pay the points with other funds to secure a full deduction in the year of payment. Points paid by the seller are not treated as paid directly to the lender but rather are viewed as an adjustment to the purchase price of the home.

DEDUCTIBLE OVER THE TERM OF THE LOAN

As long as the payments meet the definition of points (e.g., are not fees for services performed by the lender), but cannot be deducted in full in the year of payment (or you opt not to deduct them in full), they are deducted ratably (evenly) over the term of the loan.

Example

In January 2025, you pay points of $3,600 to obtain a 30-year mortgage for your vacation home. You must amortize the points over 360 months and can deduct $10 per month each year until you've deducted all of the points or pay off the mortgage.

The following are situations in which you amortize the points rather than fully deduct them in the year of payment:

- To buy a second home.
- To substantially improve your main home but the points are withheld from the mortgage.
- To refinance an existing mortgage.
- To buy your main home but you elect to amortize the points.

Planning Tips

If you pay points to buy your main home, you are not required to deduct them in full in the year of payment. You can opt to amortize them over the term of the loan. You may wish to make this election if you can't benefit from the deduction in the year of payment. This might occur if you buy your home late in the year and your total itemized deductions do not exceed your standard deduction amount. Another reason to opt to amortize is if your acquisition indebtedness (plus points) in the year you paid the points is over your applicable dollar limit for purposes of deducting mortgage interest. Yet another reason is that you aren't itemizing now so you cannot currently benefit from the points, but may itemize in the future when part of the points could be deductible.

When you are financing a mortgage and are faced with the option of paying higher interest with little or no points or a lower interest rate but some or substantial points, which option should you select? The answer usually depends on how long you plan to remain in the home (how long you will be paying the mortgage). To help you make this decision based on your circumstances, use a mortgage points calculator (you can find one at www.dinkytown.net/java/MortgagePoints.html).

Pitfall

If you refinance your loan with a new lender and have been amortizing points over the term of a previous loan (for example, this is your second or third refinance), be sure to deduct the remaining balance of the unamortized points.

Example

In January 2021, when rates had declined below your original mortgage rate, you refinanced your outstanding balance for a new 15-year mortgage, paying $1,800 in points. In July 2025, you refinance again. On your 2025 return, be sure to deduct the unamortized points of $1,260: $1,800 ÷ 180 months = $10 per month; 4 years, 6 months × $10 = $540; $1,800 − $540 = $1,260.

Where to Claim the Deduction

You deduct points along with your home mortgage interest on Schedule A of Form 1040 or 1040-SR. There is a separate line on Schedule A to list your points if they are not included on Form 1098 with your other home mortgage interest.

Prepayment Penalties

It costs a lender money to make a loan, which it expects to recoup through interest collected during the term of the loan. But if a borrower pays off a loan within a short time of obtaining it (generally under 2 years), the lender has not had time to recoup its lending costs. To protect the lender against a quick payoff, prepayment penalties may be owed. The prepayment penalties are spelled out in the mortgage note at the time of obtaining the mortgage. From the borrower's perspective, the tax law looks favorably on prepayment penalties, allowing them to be deductible if certain conditions are met.

Benefit

If you pay off your mortgage before you are required to, there may be a prepayment penalty as specified in your mortgage papers. Prepayment penalties are treated as deductible interest. They are a set amount of interest: for example, 6 months of interest on 80% of your outstanding loan balance if you pay off the mortgage before a set term (usually one to 2 years). For the rules on deducting interest on your home or second home, see earlier in this chapter.

Conditions

There are no special conditions to meet for deducting prepayment penalties, other than itemizing rather than claiming the standard deduction. Simply refer to the rules discussed earlier in this chapter on how to treat mortgage interest.

Planning Tip

Think ahead. When taking out a mortgage, check whether there are any potential prepayment penalties. You may be able to get the lender to delete these from the loan agreement. This is important because you may have to relocate before you had planned and do not want to incur this needless cost.

Pitfall

Don't sign any mortgage loan agreement before finding out if there are prepayment penalties. One common scam by unscrupulous lenders is nondisclosure of prepayment penalties, which can run as much as 6 months of interest on up to 80% of the outstanding loan balance. Such a high penalty can keep you locked into a mortgage when you otherwise could have refinanced for a lower mortgage rate.

Where to Claim the Deduction

Assuming that the prepayment payment penalty is deductible, you claim it with your home mortgage interest on Schedule A of Form 1040 or 1040-SR. The amount of mortgage interest is reported annually to you by the lender on Form 1098, *Mortgage Interest Statement*.

Late Payment Penalties

Under the terms of a loan, if a payment is late for any reason, the borrower may owe additional amounts called late payment penalties. There are different types of late payment penalties: a *flat fee*, such as $50, charged without regard to the amount of the late payment or how long it is outstanding, and a *percentage fee*, fixed with regard to the late payment. The percentage fee continues to be assessed each month that a payment remains delinquent. Only late payment penalties qualifying as "interest" may be deductible.

Benefit

If you are late in making a payment, you may be charged a penalty by the lender. Generally, penalties for delinquent payments are treated as deductible interest, which can be written off if you itemize your deductions.

Example

Your monthly mortgage payment is $1,000, which is subject to a 2% late payment penalty. Due to unexpected financial reverses, you fail to make your payment for June, July, and August. In September, you're back on your feet and pay up all outstanding amounts, including the late payment penalties of $120 (June payment: 2% of $1,000 × 3 months; July payment: 2% of $1,000 × 2 months; August payment: 2% of $1,000 × 1 month). Since the late payment penalties are an interest charge, they are deductible.

Condition

Late payment penalties are treated as deductible interest as long as they are not imposed for a specific service provided by the lender. If they are a flat charge imposed regardless of how late the delinquency may be, they are viewed as a nondeductible service charge rather than as deductible interest.

Planning Tip

Even though late payment penalties can be deductible, you should try to avoid them if possible. The deduction does not fully offset your payment. One way to do so is to arrange for mortgage payments to be debited automatically from your checking account.

Pitfall

Being late on making your mortgage payments can cost you more than late payment penalties. Being late can adversely affect your credit rating (a decrease of as much as 180 points) and hurt your ability to obtain a loan or even get a job within 2 years or so of the late payment. Usually if your payment is no more than 30 or 60 days late, it likely won't seriously affect your FICO score if it occurs only once or twice, although it may stay on your credit report for about 2 years. If you are 90 days late even once, your credit rating will suffer; the late payment will stay on your credit report for up to 7 years.

Where to Claim the Deduction

Assuming that the late payment penalty is deductible, you claim it with your home mortgage interest on Schedule A of Form 1040 or 1040-SR. The amount of mortgage interest is reported annually to you by the lender on Form 1098, *Mortgage Interest Statement.*

Reverse Mortgages

Homeowners who are at least 62 years old and have little or no mortgage left on their primary residence can access the equity that has built up in their home over the years by obtaining a reverse mortgage. As the name implies, you receive money from a lender but do not have to repay it immediately; usually repayment is postponed until you move from your home or die. Proceeds of the mortgage can be made to you in a lump sum, as monthly payments, or as a line of credit that you can draw on to the extent needed.

Benefit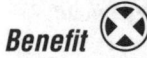

Proceeds received from a reverse mortgage are tax free. There are no dollar limits on the amount that is tax free, but there are limits on how much of a reverse mortgage you can obtain, based on your age, the current interest rate, and the appraised value of your home.

Conditions

To qualify for a reverse mortgage, you must be at least 62 years old and own a primary residence. There are no income limits on eligibility.

Planning Tip

To learn more about reverse mortgages from the U.S. Department of Housing and Urban Development (HUD) (called home equity conversion mortgages for seniors), go to https://www.hud.gov/program_offices/housing/sfh/hecm/hecmhome.

Pitfalls

Even though interest accrues on funds borrowed under a reverse mortgage, no deduction can be claimed until repayment is made.

A reverse mortgage can adversely affect Medicaid eligibility, which may be needed for long-term care assistance. The proceeds from the reverse mortgage are treated as assets for Medicaid eligibility purposes.

Where to Claim the Benefit

You do not have any tax reporting with a reverse mortgage when you obtain the loan proceeds. You report (and deduct) interest only when you actually pay it. Reporting rules on mortgage interest are explained earlier in this chapter.

Cancellation of Mortgage Debt

During the subprime mortgage debacle more than a decade ago, thousands of Americans lost their homes. During the pandemic, millions of homeowners stopped paying their mortgages, although some were given reduced or suspended mortgage payments. A report by Attom in mid-2025 showed mortgage foreclosures were rising, as compared to the previous year, but it's unclear what will happen going forward.

Homeowners are usually personally liable for the amount of the mortgage, even though the lender can foreclose, sell the home, and use the sale proceeds to pay down the debt. Unfortunately, the borrower may still owe money on the loan after foreclosure (the home sale may not cover what's due). Generally, when the lender forgives a portion of the outstanding mortgage, a practice that lets the borrower off the hook, this debt forgiveness is considered to be ordinary income for tax purposes. Under a special law, forgiven debt on a main home may not be taxable.

Benefit ✪

If you are not personally liable on the mortgage debt, then forgiveness of debt does not result in any income. There are more than a dozen states with anti-deficiency laws that make the forgiven debt to a homeowner not recourse and, therefore, nontaxable.

If you are personally liable on the debt, forgiveness is treated as tax-free income within the limits that follow.

Conditions

There are 2 conditions for tax-free treatment:

1. The forgiven debt must have been used to buy, build, or substantially improve your main home and the debt must have been secured by the home. If a debt has been refinanced, the amount qualifying for this tax break is limited to the mortgage principal immediately before the refinancing.
2. The limit in 2025 on qualifying debt is $750,000 ($375,000 for a married person filing separately).

Looking Ahead

After 2025, the ability to exclude cancellation of debt income on a principal residence expires, so forgiveness in 2026 will trigger taxable income unless Congress extends the law.

Planning Tip

Debt forgiveness can apply to a so-called short sale, which occurs when the amount of the outstanding debt is greater than the value of the home (what a lender would realize if the home were sold). The short sale avoids the need for foreclosure. Also, some lenders will work with a homeowner to reduce the mortgage balance or change the terms of the loan so the homeowner can stay in his or her home. If there is any cancellation of debt, it can be tax free to the same extent as cancellation related to a foreclosure.

Pitfalls

The tax break on forgiven debt does not apply to a second home, rental property, or business property.

You may still have to recognize gain if the home was foreclosed upon and the amount realized on the sale is greater than your basis in the home. The fair market value of the property (reported to the borrower in Box 7 of Form 1099-C, *Cancellation of Debt*) is treated as the amount realized on the sale.

If you sell your home at a loss, you cannot deduct the loss; it is a nondeductible personal loss. If any part of the mortgage is forgiven in conjunction with the sale, the resulting income can be excluded if the conditions stated earlier apply.

Where to Claim the Benefit

Forgiven debt is reported to you by the lender on Form 1099-C. To claim the exclusion, complete Form 982, *Reduction of Tax Attributes Due to Discharge of Indebtedness* (instructions to the form point out the specific lines applicable to home mortgage debt forgiveness if you are preparing a paper return). There is no income from debt cancellation to report on the return; just attach the completed Form 982 to the return.

Penalty-Free IRA Withdrawals for Home-Buying Expenses

If you thought IRAs were for retirement only, you'd be wrong. The tax law lets you tap into your IRA for certain special reasons without incurring any penalty (although withdrawals are subject to tax). One of those reasons is to buy a home.

Benefit ⦿

You may be able to use money in your IRA toward the cost of buying a home without incurring an early distribution penalty from your IRA. The withdrawal is subject to regular income tax, but you avoid the 10% early distribution penalty on withdrawals before age 59 ½.

Condition

You can withdraw only up to $10,000 free from penalty from your IRA. This is a once-in-a-lifetime opportunity. If you have already used this break to buy a previous home, you can't use it again.

You must spend the $10,000 on qualified first-time home-buying expenses, such as a down payment to purchase a home. These are expenses used to buy, build, or rehabilitate a main home for yourself, your spouse, child, grandchild, or ancestor (parent or grandparent) of you or your spouse. Such person cannot have had an ownership interest in a principal residence within 2 years before the purchase, construction, or renovation of the new home.

Planning Tip

Use this tax break only as a last resort. Once you withdraw the funds from the IRA and spend them on home-buying expenses, you cannot replace the funds in your retirement savings account. In effect, you lose the opportunity to build up your retirement savings.

Pitfalls

If you take a withdrawal from your IRA with the intention of using the money to buy a home but the sale falls through, you become taxed on the money unless you redeposit it back in the IRA. You have 120 days from your initial withdrawal to redeposit the funds. And, if you're under age 59 ½, the distribution is also subject to a 10% penalty unless timely redeposited.

When a couple is buying a home together and the sale falls through, each must be a first-time homebuyer for the penalty exception to apply.

Using IRA funds for buying a home should be a last resort because it diminishes retirement savings. A withdrawal cannot be replaced in the IRA after 60 days (120 days if the sale falls through), which means those funds—and what could be earned on them—won't be available in retirement.

Where to Claim the Benefit

If you take money from your IRA, you must file Form 5329, *Additional Taxes on Qualified Plans (Including IRAs) and Other Tax-Favored Accounts*. You report total early distributions from your IRA. You can then subtract those exempt from the 10% penalty because you used them for qualified first-time home-buying expenses. You must indicate which exception to the 10% penalty you are relying on (a number is assigned to each exception, and these numbers are listed in the instructions to this form if you are preparing a paper return).

Real Estate Taxes

Property owners are charged real estate taxes to cover government services related to the property. Local property taxes may include city, town, and/or county taxes; school taxes; and even other charges (such as fire or sewer district taxes). Fortunately, the tax law allows property owners to deduct these taxes as an itemized deduction, subject to an overall limit on the deduction for state and local taxes.

Benefit ⊜

Your burden of paying local property taxes, including city, town, and/or county taxes and school taxes, can be eased somewhat by deducting your payments.

If you itemize deductions, you can deduct real estate taxes you pay on your main home and any other home you own. There are no limits on the number of homes for which you can claim the deduction. But the deduction for all state and local taxes, referred to as SALT (real estate taxes, income or sales taxes, and personal taxes) is capped for 2025 at $40,000 ($20,000 for married persons filing separately) and there is an income cap (see Chapter 15). The deduction for real estate taxes on your residence and vacation homes is claimed as an itemized deduction; you cannot use this benefit if you claim the standard deduction.

If you pay real estate taxes on a rental property, it is deductible against your rental income, regardless of whether you itemize your personal deductions.

Conditions

You must be the owner of the home so that you are obligated for the payment of the tax. If you buy the property at a tax sale, you cannot start to deduct property taxes until you receive title to the property under state law (typically following a redemption period).

If you pay the seller's unpaid back taxes when you purchase the home, you cannot deduct this payment as your taxes. You can add the payment to your basis in the home used for figuring gain or loss when you sell it.

In the year that property is sold, real estate taxes must be allocated between the buyer and the seller. Usually this allocation is reflected in your closing documents.

- The seller can deduct taxes for the portion of the year through the day before the date of sale.
- The buyer can deduct taxes for the portion of the year commencing with the date of sale.

Generally, if you rent rather than own your home, you cannot deduct the portion of the rent that the landlord uses to pay the property taxes. But in Hawaii you can do so if the lease runs for 15 years or more. Also, as a tenant in California you can deduct your payments if you have your name placed on the tax rolls and agree to pay the tax directly to the taxing authority.

Planning Tips

Consider prepaying an upcoming tax bill before the end of the year to increase your current deductions. For example, you can pay your January 2026 property tax bill in December 2025 to increase your deductions for 2025, assuming this does not put you over the SALT cap (see Chapter 15); you'll likely obtain a discount for paying early.

If you are self-employed and claim a home office deduction, part of the real estate taxes is taken into account in figuring that deduction. But because of the SALT cap, there are certain computational complications (see Chapter 10).

Ask your city or town whether you qualify for any property tax reductions or rebates. Some areas provide them on the basis of age (reduction for seniors), veteran status, or for some other reason (becoming a widow or widower). Some locations even suspend real estate taxes for seniors entirely until the home is sold (e.g., when the owner dies or relocates). Generally, a reduction or rebate is not automatic; the homeowner must apply for it. The amount saved because of a property tax reduction or rebate is *not* treated as income; it merely lowers the amount you pay for real estate taxes and, in turn, the amount of your itemized deduction for real estate taxes. If you are a distressed homeowner who receives assistance from HAF to pay your real estate taxes (and certain other expenses), use the IRS safe harbor to determine the extent of payments you make that are deductible. This safe harbor is explained earlier in this chapter (see Home Mortgage Interest).

Pitfalls

If you make payments to the lender that are held in escrow and disbursed to the taxing authority, you can only deduct real estate taxes when the lender makes the disbursements (not when you pay the lender).

If the title to your home is in the name of one spouse and the other spouse pays the real estate tax bill, the deduction can be claimed only if you file a joint return. Since the party paying the tax isn't the legal owner of the home, the tax may not be deducted on a separate return.

Special assessments by homeowners associations for the purpose of maintaining common areas or special assessments by municipalities for certain government services (water, sewage, or garbage collection) are not deductible as real estate taxes.

Do not prepay real estate taxes if you itemize and are subject to the alternative minimum tax (AMT). Since taxes are not deductible for AMT purposes, prepaying them can trigger or increase your AMT liability. You effectively lose the benefit of claiming the deduction.

If you receive a homestead tax credit from your state based on a percentage of your real estate taxes, the IRS says that the credit is treated for federal tax purposes as a reduction in your state income tax. This limits the amount of state income tax you can claim as an itemized deduction on your federal income tax return; it doesn't change your deduction for real property taxes.

The majority of states have enacted a Pass-Through Entity Tax (PTET) to enable business owners to optimize their deduction for state and local taxes (see Chapter 15). Some states have tried to create workarounds for the SALT limit using charitable contribution deductions. The IRS has nixed the charitable contribution workaround, other than for a de minimis amount (see Chapter 6).

Where to Claim the Deduction

You deduct your payment of real estate taxes on your residence and vacation homes as an itemized deduction on Schedule A of Form 1040 or 1040-SR. You deduct real estate taxes on rental properties on Schedule E of Form 1040 or 1040-SR.

In the year you sell property, if your share of real estate taxes is paid in advance by the buyer, the lender or real estate broker will generally include this information on Form 1099-S, *Proceeds from Real Estate Transactions*. But this form is not required to be filed for all sales, so you should keep track of this information (check your settlement papers).

Each year that you own property you do *not* receive any official information return notifying you of the amount of taxes you paid during the year. As a practical matter, if you make payments to a commercial lender to cover real estate taxes, your annual tax payments will be detailed in a year-end statement sent to you by the lender.

Cooperative Housing

Cooperative housing, also called a co-op, is a form of home ownership. You become a tenant-stockholder in a cooperative housing corporation (CHC) that owns and runs a multiunit housing complex. Your shares entitle you to exclusive use of your housing unit, plus access to common areas. There are tax breaks unique to this form of home ownership.

Benefits

You may experience 2 levels of deductions—one that is allocated to you from the CHC and the other that you obtain through your direct payments. For example, you may incur 2 interest deductions—one for your share of interest on debt of the CHC (e.g., for common areas) and one for the purchase of your unit that you financed through a bank. This section discusses only your allocated deduction; deductions for your direct payments are included in other sections of this chapter (e.g., home mortgage interest).

Condition

The only condition for claiming a deduction for CHC expenses allocated to you is ownership of shares in the CHC.

Planning Tip

Tenant-stockholders in cooperative housing corporations are usually treated the same in the tax law as homeowners of condominiums and single-family homes.

Pitfalls

While a tenant-shareholder of an apartment in a cooperative housing corporation can deduct his/her share of the co-op's real estate taxes (subject to the SALT cap), a federal appeals court has decided that these taxes are *not* deductible for purposes of the alternative minimum tax (AMT). Even though the AMT rules do not specifically bar a deduction, these taxes are treated in the same manner as if the taxes had been paid directly by the owner of a single-family home. There had been speculation that coop owners could skirt the SALT cap, but an IRS letter to a Congressional office said that the limit on deducting state and local taxes applies to taxes allocated to coop owners and deducted on their returns.

Where to Claim the Deduction

You claim a deduction for your share of the CHC's mortgage interest and real estate taxes allocated to you on Schedule A of Form 1040 or 1040-SR as a miscellaneous itemized deduction.

The CHC should provide you with Form 1098, *Mortgage Interest Statement*, to show your share of these expenses.

Minister's Housing Allowance

Members of the clergy of any recognized faith or denomination who receive assistance with their housing costs, through free use of a home or payments toward these living costs, may qualify for a tax break. Their housing allowance, sometimes referred to as a parsonage allowance, may be a nontaxable fringe benefit of their job.

Benefit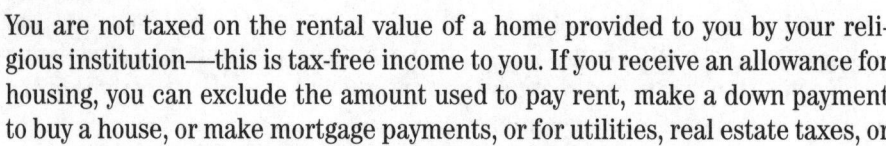

You are not taxed on the rental value of a home provided to you by your religious institution—this is tax-free income to you. If you receive an allowance for housing, you can exclude the amount used to pay rent, make a down payment to buy a house, or make mortgage payments, or for utilities, real estate taxes, or repairs to the home. There is no dollar limit on this exclusion.

Conditions

You must be a duly ordained minister and acting in that capacity. A rabbi or cantor as well as an imam are treated as ministers for purposes of this exclusion. Retired ministers can qualify for the exclusion if the housing allowance is made in recognition of past services. A minister acting as a teacher or an administrator of a parochial school or seminary qualifies for the exclusion if the school is an integral part of a church organization.

Church officers who are not ordained cannot qualify for the exclusion. Ordained ministers who are working as executives of nonreligious organizations cannot claim the exclusion even if they perform religious duties. For example, in one case a minister-administrator of an old age home not under church authority could not claim the exclusion.

The religious institution (e.g., church or local congregation) must designate the part of your compensation that is the housing allowance. This designation must be made in advance of the payments to you. Designation can be made in an employment contract, minutes, a resolution, or a budget allowance.

Planning Tip

If you pay mortgage interest and/or real estate taxes, you can claim deductions for these payments even if you finance them with the tax-free housing allowance. You must itemize your deductions to write off mortgage interest and real estate taxes on your home, as explained in this chapter.

Pitfalls

Even though the housing exclusion is not subject to income tax, it is treated as self-employment income for purposes of Social Security and Medicare taxes. If you use a church-provided home tax free, figure the rental value for purposes of self-employment taxes at what you would pay for similar quarters in your area, including utilities and garage or parking space, if any.

Claiming the housing allowance can have an adverse impact on your business deductions. The portion of business deductions allocable to the tax-free housing allowance is not deductible.

Example

Your salary as a minister is $40,000. You also receive a $20,000 housing allowance. Your work-related expenses are $6,000. You can deduct only $2,000. Since one-third of your income is tax free, only one-third of the expenses are deductible.

Where to Claim the Exclusion

If you can exclude the benefit, you do not have to report anything on your return. If you receive an allowance in excess of the amounts used for housing expenses, you must include the excess as part of your salary reported on Form 1040 or 1040-SR.

Home Sale Exclusion

Homeowners are highly favored under the tax law. Not only can they deduct certain costs of home ownership, such as mortgage interest and property taxes as explained earlier in this chapter, but they can also receive tax-free income when they sell their homes. A special rule permits a limited amount of gain from the sale of a main home to escape federal income tax. And this tax break can be used over and over again within certain limits.

Benefit ⊗

If you sell your home for a profit, you may avoid tax on some or all of your gain as long as you meet certain conditions. More specifically, you do not pay any tax on a gain up to $250,000 from the sale of your home ($500,000 on a joint return or by a surviving spouse if the sale is within 2 years of the other spouse's death) if you owned and used the home as your main residence for at least 2 of the 5 years preceding the date of sale. The amount you exclude is tax-free income to you.

Conditions

To be eligible to use the full exclusion amount of $250,000 ($500,000 on a joint return or for a surviving spouse), you must meet all 3 conditions:

1. The home must be your main home ("principal residence").
2. You owned your home for at least 2 years prior to the sale.
3. You used your home as your main home for at least 2 years prior to the sale.

If you acquired your home in a tax-free exchange, the ownership and use periods must be 5 full years (instead of 2 of 5 years) before qualifying for the exclusion.

If you are a member of the uniformed services, Foreign Service, or intelligence community, or are a Peace Corps volunteer, you can elect to suspend the 5-year testing period for the ownership and use tests for up to 10 years.

MAIN HOME

Your main home is the one in which you primarily dwell. If you own 2 or more homes, you must determine which one is your primary residence. This determination is usually based on which one you live in for the greater part of the year. There isn't a bright line test; you can use other factors to show that the home you used less of the time is your main home. Such factors include:

- Where you work or own a business
- Where your family members reside
- The address you use for your federal and state income tax returns
- The address you use for your bills and correspondence
- Where you have your driver's license and voter registration
- The location of religious institutions and clubs you belong to

Your main home isn't limited to a single-family dwelling. You can treat as your main home a mobile home, trailer, houseboat, or condominium apartment used as your primary residence. Even stock in a cooperative housing corporation is subject to this rule as long as you live in the cooperative apartment or house as your main home.

If you change the title to your home, you don't necessarily lose the opportunity to claim the exclusion.

- If you transfer ownership of your home to a grantor trust, one in which you are treated as the owner of the trust and report all of the trust's income on your personal tax return, the trust can use the exclusion provided you meet the ownership and use tests.

- If you transfer ownership of your home to a single-member limited liability company, again, the LLC can use the exclusion provided you meet the ownership and use tests. The LLC is treated as a "disregarded entity" for tax purposes so you report all of the LLC's income on your personal tax return.
- If you divorce and the title to the home is changed from your spouse's name or joint name to your name alone, you can include the period of your spouse's ownership in meeting the ownership test.
- If you are a surviving spouse, you can use the $500,000 exclusion amount if you sell the home within 2 years after your spouse's death. But if you sell in a later year, you are limited to the $250,000 exclusion.

OWNERSHIP TEST

You must own your home for at least 2 years in the aggregate prior to the date of sale. This means that you owned the home for a full 24 months or 730 days (365×2) during the 5-year period that ends on the date of sale. The periods of ownership and use need not be continuous or identical.

If you are married and file a joint return, only one spouse is required to meet the ownership test to qualify for the exclusion as long as both satisfy the use test.

USE TEST

You must use your home as your primary residence for at least 2 years in the aggregate prior to the date of sale. This means that you lived in the home for a full 24 months or 730 days (365×2) during the 5-year period that ends on the date of sale. The periods of ownership and use need not be continuous or identical.

Example

In November 2021, you purchased your home and lived there until September 2023, when you took a 1-year sabbatical overseas. You returned to your home in September 2024 and lived there until you sold the home in December 2025. You meet the use test because you lived in your home for 26 months (10 months before the sabbatical and 16 months after it).

Temporary absences, such as a 3-week vacation, are ignored. This is true even if you rent out your home while you are away.

If a homeowner becomes incapacitated before meeting the 2-year use test and resides in a licensed care facility, the full home sale exclusion can be used as long as the homeowner used the home for at least 1 year prior to moving from the home and meets the 2-year ownership test.

PARTIAL EXCLUSION

Even if you sell before meeting the full 2-year ownership and use tests, you may be eligible to use a prorated exclusion amount for the period of your ownership and use. A partial exclusion is allowed if you sell early because of:

- *Change in jobs.* If you relocate for a new job or a new business (if self-employed), you automatically are treated as having a qualified change in jobs if the distance test used for the moving expense deduction (explained later in this chapter) is met. The distance between your new job location and your former home must be at least 50 miles greater than the distance between your old job location and your former home. If your spouse, co-owner, or person who resides with you has a change of jobs, you can qualify for the exclusion.

- *Health reasons.* The change must be medically motivated (for example, your doctor recommends a change so you can receive medical or personal care for an illness or injury). A change that is merely beneficial to your health, such as moving to a warmer climate, isn't viewed as a health reason for purposes of using the partial exclusion. Again, the health of your spouse, co-owner, or person who resides with you can be taken into account in determining your eligibility for the partial exclusion.

- *Unforeseen circumstances.* If you are forced to sell because of events beyond your control, you can use the partial exclusion. Such events include, but are not limited to: Your home is destroyed through acts of war or terrorism, someone in your household dies or goes on unemployment benefits, you become unable to pay basic living expenses because of a change in employment (e.g., being furloughed for 6 months) or self-employment, there is a legal divorce or separation, you have multiple births resulting from the same pregnancy, you must have a larger home to meet adoption agency requirements, you received death threats at the current address, you must leave a senior retirement home so your young grandchild can live with you, you must move to a home that can accommodate your paralyzed mother's disability, you are forced to sell because of pressure from neighbors, you experience excessive airport noise that was not disclosed by the seller, or you become part of a blended family or have additional children that cannot be accommodated in your current home.

Planning Tips

If you have owned your home for a long time and paid down the mortgage, your gain may exceed your exclusion amount. You can minimize your gain by adding to the basis of your home any capital improvements you've made to it.

EXAMPLES OF CAPITAL IMPROVEMENTS

- Addition of a deck, garage, porch, or room
- Appliances
- Duct work
- Fencing
- Heating and cooling systems
- Kitchen and bathroom modernization
- New roof
- Paving the driveway
- Propane tank installed underground
- Retaining wall
- Satellite dish
- Security system
- Septic system
- Smart home features (LED lighting, smart locks)
- Soft-water system
- Storm doors and windows
- Walkway
- Well
- Wiring upgrade

If you subdivide your property, selling off vacant land separately from the parcel on which the home is situated, you can claim the exclusion for the sale of the vacant land and the sale of the home provided they occur within 2 years of each other. Only one exclusion amount applies to both sales.

Example

You are single in 2025 and subdivide your property and sell the vacant land for a profit of $100,000 (you must allocate the basis in your home between the vacant land and the parcel with the home to determine your gain on the sale of each parcel). You can exclude this gain on your 2025 return. In 2026, you sell the parcel containing your home for a profit of $200,000. You can exclude $150,000 of this $200,000 gain on your 2026 return (you already used $100,000 of the exclusion on your 2025 return). You must report and pay tax on the remaining $50,000 profit.

If you have been claiming a home office deduction for a portion of the home, you can still apply the exclusion to the home office portion as long as both the personal and business portions are part of the same dwelling. But there is depreciation recapture, as explained under "Pitfalls."

You can use the exclusion over and over again. As long as you meet the 2-year ownership and use tests for each residence, you can avoid tax on gains from each one. One exclusion can be claimed every 2 years.

If your home is destroyed by a casualty, and insurance proceeds exceed the basis of your home, resulting in a taxable gain, the transaction may qualify as a home sale for purposes of the home sale exclusion. The damage to the home must be sufficient to constitute a "destruction."

Pitfalls

The home sale exclusion applies only to "qualified use" of a residence. "Nonqualified use" includes any period after December 31, 2008, in which the home is not used as a principal residence. If you stop using the home as your main home and use it only as vacation property, or if you rent it out, gain related to this period does not qualify for the home sale exclusion. Temporary absences are not treated as nonqualified use; they're disregarded.

If you have been claiming a home office deduction for a portion of your home, you must recapture depreciation you have claimed for the office after May 6, 1997. This is so even though you can use the exclusion for gain on this part of the home. "Recapture" means you pay tax on all the depreciation claimed after May 6, 1997, at the rate of 25% (assuming your tax bracket is at or above this rate). Home office deduction rules are discussed in Chapter 10.

You must reduce the basis of your home by the amount of any energy credit claimed.

Example

If you claimed a $1,200 energy efficient home improvement tax credit back in 2023 for adding attic insulation, you must subtract $1,200 from the basis of your home.

If you fail the 2-year ownership and use test, you cannot claim a partial home sale exclusion based on unforeseen circumstances merely because a job promotion, house appreciation, or winning the lottery enables you to buy a bigger home.

Where to Claim the Exclusion

If your gain is fully excludable, you do not have to report the sale of your home on your return. If some of the gain is taxable because it exceeds the exclusion amount (or all of your gain is taxable because you opt *not* to use the exclusion), you report the sale on Form 8949, *Sales and Other Dispositions of Capital Assets*, which is carried over to Schedule D and then to Form 1040 or 1040-SR.

You can use a worksheet in IRS Publication 523 to figure your gain and whether any portion of the gain is excludable.

Moving Expenses for Active Duty Military Personnel

According to the U.S. Census Bureau, 25.87 million people in the U.S. moved in 2024. It's estimated that individuals will move 11.7 times during their lives. The cost of a move varies considerably with such factors as location, amount of furniture and other household goods to be moved, and services provided (e.g., packing). The cost may be lower for DIY (e.g., renting or borrowing a truck or using a pod). You can deduct your moving costs only if you are in the armed services and meet certain requirements.

Looking Ahead

Starting in 2026, the moving expense deduction is applicable to members of the intelligence community (e.g., CIA, NSA, ODNI).

Benefit

If you are member of the U.S. Armed Forces, you can deduct your moving expenses as an adjustment to gross income, even if you don't itemize your other personal expenses. If you are reimbursed or receive an allowance for moving expenses, you are not taxed on these payments. There is no dollar limit on this benefit.

Deductible amounts include amounts paid to pack, crate, and move your household goods and personal effects. Storage and insurance costs can be treated as deductible expenses for any period within 30 days after the items were moved from your old home but before they were delivered to your new home. If you are stationed overseas, there is no limit on storage and insurance costs while you work at your overseas location. The cost of connecting or disconnecting household appliances is a deductible moving expense, but the cost of installing a landline in your new home is not deductible.

Deductible amounts also include travel expenses for you and members of your household.

EXAMPLES OF DEDUCTIBLE TRAVEL EXPENSES FOR THE MOVING DEDUCTION

- Lodging en route from the old home to the new home. Include the cost of lodging before you depart for one day after your old residence is unusable as well as lodging for the day of arrival at your new location before you move into your home. But the cost of meals is not deductible.
- Transportation from the old home to the new home. You and members of your household do not have to travel together; simply add up the costs for each person. If you drive, you can figure your cost for moving at 21¢ per mile in 2025.
- The cost of moving your pets. Pets are viewed as household items, not as members of your family; the cost of moving them is still deductible.

Condition

To be treated as a deductible expense (or to qualify for an exclusion for reimbursement or an allowance for moving expenses), you or your spouse must be on active duty and the move must be because of a military order and incident to a permanent change of station.

Planning Tip

Even if you can deduct your moving costs, it still makes sense to keep them as low as possible. When planning a move, to get a rough idea of moving costs, get an estimate using a calculator from Moving.com (https://www.moving.com/ movers/moving-cost-calculator.asp). Be sure to get several binding quotes from reputable moving companies before contracting with one of them. Finally, put everything you agree to in writing and include adequate insurance for loss, breakage, and other damage. Learn about moving, including how to insure the move, in *The Ultimate Moving Guide* from SmartMove (https://www .smartmove.us/resources/moving-guide).

Pitfalls

You cannot take the deduction if you are a civilian military contractor, even if you receive official orders directing the move.

Even if you are in the military and move because of a military order, not every move-related expense is deductible.

EXAMPLES OF NONDEDUCTIBLE MOVING EXPENSES

- Any part of the purchase price of a new home
- Car registration tags
- Driver's license
- Expenses of buying or selling a home

- Expenses of getting or breaking a lease (lease cancellation fee)
- Home improvements to sell your home
- Losses from disposing of club memberships
- Meal expenses
- Mortgage penalties (but they may be deductible as an itemized mortgage interest expense as explained earlier in this chapter)
- Premove house-hunting expenses
- Real estate taxes (but they may be deductible as an itemized expense)
- Refitting of carpets and draperies
- Security deposits forfeited
- Storage charges except those incurred in transit and for foreign moves
- Temporary living expenses

Where to Claim the Deduction

If your employer (the federal government) pays your moving costs and you are eligible to exclude this benefit from your income, you do not report them on your return.

If you deduct your expenses, figure the deduction on Form 3903, *Moving Expenses*, which you attach to your return. Enter the deductible amount on Schedule 1 of Form 1040 or 1040-SR.

Energy Improvements

Homeowners can claim various tax credits for making certain energy-saving improvements. In view of currently high energy costs, consider taking advantage of tax breaks to save money on taxes and energy costs.

Benefit ⊕

For 2025, there are 2 tax credits that a homeowner may claim for making certain energy improvements to the home. These include a 30% credit for adding qualified energy efficiency improvements (called the energy-efficient home improvement credit) and a 30% credit for solar and fuel cell property (called the residential clean energy credit). Both credits are nonrefundable (they can't exceed your current tax liability to generate a refund). Both credits end on December 31, 2025, so they apply only to property placed in service by that date.

Conditions

The law requires that these improvements meet certain energy-saving standards and cannot exceed certain dollar limits. Different requirements apply to energy improvements and to solar energy and fuel cell power plants.

Credits generally are meant for a homeowner's principal residence. The credits may be claimed for a second home, but there are limitations. The credits may never be claimed for a home that is rented, because it's not used as the taxpayer's residence. But tenants who make improvements to their principal residence may qualify for a credit, with limitations. Credit availability based on use of a home is explained in IRS FAQs at https://www.irs.gov/credits-deductions/ frequently-asked-questions-about-energy-efficient-home-improvements-and- residential-clean-energy-property-credits-qualifying-residence.

ELIGIBLE ENERGY-EFFICIENT ITEMS

The U.S. Department of Energy has a list of things that are eligible for the credit at https://www.energy.gov/policy/articles/making-our-homes-more- efficient-clean-energy-tax-credits-consumers. These include:

- Insulation systems that reduce heat loss/gain
- Exterior windows (including skylights)
- Exterior doors
- Advanced main air-circulating fan
- Qualified natural gas, propane, or oil furnace or hot water heater
- Electrical panel upgrades

These items are listed in the law, but they are not the only ones to qualify for the credit; other items meeting certain energy standards can also qualify. It is up to the manufacturer to obtain certification for its products. For example, certification has been obtained for a qualifying wood or pellet stove, fireplace, and fireplace insert by various manufacturers. Other items meeting certain energy standards include central air conditioners.

Property *not* qualifying for the energy-efficient home improvement credit includes:

- Window treatments (e.g., blinds, shutters, tinting)
- Roofs. There has been no ruling yet on whether COOLWALL heat-reflective wall coating (a type of exterior paint),which reduces a home's cooling costs, qualifies for the credit.
- Items installed by a tenant in a rented home or by an owner in a second home or a primary residence in a foreign country, or by a landlord on a

home that he or she doesn't live in (only items installed by an owner on a principal residence located in the U.S. can qualify).

- Items installed during construction of a home; only expenditures incurred for an existing home or for an addition or renovation of an existing home can qualify.

Labor costs. The costs can be taken into account for the credit only for certain expenditures. Labor costs may *not* be included with respect to exterior windows or skylights; exterior doors; and insulation materials and systems (including air sealing materials or systems).

LIMITATIONS ON ENERGY-EFFICIENT ITEMS

The credit is 30% of the cost of expenditures, up to a maximum annual credit of $1,200. For example, the maximum credit for adding insulation or air sealing material is $1,200.

There are various limits applied per expenditure:

- $600 for any single qualifying energy property item
- $600 for new windows
- $500 for new exterior doors in the aggregate ($250 per door)
- $600 for electrical panel upgrades
- $150 for a natural gas, propane, or oil furnace or hot water boiler

Notwithstanding the annual and per item limits, the credit for qualifying expenditures on biomass stoves or water heaters and/or heat pumps powered by electricity or natural gas is capped at $2,000.

The credit also covers the cost of written home energy audits that identify the most significant and cost-effective energy efficiency improvements to the residence, including an estimate of the energy and cost savings to each improvement. The credit for home energy audits is capped at $150, so a $500 audit, 30% of which is deductible, results in the maximum credit. The home energy audit must be substantiated by a qualified home energy auditor, who is someone certified by a program recognized by the U.S. Department of Energy.

Dwelling unit also used for business. In claiming the credit for a residence that is also used for business purposes (e.g., a dwelling unit in which you conduct business), the full credit may be claimed if business use is not more than 20% of total use. If business use exceeds 20%, the credit is limited to the portion of expenditures allocable to the portion of the residence used for nonbusiness purposes.

Co-ops and condos. For owners of a co-op or condominium where qualified expenditures are paid by the co-op or condominium board or management association, they are treated as having paid their proportionate share.

Example

X, a cooperative housing corporation, has 10 tenant-stockholders who are all individuals. Each tenant-stockholder owns 1 share of stock. In 2025, X pays $2,000 for a new exterior door for the building. Each tenant-stockholder is treated as having paid $200 ($2,000 × (1 share of stock per tenant-stockholder/ 10 total shares of stock)) for the exterior door. Each tenant-stockholder is entitled to claim a tax credit of $60 ($200 × 30%) for the exterior door.

Example

Y, a condo, has 50 resident owners and in 2025, pays $2,000 for a new exterior door for the building. The organizational documents for Y include a Declaration that lists each resident's percentage interest in common elements based on the proportion of square footage of each dwelling unit to the total square footage of all dwelling units in the building. The Y Declaration shows that Z, an individual dwelling unit owner in Y, has a 10% interest in the common elements, so the Y Board of Directors can determine that Z's proportionate share of the expenditure for the exterior door is $200 ($2,000 × 10%). Z is treated as having paid $200 for the exterior door. Z's credit for 2025 for the exterior door is $60 ($200 × 30%).

Incentives, grants, or rebates by the government or a public utility. Determine whether they are taxable or tax free and whether a credit can be claimed with the funds:

- *Subsidies from a public utility*: no credit allowed (the subsidies are not taxable to the homeowner).
- *Rebates*: reduction in the purchase price of the property, effectively reducing the amount of the credit.
- *Grants and other state incentives*: Generally, a homeowner is not required to reduce the purchase price or cost of property acquired with a governmental energy-efficiency incentive unless that incentive qualifies as a rebate under federal income tax law. While many states label their energy-efficiency incentives as "rebates" that reduce the purchase price, these incentives may not qualify as rebates under federal income tax law, and the amount of the incentive could be included in the homeowner's income for federal income tax purposes.

SOLAR POWER AND FUEL CELLS

There is a 30% residential clean energy credit for solar panels, solar water heating equipment, a geothermal heat pump, a small wind property, a fuel cell power plant, and battery storage technology added to your home in the United States.

But different eligibility rules apply for the residential clean energy property credit. For example, the credit may be claimed for a home that is rented or is a second home, as long as it's used as the taxpayer's residence. Landlords can never claim the credit (but they may qualify for an investment tax credit for installing solar panels, etc.). The credit can apply for an existing or newly constructed home. And any unused credit, though not refundable, may be carried forward indefinitely.

In general, a qualified fuel cell power plant converts a fuel into electricity using electrochemical means, has an electricity-only generation efficiency of more than 30%, and generates at least 0.5 kilowatts of electricity.

You can claim one credit equal to 30% of the qualified investment in a solar panel and another equivalent credit for investing in a solar water heating system.

Additionally, you are allowed a 30% tax credit for the purchase of qualified fuel cell power plants. The credit may not exceed $500 for each 0.5 kilowatt of capacity.

Planning Tips

How can you know whether energy-efficient improvements to your home will qualify for these tax credits? Obtain a manufacturer's certificate that the item has been approved by the IRS as qualifying for the credit. You can find helpful information at www.EnergyStar.gov.

If you can't fully use the residential clean energy credit in 2025, you can carry the unused credit forward; there is no limit on this carryforward period. But there is no carryforward for the energy-efficient home improvement credit.

There may be tax breaks—credits, sales tax exemptions, property tax exemptions—at the state and local level for making certain energy improvements. Check with DSIRE at https://www.dsireusa.org/.

Pitfalls

You must reduce the basis of your home by the amount of any energy credit claimed. For example, if you claim a $1,200 energy-efficient home improvement credit in 2025, you must subtract $1,200 from the basis of your home for determining gain or loss on the sale of the home in the future.

If the credit cannot be used in whole or in part in 2025 because there is insufficient tax liability to offset it, the energy-efficient home improvement credit may not be carried forward; it is simply lost.

Where to Claim the Credits

You figure the credit on Form 5965, *Residential Energy Credits*. You must include the PIN of a qualified manufacturer on the form. Check the IRS's Energy Credit Online Portal listing of qualified manufacturers (QMs) of specified energy property (it does not include insulation). The credit is then entered on Schedule 3 of Form 1040 or 1040-SR.

ABLE Accounts

If you have a disabled child or are under age 26 (starting in 2026 it's 46) and meet certain eligibility conditions, you can have a special savings account that generally does not adversely impact eligibility for means-tested government programs (e.g., Medicaid). An ABLE account can be used on a tax-free basis for housing, as well as other qualified disability expenses. See details in Chapter 2.

Disaster Rules for Casualties to Your Home

These special rules are explained in Chapter 12.

Government Assistance

Federal, state, and local governments provide various forms of assistance to homeowners.

General assistance. If you received government assistance in 2025 to pay your rent, utilities, or home energy expenses under any federal or state law (e.g., Homeowner Assistance Fund, or HAF) you are not taxed on this assistance. For example, Maine's one-time $450 winter energy relief payment to residents is not taxable. This is so, whether payments were made to you and you used them for rent, utilities, and/or home energy expenses or the payments were made directly to your landlord and/or utility companies.

Energy-saving retrofits and high-efficiency home electrification projects. Two Department of Energy programs give homeowners rebates for certain retrofits to homes that reduce energy consumption. For example, homeowners can receive up to $8,000 for upgrades that reduce energy usage by 20–35%, with income limits and eligibility criteria varying by state. These rebates are treated as a reduction in the purchase price of the costs of products and equipment under these projects. The tax basis of the home is reduced by the rebate amount.

Example

A $500 rebate is provided at the time of the sale of eligible equipment with a sales price (before the rebate) of $600. The homeowner's cost basis in the property is only $100 (not $600).

In figuring the residential energy clean property credit (explained in this chapter), expenditures used to figure the credit are reduced by the tax-free rebate amounts.

Example

A taxpayer purchases an eligible product for $400 and receives a $100 rebate for this purchase through a DOE Home Energy Rebate Program. The taxpayer may claim a 30% credit with respect to the remaining $300 of qualifying expenditures. The credit amount is $90, not $120.

If a homeowner purchases an item or items eligible for the energy-efficient home improvement credit and residential energy clean property credit, the homeowner can make a pro rata allocation of amounts received as rebates to individually itemized expenditures as a share of total project cost in determining the amounts paid or incurred for such items for the credits.

Example

A $2,000 rebate for a whole-house energy-saving retrofit is proportionately allocated 60% to $3,000 in qualifying expenditures for a heat pump ($1,200 of the $2,000 rebate) and 40% to $2,000 in qualifying expenditures for insulation ($800 of the $2,000 rebate). The homeowner may treat the amount paid or incurred for the heat pump and the insulation as $1,800 ($3,000 less the $1,200 allocated portion of the rebate) and $1,200 ($2,000 less the $800 allocated portion of the rebate), respectively.

Home Office Deduction

If you work from home, you may be eligible to claim a home office deduction. This write-off includes personal expenses that would not otherwise be deductible, such as utilities and home repairs. This deduction, which is limited to self-employed individuals, including independent contractors, is explained in Chapter 14.

Retirement Savings

Your Social Security benefits alone, or even retirement benefits derived from employer contributions to retirement plans on your behalf, probably won't provide you with the financial security you want for your retirement years. You need to save so that you'll have the assets to generate income after you stop working. Fortunately, the tax law provides important incentives to encourage your personal savings in special retirement accounts. You may be able to write off your savings (contributions) as well as qualify for special treatment when you start drawing from these savings.

There are many different types of retirement plans that you may be able to use to save for your future. Contributions are subject to limits; if your income is high enough, it may bar you from contributing to some plans but not to others.

SECURE Act 2.0, which was signed into law at the end of 2022, made a number of favorable changes in retirement plan rules, some of which are effective for 2025 and beyond. The One Big Beautiful Bill Act in 2025 did not make any direct changes to retirement plans and IRAs.

This chapter explains the tax breaks you may be entitled to when you save for retirement using tax-advantaged ways. If you are an employer, you may be eligible for a tax credit for starting a qualified retirement plan for your business. This credit and other credits related to retirement plans are explained in Chapter 14.

For more information, see IRS Publication 560, *Retirement Plans for Small Business*; IRS Publication 575, *Pension and Annuity Income*; IRS Publication 590-A, *Contributions to Individual Retirement Arrangements (IRAs)*; IRS Publication 590-B, *Distributions from Individual Retirement Arrangements (IRAs)*; and IRS Publication 4333, *SEP Retirement Plans for Small Businesses*.

Traditional IRAs

The Employee Retirement Income Security Act of 1974 (referred to as ERISA) created individual retirement accounts (IRAs) to enable taxpayers to save for their own retirement largely because company pensions could no longer be relied upon for retirement income. With an IRA, the government effectively contributes to your retirement savings by permitting a tax deduction for contributions if certain conditions are met. The tax savings are the government's contribution. For example, if you are in the 32% tax bracket, the government contributes almost one-third of your contributions to a traditional (deductible) IRA by means of tax savings from the total contribution amount; you only have to come up with about two-thirds of the contribution.

Benefit

If you work as an employee or have net earnings from self-employment, you can contribute to an IRA. The contribution limit for 2025 is $7,000, or $8,000 if you are age 50 or older by the end of 2025, as long as you earn at least this dollar amount.

If you are single, under age 50, and earn at least $7,000, you can make a full contribution regardless of your income (the income limitation is explained later in this chapter). If you work part-time and earn only $5,000, your contribution is limited to $5,000. *Making* a contribution is different from *deducting* one. This is explained later in this chapter.

If you have a spouse who does not work for compensation, you can contribute to an IRA for your spouse based on your own earnings. The IRA for a nonworking spouse is called the Kay Bailey Hutchison Spousal IRA. The same dollar limit of $7,000 (or $8,000 if age 50 by the end of 2025) applies to a spousal IRA. This means that if you have sufficient earnings and both you and your spouse are under age 50, you may contribute up to $14,000 ($7,000 for yourself and $7,000 for your spouse) for 2025.

If you do not participate in another qualified retirement plan, such as a 401(k) plan, or if you do participate but your income is below a set amount, you can deduct your contributions. The deduction is claimed as an adjustment to gross income; you claim it regardless of whether you itemize your other deductions.

Earnings on IRA contributions build up on a tax-deferred basis (no tax is owed annually on the earnings of an IRA although there are exceptions if the account holds certain investments). You are required to take certain withdrawals from the IRA starting at a certain age or, regardless of your age, if you inherit an IRA. The starting age for an account owner for those born between 1951 through 1959 is now age 73.

The starting age for commencing required minimum distributions increases to 75 in 2033. This applies to those born in 1960 or later.

If you fail to take these required amounts (called required minimum distributions or RMDs), you may be subject to a 25% penalty of the amount you should have taken (10% if the RMD is received and the tax paid before receiving a notice of assessment from the IRS and this is within 2 years of the missed RMD).

Conditions for Making Contributions

There are 2 conditions for making a contribution:

1. Earned income
2. Cash contributions

EARNED INCOME

Earned income for purposes of making IRA contributions means taxable wages (including tips, commissions, bonuses, and jury duty fees) and net earnings from self-employment. Earned income for purposes of making IRA contributions also includes taxable alimony, tax-free combat pay, and stipends and non-tuition fellowship payments to graduate and postdoctoral students.

You must earn the income. If you live in a community property state where one-half of your spouse's earnings is viewed as income, you cannot use your share of your spouse's income as the basis for making your IRA contribution.

Earned income does *not* include:

- Conservation Reserve Program (CRP) payments even though they are reported as income for self-employment tax purposes.
- Deferred compensation, pensions, or annuities.
- Investment income, such as dividends or interest.
- Income earned abroad for which the foreign earned income exclusion has been claimed.
- Partnership income from a business for which you do not provide services that are a material income-producing factor.
- Social Security benefits.
- Unemployment compensation.

CASH CONTRIBUTIONS

All contributions must be made in cash, which includes payments by check or cash transfers from a financial account. If you currently own investments that you want to use as your contributions, you must first liquidate them. Your IRA can then reacquire the same investments (provided they are not prohibited investments discussed later). Contributions can also be made using a federal income tax refund (explained later in this chapter).

Contributions cannot be made using digital assets. The IRS views cryptocurrency as property and not as cash.

Condition for Claiming a Deduction

Just because you meet all the conditions for making an IRA contribution does not mean that you can claim a deduction for the contribution. Even if you qualify to make a contribution, there is an additional condition in order to deduct your contribution.

There is no income cap for taking a deduction for a contribution if you do not participate in a 401(k) or other qualified retirement plan. But to deduct a contribution if you are an active participant in a qualified retirement plan, your modified adjusted gross income (MAGI) cannot exceed a phaseout range. The deduction amount phases out for MAGI within the phaseout range. No deduction can be claimed if MAGI exceeds the phaseout range. MAGI for this purpose is adjusted gross income, increased by exclusions for interest on U.S. savings bonds used for higher education, employer-paid adoption assistance, and foreign earned income as well as the deduction for interest on student loans. Table 5.1 shows the phaseout ranges for 2025.

Example

You are single, age 42, and participate in your company's 401(k) plan. If your AGI is $75,000, you can fully deduct your IRA contributions. If your AGI is $84,000, your basic deduction for 2025 is limited to $3,500 (½ of $7,000). If your AGI is $89,000 or more, you cannot deduct your IRA contributions.

If one spouse is an active participant, the other spouse is permitted to make a deductible IRA contribution only if the couple's MAGI is below a set limit. For 2025, the MAGI limit in this case is $236,000. The nonactive participant's spouse's contribution is reduced when the couple's MAGI exceeds $236,000; it is fully phased out when MAGI reaches $246,000.

TABLE 5.1 2025 MAGI Phaseout Range for Active Participants Deducting IRA Contributions

Filing Status	MAGI
Married filing jointly and surviving spouse	$126,000–146,000
Single and head of household	$79,000–89,000
Married filing separately	$0–$10,000*

*A married person filing separately who did not live with a spouse at any time during the year is subject to the MAGI limits for singles.

Planning Tips

You have until the deadline for filing the return to make an IRA contribution. For example, you have until April 15, 2026, to make an IRA contribution for 2026. But even if you obtain a filing extension, you do not gain any additional time to make your annual contribution.

Just because you have more time to act doesn't mean it's a good idea to delay. The earlier in the year you make your contribution, the sooner you begin to earn tax-deferred income. For example, if you make your 2025 contribution on January 15, 2025, rather than on the due date of the 2025 return, you gain an additional 15 months of tax-deferred investment buildup in the IRA.

You may fund your IRA contribution with a tax refund from your return. You do this by filing Form 8888, *Allocation of Refund (Including Savings Bond Purchases)*, to indicate the amount of the refund to be directly deposited into your account (the account must already be set up). If you file your return early enough, the refund may be applied toward a current year contribution.

Example

You file your 2025 return on March 1, 2026, which shows a tax refund of $8,000. On the return you claim a $7,000 IRA contribution (the amount for which you are eligible) even though you have not yet made the contribution. On your return you provide deposit information to put $7,000 of your 2025 refund into your IRA for 2025 and you instruct your IRA custodian to be sure to credit the direct deposit for 2025.

Some brokerage firms assume the direct deposit should be applied to the current calendar year (which would mean a contribution for the year after the year of the return), but don't let this assumption apply if you don't want it to. Instruct your IRA custodian or trustee on the year for which the funds are being deposited.

You can help your child jump-start his or her retirement savings by providing the funds for an IRA contribution. As long as your child has earned income (e.g., from a part-time or summer job), you can make a gift of the contribution amount to your child.

Example

Your child earns $1,800 from a summer job and uses her earnings as spending money for the year. You can give your child $1,800 to make an IRA contribution.

The IRA contribution amount and MAGI limits can be increased for inflation, so check the Supplement for any changes for 2026.

If, in the course of a marital dissolution, an IRA is awarded to a spouse or former spouse, the IRA owner can avoid tax on the transfer by retitling the account in the spouse's name or making a direct trustee-to-trustee transfer. A distribution followed by a transfer to the spouse is taxable to the owner.

If you are age 70½ or older, you can opt to make a one-time transfer of up to $54,000 in 2025 from your IRA to a charitable gift annuity. This is considered a qualified charitable distribution (see Chapter 6). This option benefits a charity while providing you with a guaranteed income for life, although it may not be substantial (check the guaranteed interest rate that the school or other charitable organization is offering).

Pitfalls

IRAs are designed to be long-term investments for you. Don't make contributions if you know you'll need the funds within a short time (say, this year or next); early withdrawals may trigger a tax penalty and possibly an investment-related penalty (such as bank charges for cashing in a certificate of deposit before maturity). Early distribution penalties and the exceptions to them are discussed next.

Also, use care in figuring how much you can put into the IRA each year and how much you may be required to withdraw annually. Again, there are penalties for putting in too much or taking out too little under certain circumstances (discussed later).

You cannot treat dividend reinvestments in your IRA as additional contributions and claim a deduction for them. Dividend reinvestments are merely investment returns on your contributions.

Early distribution penalties. If you need funds from your IRA before you retire, you may be subject to a 10% early distribution penalty. This penalty applies if you take money out before age 59½, unless you meet one of the following exceptions to the penalty:

- You become disabled (or die and your heirs take out the money).
- You take the money in a series of substantially equal periodic payments. This essentially means you take withdrawals in even amounts for at least 5 years or until you attain age 59½, whichever is later.
- You use the money to pay medical expenses exceeding 10% of your adjusted gross income.

- You are unemployed and receiving unemployment benefits for at least 12 consecutive weeks (or if you had been self-employed, you would have received such benefits due to lack of work).
- You use the money to pay higher education expenses (this exception to the 10% penalty is explained more fully in Chapter 3).
- You take out no more than $10,000 and use it to pay first-time home-buying expenses (this exception to the 10% penalty is explained more fully in Chapter 4).
- The IRS places levies on your IRA for back taxes.
- You are a reservist called to active duty.
- You pay birth or adoption expenses up to $5,000.
- You take a distribution up to $22,000 for expenses related to a federally declared disaster within 180 days of the event. Qualified disaster distributions are explained later in this chapter.
- You have a terminal illness (death is expected to result in 84 months as certified by a physician).
- You are a victim of domestic abuse and take distributions up to the lesser of $10,300 or 50% of the account balance.
- You take up to $1,000 for personal or family emergency expenses due to unforeseen circumstances or immediate financial need.

Looking Ahead

Starting in 2026, the 10% penalty does not apply to withdrawals for long-term care insurance premiums up to $2,500 per year.

There is no exception to the penalty for paying income taxes, even if this is done to avoid a levy on the IRA (which is a penalty exception).

Excess contributions penalty. If you are an active participant who contributed to an IRA but after the close of the year you find out your AGI is too high for a deductible contribution, you have several options to correct the contribution and avoid a 6% excise tax on excess contributions. The 6% excise tax applies each year until you correct the excess contribution.

You can treat the contributions as nondeductible IRA contributions. Alternatively, you can withdraw the excess contribution (plus any earnings on it) by the due date of your return (plus extensions). If you miss this deadline, you can limit the tax penalty to one year by withdrawing the excess by December 31 of the year following the year of the contribution.

Example

In 2025, you are 48 years old, and are an active participant in a qualified retirement plan. You anticipate your AGI for the year to be low enough to make a deductible IRA contribution. You contribute $7,000 to your IRA on November 15, 2025, intending to take a deduction for it on your 2025 return. In December you receive unexpected income (e.g., a year-end bonus, a large distribution from a mutual fund) that makes your AGI exceed the limit for making a deductible contribution in 2025. You can treat the contribution as a nondeductible IRA for 2025. You can withdraw the contribution (and earnings on it) by April 15, 2026, and avoid the penalty. You can withdraw the contribution (and earnings on it) by December 31, 2026; you'll owe the penalty for 2026.

If you contribute to an IRA but later determine that your income prevents you from claiming the IRA deduction reported on your return (for example, you are an active plan participant and a later IRS audit increases your MAGI above the phaseout range), you are subject to a 6% excise tax, called an excess contributions penalty. This tax continues to apply every year in which the excess contribution (and earnings on such contribution) remains in the IRA.

You can designate that the excess contribution be treated as your IRA contribution in a subsequent year, assuming you're eligible to make a contribution at that time.

Example

In 2026, you deduct your $7,000 IRA contribution for 2025 on your return. In 2027, the IRS audits your return and increases your MAGI to an amount that makes your contribution nondeductible. You were not eligible for a deductible contribution in 2026 but can make a fully deductible contribution in 2027. Designate the 2025 contribution as your 2027 deductible contribution to limit the 6% penalty to 2025 and 2026.

Penalty for insufficient withdrawals. Usually, starting in the year in which you attain the required starting age discussed earlier, you must take required minimum distributions (RMDs). If you don't take RMDs, you can be subject to a 25% penalty on the amount you failed to take.

The penalty is reduced to 10% if you correct the error within 2 years. And the penalty may be avoided altogether if you can show the shortfall was due to reasonable cause and you're taking steps to correct the error.

The penalty also applies to heirs who fail to take RMDs from inherited accounts. The rules for RMDs for beneficiaries are very complicated. Final regulations issued in 2024 clarify these rules. Those who inherited accounts from an owner who died in 2020, 2021, 2022, or 2023 won't be penalized for failing to take RMDs in 2022 through 2024; they must begin RMDs in 2025 to avoid future penalties.

IRS FAQs explain the penalty for account owners and beneficiaries at https://www.irs.gov/retirement-plans/retirement-plan-and-ira-required-minimum-distributions-faqs.

Investment limitations. You can invest your IRA contributions in a wide array of investment vehicles, including certificates of deposit, stocks, bonds, and mutual funds. You can even invest in real estate if you avoid self-dealing and other prohibited transaction rules.

The law places certain limits on the types of things you can invest in. If you opt to invest in a prohibited vehicle, you are treated as having taken a distribution; you are taxed on the amount and, if under age 59 ½, subject to a 10% penalty. You are prohibited from putting your IRA money into collectibles, which include:

- Antiques
- Art works
- Coins (other than state-issued coins or certain U.S. minted gold, silver, or platinum coins)
- Gems
- Guns
- Metals (other than gold, silver, platinum, or palladium bullion held by your IRA trustee)
- Nonfungible tokens (NFTs)
- Stamps

Technically, you are permitted to own realty in an IRA, but you must do so through a self-directed IRA that permits such investment. And you cannot mortgage the property (IRAs are barred from any borrowing, as explained later).

Also, even though there is no law preventing you, it makes no sense to put IRA money into tax-exempt municipal bonds. Since the IRA is already tax deferred, you don't gain any benefit from the tax-free interest on the bonds. And when you take distributions from the IRA, they will all be treated as ordinary income (even though the underlying investment producing the earnings was tax-exempt bonds).

It may also be advisable to avoid foreign investments because foreign taxes paid from the IRA do not qualify for a deduction or credit; they only reduce the funds within the account. Another type of investment you may want to avoid is a master limited partnership (MLP). If you invest IRA funds in an MLP, you may have reportable income even though you haven't taken any distribution. When the MLP has unrelated business taxable income (UBTI) over $1,000 from operations or the sale of units, you have to file Form 990-T, *Exempt Organiza-tion Business Income Tax Return*, for your IRA and pay required taxes. There are also basis adjustments as well as other complications for MPL losses in your IRA.

The IRS has not classified cryptocurrency as a collectible, so it is a type of property that appears to be permissible to be held in an IRA. There are compa-nies offering self-directed IRAs that allow you to invest in cryptocurrency, but caution is advised.

Borrowing limitations. You are prohibited from borrowing from your IRA or using it as collateral for a loan. If you do borrow from your IRA, the amount borrowed or used as collateral is treated as a taxable distribution to you (and can be subject to penalty if you are under age 59½). If you take a loan from the IRA, the value of the entire account as of the first day of the year in which the loan is taken is includible in your income. If you pledge part of the account, that part of the account is includible in your income. What's more, the taxable amount may be subject to a 10% penalty if you are under age 59½.

But you can have access to the funds for a short time without any adverse tax consequences. You can take a distribution and use it for 60 days; as long as the funds are replaced by the end of 60 days, there is no taxable distribution.

Account losses. If you lose money—the money you put into the IRA is worth less now—you can't deduct the loss.

Where to Claim the Deduction

You deduct your IRA contribution on Form 1040 or 1040-SR. If you receive Social Security benefits in a year in which an IRA contribution is made, which can impact the deductible amount, there is a special worksheet in IRS Publication 590-A for figuring the IRA deduction in this case. If you are using a tax refund to fund your IRA, you must file Form 8888, *Allocation of Refund (Including Savings Bond Purchases)*, to indicate the amount of the refund to be directly deposited into your account.

If you are treating the contribution as a nondeductible IRA, you must com-plete Form 8606, *Nondeductible IRAs*. The purpose of this form is to help you keep track of nondeductible contributions so that when distributions are later taken, you won't pay tax on these after-tax contributions.

If you are subject to any penalty with respect to your IRA, you must file Form 5329, *Additional Taxes on Qualified Plans (including IRAs) and Other*

Tax-Favored Accounts, and enter the penalty on Schedule 2 of Form 1040 or 1040-SR.

A 2024 report from the Treasury Inspector General of Tax Administration found that while about 6.2 million taxpayers took early distributions, 2.8 million did not pay the 10% that was owed. In light of this report, expect the IRS to be scutinizing Form 1099-Rs and checking whether taxpayers have properly reported distributions on their returns.

Roth IRAs

Roth IRAs (named after U.S. Senator William Roth, who sponsored the law) are an alternative personal retirement savings account that debuted in 1998. While these accounts offer no immediate tax break since contributions are not deductible, they offer long-term tax savings.

Benefit

For 2025, you can contribute up to $7,000 ($8,000 if you are 50 or older by December 31, 2025) to a special type of retirement savings account that allows you to build up tax-free income. While there is no current tax deduction for your contributions, you have access to your contributions and can withdraw them at any time tax free (after all, you made those contributions with after-tax dollars). But you can also withdraw earnings on those contributions tax free after 5 years if certain conditions discussed later are met. You can also create a Roth IRA by converting some or all of a traditional IRA or qualified retirement plan, with no dollar limit, which is discussed later in this chapter.

Conditions for Making Roth IRA Contributions

To be eligible to make contributions to a Roth IRA, you must meet 2 conditions:

1. You must have earned income (as explained earlier under traditional IRAs).
2. Your modified adjusted gross income (MAGI) cannot exceed a set limit.

Whether or not you are an active participant in a qualified retirement plan has no bearing on eligibility to contribute to a Roth IRA.

MAGI LIMIT

Your MAGI in 2025 cannot be more than the limit for your filing status shown in Table 5.2. A partial contribution can be made if your MAGI falls within the phaseout range.

TABLE 5.2 2025 MAGI Phaseout Range for Roth IRA Contributions

Filing Status	MAGI
Married filing jointly and surviving spouse	$236,000–246,000
Single and head of household	$150,000–170,000
Married person filing separately	$0–$10,000

Example

You are single, age 40, with MAGI in 2025 of $75,000. You can contribute up to $7,000 to a Roth IRA in 2025. If your MAGI is over $170,000, no contribution is allowed, even if your company doesn't have any qualified retirement plan. If your MAGI falls within the phaseout range, you can make a partial contribution. You figure your allowable limit using Worksheet 5.1, adapted from IRS Publication 590-A.

WORKSHEET 5.1 Reduced Roth IRA Contribution Limit for 2025

1. Enter your MAGI.	1. _____
2. Enter: • $236,000 if you file a joint return or are a surviving spouse. • $0 if you are married filing a separate return and you live with your spouse at any time during the year. • $150,000 for all other taxpayers.	2. _____
3. Subtract line 2 from line 1.	3. _____
4. Enter: • $10,000 if you file a joint return or are a qualifying widow(er). • $15,000 for all other taxpayers.	4. _____
5. Divide line 3 by line 4. Enter the result as a decimal (carried to 3 places). If the result is 1.000 or more, enter 1.000.	5. _____
6. Enter the lesser of: • $7,000 ($8,000 if 50 or older), or • Your taxable compensation.	6. _____
7. Multiply line 5 by line 6.	7. _____
8. Subtract line 7 from line 6. Round the result up to the nearest $10. If the result is less than $200, enter $200.	8. _____
9. Enter contributions for the year to other IRAs.	9. _____
10. Subtract line 9 from line 6.	10. _____
11. Enter the lesser of line 8 or line 10. *This is your reduced Roth IRA contribution limit.*	11. _____

This MAGI limit applies whether or not you participate in another qualified retirement plan.

There is no age limit for making Roth IRA contributions. As long as you continue working, you can continue to put money into a Roth IRA (assuming your MAGI is below the limit).

You can choose to convert some or all of your retirement plan account or IRAs at any time; there is no deadline for making a conversion.

Tax-Free Income Withdrawals

You can withdraw your contributions at any time tax free, but the withdrawal of earnings on your contributions are tax free only after 5 years and you meet *any* of the following 3 conditions:

1. You are over age 59 ½.

2. You become disabled.

3. You withdraw no more than $10,000 and use the money for qualified first-time home-buying expenses. (Qualified first-time home-buying expenses are explained in Chapter 4.)

For contributory Roth IRAs (in contrast to converted Roth IRAs explained later), the 5-year period runs from the first day of the year to which your contributions relate. For example, if you contribute $7,000 to a Roth IRA for 2025 on April 15, 2026, the 5-year period commences on January 1, 2025. For Roth IRAs established through conversions, the 5-year period used to determine whether the 10% penalty applies if you are under age 59 ½ at the time of the conversion, the period starts on the first day of the year in which the conversion is made.

Example

On April 15, 2021, you contributed $4,000 to a Roth IRA for 2020. If you are at least 59 ½ in 2025, you can now withdraw the earnings you have built up in the account completely tax free—no income tax and no early distribution penalty. The 5-year period began on January 1, 2020. If, instead, you converted the Roth IRA on April 15, 2021, the 5-year period would have begun on January 1, 2021.

Planning Tips

The deadline for 2025 Roth IRA contributions is April 15, 2026. This is the same deadline for traditional IRAs discussed earlier in this chapter.

You can fund a Roth IRA with a tax refund, as explained earlier in this chapter for traditional IRAs.

Assuming your income gives you the option of choosing between making a deductible IRA contribution or a nondeductible Roth IRA contribution, which alternative makes more sense for you? In most cases, choosing to make the Roth IRA contribution is wiser because the value of the IRA deduction you are forgoing is much smaller than the value of receiving tax-free income from the Roth IRA in the future.

Example

You are eligible to make either a deductible IRA contribution or a Roth IRA contribution. Assuming you are in the 24% tax bracket, a $7,000 deduction to a deductible IRA would save you $1,680 this year. But let's also assume that a $7,000 contribution can quadruple in the next 25 years to $28,000 (of which $21,000 is earnings on your contribution). If you opt for the Roth IRA, then when you withdraw the funds (assuming you are over age 59½), you won't pay any income tax on the earnings—a $5,040 tax savings if you are still in the 24% tax bracket.

Survivors of military personnel who died from injuries now can contribute the proceeds from Servicemembers' Group Life Insurance (SGLI) to a Roth IRA without regard to the annual contribution limit and without regard to the MAGI limit. This contribution is treated as a rollover contribution and must be made no later than one year after receipt of the SGLI proceeds.

Contributions you make to a designated Roth account within a 401(k) plan have no impact on your ability to contribute to a Roth IRA. For example, say in 2025, you contribute $23,500 to a designated Roth account 401(k) within your employer's plan (you're not 50 years old or older). You can also contribute $7,000 to a Roth IRA (assuming your income does not exceed the limits).

There is a tax strategy referred to as a "backdoor Roth IRA," which is a way for those with income too high to deduct contributions to an IRA to create a Roth IRA. It is discussed under Roth IRA Conversions later in this chapter.

Pitfalls

If a long-term 529 plan is rolled over to a Roth IRA, the rollover reduces the annual contribution limit for the beneficiary. For example, if $5,000 is rolled over from a long-term 529 to the beneficiary's Roth IRA in 2025, the beneficiary's contribution limit for 2025 is $2,000 ($7,000 – $5,000). Long-term 529 plan rollovers are discussed in more detail in Chapter 4.

Beneficiaries who inherit a Roth IRA must take RMDs and can be penalized for failing to do so. But there's one big difference in RMDs for traditional IRAs versus Roth IRAs: beneficiaries of Roth IRAs don't have to take RMDs over the

10-year period mandated for traditional IRAs; they can wait until the end of the 10 years to completely drain the account. And, like Roth IRA owners, beneficiaries are not taxed on their distributions.

Where to Claim the Benefit

You do not report contributions you make to a Roth IRA on your return (remember, they are not deductible).

If you make excess contributions to the Roth IRA, you are subject to a 6% excise tax and must file Form 5329, *Additional Taxes on Qualified Plans (Including IRAs) and Other Tax-Favored Accounts*. Enter the excise tax on Schedule 2 of Form 1040 or 1040-SR.

Roth IRA Conversions

You can convert your existing IRA or qualified retirement plan account (e.g., 401(k) account) to a Roth IRA. There is no dollar limit on the amount you can convert and no income limits on conversion eligibility. If there were no nondeductible contributions made to your IRA or if all of the 401(k) was funded with pre-tax dollars (salary reduction amounts by you as well as employer contributions that the employer deducted, neither of which you've paid taxes on), then all of the amount converted is taxable income. In effect, the conversion is treated just like a distribution. Fortunately, there is no 10% early distribution penalty if you're under age 59½ at the time of the conversion, as long as the funds remain in the Roth IRA for at least 5 years.

You can also convert funds from a traditional 401(k) plan to a designated Roth account if the plan allows for such conversions. These are referred to as in-plan rollovers. They are essentially the same as conversions to Roth IRAs.

Benefit

There is no current tax benefit to making the conversion; only a current tax cost. The benefit from the conversion results from building up potentially tax-free income for retirement.

Conditions for Making a Roth IRA Conversion

There are no conditions for making a conversion. There is no age or income limit. There is only the decision on whether it makes sense to do the conversion. Factors to consider:

- *Your age*. The younger you are, the longer you will have to build up tax-free income.
- *Your income*. The more modest your income, the less tax on the conversion.
- *Your ability to pay the tax on the conversion*. It's advisable to have sufficient funds to pay the tax resulting from the conversion.

Planning Tips

Making a Roth IRA conversion for the year does not automatically prevent you from also making a Roth IRA contribution if you are otherwise eligible to do so. Of course, the resulting income from the conversion may impact your eligibility for making an annual contribution because it increases your MAGI. Don't have an IRA that can be converted? The "backdoor Roth IRA" is a strategy for creating a Roth IRA other than through annual contributions. It involves contributing to a traditional IRA and then converting it to a Roth. Those who are active participants and have income too high to contribute to a deductible IRA can contribute to a nondeductible IRA and then make the conversion. Whether this strategy makes sense depends upon the situation, factoring in the tax cost for the conversion and the time frame for future buildup on the Roth IRA.

The decision to convert isn't an all-or-nothing proposition. You can convert part of your IRA to a Roth IRA. In fact, you can do this every year until you've converted the amount you've targeted for this purpose.

If you convert a 401(k) or similar account to a Roth IRA (assuming the plan allows this), be sure to do so using a direct transfer by the plan administrator to your Roth IRA. This avoids the mandatory 20% withholding that applies to qualified retirement plan distributions.

Pitfalls

The income resulting from the conversion may push you into a higher tax bracket and prevent or curtail the ability to use other tax benefits, including deductions or tax credits. Because the conversion increases MAGI, it may mean additional Medicare premiums for Parts B and D 2 years from now. The income from a conversion in 2025 may cause additional Medicare premiums in 2027.

A conversion can't be undone. In the past, you were allowed to change your mind, but this is no longer so; a conversion is permanent.

You cannot convert funds that are required minimum distributions (RMDs). They have to be taken out of traditional IRAs and qualified retirement plans (e.g., 401(k) plan) and cannot be put into Roth IRAs.

Don't confuse a Roth IRA with a Roth 401(k) (called a designated Roth account). The rules for a designated Roth account are separate and distinct from the rules for a Roth IRA.

If you take a distribution from your IRA to make a conversion, have sufficient funds to pay the tax so you don't eat into the conversion amount.

Example

In 2025, when you are 40 years old, you want to convert your $100,000 IRA to a Roth IRA. Assuming you're in the 24% tax bracket (after factoring in this distribution), the conversion costs you $24,000. If you use $24,000 of the $100,000 to pay the tax, then you have only $76,000 in your Roth IRA. And the $24,000 not converted to the Roth IRA is subject to a 10% penalty because you are under age 59½, costing you an additional $2,400 in tax.

Where to Report the Roth IRA Conversion

Income from a conversion to a Roth IRA is reported on Form 1040 or 1040-SR. If you use a portion of your IRA to pay the tax and are subject to the 10% penalty on this amount, file Form 5329, *Additional Taxes on Qualified Retirement Plans (Including IRAs) and Other Tax-Favored Accounts,* and enter the penalty on Schedule 2 of Form 1040 or 1040-SR.

IRA Rollovers

IRAs are highly portable—they can be transferred from one investment company to another with no immediate tax consequences if certain conditions are met. This allows taxpayers to move accounts from a bank to a mutual fund or from one brokerage firm to another. The same rules applicable to rollovers of traditional IRAs also apply to rollovers of Roth IRAs.

Benefit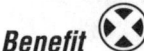

You can transfer funds from one IRA to another without any current tax. There are no dollar limits on the amount you can roll over each year.

There are 2 ways in which to make the transfer:

1. *Direct transfers.* You can instruct the custodian or trustee of your IRA to transfer funds directly to the custodian or trustee of another IRA.
2. *Distribution and reinvestment.* You can take a withdrawal of funds from your IRA and replace the funds within 60 days.

Conditions

The transfer method you use determines the conditions you must meet to achieve tax-free treatment.

DIRECT TRANSFERS

You instruct the custodian or trustee of your IRAs to complete the action; you cannot receive any funds that are part of the transfer. There is no time requirement for your fiduciaries to complete the transaction. There is no limit on the number of direct transfers you can make each year.

DISTRIBUTION AND REINVESTMENT

You must complete the transaction within 60 days. Generally, the IRS cannot extend this period. But you may qualify for a waiver of the 60-day deadline in limited circumstances detailed later under "Pitfalls."

You are permitted to make only one rollover per 12-month period (this rule is called the one-rollover-per-year rule even though technically it's a 12-month period). This rule applies per taxpayer, so only one rollover can be made within the period, regardless of how many separate IRA accounts you may have.

Note: Regardless of which method you select, rollovers are handled separately from annual contributions to IRAs and Roth IRAs. So, you may make a rollover even if you also make a deductible IRA contribution for the year.

Planning Tips

You can use funds in your IRA as a short-term loan. While borrowing against an IRA is not permitted, you can take a distribution and avoid current tax if you replace the funds within 60 days.

Example

In early February 2025 you were out of work and didn't have money to pay the rent, so you used funds from your IRA for this purpose. Later in March 2025, you found a job and used some earnings to replace your IRA withdrawal. Because you did this within 60 days, it is not treated as a taxable distribution.

You may want to roll your IRA over to a company retirement plan, such as a 401(k) plan. This may make sense for several reasons. Company investment options may entail lower fees than what you pay if you invest through a personal IRA. If you are nearing age 73 (the current age for which RMDs must commence for those born in 1951 through 1959) and still working for a company that has a qualified retirement plan deferring required minimum distributions (RMDs) until actual retirement, ask whether it accepts rollovers from your IRA. If so, you may want to take advantage of the opportunity to add to your company's retirement plan and delay RMDs until you retire. (This strategy does not work for anyone who owns 5% or more of the company.) And, the 401(k) may allow you to borrow from the plan, which is something you can't do with an IRA (although it isn't the best thing to do with a 401(k) if building up retirement savings is your goal).

If you have a long-term 529 plan, you can roll over the funds to the beneficiary's Roth IRA. The details of rollovers from long-term 529 plans are discussed in Chapter 4.

If you try to complete the rollover on time but outside events prevent you from doing so, you may be able to obtain an extension to the 60-day limit. The limit is automatically extended if the account is frozen, if you are serving in a combat zone, are in a federal disaster area, or a victim of terrorist or military action. The limit is also extended if you meet all of the following conditions:

1. You were not previously denied a waiver request for a rollover by the IRS.
2. Your reason for missing the 60-day deadline is one of the following:
   - Your financial institution made an error.
   - You misplaced the distribution check and never cashed it.
   - You deposited the distribution in an account you thought was an eligible retirement plan.
   - Your principal residence was severely damaged.
   - A member of your family died.
   - A member of your family was seriously ill.
   - You were incarcerated.
   - You were subject to restrictions imposed by a foreign country.
   - There was a postal error.
   - The distribution was made on account of an IRS levy and the proceeds have been returned to you.
   - The party making the distribution delayed providing information required by the receiving plan or IRA despite your best efforts to obtain it.
   - The distribution was made to a state unclaimed property fund.
3. You complete the rollover as soon as practical. There is a 30-day safe harbor, which means doing so within 30-days after the occurrence of the condition that prevented the rollover.

If you qualify for this self-certification, send a written letter to the plan administrator or IRA trustee stating that you satisfy the conditions for relief. There's a sample letter for this purpose in the Appendix to Revenue Procedure 2016–47.

Even if you can't use the self-certification process, you may still obtain relief for missing the 60-day rollover deadline in some situations. For example, the Tax Court allowed more time for a person suffering from depression to complete a rollover.

Pitfall

If you take a distribution and plan to reinvest within 60 days, make sure to watch the calendar closely. If you miss the deadline by even one day (and don't qualify for relief explained earlier), the entire distribution becomes taxable to you.

Where to Claim the Benefit

IRA rollovers that are distributed to you are reported to you (and the IRS) on Form 1099-R, *Distributions from Pensions, Annuities, Retirement or Profit-Sharing Plans, IRAs, Insurance Contracts, Etc*.

You must report the distribution on line 4a on page 1 of Form 1040 or 1040-SR, but if you successfully completed the transfer within 60 days, check box on line 4c1 and enter only zero on line 4b of Form 1040 or 1040-SR.

Overview of 401(k) and Similar Plans

Pensions used to be the responsibility of employers, but that responsibility has shifted to employees. To make it easier for employees to pay for their own retirement savings, the tax law has created special retirement plans. Companies set up the plans, but employees fund them (in whole or in part) by contributing a portion of their salary each year. Employees decide how their contributions are to be invested by selecting from a menu of investment options provided by the employer. The tax law encourages employee contributions by allowing them to escape immediate taxation.

There are different types of 401(k)s: Starter 401(k)s, which first became available in 2024, and regular 401(k)s, which have been around since 1978.

The rules discussed here refer to 401(k) plans, but most of them also apply to other similar plans, such as 403(b) and 457 plans. These other plans are not discussed separately. If you are in or considering participation in one of these other plans, specific questions should be addressed to your plan administrator.

Starter 401(k)

Because so many workers don't have access to retirement savings in the workplace, a new type of retirement plan was created by SECURE Act 2.0 and became effective in 2024. If you work for a small employer, you may have access to retirement savings through a Starter 401(k). This plan is funded *entirely* by employee salary reduction contributions; employer contributions are not permitted.

Benefit

You are automatically enrolled in the plan if you are eligible to participate. The amount of your salary reduction contributions to the plan is not treated as taxable compensation.

Conditions

The only condition for making contributions is being an eligible employee. This means meeting your company's age and service requirements for participation. Usually, this means being at least 21 years old and having at least one year of service with the company; but the employer may adopt less stringent conditions. If you are covered by a collective bargaining agreement, you can't contribute to the Starter 401(k).

The plan must set a contribution amount of at least 3% of compensation. It can be as high as 15% of compensation. You can opt to reduce the plan's automatic contribution level or opt out entirely. Your elections are made year by year.

The maximum contribution for 2025 is $6,000 (the same limit as in 2024). Those age 50 and older can add another $1,000. The contribution amount can be indexed for inflation; check the Supplement for the 2026 limit.

Planning Tips

If you've been having salary reduction amounts added to a state-run plan, your employer may choose to roll them over to the Starter 401(k).

If you contribute to a Starter 401(k), you may be eligible for the retirement saver's credit (discussed later in this chapter).

If you leave the job, you are fully vested in your account balance and can opt to roll over your account to an IRA or another qualified retirement plan.

Pitfall

If you contribute to a Starter 401(k), you are considered an active participant. This may impact eligibility to make deductible IRA contributions, explained earlier in this chapter.

Where to Claim the Benefits

The same reporting for conventional 401(k)s discussed next applies for Starter 401(k)s.

Regular 401(k)

Benefit

If you are eligible to participate in your employer's 401(k), you can agree each year to contribute a portion of your salary as your contribution to the plan. You can change your contribution from year to year; you may also be able to reduce it within a year. Depending on your employer's plan, you may be automatically enrolled and then have the opportunity to change the default contribution made by you (you can even opt out entirely from contributing) or be offered the opportunity to participate and make contributions within the limits discussed later.

Your contribution is called an elective deferral or salary reduction amount. This amount is *not* treated as compensation to you for the year. You do not pay income tax on your elective deferral, but you do pay Social Security and Medicare taxes—FICA—on the elective deferral.

Example

If your wages this year are $45,000 and you contribute $8,000 to your company's 401(k) plan, only $37,000 of your wages for purposes of income taxes is reported on your Form W-2; you only pay income taxes on $37,000 this year.

If you are in a 401(k), you may be able to direct contributions to a designated Roth account. Contributions to a designated Roth account within a 401(k) plan are not treated as elective deferrals; they are made with after-tax contributions. A designated Roth account, which offers the opportunity to create tax-free income for the future, is similar but not identical to a Roth IRA.

Conditions

Eligibility requirements to make elective deferrals are spelled out in your company's plan. You should receive a summary of the plan from your employer and be given an opportunity to designate your elective deferrals for the year (typically within a month or so before the start of a new year or upon becoming eligible to participate in your company's plan).

ELECTIVE DEFERRAL LIMITS

The law fixes the *maximum* elective deferral limits for each year. If you have the designated Roth account option, you can split elective deferrals between pre-tax and after-tax contributions; the total cannot exceed annual limits. Your plan may place other restrictions or limits on how much you can contribute annually to the plan.

The law allows you to contribute up to 100% of your earnings to the plan, up to a dollar limit on contributions. The elective deferral contribution limit for a 401(k) plan in 2025 is $23,500. Those who are at least 50 years old by the end of 2025 can make an additional catch-up contribution:

- The basic catch-up contribution limit is $7,500.
- Those who are age 60, 61, 62, or 63 in 2025 can make a catch-up contribution of $11,250.

Example

In 2025, you are 28 years old and earn $60,000 from your employer offering a 401(k) plan. Your maximum contribution, assuming you can afford to make it, is $23,500 (although your plan may restrict contributions to a percentage of your compensation). If the plan has a designated Roth account option, you can split the $23,500 contribution amount between the regular and Roth parts; you can even put the entire amount into the designated Roth account. You are a self-employed person, age 52, who wants to optimize retirement plan contributions. For 2025, assuming you have sufficient net income from self-employment, you can contribute up to $77,500 (elective contribution [$23,500 + $7,500] and employer contribution [$46,500]).

Looking Ahead

Starting in 2026, catch-up contributions for those with wages for FICA purposes of $145,000 or more in 2025 can only be made to designated Roth accounts.

Planning Tips

If you are pressed for funds and find it difficult to take full advantage of the elective deferral opportunity, at least contribute what is necessary to obtain your employer's matching contribution if available. Your employer's matching contribution is, in effect, "free money" to you, and it would be unwise to ignore it.

Example

In 2025, you are permitted under the plan to contribute $23,500 through elective deferrals. Your employer will match 50% of your contributions up to 6% of your compensation. If you earn $40,000, you must contribute at least $4,800 to obtain your employer's top contribution on your behalf of $2,400.

If your employer has an automatic enrollment plan, a set percentage of your pay is put into the plan for the year. But you must be given the option before the start of the plan year to reduce the automatic contribution or opt out entirely.

If you are self-employed and have no employees, you can set up a solo 401(k) to maximize your retirement plan contributions. You effectively make both employee and employer contributions (even though you are self-employed). This means you can contribute a total of up to $70,000 with a combination of the so-called elective deferral amount plus a so-called employer contribution. Employer matching contributions can be directed toward a designated Roth account. But, like your own contributions to the designated Roth account, employer matching contributions to the designated Roth account are currently taxable.

As explained earlier, 401(k) plans can offer a designated Roth account option. If your plan allows it, you can choose to make after-tax contributions to a designated Roth account so that withdrawals can become tax free (like withdrawals from Roth IRAs). Contributions to a traditional and/or designated Roth cannot exceed the annual limit. For example, you are under age 50 and choose to split your contribution between a regular 401(k) and a designated Roth account—say, $13,500 to a regular 401(k) and $10,000 to a designated Roth account; total contributions cannot exceed annual limits.

Keep in mind that taxes are only the tail that wags the investment dog. If you have a 401(k), be sure to monitor investment performance as well as fees for investment choices to optimize your retirement savings.

Pitfalls

Once you have made your elective deferral contributions, access to your money is limited by the terms of the plan and the tax law. Generally, you can't receive the funds until you retire from the company. You may be permitted to withdraw funds. There is a 10% penalty for distributions before age 59½ unless a penalty exception applies. Some of the exceptions are the same as those for IRAs, but some IRA exceptions do not apply for 401(k)s and some exceptions only apply to 401(k)s. Exceptions that apply to 401(k)s include:

- Death
- Disability
- Series of substantially equal periodic payments
- Payments under a qualified domestic relations order (QDRO)
- Payment of unreimbursed medical expenses exceeding your applicable AGI threshold
- Separation from service during or after the year you become age 55 (age 50 for public safety employees)

- Certain distributions to qualified military reservists called to active duty
- Birth or adoption expenses up to $5,000 IRS levy
- Distribution up to $22,000 for expenses related to a federally declared disaster within 180 days of the event
- Terminal illness (death is expected to result in 84 months as certified by a physician)
- Victim of domestic abuse. The penalty-free distribution is limited to the lesser of $10,300 or 50% of the account balance.
- Distributions up to $1,000 for personal or family emergency expenses due to unforeseen circumstances or immediate financial need.

Looking Ahead

Beginning in 2026, the 10% early distribution penalty does not apply to withdrawals from qualified retirement plans used to pay long-term care insurance premiums up to $2,500 per year.

You may be able to borrow from the plan or take a "hardship distribution." Plan loans are discussed in Chapter 11; hardship distributions are discussed later in this chapter.

Even though you are not taxed on your elective deferral amount (it is subtracted from your taxable compensation), such amount is still subject to Social Security and Medicare (FICA) taxes, which are withheld from your pay.

Where to Claim the Benefit

You do not have to report anything on your tax return. You will note that your elective deferral amount is subtracted from your pay so that only the reduced amount is reported as taxable compensation to you on Form W-2, which you then report as wages on Form 1040 or 1040-SR.

403(b) Plans

Retirement plans offered by public schools, colleges, and universities; churches; and certain tax-exempt organizations are designated as 403(b) plans. They're also called tax-sheltered annuities or TSA plans. The rules for employee elective deferrals, including those to designated Roth accounts, as well as for employer contributions follow the same rules as those for 401(k) plans. There are some minor differences, such as treating a self-employed minister as employed by a tax-exempt organization so that the minister can have a 403(b) plan. Refer to the previous discussion of Regular 401(k) plans for details.

457(b) Plans

Retirement plans offered by certain state and local governments and non-governmental tax-exempt entities are called 457 deferred compensation plans. The rules for employee elective deferrals to 457(b) plans, including those to designated Roth accounts, as well as for employer contributions follow the same rules as those for 401(k) plans. There are some minor differences. Refer to the previous discussion of Regular 401(k) plans for details.

Self-Employed Retirement Plans

If you are self-employed, you have to take care of your retirement savings; there is no employer to help with this. Just like retirement plan options for companies, self-employed individuals have options too. On the tax return, you see them listed as *self-employed SEP, SIMPLE, and qualified plans.*

Benefit

If you are a sole proprietor or independent contractor and have a profitable year, you can contribute to a qualified retirement plan. There are 2 main types of plans:

1. *Defined contribution plan.* The funds you have on retirement are based solely on what you've contributed and how well your investments have performed. A profit-sharing plan is a defined contribution plan.

2. *Defined benefit plan.* At retirement, you receive a pension based on your earnings (each year before retirement your contribution is determined by an actuary to be sufficient to pay this pension at a specific age, assuming a certain return on your investments).

You claim a deduction for your contribution. For a defined contribution plan in 2025, you can deduct 25% of compensation or $70,000, whichever is less. For self-employed individuals, net earnings from self-employment (the figure on which contributions are based) must be reduced by the contribution itself, so that the effective contribution rate is only 20% (not 25%). Also, you must reduce your net earnings from self-employment by the employer equivalent portion of your self-employment taxes. It may sound complicated to figure your allowable deduction, but you can use Worksheet 5.2, adapted from IRS Publication 560, to guide you (if you use tax preparation software, this is done automatically for you).

For a defined benefit plan, your deduction is based on what is actuarially required to fund the promised pension. You need the actuary to tell you what your contribution is, based on plan assumptions (e.g., at what age you expect to retire).

WORKSHEET 5.2 Figuring Your 2025 Contribution to a Defined Contribution Plan

1. Enter your net earnings from self-employment.	1. _____
2. Enter your deduction for self-employment tax (employer equivalent portion of the tax).	2. _____
3. Subtract line 2 from line 1.	3. _____
4. Enter your effective contribution rate (no more than 20%).	4. _____
5. Multiply line 3 by line 4.	5. _____
6. Multiply $350,000 by your actual contribution rate (no more than 25%).	6. _____
7. Enter the smaller of line 5 or line 6.	7. _____
8. Contribution dollar limit.	8. $70,000
9. Enter the smaller of line 7 or line 8. *This is your contribution.*	9. _____

Conditions

There are many conditions for starting and maintaining a qualified retirement plan. Some are highly complex and well beyond the scope of this book. But here are some things to watch out for:

- The plan must be set up by the extended due date of your return.

Example

In 2025, you are self-employed and profitable. You want to contribute to a profit-sharing plan for the year. You have until April 15, 2026 (or later if you obtain a filing extension) to set up and contribute to the plan.

- You must cover employees if they meet certain requirements. This raises the cost of having a plan. But you deduct contributions on behalf of your employees from your business income, reducing your net earnings from self-employment.
- You *may* have to file an annual information return with the U.S. Department of Labor. The filing obligation is explained under Pitfalls.

Example

In 2025, you have net earnings from self-employment (your profits on Schedule C) of $80,000 and your plan sets a contribution limit of 25%. Assume you did not defer any part of self-employment tax for 2025. Your contribution for 2025 on your behalf is $14,870, figured as follows:

1. Enter your net earnings from self-employment.	1. $80,000
2. Enter your deduction for self-employment tax (employer equivalent portion of the tax).	2. 5,652
3. Subtract line 2 from line 1.	3. 74,348
4. Enter your effective contribution rate (no more than 20%).	4. 20%
5. Multiply line 3 by line 4.	5. $14,870
6. Multiply $350,000 by your actual contribution rate (no more 20%, which is the plan contribution limit of 25%).	6. 70,000
7. Enter the smaller of line 5 or line 6.	7. 14,870
8. Contribution dollar limit.	8. $70,000
9. Enter the smaller of line 7 or line 8. *This is your contribution.*	9. $14,870

Planning Tips

You may want to consult with a benefits expert to help you decide which type of retirement plan is best for you, based on your profitability, age, the nature of your business, and other factors, including your desire to optimize contributions.

If you choose to use a solo 401(k), you are not forced to put catch-up contributions into a designated Roth account. This is so regardless of your income.

Pitfalls

Be aware that deductible contributions to your account claimed as an adjustment to gross income on your personal return are a reduction to qualified business income (QBI). The deduction reduces your QBI deduction (see Chapter 14).

Having a qualified retirement plan means you are subject to annual reporting requirements referred to earlier; the government wants to know some details about your plan. A simplified annual return is used for plans covering fewer than 25 participants. If you (or you and your spouse) are the only participants, you must file Form 5500-EZ, *Annual Return of One Participant (Owners and Their Spouses)*. But you are exempt from filing if plan assets at the end of the year do not exceed $250,000. You are not exempt and a return must be filed for the final year of a plan, even if assets are below the $250,000 limit.

If you are required to file, you cannot download the form from the Internet like most other tax forms because Form 5500-EZ is a scannable form that must be obtained by mail or at an IRS office. Usually it is sent to you automatically if you have filed one in the past; otherwise, you can request one from the IRS by calling 800-829-FORM. Form 5500-EZ can be filed electronically.

The form usually must be filed under the ERISA Filing Acceptance System (EFAST2) (www.efast.dol.gov). The form is due by the last day of the seventh month following the close of the plan year (e.g., July 31, 2026, for the 2025 year of a calendar-year plan). You can obtain an automatic extension to October 15, 2026 (the same extended due date for federal income tax returns on extension) by filing Form 5558, *Application for Extension of Time To File Certain Employee Plan Returns*. If you obtain an extension of time to file your 2025 income tax return, then you don't have to file Form 5558; you get an automatic extension for your Form 5500-EZ to October 15, 2026, as long as you and your plan have the same taxable year (retain a copy of Form 4868 used to obtain the income tax filing extension with your records for your qualified retirement plan).

If you are delinquent in filing Form 5500-EZ, you may obtain relief from penalties that would otherwise apply. Follow the steps in Revenue Procedure 2015–32.

Where to Claim the Benefit

You deduct contributions to the plan for your employees on Schedule C (such contributions are a business expense). You deduct your own contributions on Schedule 1 of Form 1040 or 1040-SR.

SEPs

A simplified employee pension (SEP) is a type of IRA that any business, whether self-employed or incorporated, can use for retirement savings. It is "simplified" because it is easy to set up and there are few administrative requirements (for example, there is no annual reporting to the government as is the case with most other company-sponsored retirement plans). The business sets up the plan and makes tax-deductible contributions to participant accounts.

Benefit

If you are self-employed (sole proprietor, independent contractor, partner, or limited liability company member) and have a profitable year, you can make deductible contributions to a simplified employee pension plan, or SEP. This is a type of IRA to which you can contribute more to than a traditional IRA. The same rules that apply to sole proprietors also apply to partners and LLC members.

You claim a deduction for the contribution on your behalf as an adjustment to gross income (not as a business expense). For 2025, the top deduction is 25% of your compensation or $70,000, whichever is less. Compensation if you are self-employed means your net earnings from self-employment, reduced by the employer equivalent portion of self-employment tax (one-half of the tax) and by the contribution for yourself; your effective percentage rate becomes 20% in this case.

Example

In 2025, you are a consultant (sole proprietor) and have net earnings from self-employment of $50,000 (after reduction for one-half of self-employment tax). Your maximum deductible contribution is $10,000 ($50,000 × 20%).

Unlike qualified retirement plans, there is no annual reporting requirement for SEPs.

Conditions

You must meet 2 conditions to deduct your SEP contributions:

1. You must have profits if you are self-employed or receive a salary if you are an S corporation.
2. You must include your employees within the plan if they (1) are at least age 21, (2) earn more than $750 in 2025, and (3) have worked for you at least 3 of the past 5 years. If they are included in the plan, you must make contributions on their behalf based on their compensation.

Planning Tips

You can set up and contribute to a SEP up to the extended due date of your return.

Example

You are an independent contractor in 2025. You can set up and make your contributions to a SEP through April 15, 2026, or if you obtain an automatic 6-month filing extension for your 2025 return, to October 15, 2026.

You can convert a SEP to a Roth IRA if you meet the eligibility requirements discussed earlier in this chapter. Conversion allows all future earnings on the money to become tax free when you take withdrawals from the Roth IRA (but you must now pay a tax on the converted amount).

Pitfalls

You cannot contribute to a SEP if you also have a self-employed qualified retirement plan; you must choose which plan is more favorable to you. Excess contributions are subject to the same penalties discussed earlier under IRAs. You must take required minimum distributions (RMDs) from your SEP, even if you are still working and contributing to it. You cannot postpone RMDs until retirement.

Where to Claim the Benefit

You deduct contributions to the plan for your employees on Schedule C (such contributions are a business expense). You deduct your own contributions on Schedule 1 of Form 1040 or 1040-SR. No special form or schedule is required to figure your deduction.

SIMPLEs

Savings Incentive Match Plan for Employees, or SIMPLE, is a type of retirement plan that allows businesses to share the cost of funding retirement savings. The company sets up the plan and employees are given the option of contributing, within set limits, a portion of their salaries to the plan. The company must make certain contributions according to a formula fixed by the tax law. The reason this type of retirement plan is SIMPLE lies in the ease of setting it up and administering it.

Benefit 🔼

If you are self-employed or a shareholder in a corporation, the business can set up a SIMPLE plan that allows you (and your employees) to make elective deferrals (salary reduction contributions) to the plan. Such amounts are excluded from your income. As an employer, you must contribute a set amount for each plan participant; you deduct your employer contribution as a business expense.

Whether you are the owner of the business or merely a rank-and-file employee, you can make elective deferral contributions to the plan. Like 401(k) plans discussed earlier, the portion of your compensation that you treat as your elective deferral is not included in your income for the year. (Limits on elective deferrals and required employer contributions are explained next under "Conditions.")

Earnings on contributions build up on a tax-deferred basis.

A SIMPLE can be set up as either a SIMPLE-IRA or a SIMPLE-401(k) plan. For purposes of the following discussion, only the SIMPLE-IRA, the more popular type, is examined.

Conditions

There are only 2 key conditions for setting up a SIMPLE plan:

1. You must be a "small employer." You must have had 100 or fewer employees who received $5,000 or more in compensation from you in the preceding year. If you set up the plan but in a later year exceed the 100-employee limit, you have 2 more years to continue the SIMPLE plan; after 2 years, you no longer qualify for a SIMPLE plan because you are no longer a small employer. You can also set up a plan if you are self-employed (even though you don't have any employees).

2. You do not maintain any other qualified plan. If, for example, you already have a profit-sharing plan, you can't also have a SIMPLE plan.

ELECTIVE DEFERRAL LIMIT

Whether you are the owner of the business or just an ordinary employee who is eligible to participate, you can agree to contribute a portion of your annual compensation to the SIMPLE plan. Your contribution, or elective deferral amount, is limited in 2025 to $16,500 if you are under age 50 or older by the end of 2025. Your contribution cannot exceed 100% of your compensation.

> ### Example
>
> In 2025, you are under age 50; you can contribute $16,500 whether your wages are $16,500, $40,000, or even $100,000. You can contribute up to 100% of your compensation, but no more than $16,500.

The deferral limit may be increased in 2025 to $18,150 (110% of the $16,500 limit) if the employer has 25 or fewer employees who earned $5,000 in compensation, or has more than 25 employees. This higher limit also applies for employers with more than 25 but not more than 100 employees if the employers make a 4% matching contribution or a 3% nonelective contribution.

Catch-up contributions. If you are at least 50 years old by the end of 2025, there are 3 different catch-up contributions that you may be eligible to make:

- *Basic catch-up contributions:* $3,500. This can be used by any employee eligible to make an elective deferral.
- *Higher catch-up if the increased deferral limit applies:* $3,850. This depends on the number of employees in the business and other factors.
- *Still higher catch-up for those age 60, 61, 62, and 63:* $5,250. This applies regardless of the number of employees in the business.

> ### Example
>
> You participate in your employer's SIMPLE IRA. There are 20 employees in the company and you age 62 years old. Your elective deferral for 2025 can be up to $23,750 ($18,500 increased elective deferral plus $5,250 special catch-up for age).

You may opt to have your elective deferrals treated as Roth contributions. This means the amount allocated to a designated Roth account that is part of the SIMPLE IRA is made with after-tax dollars (you're taxed on the salary allocated to this). But funds in the Roth account build up tax free; you won't be taxed on the contributions and earnings withdrawn after age 59 ½ or under certain other circumstances.

REQUIRED EMPLOYER CONTRIBUTION

Like other retirement plans, the plan must meet certain nondiscrimination requirements; it cannot favor you as the owner and other highly paid employees. SIMPLE plans don't have any complicated nondiscrimination formulas. Instead, if you are the owner and make the required employer contribution on behalf of each employee who is eligible to participate, your plan is viewed as nondiscriminatory.

You must adopt one of these 2 contribution formulas and make contributions accordingly:

1. Employer matching contribution on a dollar-for-dollar basis
2. Nonelective contributions of 2% of compensation

In an employer matching contribution arrangement, you match employee contributions on a dollar-for-dollar basis up to 3% of employee compensation. If an employee does not make an elective deferral, you do not have to contribute anything on behalf of the employee.

> ### Example
>
> Your employee makes an elective deferral contribution to the SIMPLE of $5,000. Her annual compensation is $40,000. You must contribute $1,200 on behalf of this employee (matching her contribution of $5,000 up to 3% of $40,000).

> **Example**
>
> You make an elective deferral of $16,500, the maximum generally permitted in 2025. Your compensation is $550,000. The matching contribution in this case is $16,500 (matching your contribution of $16,500, which is less than 3% of $550,000 [$16,500]).

If the formula requires nonelective contributions of 2% of compensation, these contributions must be made without regard to any employee elective deferrals. Even if the employee makes no elective deferral, the employer must still contribute 2% on the employee's behalf if the employee is eligible to participate in the SIMPLE plan. No more than $350,000 of compensation can be taken into account in figuring nonelective contributions.

> **Example**
>
> Your employee makes an elective deferral contribution to the SIMPLE of $5,000. Her annual compensation is $40,000. You must contribute $800 (2% of $40,000).

> **Example**
>
> You make an elective deferral of $16,500, the maximum generally permitted in 2025. Your compensation is $375,000. Your nonelective contribution in this case is $7,000 (2% of $350,000).

Employers can choose to make additional contributions to each employee of the plan in a uniform manner. The contribution in 2025 may not exceed the lesser of up to 10% of compensation or $5,100. Check with your employer or plan administrator for details.

Planning Tips

SIMPLEs may be the most cost-effective plan to use if you have employees. Discuss your retirement plan options with a benefits expert.

If you have made contributions to a SIMPLE-IRA, you can convert it to a Roth IRA (see earlier in this chapter). But you must wait at least 2 years following the contribution to make the conversion or be subject to a 25% early distribution penalty if you are under age 59 ½.

Pitfall

Distributions from SIMPLE-IRAs before age 59 ½ are subject to a higher early distribution penalty than the penalty imposed on traditional IRAs. Instead of the usual 10% early distribution penalty, you may be subject to a penalty of 25% for distributions within 2 years of SIMPLE-IRA participation if you are under age 59 ½.

Where to Claim the Deduction

You deduct contributions to the plan for your employees on Schedule C of Form 1040 or 1040-SR (such contributions are a business expense). You deduct your own contributions on Schedule 1 of Form 1040 or 1040-SR. You do not have to complete any form or schedule to claim the deduction.

Retirement Saver's Credit

A worker's wages just don't seem to stretch far enough to pay the bills *and* save for retirement. The tax law tries to encourage those having the most difficulty—lower-income taxpayers—to make retirement plan contributions by offering a special tax credit. Those qualifying for this credit also enjoy other tax benefits from making the contributions, such as a deduction for IRA contributions. This is one of the few instances in the tax law where you get to "double dip" with a tax deduction or exclusion, plus a tax credit, for the same action (your retirement plan contribution). At the end of the road, taxpayers taking advantage of these breaks have not only enjoyed current tax savings but have also built up their personal retirement savings.

Benefit

If you contribute to a retirement plan through your company or to an IRA, you may be eligible to claim a tax credit of up to 50% of contributions up to $2,000, for a top credit of $1,000. This credit is in addition to any other benefit to which you may be entitled, such as salary reduction for a 401(k) plan contribution or a deduction for an IRA contribution.

Looking Ahead

Starting in 2027, the retirement saver's credit will be replaced by a government matching program. The match will be 50% of IRA or retirement plan contributions up to $2,000 per individual. The match will phase out between $41,000 and $71,000 in the case of taxpayers filing a joint return ($20,500 to $35,500 for single taxpayers and married filing separate; $30,750 to $53,250 for head of household filers).

Conditions

There are 3 conditions for claiming the retirement saver's credit. In order to claim the credit you must:

1. Have qualified retirement savings contributions or ABLE account contributions for the year
2. Be an eligible individual
3. Have adjusted gross income below a set amount

QUALIFIED RETIREMENT SAVINGS CONTRIBUTIONS

Retirement savings can come from several sources; you total your contributions to all of the following:

- IRA contributions (whether they are deductible or nondeductible)
- Roth IRA contributions
- Elective deferrals (salary reduction contributions) to 401(k) plans, Starter 401(k)s, 403(b) annuities, or 457 plans
- Voluntary contributions to any qualified retirement plan of your employer
- ABLE account contributions

You must reduce your qualified contributions and elective deferrals by distributions included in your income that you receive from any qualified retirement plan of your employer or from a deferred compensation plan of your employer (if your employer is a state or local government or tax-exempt organization). You must also reduce your qualified contributions and elective deferrals by distributions from Roth IRAs during the 5 years following your contributions to such accounts or from a rollover to a Roth IRA. You must include not only distributions in the current year, but also those made in the 2 preceding years and in the period after the year for which you are figuring the credit up to the due date of the return (including extensions).

Example

You want to claim the retirement saver's credit for 2025. In determining your eligible contributions and elective deferrals for 2025, you must look to distributions taken in 2023 and 2024, plus any distributions you take in 2025 and up to April 15, 2026 (assuming you file your return by this deadline).

You don't have to reduce your qualified contributions and elective deferrals by the following distributions:

- Amounts treated as loans from a qualified plan
- Excess contributions
- Deductions for dividends paid on certain employer securities
- Contributions returned to you before the due date of your return
- IRA accounts converted to a Roth IRA

ELIGIBLE INDIVIDUAL

To be eligible to claim the credit you must:

- Be at least 18 years old by the close of the year. Even though someone who is 14 can contribute to an IRA, he or she isn't old enough to claim this credit.
- Not be claimed as a dependent of another taxpayer.
- Not be a full-time student (someone who is enrolled full time for at least 5 calendar months during the year).

MAGI LIMIT

To claim the top credit, your modified adjusted gross income (MAGI) must be below a set amount. If your MAGI is more modest, you may be entitled to a smaller credit. No credit can be claimed if your MAGI in 2025 exceeds a set limit, detailed in Table 5.3. MAGI for this purpose is your adjusted gross income increased by the foreign earned income exclusion, the foreign housing exclusion, or the exclusion for income from U.S. possessions or Puerto Rico.

TABLE 5.3 MAGI Limits in 2025 for Retirement Saver's Credit

Modified Adjusted Gross Income						
Joint Return		Head of Household		All Others		Applicable
Over	Not Over	Over	Not Over	Over	Not Over	Percentage
$ 0	$47,500	$ 0	$35,625	$ 0	$23,750	50%
47,500	51,000	35,625	38,250	23,750	25,500	20
51,000	79,000	38,250	59,250	25,500	39,500	10
79,000		59,250		39,500		0

In 2025, you are single with MAGI of $38,000. Your elective deferral to your company's 401(k) plan for the year is $3,000. You may claim a tax credit of $200 (10% of $2,000, the maximum contribution taken into account in figuring the credit).

Planning Tip

The credit can be claimed in addition to other benefits that contributions entitle you to. For example, even though you excluded your 401(k) plan contributions from income, you can still claim the credit with respect to those same contributions. Similarly, even though you deducted your IRA contributions, you can also base the credit on the same contributions.

Pitfalls

You may meet all conditions for claiming the credit, but lose out on the opportunity to use it if you claim certain other credits that offset your tax liability. The retirement saver's credit cannot exceed your regular tax liability, plus your alternative minimum tax liability, reduced by the sum of all credits to which you may also be entitled other than the child tax credit, the adoption credit, and the foreign tax credit. You cannot receive a refund from the retirement saver's credit, and you cannot carry forward the unused amount to a future year.

Lower-income individuals who qualify for the 50% credit may not have sufficient tax liability to use the entire credit (even assuming they can afford to make retirement plan contributions).

A married couple has MAGI of $39,000, so they are entitled to a maximum credit of $1,000 ($2,000 x 50%). Since their tax liability is only $900 (10% of [$39,000 MAGI − $30,000 standard deduction]), and their credit is limited to $900.

Where to Claim the Credit

You figure the credit on Form 8880, *Credit for Qualified Retirement Savings Contributions*, which you attach to the return. You enter the amount of your credit on Schedule 3 of Form 1040 or 1040-SR.

Custodial/Trustee Fees

Having an IRA isn't necessarily free—there may be charges for maintaining an account with a brokerage firm or mutual fund that acts as the IRA's custodian or trustee. Some firms charge only for trades that you make in the account, while others charge a flat management fee based on the value of assets in the account (e.g., 1% or more; lower for "robo advisers" providing computerized plans but no investment advice). These fees are not deductible. This is so even if the fees are separately billed and you pay them with funds outside of your IRA.

Employer-Paid Retirement Planning Advice

Retirement planning is a difficult and confusing subject. Employees nearing the end of their careers often must make important decisions regarding their company retirement plans and their personal retirement savings in order to maximize their retirement income and minimize their taxes. Companies may step in to assist these employees by bringing in outside professional assistance to provide retirement planning advice. Employees taking advantage of this expertise may enjoy the fringe benefit tax free.

Benefit

You are not taxed on the value of retirement planning advice you (and your spouse) receive through your employer. You can exclude this benefit from your income. There is no dollar limit on what you can exclude.

Conditions

This fringe benefit must be provided to you by your employer on a nondiscriminatory basis (i.e., the benefit cannot be limited to owners and highly paid employees). Whether the benefit is discriminatory is something determined by your employer, not by you.

The tax-free benefit is limited to employer-paid retirement education services that you can use to make more informed investment decisions for your retirement plan contributions as well as decisions regarding distributions upon termination of employment. You may not exclude the value of related services, such as tax-preparation, accounting, legal, or brokerage services.

Planning Tip

Many companies are now offering free online investment information related to their retirement plans; take advantage of any advice offered.

Pitfall

There is no downside to taking full advantage of any advice and information your employer offers you. If you believe the advice you have received is not suitable or helpful, then talk to your own retirement-planning adviser.

Where to Claim the Benefit

Since the benefit is not included in your income, you do not have to report it on your return or complete any form or schedule to claim it.

Charitable Transfers of IRA Distributions

There is a special tax break that allows those age 70 ½ and older to make tax-free transfers from their IRAs to a public charity. Technically, the transfer is called a qualified charitable distribution (QCD). It is a way to benefit your favorite charities while obtaining a tax break (the exclusion from income for the transfer).

Benefit ⊗

You may exclude up to $108,000 in 2025 for a direct transfer from your IRA to a public charity. You can make such transfers year after year if you desire. The contribution can count toward your required minimum distribution (RMD) for the year.

Example

Your RMD for 2025 is $8,990. You instruct your IRA custodian to transfer $7,500 to the American Red Cross. Of the $8,990 RMD, $7,500 is tax free; the balance is taxable as ordinary income.

Conditions

There are 5 conditions for a QCD:

1. You must be at least age 70 ½. This age applies even though your starting age for RMDs is older.
2. You must be the owner of the IRA (i.e., not a beneficiary who inherited the IRA).
3. The distribution must be from a qualified account. This is a traditional IRA, or a SEP or SIMPLE-IRA that is not ongoing (i.e., no current contributions are being made). It does not include accounts in other types of qualified retirement plans, such as 401(k)s.

4. The funds must be transferred directly to a qualified charity by December 31. This is a public charity. Donor-advised funds and supporting organizations are not eligible recipients for a QCD.

5. You must obtain a written acknowledgment from the qualified charity for any QCD of $250 or more.

One-time special QCD. You can make a one-time $54,000 distribution from an IRA to charity through charitable gift annuities, charitable remainder unitrusts, and charitable remainder annuity trusts. To the extent this one-time option is used, it reduces the annual QCD limit.

Example

You transfer $54,000 to the charitable gift annuity at the American Red Cross. Your limit for other QCDs in 2025 is $54,000 ($108,000 – $54,000).

Planning Tips

If you made nondeductible contributions to your IRA, a special rule treats amounts distributed to charities as coming first from taxable funds, instead of proportionately from taxable and nontaxable funds, as would be the case with regular IRA distributions.

If you want to make a QCD, contact your IRA custodian or trustee to determine what steps you must take. Some financial institutions require an IRA owner to submit written instructions for a QCD; others will make a transfer based on oral instructions. Be sure that the transfer identifies you to the charity (or you should notify the charity about the transfer so it knows it came from you and where to send acknowledgments).

Pitfalls

You must obtain a written acknowledgment from the organization receiving your QCD, even though no charitable contribution deduction is allowed. You cannot exclude the QCD without a written acknowledgment for any amount of $250 or more.

A QCD can only be made from an IRA or a Roth IRA (although there is no tax reason to transfer funds from a Roth IRA). You cannot make a QCD from IRA-like retirement plans, such as a SIMPLE-IRA or a SEP-IRA, that you're still funding.

You cannot take a charitable contribution deduction for a QCD. The tax benefit is the exclusion from income for the IRA transfer.

> **Example**
>
> On December 23, 2025, an individual, age 75, directs the trustee of his IRA to make a distribution of $25,000 directly to a qualified charitable organization. The total value of the IRA is $30,000 and consists of $20,000 of deductible contributions and earnings and $10,000 of nondeductible contributions (basis). The QCD is $20,000 (deductible contributions and earnings).

If you make deductible IRA contributions after age 70 ½, they reduce the QCD.

> **Example**
>
> An individual, who was over age 70½ in 2024, made a deductible IRA contribution of $7,500. In 2025, the individual makes a QCD of $25,000. The maximum amount excludable is $17,500 ($25,000 – $7,500).

Where to Claim the Exclusion

You will receive Form 1099-R reporting your distribution the taxation. Code y indicates that the distribuiton is a QCD. The full amount of the QCD is shown on line 4a of Form 1040 or 1040-SR. Check the box on line 4c2 of Form 1040 or 1040-SR to indicate the QCD.

Qualified Longevity Annuity Contracts

A qualified longevity annuity contract (QLAC) is an annuity contract purchased from an insurance company with funds from a qualified retirement plan or IRA (other than a Roth IRA). The QLAC is a special limited option for postponing required minimum distributions and ensuring retirement income for life.

Benefit

The value of the QLAC is excluded from the account balance used to determine required minimum distributions.

Conditions for a QLAC

There are 3 conditions for continued deferral on funds within the QLAC:

1. A maximum investment.
2. A limit on the deferral period.
3. A bar to any commutation benefit, cash surrender value, or other feature as well as a bar to any benefits payable after death.

MAXIMUM INVESTMENT

There is a dollar limit on how much can be invested in a QLAC. The QLAC limit for 2025 is $210,000. This is a lifetime limit. If you bought a QLAC when the cap was lower (e.g., $125,000 in 2014–2017; $130,000 for 2018–2019; $135,000 for 2020 and 2021; $145,000 in 2022; $200,000 in 2023 and 2024), you can add to your existing policy (up to the new limit) or obtain a separate QLAC from another insurer for the additional amount.

DEFERRAL PERIOD

When going into a QLAC, you can specify the beginning annuity date (e.g., age 75). But the contract must provide that distributions begin no later than the first day of the first month after your 85th birthday.

BAR TO OTHER DISTRIBUTIONS

The only benefits payable to you from the QLAC are annuity payments commencing at the annuity starting date. So, once you commit to a QLAC, that's it.

If you die on or after the annuity starting date and have a surviving spouse, a life annuity can be paid to the surviving spouse where the annuity payment is not in excess of 100% of the annuity payment that is payable to you. If you die before the annuity starting date, the annuity for the surviving spouse is permitted to exceed 100% of the annuity payment that would have been payable to you to the extent necessary to satisfy the requirement to provide a qualified preretirement survivor annuity. The annuity to the surviving spouse must commence no later than it would for you. Other rules apply for non-spouse beneficiaries.

Instead of a life annuity payable to a beneficiary, a QLAC can permit the return of premiums after your death. The refund of premiums to the beneficiary is limited to what you paid minus any annuity payments you already received.

Planning Tips

A QLAC isn't for everyone, so think whether one makes sense for your situation. Factor in your health (and your family's health history) to project your longevity. Also consider your concerns about outliving your income and having insufficient Social Security benefits to sustain you past age 85.

You can add a cost-of-living adjustment to your QLAC so eventual annuity payments will keep pace with inflation.

Pitfalls

Once you buy it, your funds are locked in until the annuity commences. If you need the money for any reason, you're out of luck.

While the QLAC protects you from stock market downturns, you can't benefit from any upswings; your future payouts are locked in up front.

As with any annuity or similar investment product, there are investment fees involved that reduce your investment return.

Where to Report the QLAC

Information about QLACs—your annuity starting state, total premiums, and the fair market value of the QLAC at the end of the year—are reported to you on Form 1098-Q, *Qualified Longevity Annuity Contract Information*. But information about distributions from QLACs is reported on Form 1099-R. The taxable amount of QLAC payments are reported on line 4d of Form 1040 or 1040-SR.

Loans from Qualified Retirement Plans

If, for any reason, you need immediate cash, you may be able to borrow it from a qualified retirement plan in which you participate. You don't have to give a reason; you simply must meet certain conditions. As with any type of loan, the proceeds are tax free.

Certain limitations apply for these loans. See Chapter 11.

PLESAs

Pension-linked employee savings accounts, or PLESAs, are like sidecars to qualified retirement plans. They can only exist if your employer has a defined contribution plan, such as a 401(k), and chooses to allow it.

Benefit ⊗

If your employer has a qualified retirement plan that includes a PLESA, you may make after-tax contributions to a designated Roth account from which you can take tax-free withdrawals when you want. This can be at least once per calendar month. The withdrawals are tax free under the designated Roth account rules discussed earlier in this chapter, even if you are under age 59½.

Conditions

The maximum you can contribute is funding to an account balance up to $2,500, or less if your employer sets a lower amount. You can contribute to the PLESA even if you don't participate in the basic retirement plan. But you cannot have a PLESA if you are highly compensated in 2025, meaning you earned $155,000 or more in 2024 or, regardless of compensation, owned 5% or more of the business at any time in 2024 or 2025.

Once you have the PLESA, you can take distributions from the account as often as you like without incurring any penalties. You do not have to demonstrate or certify any need for the funds; they're yours at your discretion.

Looking Ahead

The $2,500 cap on contributions, as well as amount of earnings that determine a highly compensated employee, may be adjusted for inflation for 2026. See the Supplement for 2026 limits.

Planning Tips

Your employer may have automatic enrollment in the PLESA, with a set contribution from you. This can be no more than 3% of compensation. However, you are allowed to opt out and withdraw any money in the account with no fee, or change the automatic contribution amount.

If your employer makes matching contributions to the plan of which the PLESA is part, then matching contributions must be made with respect to your PLESA contributions at the same rate.

Pitfalls

Once the funds are withdrawn, they cannot be redeposited. Over time, this reduces your retirement savings.

If you've made contributions as a non-highly compensated employee but become highly compensated, you can use the PLESA in the same manner, but no additional contributions can be made.

Your employer may impose fees on withdrawals if they exceed 4 withdrawals within a year.

Where to Report Contributions and Distributions

Contributions to the PLESA are reported on Form W-2; they are part of your taxable compensation. Withdrawals from your PLESA are reported on Form 1099-R. Look for Code B in Box 7 (designated Roth account distribution).

Hardship Distributions from Retirement Plans

Hardship distributions are distributions that a qualified retirement plan can make to you under special circumstances without losing its qualified status. It was reported that in 2024, nearly 5% of participants in 401(k) plans took a hardship distribution. Generally, the distributions are treated as any other distributions (e.g., taxable and, if under age 59 ½, subject to a 10% penalty unless some other penalty exception applies). Hardship withdrawals cannot be put back into the plan.

Your employer may also offer the option of withdrawing up to $1,000 per year for personal or family emergency expenses. You self-certify the need; the employer doesn't check up on this. The withdrawal is not subject to the 10% early distribution penalty even if you are under age 59 ½, but, like a hardship distribution, it's included in gross income and subject to tax. You may recontribute the withdrawal within 3 years. If you do, you may need to file an amended return to back out the income and recoup any taxes that were paid on the initial withdrawal.

An employer may include emergency savings accounts—PLESAs—linked to the company's retirement plan. This was discussed earlier in this chapter.

Special Rules for Federal Disasters

If you live in a federally declared disaster area and have an economic loss (e.g., damage to your home; temporary or permanent layoff), a qualified retirement plan or IRA may permit a disaster distribution up to $22,000. The distributions are not subject to the 10% additional tax and are taken into account as gross income over 3 years unless you opt to report all the income in the year of the disaster. Additionally, amounts distributed prior to the disaster to purchase a home can be recontributed, and an employer is permitted to provide for a larger amount to be borrowed from a plan (up to $100,000) by affected individuals and for additional time for repayment of plan loans owed by affected individuals.

If you received a qualified disaster distribution, you have 3 years from the date it was received to repay all or part of it to the same or other retirement plan. Doing this cancels any tax paid on the original distribution to the extent of the recontribution. You must file amended returns to recoup the taxes paid.

Again, the same treatment applies for a recontribution of a qualified disaster distribution that was subject to a 3-year repayment rule.

In addition to filing an amended return or two amended returns, you must also file Form 8915-F, *Qualified Disaster Retirement Plan Distributions and Repayments*.

Charitable Giving

Americans are very generous people. Aside from the good feeling you get from following your philanthropic nature, the tax laws reward you for making donations. Americans donated $592.50 billion to charities in 2024 (according to estimates by Giving USA 2025) and more than 75 million people in the U.S. did volunteer work for charities.

This chapter covers the basic rules for claiming charitable contribution deductions, including the limits on different types of contributions and the substantiation required to support the deductions. This chapter also contains a record keeper that you can use to track your cash contributions throughout the year.

For more information, see IRS Publication 526, *Charitable Contributions*; IRS Publication 561, *Determining the Value of Donated Property*; IRS Publication 1771, *Charitable Contributions—Substantiation and Disclosure Requirements*; and IRS Publication 4303, *A Donor's Guide to Vehicle Donations*.

Cash Donations

Donations by cash, check, or credit card to charities or government bodies are deductible within set limits if certain conditions are met. The impact of this deduction is that Uncle Sam becomes your partner in making contributions. For example, if you are in the 32% tax bracket, the government is effectively making almost ⅓ of your contribution through the tax savings you enjoy from the donation. But the deduction only applies for those who itemize their personal deductions. Congress could allow non-itemizers to claim a deduction as was done in the past; check the Supplement for any update.

Benefit

You can deduct the cash donations you make to public charities, private foundations other than nonoperating private foundations, and the government. You can annually write off your cash donations up to 60% of your adjusted gross income (AGI) if you itemize your deductions in 2025.

Example

In 2025, you donate $50,000 cash to charity and itemize your deductions. You deduct $30,000 (60% of $50,000).

For those who itemize, donations made in prior years in excess of percentage cap based on your AGI can be carried forward for up to 5 years.

Example

Same as the example above. The unused contribution amount of $20,000 ($50,000 contributed minus $30,000 deducted) is carried forward to next year (it is deductible next year depending on your AGI). There is a 5-year limit on carryforwards.

Looking Ahead

Starting in 2026, those who claim the standard deduction can deduct cash contributions up to $1,000 ($2,000 for married persons filing jointly). There is no income limit for claiming this deduction. But those who itemize face a new limit on their deduction for contributions. The first 0.5% of adjusted gross income cannot be deducted. For example, if an individual has adjusted gross income of $240,000 in 2026, only contributions in excess of $1,200 (0.5% of $240,000) are deductible. What's more, those in the top tax bracket of 37% can only effectively deduct 35% of the contribution in excess of the 0.5% threshold.

Starting in 2027, there is a tax credit of up to $1,700 for contributions to a Scholarship Granting Organization (SGO). This is designed to help families with adjusted gross income up to 300% of the area median income to receive scholarship support.

Conditions

To claim a deduction for your cash contributions to charity, you must meet all 4 conditions:

1. Donations must be made to a qualified charity.
2. You cannot deduct donations exceeding 60% of your adjusted gross income.
3. You must itemize deductions in 2025 and can't claim the standard deduction.
4. You must have proof of your donations (you meet substantiation requirements).

QUALIFIED CHARITY

Just because a charity calls itself one does not mean it is tax-qualified; it must receive IRS approval to be a tax-exempt organization to which contributions are tax deductible. The charity must be a domestic nonprofit organization, trust, community chest, fund, or foundation that is operated exclusively for one of the following purposes:

- Charitable purposes
- Fostering amateur sports competition
- Prevention of cruelty to children or animals
- Religious purposes
- Scientific, literary, and educational purposes

Other organizations or places to which you can make tax-deductible contributions are:

- Domestic fraternal groups operating under a lodge system
- Domestic nonprofit veterans' organizations or auxiliary units
- Legal services corporations set up under the Legal Services Corporation Act
- Nonprofit cemetery and burial companies (as long as voluntary contributions benefit the whole cemetery and not merely your plot)
- U.S. government; government of a U.S. possession, state, city, or town; or Indian tribal government

Certain well-known charities, such as the American Red Cross, the United Way, the Boy Scouts and Girl Scouts, and the Salvation Army, are clearly authorized to accept tax-deductible contributions. Some charities may be less known, and the IRS warns taxpayers to beware of fake charities. If you have any question about an organization's status, ask about its status or check with the IRS, which maintains an online database in IRS Publication 78, *Cumulative List of Organizations*, at www.irs.gov/charities-non-profits/exempt-organizations-select-check.

Once you determine that an organization is eligible to receive a tax-deductible contribution, you may want to check whether the organization is worthy. You can see how much of your contribution goes to the purpose you intend versus being used for administrative costs (e.g., advertising, salaries) of the organization at Charity Navigator at www.charitynavigator.org, GuideStar at www.guidestar.org, or Better Business Bureau Give.org at www.give.org.

AGI LIMIT

Your deduction is limited to 60% of your adjusted gross income (AGI), a tax concept explained more thoroughly in the introduction to this book after taking into account all other charitable contributions for the year.

Note: There are some organizations to which donations are limited to 30%, but this is not the usual case. To find out more about so-called "30% charities," see IRS Publication 526, *Charitable Contributions*, at www.irs.gov.

SUBSTANTIATION

You must have proof of your donations in the event your return is questioned. The tax law is very specific about the type of proof (called substantiation in the tax law) that is recognized by the IRS.

Donations in *any* amount must be substantiated, such as with a credit card statement. Organizations that accept weekly cash donations may make arrangements to substantiate these donations, such as providing you with a monthly acknowledgment of total donations for the period. The Salvation Army offers "Kettle Pay," which allows cash donations at sidewalk red kettles to be made with the tap of a smartphone, which creates a record via the credit card to which Apple Pay or Google Pay are linked.

Charitable donations through payroll deductions are treated as substantiated by a variety of means, including pay stubs, W-2 forms, or other written statements from an employer.

If the donation is more than $75, get a disclosure statement from the charity stating the value of any benefit received from the organization. Donations of $250 or more require a written acknowledgment from the charity; a canceled check is not enough proof in this case. More details on this statement may be found later in this chapter.

EXAMPLES OF DEDUCTIBLE CONTRIBUTIONS

- Checks payable to charity
- Collection plate contributions substantiated by the charity
- Credit card donations
- Rebates applied through credit card programs
- Withholding from wages for charitable purposes
- License plate fee above the normal plate cost if the state gives the extra amount to a qualified charity
- Voluntary contributions to a qualified charity made in the space provided on your state income tax return (you effectively make the donation by increasing your state income tax payment or reducing your state income tax refund)

Planning Tips

You can use the record keeper at the end of this chapter to track your total distributions for the year. Be sure to obtain substantiation for all donations.

TIMING ISSUES

You can deduct contributions made up to the last day of the year. In making year-end contributions, keep these points in mind:

- Contributions by credit card are deductible in the year you charge them, not in the year you pay your credit card bill. If you charge the gift by December 31, 2025, it is deductible in 2025 even though you pay the credit card company in 2026.
- Contributions by check that are mailed before December 31 are deductible in the year of mailing even though the charity receives the check and cashes it in the following year.
- A pledge to make a charitable contribution is not deductible until you pay the pledge.
- Contributions made through a pay-by-phone bank account are not deductible when you make the call but rather as of the payment date on the bank statement.

If you have not received a written acknowledgment from the charity by the deadline for filing your return, obtain a filing extension. This will allow you to meet substantiation requirements.

AGI PLANNING

Generally, tax planning dictates that you try to *reduce* your adjusted gross income to boost your deduction for medical expenses as well as eligibility for certain exclusions and credits. But if you make sizable donations and itemize your deductions, you may not want or need to adopt strategies to reduce your AGI. By claiming your charitable deduction, you effectively reduce or eliminate the tax on your income.

Example

In 2025, you donate $50,000 in cash to a charitable organization and are itemizing your deductions. Your AGI is $100,000 so $60,000 of the contribution is deductible. You can try to reduce your AGI to reduce your tax bill, but it lowers the current deduction for the contribution. And if you have a carryover of charitable contributions from 2024, don't reduce your AGI below an amount that will allow you to use it completely.

Pitfalls

Despite your generous nature and good intentions, you can easily slip up on technicalities that can prevent you from claiming a deduction. Be sure to follow all requirements for deducting your cash contributions. Don't overlook appraisal requirements.

NONQUALIFIED ORGANIZATIONS

An organization may seem like a charity and still not be one. Don't assume that a hospital or school is automatically qualified to accept deductible donations. If it is operated for profit, your contributions are not deductible.

You may not deduct donations to foreign charities unless allowed by international treaties (for example, donations to charities in Mexico and Canada can be deductible). But a domestic charity set up to distribute funds abroad may be a qualified organization under the rules discussed earlier.

Other organizations that are *nonqualified* include:

- Sororities and fraternities.
- Civic leagues, chambers of commerce, business leagues, or labor unions. But you may be able to treat contributions to these organizations as deductible business expenses (see Chapter 14).
- Professional associations of attorneys, doctors, and accountants. Some unrestricted gifts to state bar associations may be deductible (the bar association reports to you the portion of annual dues treated as charitable contributions).
- Foreign organizations other than certain Canadian, Israeli, or Mexican charitable organizations.
- Homeowners' associations.
- Political organizations and candidates.

OTHER NONDEDUCTIBLE DONATIONS

You cannot deduct a donation you make directly to an individual, no matter how worthy the person is. For example, suppose your neighbor's house was severely damaged by a fire and you give your neighbor $1,000 to help him through the days following the fire. Your generosity does not warrant a tax deduction.

You cannot claim a deduction for a qualified charitable distribution (QCD) from your IRA (discussed in Chapter 5 and later in this chapter). You cannot deduct donations made on your behalf that are based on the purchases you make; these charitable contributions are made at no additional cost to you. For example, the 0.5% donations made through AmazonSmile or the donations (3% on average) through iGive based on your purchases are not deductible by you.

If you donate unused frequent flyer miles to Make-a-Wish Foundation, you cannot deduct them. According to the charity, frequent flyer miles are "a gift or an award from the corporation to the individual" (which means a taxpayer has no basis in them on which to figure a deductible amount).

EXPIRATION OF CARRYOVER

Unlike other carryovers in the tax law that run indefinitely, the carryover of excess charitable contributions is limited to 5 years. If you have such carryovers, don't let the 5 years expire causing you to waste potential write-offs. Consider realizing sufficient income to allow you to use up your carryovers.

Where to Claim the Deduction

Because you itemize your deductions, report your charitable deduction for your cash donations on Schedule A of Form 1040 or 1040-SR. If you make only cash donations, you do not need any additional form or schedule other than Schedule A to report your charitable contributions.

Appreciated Property Donations

The government encourages donations of appreciated property held for more than one year by allowing tax deductions at the property's value (rather than limiting them to the donor's cost or other tax basis) as long as certain conditions are met.

Benefit

You can claim a charitable contribution deduction *and* avoid capital gains by donating appreciated property to charity. You also avoid the net investment income tax that could apply to capital gains if you are a high-income taxpayer. As long as the property has been held for more than one year, the charity is qualified, and other conditions are met, the donation is based on the property's value.

> ### Example
>
> You own stock you bought years ago for $2,000 that is now worth $10,000. If you donate it to a tax-exempt organization, you can claim a charitable contribution deduction of $10,000, the current value of the stock. What's more, you don't have to pay capital gains tax on your $8,000 of appreciation ($10,000 − $2,000), which would have cost you $1,200 ($8,000 × 15%). If you are in the 24% tax bracket, your deduction saves you $2,400 in taxes ($10,000 × 24%). Your total savings from your generosity is $3,600 ($1,200 capital gains tax saved plus $2,400 tax savings from the deduction).

Donations of appreciated property are limited to 30% of your adjusted gross income for the year, in most cases. Donations in excess of this limit can be carried forward for up to 5 years.

Donations of appreciated property that do not meet the conditions listed next are deductible only to the extent of your cost.

Conditions

To claim a deduction for the value of the property you donate to charity, you must meet all 4 conditions:

1. The property must be held long term ("holding period").
2. If the property is tangible personal property, such as artwork, cars, and equipment, the charity must put the property to use in its exempt purpose ("tangible property used in the charity's exempt purpose").
3. The property cannot be "ordinary income property" (which is property that would generate ordinary income rather than capital gain if it were sold instead of donated).
4. You must comply with substantiation requirements.

Remember that donations to only a qualified charity produce a tax deduction for you. Which organizations are qualified charities, and which are not, is discussed earlier in the chapter under "Cash Donations."

HOLDING PERIOD

To meet the long-term holding period, you must own the property for more than one year prior to the date of the donation.

TANGIBLE PROPERTY USED IN THE CHARITY EXEMPT PURPOSE

If you give property other than securities or real estate, you are giving tangible personal property. Items commonly donated in this category include works of art, books, antiques, furniture, equipment, and collectibles.

Use of the property in the charity's exempt purpose means that the use serves a function related to the charity's exemption. For example, if you donate art to a school and the school displays the work in the library or school museum so that students can study it, the property is being used in the charity's exempt purpose.

If the charity sells the property you donate, you don't meet the related use test even though the proceeds certainly serve the charity's exempt purpose. The tax law treats the sale as an unrelated purpose (see "Planning Tips" for protection).

PROPERTY IS NOT ORDINARY INCOME PROPERTY

If you donate appreciated property that would produce ordinary income if it were sold rather than donated, you cannot deduct the property's value; your donation is limited to your cost. Examples of ordinary income property include inventory, stock in trade, farm crops, and works of art or music, books, and memoranda donated by the person who created them. But businesses, whether or not incorporated, can claim an enhanced charitable contribution for donations of their food inventory.

SUBSTANTIATION REQUIREMENTS

Substantiation means proof of your donation. The tax law is very specific on the type of substantiation. It varies with the amount and nature of the donation.

More than $500. If the total deduction claimed for your property donations is more than $500, you *must* attach Form 8283, *Noncash Charitable Contributions*, to your return.

More than $5,000. If you make a donation exceeding $5,000 (one item or a collection), you must obtain a written appraisal for your donation. Donations of cryptocurrency valued over $5,000 require a qualified appraisal. An appraisal is also required for a donation of used clothing or a household item valued at over $500 that is not in good used condition or better. The appraisal is summarized on the form.

You do not need a written appraisal if the donation is:

- Publicly traded securities—you simply use the market value on the date of the donation.
- Nonpublicly traded stock (stock in a private corporation) if valued at $10,000 or less. You do need an appraisal if the value exceeds this amount.

Obtain the appraisal no earlier than 60 days before you make the donation. You must have the appraisal in hand by the time you file your return (including extensions). In addition to obtaining the appraisal, the charity must acknowledge on Form 8283 that it received your donation (so leave enough time to obtain this acknowledgment before filing your return).

Art valued at more than $20,000. If you donate art valued at $20,000 or more, you must attach the written appraisal to the return, along with a color photo or slide, if the IRS asks for it.

Planning Tips

If you are concerned that the charity may sell the tangible property you donated, which would limit your deduction to your cost, ask the charity for a letter stipulating that it has no immediate intentions of selling. Then your deduction for the value of the property would be protected even if the charity later changes its intentions and sells your donation.

Donations of collectibles can yield even greater tax savings than donations of securities. The reason: Gain on a sale of collectibles is taxed up to 28%, compared with a top 15% (or 20% for those essentially in the top tax bracket) rate of gain from a sale of securities. Donations avoid the capital gains tax entirely.

ELECTION TO CHANGE AGI LIMIT

If you qualify to deduct the fair market value of your property, you can elect to reduce the gift by its appreciation and instead use a 50% AGI limit (instead of the 30% AGI limit that is usually required). This election makes sense when there is little appreciation on the property, and opting to reduce the deduction by appreciation still gives you a greater write-off.

Example

You donate stock valued at $100,000 that cost you $90,000. Your AGI is $180,000. If you do nothing, your deduction for your $100,000 is limited to $54,000 (30% of $180,000). But if you make the election to reduce the deduction by its appreciation so that it is limited to your cost of $90,000, you can deduct it in full; your limit in this case is 50% of AGI or $90,000.

You make the election simply by attaching your own statement to your return explaining that you are making the election; no special IRS form or schedule is required. But you can't void the election unless it was based on a material mistake; you can't change your mind simply because you later reconsider the situation and prefer to carry forward the unused deduction that you could have claimed.

IRS APPRAISAL

For example, an owner of a nationally well-known tax preparation company donated privately-held stock to charity. Since the value of the donation was never in question, he never bothered to obtain a qualified appraisal as required by the tax law. This tax-savvy taxpayer lost out on a sizable deduction for his stock donation because he overlooked a basic requirement for claiming it and the IRS caught him.

If you are donating very expensive works of art valued at $50,000 or more, you can protect your deduction from IRS questioning by obtaining an advance valuation of the art from the IRS's Art Advisory Panel. If the IRS agrees to give you this advance valuation, you'll receive an IRS Statement of Value (SOV) that you attach to your return to support your deduction. There is a fee of $8,400 for one to 3 items, and $800 for each additional item, and obtaining an SOV can take as long as a year. The fee must be paid by direct debit from a bank account through Pay.gov. The good news is that an SOV avoids hassles with the IRS over valuation later on. But the bad news is that if you don't agree with the SOV, you are left with no alternative but to litigate the issue (you still must attach it to your return, even if you claim a higher deduction than the SOV).

Pitfalls

Donations of appreciated property can produce important tax savings for you, but here are some things to watch out for.

SUBSTANTIATION

As explained earlier, property donations must meet substantiation requirements to be deductible. The Tax Court recognized that a deed of gift for the transfer of property to charity may be considered a "contemporaneous written acknowledgment," but only if it also says that no goods or services were received in exchange.

PENALTY FOR OVERVALUATIONS

Valuing property isn't an exact science. When making charitable donations, you hope that the property is valued as highly as possible to boost your deduction. But don't be too generous in your estimations; substantial overvaluations of charitable donations resulting in a tax underpayment exceeding $5,000 can lead to a penalty.

- If the value claimed is 200% or more of the correct value (and results in an underpayment exceeding $5,000), the penalty is 20% of the underpayment.
- If the value claimed is 400% or more of the correct value (and results in an underpayment exceeding $5,000), the penalty is 40% of the underpayment.

Example

Assume you are in the 32% tax bracket. You donate an oil painting to charity and estimate that its value is $35,000. In truth, it is actually worth only $10,000. Since the value claimed is more than 200% of the correct value and your valuation results in your underpaying tax by more than $5,000, you are subject to a 20% penalty of the resulting underpayment of tax. In this case, because you are in the 32% tax bracket, there would be an $8,000 underpayment ([$35,000 − $10,000] × 32%) so your penalty would be $1,600 ($8,000 × 20%). If you had valued the painting at $40,000, your penalty would have been 40% of the underpayment.

The penalty is applied on an item-by-item basis. So, for example, if you donate 2 objects, overvaluing one item and undervaluing the other, you cannot offset the undervaluation by the overvaluation.

DONATIONS OF PROPERTY THAT HAS DECLINED IN VALUE

If you donate property that meets all of the conditions discussed, your tax deduction is based on the value of the property, even if you paid more for it. In effect, you get no benefit from the loss in value.

Unless the charity has a specific need for your item, it is advisable to sell the property rather than donate it if you can claim a tax deduction for your loss (for example, the property is investment property on which a capital loss can be claimed). You can then donate the proceeds so that the charity receives the same benefit. By selling the property, you to take a tax loss on the sale.

Example

You own stock you paid $10,000 for years ago. It is now worth $2,000. If you donate the stock, your deduction is limited to $2,000. If you sell the stock and donate the proceeds, the charity receives the same $2,000. You can claim a tax loss of $8,000 ($10,000 − $2,000). You can use this loss to offset your capital gains and then up to $3,000 of your ordinary income; excess capital losses can be carried forward indefinitely and used in future years.

This strategy does not apply to personal-use (noninvestment or nonbusiness) items, such as your personal car, because you cannot take a capital loss deduction on their sale.

APPRAISALS AND ADDITIONAL COSTS

You may have costs over and above the property you're donating. There may be appraisal costs for determining the value of the donation so you know how much to deduct. There may be packing, shipping, and insurance costs to send donated items to a charitable organization. These costs are not deductible.

Where to Claim the Deduction

Like cash donations, you report property donations on Schedule A of Form 1040 or 1040-SR.

But you may also have to complete Form 8283, *Noncash Charitable Contributions*, as explained earlier under "Substantiation."

Used Clothing and Car Donations

Clothing that no longer fits, appliances and sporting equipment that are no longer used, and cars being replaced may be of great benefit to someone else. The tax law rewards donations of these items to charities that can put them to continued good use by permitting a tax deduction for those who itemize if certain conditions are met.

Benefit

Your used clothing, linens, toys, cars, and other items can be of benefit to others. Consider donating them to charity and taking a tax deduction for your efforts. A deduction of these items is generally subject to the 50% of adjusted gross income limit minus cash contributions subject to the 60% limit discussed earlier in this chapter. This means that donations of these items are included along with your cash contributions to determine your annual limit.

Conditions

The items must be donated to a qualified charity (see the explanation of a qualified charity under "Cash Donations" earlier in this chapter).

For donations of used clothing and household items, no deduction can be claimed unless the items are in "good used condition or better." If a single item is appraised at over $500, it can be deducted even though it is not in good used condition (although condition certainly affects its value).

Special rules for vehicles. Special substantiation rules apply to donations of cars, boats, and planes valued at over $500. You must obtain a written acknowledgment, Form 1098-C, *Contributions of Motor Vehicles, Boats, and Airplanes*, within 30 days of the date of contribution or the date that the organization sells the vehicle without using it in any significant way (e.g., driving a car to deliver meals to the needy for one year). If the organization sells the vehicle without using it in a significant way in its charitable activities or making any improvements to the vehicle, your donation is limited to the sale proceeds that the organization receives from a sale. Information about the sale is provided to the IRS. Use of Form 1098-C is mandatory for these donations; a thank-you letter from the charity is no substitute.

If you value a car over $250 but not over $500 (something very rare today) and the charity sells it, you can deduct the actual fair market value; you are not limited to the sales proceeds. But if you value the car over $500 and the charity sells it for less than $500, your maximum deduction is $500. For example, if you value the car at $650 and the charity sells it for $450, you can deduct $500.

Planning Tips

Don't know what your used items are worth? Here are some resources you can turn to for help:

- Used cars: Kelley Blue Book at https://kbb.com and Carvana at https://www .carvana.com/sell-my-car provide free online prices for used cars, based on the vehicle's mileage, condition, and other factors.

- Used clothing and household items: The Salvation Army's Valuation Guide at https://satruck.org/Home/DonationValueGuide is a free online guide to valuing used clothing, appliances, furniture, and other household items. The Valuation Guide for Goodwill Donor at https://goodwillnne.org/donate/donation-value-guide is another free online guide.
- Used computers, smartphones, and other electronics: Gadget Value at www.gadgetvalue.com provides values for old PCs.

In one case, a court allowed a donation for used clothing valued at $25 per bag.

There are some apps to help with valuation, such as TurboTax's ItsDeductible Donation Tracker and Donation Assistant by Tax Act, which are free. You can use your smartphone to take photos of the donated items to keep with your records.

Pitfalls

You cannot claim a deduction if you donate items directly to an individual, no matter how much in need that person may be. For example, if a fire destroys a neighbor's home and you provide your neighbor with clothing and other items, you cannot claim a charitable contribution deduction for your generosity.

Don't expect the charity to provide you with a valuation of your donation. It's up to you to assess the value of the items you donate; the charity merely confirms that you actually made the donation.

Don't include in the amount of your charitable contribution any appraisal fees or the cost of packing and shipping you incur when making property donations. These expenses are not deductible.

Where to Claim the Deduction

For information about where to claim a deduction for your donation, see the rules under "Appreciated Property Donations" earlier in this chapter, including the rules on substantiation and filing Form 8283, *Noncash Charitable Contributions*. Also attach Form 1098-C, *Contributions of Motor Vehicles, Boats, and Airplanes*, if you donated such an item valued at over $500.

Intellectual Property Donations

If you give a patent, a certain copyright, or other intellectual property to charity, you can not only deduct the initial contribution, but can also claim deductions in future years for a percentage of the income that the charity derives from the property.

Benefit

You can claim an itemized deduction for donations of intellectual property to charity of:

- The fair market value of the donation in the year of the donation for intellectual property that you did not create (or, for self-created property, the amount that would have been ordinary income had you sold it rather than donated it).
- A percentage of the income derived from the property for up to 10 years following the year of the donation. The percentage is based on Table 6.1 (the table runs for 12 years because of the potential for a donee to have a fiscal year or a short tax year).

Condition

At the time of the donation, you must tell the charity that you intend to claim the additional deductions. This is done by providing the charity with your personal written statement of your intention to treat the contribution as a qualified intellectual contribution. This statement must also describe the property and the date of the donation.

TABLE 6.1 Deduction for Income from Intellectual Property Donations

Year Ending after Date of Contribution	Applicable Percentage
1st	100%
2nd	100
3rd	90
4th	80
5th	70
6th	60
7th	50
8th	40
9th	30
10th	20
11th	10
12th	10

Planning Tip

The additional deduction applies to all types of intellectual property. This includes not only patents and certain copyrights, but also trademarks, trade names, trade secrets, know-how, certain software, and certain applications or registrations of this property.

Pitfalls

The additional deductions can be claimed for up to only 10 years following the year of the intellectual property donation. If the life of the property is shorter than 10 years, you cannot claim additional deductions beyond this life.

The additional deduction does not apply to donations of intellectual property to a private foundation other than an operating private foundation.

Where to Claim the Deduction

Each year the charity informs you (and the IRS) of the income derived from your donation on Form 8899, *Notice of Income from Donated Intellectual Property*.

To claim a charitable contribution deduction, complete Schedule A of Form 1040 or 1040-SR. You may also have to complete Form 8283, *Noncash Charitable Contributions*, as explained earlier in this chapter under "Substantiation Requirements" for appreciated property donations.

Real Estate Donated for Conservation Purposes

Real estate development has gobbled up open spaces and turned them into houses, shopping malls, parking lots, and office buildings. But the government wants to encourage the maintenance of green spaces and does so by permitting tax deductions for donations of certain property interests for this purpose.

Benefit

Certain donations of partial interests in real property to government agencies or publicly supported charities for exclusively conservation purposes may entitle you to a deduction. Such donations include:

- Your entire interest in real property other than retained rights to subsurface oil, gas, or other minerals. For example, you own land and donate it to your town, retaining these mineral rights.

- A remainder interest in real property. For example, you own land. You keep the right to use it for the rest of your life, giving your town the remainder interest in the property. You do this by deeding the remainder interest to the town.

- An easement, restrictive covenant, or similar property restrictions granted in perpetuity (meaning forever). For example, you own property but give your town an easement limiting the use of a portion of it for a bird sanctuary forever. Even if you later sell the property, the new owner must continue to respect the easement and keep the use as a bird sanctuary.

Conditions

Only donations for qualified conservation purposes entitle you to a deduction. Qualified conservation purposes include:

- The preservation of land areas for outdoor recreation, education, or scenic enjoyment.
- Preservation of historically important land areas or structures.
- Protection of plant, fish, and wildlife habitats or similar natural ecosystems.

For a conservation easement contribution that relates to a building in a registered historic district, there is a $500 filing fee if the claimed deduction is more than $10,000. This payment is accompanied by Form 8283-V, *Voucher for Filing Fee Under Sec. 170(f)(13)*. But don't attach the voucher and check to the return. Instead, mail Form 8283-V and your check made payable to the U.S. Treasury to Internal Revenue Service, P.O. Box 9002, Becky, WV 25802-9002.

Planning Tips

To make the donation of an easement on your property, you probably need to pay an attorney to handle the legal work involved.

Donations are deductible up to 50% of the contribution base (which is essentially adjusted gross income), instead of the usual 30% limit (provided the use of the donated property does not prevent farming or ranching). Farmers and ranchers have a 100% limit. Unused contributions because of this limit can be carried forward for up to 15 years.

Pitfalls

Once you give away this interest, you can't change your mind and get it back. As explained earlier, the donation must be in perpetuity (forever). Here is a list of actions that run counter to the rule about perpetuity and can cost you a deduction for any conservation easement donation:

- Failing to subordinate a mortgage to the easement (making the interests of the lender secondary to those of the easement, which requires the consent of the lender)

- Making a conservation easement in North Dakota, which limits the term of an easement to 99 years
- Providing (even informally) that the property be returned if the IRS denies a tax deduction
- Retaining the right to substitute property (even though no property is ever returned to you)
- Having a right to a subtraction for post-donation improvements in the event of a judicial extinguishment of the easement (although one federal appellate court said this did not violate the rule about perpetuity).

If a deed of gift contains a defect that means the perpetuity requirement is not met, there is an opportunity to correct the defect. This does not apply to easements involving abusive transactions, explained next.

If you are an owner in a pass-through entity (i.e., partnership, limited liability company, S corporation) that donated a conservation easement, your deduction may be disallowed if the arrangement is viewed as an abusive transaction. No deduction for a donation of a conservation easement is allowed if the deduction claimed exceeds 2 ½ times the sum of each owner's relevant basis in the contributing entity unless any of the following conditions apply:

- The contribution meets a 3-year holding period
- Substantially all of the contributing entity is owned by members of a family
- The contribution relates to the preservation of a certified historic structure and special reporting requirements are met

Where to Claim the Deduction

For information about where to claim a deduction for your donation, see the rules under "Appreciated Property Donations," earlier in this chapter, including the rules on substantiation and filing Form 8283.

Bargain Sales

Taxpayers can have their cake and eat it, too—recoup their investments in property while obtaining tax deductions to boot—by making bargain sales of property to charity. It's a bargain because the charity is paying only a portion of the property's actual value, typically the donor's original cost for the property. It's a sale because the donor is receiving payment for the transaction and not merely donating the entire value of the property. Even so, a partial tax deduction is permitted under certain conditions.

Benefit

If you have appreciated property, you can recoup your investment while obtaining a tax deduction when you make a bargain sale to charity. In effect, the donation is viewed as 2 transactions: part sale and part gift.

You figure your gain on the sale by allocating the basis between the sale and the gift part as follows:

Step 1: Divide the sales proceeds by the fair market value of the property (include any outstanding debt as sales proceeds).

Step 2: Apply the percentage in Step 1 to the adjusted basis of the property to find the portion of the basis allocated to the sale.

Step 3: Subtract the resulting basis of Step 2 from the sales proceeds to find your gain.

Example

You sell property to your favorite charity for what you paid for it ($12,000). At the time of the donation, it is worth $20,000. Under Step 1, divide $12,000 by $20,000, which is 0.6 or 60%. Apply 60% to the adjusted basis of $12,000, which is $7,200, the basis allocated to the sale. Your gain is $4,800, the difference between your sales proceeds of $12,000 and this basis of $7,200. By making the donation, you have obtained a charitable contribution deduction of $8,000 (the appreciation on the property), while recouping your initial investment, so you are out-of-pocket nothing. Had you sold the property to someone other than a charity, you would have paid capital gains tax on the gain of $8,000 ($20,000 − $12,000), or $1,200 at a 15% capital gain rate (assuming this is your capital gains tax rate).

Conditions

The same conditions apply to bargain sales as to other charitable contributions (for example, the charity must be an IRS-approved organization). For conditions, see earlier in this chapter.

Planning Tip

A bargain sale can enable you to recover your cost (investment in the property) while also obtaining a deduction for any increased value in the property. Donating the property through a bargain sale saves you the time and expense of selling it to a third party in order to raise the funds to make the donation you would make if you keep your initial investment.

Pitfalls

If the property you donate is not the type of property that entitles you to a donation of the appreciation (for example, you didn't own it for more than one year), then the bargain sale doesn't produce any charitable contribution deduction. Of course, the charity still obtains the item at a bargain price.

You must allocate the basis of the property on a bargain sale even if the annual AGI limit prevents you from claiming a charitable contribution deduction.

Where to Claim the Deduction

You report the bargain sale on various forms and schedules accompanying Form 1040 or 1040-SR: Report the donation portion on Form 8283. Use Schedule D to report the sale portion and Schedule A to report the gift portion.

Details on reporting gifts of appreciated property are explained earlier in this chapter.

Volunteer Expenses

During natural disasters, the efforts of volunteers are widespread and dramatic, but volunteering has become the thing to do at any time. Americorps reported that more than 75.7 million Americans did some volunteer work in 2023 (there are no more recent statistics). While individuals bear the burden of the time and effort they put in, the government helps defray any actual out-of-pocket costs through a deduction that can be claimed if certain conditions are met.

Benefit

If you incur out-of-pocket expenses in serving your favorite charity, you can deduct these costs as part of your itemized deduction for charitable donations.

If you use your vehicle for charitable purposes, including attending meetings of organizations you serve, you can deduct your actual vehicle expenses for gas and oil or mileage at the rate of 14¢ per mile. The 14¢ per mile rate is fixed by law (unchanged since 1997); it cannot be increased by the IRS. Whichever method you select, you can also write off parking and tolls.

Conditions

As long as you incur out-of-pocket costs for a qualified charity (explained earlier in this chapter under "Cash Donations") and you itemize deductions, your costs are deductible.

EXAMPLES OF DEDUCTIBLE UNREIMBURSED EXPENSES

- Materials and supplies you furnish (e.g., stamps)
- Related costs of hosting a fundraiser (e.g., invitations, food, and beverages)
- Travel expenses, including meals and lodging for overnight trips away from home to serve as an official delegate to a convention of a church, charitable, veteran, or other similar organization
- Travel expenses to work for a charitable organization (such as Habitat for Humanity and Meals on Wheels)
- Uniforms required in serving the organization

Planning Tip

Keep track of your mileage and out-of-pocket expenses on behalf of the charity. In a diary, logbook, or app, note the odometer readings, date, destination, etc. for every charity-related trip for which your car is used.

Pitfall

Just because you are not compensated by the charity for your efforts doesn't automatically mean that every cost you incur on behalf of the charity is deductible. You *cannot* deduct:

- The value of your time and energy. Even if you perform work for the charity, you cannot deduct what you would have charged for your expertise.

Example

You are an attorney who does pro bono work for a local charity. You cannot deduct your usual hourly rate for the time spent on this charitable activity.

- The rental value of your home or vacation home that you allow the charity to use in its fund-raising activities.

Example

You own a vacation home and let the charity raffle off a one-week stay there. You cannot deduct the fair rental value of that one week's use of your vacation home.

- Babysitting expenses you paid to enable you to put in time for your charity.
- Travel costs to attend a convention for a nonprofit organization if you are not a delegate.
- Travel costs to work on a project for a nonprofit organization if there is a significant element of personal pleasure, recreation, or vacation involved.

You *must* substantiate your out-of-pocket expenses in order to deduct them. If total expenses are $250 or more, you must obtain a written acknowledgment from the charity for your activities. Without this substantiation, a deduction is limited to $249, provided there are credit card statements, canceled checks, or other documentation.

Where to Claim the Deduction

To claim a charitable deduction for your unreimbursed expenses, you must complete Schedule A of Form 1040 or 1040-SR.

Tickets to Fundraisers, Raffles, and Sporting Events

Who hasn't bought a ticket to a fundraising event or activity, such as a raffle or dinner dance, to benefit a charity? Just because the check is written out to a charity doesn't automatically entitle taxpayers to a deduction. Special rules govern the extent, if any, to which the cost of fund-raising tickets may be deductible.

Benefit

You can deduct the purchase price for raffle tickets and charity-sponsored events in excess of the regular admission price or other benefit you receive.

Example

You pay $100 for a ticket to an evening sponsored by your favorite charity that includes dinner and a show. The value of the dinner and show (what you would have paid regularly) is $75. You can deduct $25 (the excess cost over the regular price). If you don't accept the ticket, you can deduct $100.

Condition

If you pay more than $75, the charity must supply you with a written explanation of the value of the benefit you receive so that you can figure your deduction, if any.

Planning Tip

If you pay for a ticket for a charity event but don't accept the ticket, make sure that an acknowledgment you receive from the charity reflects your refusal to accept the ticket.

Pitfalls

You cannot deduct any of the cost of Girl Scout cookies you buy for your own consumption. The cost of the cookies is treated as their fair market value so you haven't made any gift. But if you leave the cookies with the troop, you may treat your payment as a deduction. Similarly, if you donate the cookies to a charity, you can deduct your cost (not the estimated retail value).

No deduction is allowed for a donation entitling you to receive the right to buy tickets or seating at college or university athletic events.

Where to Claim the Deduction

To claim a charitable deduction for your donations in connection with tickets, raffles, or other fundraisers, you must complete Schedule A of Form 1040 or 1040-SR. You do not have to attach the written explanation for your donations to your return; save them for your records with the copy of your return.

If you do not make donations of property, you do not need any additional form or schedule other than Schedule A to report your charitable contributions.

Membership Fees to Nonprofit Organizations

Anthropologist Margaret Mead said, "Never doubt that a small group of thoughtful, committed citizens can change the world. Indeed it is the only thing that ever has." Perhaps that's why so many Americans belong to organizations of all kinds, including religious, civic, and fraternal organizations. Belonging is rewarded taxwise to a certain extent by permitting the cost of dues to be deductible, within certain limits.

Benefit

If you pay dues to nonprofit organizations, you can treat the payments as cash contributions subject to the rules discussed earlier in this chapter. Examples of membership fees and offerings that are deductible include payments to religious organizations (e.g., your church, synagogue, or mosque) and fraternal organizations operating under a lodge system (e.g., Elks Club).

You must reduce your deduction by the value of any benefits (other than token amounts) you receive, such as monthly journals.

> ### Example
>
> You donate $100 to your local public broadcasting station during its annual fund drive. You receive a DVD of one of its programs. Your deduction is limited to the donation in excess of the value of the DVD (the station should supply you with this information).

You do *not* have to reduce your donation by these tokens distributed by the charity in gratitude for your gift:

- Items costing no more than $13.60 if your gift is at least $68.00 in 2025 (these figures are adjusted annually for inflation)
- Items worth no more than $2.72 (2% of $136) in 2025, regardless of the amount of your gift

If you pay $75 or less for membership that entitles you to benefits, you can fully deduct your dues if either of these alternatives applies:

- You receive membership privileges that can be exercised frequently (e.g., free or discounted parking or admission) or discounts on gift shop or mail order items.
- Your membership entitles you to admission to members-only events and the cost of each event is no more than $13.60 in 2025.

If you pay more than $75, you can exclude only those benefits that you would have excluded had you paid $75 or less; more expensive benefits are not excludable.

Student Exchange Program

Individuals who open their homes to students, serving as hosts under special programs, may be eligible for a tax break that helps to defray the cost of hospitality. To claim this tax benefit (which hasn't changed since 1960), certain conditions must be met.

Benefit

If you support a student in your home, you may deduct up to $50 per month as a charitable contribution deduction as long as you itemize your deductions and meet certain conditions. If the student is in your home for at least 15 days of a month, you can treat it as an entire month.

Conditions

To claim a deduction for supporting a student in your home, you must meet all 3 of these conditions:

1. The student must be in elementary, middle, or high school.
2. The placement in your home must be arranged under an educational program by a charitable organization and is documented by a written agreement.
3. You have records showing what you spend on the student's food, clothing, medical care, schooling, and recreation.

Planning Tip

Supporting a student in your home may entitle your child to spend time in another family's home. For example, if you accept a foreign exchange student into your home, you may not only obtain a tax deduction for that foreign student, but in addition, your child may be able to go abroad and there is no tax cost to this benefit—to you or to your child. While you may have to pay out-of-pocket for airfare, your child's living expenses abroad may be provided for free.

Pitfall

You usually cannot deduct any payments made where you receive money from the charity for the student's maintenance. For example, if the charity reimburses you for medical expenses you pay for the student, you cannot deduct the medical expenses you paid. But you are permitted to deduct your prepayment of a one-time expense, such as a medical bill or vacation for the student at the request of the student's parents or sponsoring organization for which you are later reimbursed for part of the cost.

Where to Claim the Deduction

See under "Cash Donations" earlier in this chapter.

Special Inventory Donations

Business owners may enjoy an enhanced charitable contribution deduction for donations by sole proprietors and any other businesses to public charities. The food must be apparently wholesome and meet all federal quality and labeling standards. The deduction is the lesser of (1) the item's basis in inventory plus ½ of its appreciation, or (2) 2 times the item's basis.

Donor-Advised Funds

You've heard the old saying "buy now, pay later." Well, you can donate now and deduct the contribution now, even though money is not disbursed to a charity until later. Using a donor advised fund (DAF), you make contributions to the fund and *suggest* which charity should benefit from them. The fund usually follows your recommendation, although it is not required to. You claim the deduction when money or property goes into the fund.

Benefit

You can deduct the money and property donated to the fund (see earlier in this chapter for rules on cash donations and donations of appreciated property).

Conditions

You cannot *require* the fund to disburse the money to a charity of your choice. You can only make suggestions. For example, if you have $15,000 in your fund account, you can ask that $5,000 be disbursed to the American Red Cross; the fund will usually follow your request, but does not have to.

Planning Tip

Wealthy individuals can set up private foundations or use other charitable vehicles to direct funds to the charities of their choice. If you do not have sufficient funds to create your own private foundation, you can use a commercial donor-advised fund such as:

- Fidelity Investments Charitable Gift Fund (www.fidelitycharitable.org/)
- Schwab Charitable Fund (www.schwabcharitable.org/public/charitable/home)
- The Vanguard Charitable Endowment Fund (www.vanguardcharitable.org/)

Some large charities and trusts offer donor-advised funds, which you can find through a web search.

Pitfall

No deduction can be claimed for a contribution to a donor-advised fund if the sponsoring organization is a war veterans organization, a fraternal society, or a nonprofit cemetery company.

Where to Claim the Deduction

See "Cash Contributions" earlier in this chapter.

Charitable Gift Annuities

Both you *and* a charity can benefit from your largesse with charitable gift annuities. These are arrangements in which you give something to a tax-exempt organization offering charitable gift annuities, such as Salvation Army or the Mayo Clinic, some mutual fund companies (e.g., Fidelity Charitable and Schwab Charitable), and many universities, and get a lifetime annuity in return. You benefit the organization and receive some benefit, although not as much as the annuity that could be received from a commercial annuity contract. What's more, you also can claim a charitable contribution deduction for a charitable gift annuity.

Usually, these arrangements provide for a deferred annuity—you make the gift now but don't start receiving annuity payments for some time. These arrangements are called deferred gift annuities.

Benefit

You can deduct part of what is donated to the tax-exempt organization, as long as you itemize deductions. If the organization accepts property donations for its charitable gift annuity program, then long-term capital gains are avoided; your donation is based on the value of the property when donated. The amount of the deduction is figured in part on your life expectancy and the rate of return. The deduction is the excess of the amount of the contribution over the value of the annuity at the time of purchase, which is determined using IRS life expectancy tables and assumed earnings set by the IRS.

Condition

You must enter into an agreement with an IRS-approved tax-exempt organization and make your contribution.

Planning Tips

The annuity rate varies by organization, so deciding which organization to use for a charitable gift annuity matters greatly.

If you are at least 70½, you can make a one-time transfer from an IRA to a charitable gift annuity up to $54,000 in 2025 using a qualified charitable distribution (QCD). This avoids income tax on the funds transferred from the IRA. See Chapter 5.

Pitfalls

Annuity benefits received are taxable income. These benefits are fixed at the time of entering into the charitable gift annuity and are not adjusted for inflation.

The rules for making decisions about charitable gift annuities and figuring deductions for them are very complicated and usually require the assistance of a tax professional.

Where to Claim the Deduction

The deduction is claimed on Schedule A of Form 1040 or 1040-SR. If you donate appreciated property to obtain the annuity, you must file Form 8283, *Noncash Charitable Contributions*.

Sophisticated Charitable Giving Arrangements

Wealthy individuals have a number of options for giving away substantial amounts of money and property. The reason they're essentially restricted to these individuals is the costs of setup and administration.

A full discussion of these options is beyond the scope of this book, but they include:

- *Private foundation.* This is an organization set up to further the charitable goals of the donor. The foundation must distribute annually at least 5% of the previous year's average net assets for charitable purposes. Contributions to the foundation are deductible, although cash contributions usually are limited to 30% of AGI and long-term capital gain property to 20% of AGI.

- *Charitable lead trust.* This type of donation enables the charity to receive income from the trust for the life of the donor or joint lives of the donor and spouse, or for a term of years. At the end of this period, the property remaining in the trust passes to a beneficiary named by the donor (it can revert to the donor, but this option typically isn't used). The contribution deduction is based on the charity's income interest, which is figured using a factor determined by the IRS.

- *Charitable remainder trust.* This type of donation enables the donor to retain the right to receive income for life or a term of years not exceeding 20 years. At the end of this period, the property remaining in the trust belongs to the charity. There are 2 types of charitable remainder trusts: a charitable remainder unitrust (CRUT), where annual income is a fixed percentage of the value of the trust determined each year, and a charitable remainder annuity trust (CRAT), where income is a fixed annual amount similar to a commercial annuity. The contribution deduction is based on the charity's remainder interest, which is figured using a factor determined by the IRS.

Again, setting up and managing these arrangements requires substantial professional fees. They must comply with IRS rules to avoid penalties or other tax problems. Again, such arrangements should be undertaken only with professional assistance.

IRA Transfers to Charity

Individuals age 70½ and older may make direct transfers from their IRAs to public charities up to $108,000 in 2025, called qualified charitable distributions (QCDs). No charitable contribution deduction may be claimed for the transfer, but the distribution is not taxable. The rules for QCDs are explained in greater detail in Chapter 5. This transfer option may be especially appealing to seniors who want to benefit their favorite charity but who do not itemize their deductions and could not claim a charitable deduction in any event in 2025.

Another way to benefit a charity from an IRA, as mentioned earlier, is a one-time rollover of up to $54,000 in 2025 for charitable gift annuities, charitable remainder unitrusts, and charitable remainder annuity trusts. You elect to treat this as a QCD. This is also explained in Chapter 5.

Leave-Based Donation Programs

Your employer may offer a leave-based donation program that is used to help co-workers who need help when out because of illness or other event. You give up your vacation, sick, or personal leave that other employees may use as needed. You are taxed on your contributed compensation and you cannot treat this as a charitable contribution. From time to time, the IRS may allow special treatment for employees who donate their unused leave time to a company program (e.g., in 2020 and 2021 for COVID-19 relief needs; in 2022 for Ukraine relief due to the Russian invasion; and in 2023 for victims of the August 2023 Hawaii wildfire). In this situation, employees are not taxed on their contributions to the program provided the employer donates the contributions to a charity for relief; the employer claims the charitable contribution deduction. No special designation has been made for 2025, but check the Supplement for any update.

Record Keeper for Your Charitable Giving

Use the record keeper in Table 6.2 to note cash contributions you make throughout the year. Include in this record your weekly donations in the church plate and similar donations. Obtain a written acknowledgment from the charity for these donations.

TABLE 6.2 Record Keeper for Your Cash Donations

Date	Name of Charity	Amount of Donation
		$
		$
		$
		$
		$
		$
		$
		$
		$
		$
		$
		$
		$
		$
		$
		$
		$

Your Car or Truck

Americans love their cars and trucks. According to Hedges & Company, there were 296.6 million vehicles registered in the United States as of 2024. Vehicles can be expensive to buy or lease and to operate, especially with today's high fuel prices. Federal tax law provides some relief for your vehicle use by way of tax write-offs.

This chapter explains the tax breaks you can take for your vehicle, which includes a car, light truck (pick-up), or van. For convenience, they are referred to in this chapter collectively as "car" or "vehicle." Deducting the use of your car for medical-related travel is discussed in Chapter 2. Deducting the use of your car when working as a volunteer for charity or donating the car to charity is discussed in Chapter 6.

For more information, see IRS Publication 463, *Travel, Gift, and Car Expenses* and IRS Publication 535, *Business Expenses*.

Business Use of Your Personal Car

According to the U.S. Department of Transportation's Federal Highway Administration, Americans drive their cars on average over 14,000 miles each year. The average miles for trucks is even higher. The cost of driving can be high when you factor in fuel, insurance, and other costs. But the tax law lets a portion of the cost of this mileage be deductible under certain circumstances.

Benefit

If you use your personal car or pickup truck for business and you are self-employed, you can deduct expenses related to the business use of your car. For example, if you are an independent contractor (not an employee) and use your car to drive for Uber or Lyft, you are eligible for a deduction.

There is a choice of methods for claiming your deduction: You can deduct your actual expenses, including an allowance for depreciation if you own your car or lease payments if you lease it ("actual expense method"), or you can claim the IRS standard mileage rate.

The IRS standard mileage rate is 70¢ per mile for business driving in 2025. Whichever method you select, you can also deduct parking and tolls that are business expenses (and not for personal commuting).

There is no overall dollar limit on what you can deduct for your car use each year. But if you own your car and use the actual expense method, there are dollar limits on how much you can deduct for depreciation or first-year expensing (unless your car weighs more than 6,000 pounds).

If your employer reimburses you for business use of your car under an "accountable plan," you do not have to report the reimbursements as income (the reimbursements are not even included on your Form W-2); the reimbursements are tax free. Ask your employer if reimbursements are made under an accountable plan, or check your W-2 form.

Conditions

To claim write-offs for business use of your personal car you merely have to keep good records, as explained later. Even so, *what* you can deduct may be limited by certain conditions.

STANDARD MILEAGE RATE

You can use the IRS standard mileage rate of 70¢ per mile in 2025 whether you own or lease your car. The standard mileage rate takes the place of separately deducting gas or charging station fees, oil, repairs, new tires, vehicle registration fees, insurance, and depreciation if you own the car, or lease payments if you lease the car.

You cannot base your car deduction on the standard mileage rate if you have depreciated your car or claimed first-year expensing. This would have occurred if you owned your car in a previous year and claimed the actual expense method.

If you use the standard mileage rate and own the car, you must reduce the basis of your car by a set amount—33¢ per mile in 2025.

ACTUAL EXPENSE METHOD

Instead of using the standard mileage rate you can deduct your actual costs, which is referred to as the actual expense method.

Depreciation. If you own your car and use the actual expense method, you can claim an allowance for depreciation (including bonus depreciation) or elect first-year expensing. Cars are treated as 5-year property; for depreciation purposes they have a 5-year recovery period. Because of a special rule, a part of the depreciation allowance is limited in the first year so that the balance must be claimed in a sixth year if you still own the car at that time. (Remember, you apply depreciation only to the business-use portion of the car, and you can use accelerated depreciation only if the car is used more than 50% for business; if business use is 50% or less, you are limited to straight line depreciation.)

If you use accelerated depreciation (and are not subject to a special rule called the midquarter convention, which applies if you place more than 40% of all of your depreciable property in service in the last quarter of the year), your depreciation rates are:

- Year 1 (the year the car is placed in service): 20%
- Year 2: 32%
- Year 3: 19.2%
- Year 4: 11.52%
- Year 5: 11.52%
- Year 6: 5.76%

Example

In January 2025, you buy a car for $38,000 and use it 60% for business and 40% for personal purposes. You do not use first-year expensing or bonus depreciation. Assume that your business-personal use percentages remain constant so that the business-use portion of the car for depreciation purposes is $22,800 ($38,000 × 60%). Here is your depreciation amount for each year (subject to the dollar limits discussed later).

Year 1: $4,560

Year 2: $7,296

Year 3: $4,378

Year 4: $2,627

Year 5: $2,627

Year 6: $1,313

Instead of depreciating the business-use portion of your car, you can elect to expense it in the year it is bought and placed in service. Like depreciation, this option may be restricted to a dollar limit, explained next.

Dollar limit. Unless your car has a rated weight of more than 6,000 pounds, if it is a "luxury vehicle" (the cost depends on the year it was placed in service), your allowance for depreciation (the percentages listed earlier in the chapter, including 20% for the first year) or first-year expensing is limited to a dollar amount fixed by the IRS. More specifically, the depreciation limit is the lower of 20% of the basis (cost) of the vehicle or the IRS dollar limit. Table 7.1 shows the dollar limits for passenger cars, which apply as well to light trucks and vans, placed in service in 2025.

Example

In November 2025, you buy a car costing $110,000 and use it 80% for business and 20% for personal purposes. Your dollar limit is $16,160 (80% of $20,200). The dollar limit is lower than 20% depreciation of the $17,600 (20% of $80,000) portion used for business, so the full amount of the depreciation allowance can be deducted.

The full amount of the dollar limit on depreciation applies only if the car is used 100% for business. If the car is used partly for business, you must allocate the dollar limit.

TABLE 7.1 Dollar Limit on Depreciation of Passenger Cars

Date Car Placed in Service	1st Year	2nd Year	3rd Year	4th and Later Years
2025	$20,200*	$19,600	$11,800	$7,060
2024	20,400*	19,800	11,900	7,160
2023	20,200*	19,500	11,700	6,960
2022	19,200*	18,000	10,800	6,460
2021	18,200*	16,400	9,800	5,860
2019–2020	18,100*	16,100	9,700	5,760

*$8,000 less if you elect not to use bonus depreciation.

If the vehicle weighs more than 6,000 pounds but not more than 14,000 pounds, as is the case for a heavy SUV used in business, you can elect to expense its cost up to $31,500; the dollar limits in Table 7.1 do not apply in this case.

Safe harbor method when claiming bonus depreciation. If you claimed bonus depreciation for a vehicle placed in service in 2019, 2020, 2021, 2022, or in 2025 and later you can continue to claim depreciation on it only if you follow the rules set forth in Rev. Proc. 2019-13. Essentially, this means figuring depreciation for years following the placed-in-service year using the percentage found in Appendix A of IRS Publication 946 (https://www.irs.gov/pub/irs-pdf/p946.pdf). Use Table A-1 of Appendix A if the half-year convention applies (the usual situation) or Table A-2 if the mid-quarter convention applies. The depreciation claimed each year is the lower of the amount figured using the applicable table or the dollar limit in Table 7.1.

Example

In 2022, you placed in service a car costing $60,000 for which 100% bonus depreciation was used (assume no Section 179 deduction was claimed and the mid-quarter convention does not apply). As a result, $19,200 was deducted in 2022, leaving a remaining adjusted depreciable basis for the car of $40,800 ($60,000 − $19,200). For 2023 through 2026, figure depreciation using the annual rate in Appendix A of IRS Publication 946. Assume that the rates in Table A-1 apply here. For 2023, the depreciation allowance is $13,056 (32% × $40,800), which is less than the dollar limit of $18,000 for the second year for a car placed in service in 2022 (from Table 7.1 in this chapter). Total depreciation allowed for the vehicle through its recovery period will be $51,332, as follows:

Taxable Year	Dollar Limit (Table 7.1 of This Chapter)	Depreciation under Table A-1 of Publication 946
2022	$19,200	$19,200
2023	$18,000	$13,056 ($40,800 × 32%)
2024	$10,800	$ 7,834 ($40,800 × 19.2%)
2025	$ 6,460	$ 4,716 ($40,800 × 11.52%)
2026	$ 6,460	$ 4,716 ($40,800 × 11.52%)
2027	$ 6,460	$ 2,350 ($40,800 × 5.76%)
TOTAL		$51,332

For 2028, the depreciation deduction is $6,460, which is the lesser of the adjusted depreciable basis of $8,668 ($60,000 − $51,332) or the dollar limit of $6,460. The remaining basis of $2,208 is deducted in 2029, assuming the vehicle is still owned at that time.

Non-personal use vehicles. Vans and trucks that are not suitable for personal use (e.g., they have permanent shelving, a front jump seat, or a permanent business sign) can be depreciated or expensed without any dollar limit.

SUBSTANTIATION

Whether you use the standard mileage rate or the actual expense method, you *must* keep good records to back up your deduction for business use of your car. If you fail to do so, you can lose some or all of your deduction. Here's what your records should show:

- Mileage (your odometer reading at the start and end of each trip for business purposes). A court has indicated that you cannot merely note the length of the trip (e.g., 10 miles) but must record the actual odometer readings for the trip.
- Date, destination, and purpose for the trip (when you used your car, the customers or clients you visited, and the reason for taking the trip).
- Costs for gas, oil, electric charging, and other car-related expenses. *Note:* If you claim the standard mileage rate, you do not have to keep track of these costs.

Planning Tips

At the start and end of the year, note your odometer reading in your records. Then use a diary, logbook, or app on your smartphone to record your business mileage throughout the year. Knowing your annual mileage and what part of it represents your business mileage will allow you to properly allocate your car expenses.

You can simplify your recordkeeping for car use with a method called "sampling." This allows you to keep records for only a part of the year and then extrapolate the business mileage for the entire year. You can use this method *only* if the portion of the year in which you kept records (e.g., the first quarter of the year) is representative of car use throughout the year.

If you claim the standard mileage rate for business use of your vehicle, you must reduce the basis of the vehicle by business use each year, based on a cents-per-mile rate. Table 7.2 shows you the cents-per-mile rates used to reduce the basis of the vehicle. It is a good idea to keep a running list of this information, which is needed when you sell the vehicle.

TABLE 7.2 Cents-Per-Mile Rates for Basis Reduction Purposes

Year	Cents-Per-Mile Rate
2019	26
2020	27
2021–2022	26
2023	28
2024	30
2025	33

Example

You bought your vehicle and placed it in service at the start of 2022 and drove it 15,000 for business each year. You sell the vehicle at the end of 2025. Your basis adjustment for purposes of determining gain or loss on the sale is $17,550 ($3,900 for 2022, $4,200 for 2023, $4,500 for 2024, and $4,950 for 2025).

For more details and strategies for deducting the expenses of using your car for business, see *J.K. Lasser's Small Business Taxes 2026*.

Pitfalls

If you are an employee and drive your vehicle on company business, you cannot take any deduction for your costs. This is so whether you own or lease your vehicle. There are exceptions for armed forces reservists, qualified performing artists, fee-based government officials, and disabled employees with impairment-related work expenses.

Assuming you're eligible to deduct vehicle expenses, if you own your car and you want to use the IRS standard mileage rate, you must elect to do so in the first year of use. Otherwise you are limited to deducting your actual expenses. For example, if you bought and used your car for business in 2024 and used the actual expense method for claiming a deduction for business use, you cannot use the IRS standard mileage rate in 2025 for this car.

If you lease your car and claim a deduction under the actual expense method, you may have to include a phantom amount in income. This is called the *inclusion amount* and is designed to equate write-offs for leased cars with those that are purchased. The inclusion amount is generally a modest figure that you take from an IRS table created for this purpose. You include only the portion of

TABLE 7.3 Sample Inclusion Amounts for Cars First Leased in 2025*

Fair Market Value		Tax Year during Lease				
Over	Not Over	1	2	3	4	Later
$ 62,000	$ 64,000	$13	$26	$36	$43	$50
70,000	72,000	63	136	201	240	277
80,000	85,000	135	295	437	522	604
90,000	95,000	198	434	641	768	888
100,000	110,000	277	606	898	1,076	1,242

*Figures for all inclusion amounts are at https://www.irs.gov/pub/irs-drop/rp-25-16.pdf.

the inclusion amount related to your car use. For example, if you use your car only 25% for business, you include only 25% of the applicable inclusion amount. Table 7.3 shows you some sample inclusion amounts for passenger cars, light trucks, and vans first leased in 2025.

Inclusion amounts for vehicles leased prior to 2025 can be found in IRS Publication 463, *Travel, Gift, and Car Expenses*.

Where to Claim the Benefit

As a self-employed person, if you use your car for both business and personal purposes, you can deduct expenses related to your business use on Schedule C of Form 1040 or 1040-SR.

If you own your car and are required to file Form 4562, *Depreciation and Amortization* (you are claiming depreciation on property placed in service in 2025), complete Part V of the form. Be sure to answer the question about whether you have written evidence of your claimed use.

If you are not required to file Form 4562, you must answer the questions about your car use in Part IV of Schedule C. These questions concern your mileage for business and personal use and whether you have written evidence to support your deduction.

Employer-Provided Car

Perhaps one of the most helpful employee benefits is the so-called company car, which means that the business pays for a car you are allowed to use not only for business travel but also for personal purposes. The extent, if any, to which you are taxed on use of a company car depends on several factors, including *how* you are using the car.

Benefit ⊗

If you use a company-owned car *only* on company business, you are not taxed on this use of the company car because it is for business (it is tax-free income to you). Similarly, if you use a certain type of company vehicle for personal use, you are not taxed on this benefit because the IRS views you as having limited personal use (it is tax-free income to you). Such vehicles include: ambulances; hearses; flatbed trucks; dump, garbage, and refrigerated trucks; one-passenger delivery trucks (even if there is a folding jump seat); tractors and other farm equipment; and forklifts. The same exclusion from income applies to vehicles where personal use is restricted or authorized only by a government authority: school buses, passenger buses, moving vans, and police and fire vehicles (including unmarked cars).

Unfortunately, if you are given unfettered use of a company-owned car that you use for personal purposes, you are taxed on this personal use. But the tax cost is substantially less than what it would cost you to own the car yourself. The value of this use is reported on your Form W-2.

Example

In 2025, your employer allows you to use a company car for personal purposes and you do so 25% of the time the car is used (the rest of the use is strictly for business). Assuming the car's value is $20,000, your employer includes in your income $1,400 (based on the annual lease value method for determining the value of personal use: $5,600 annual lease value of the car × 25%). If you are in the 24% tax bracket, this added income results in additional tax of $336. In effect, it costs you just $336 to use your company's car for personal purposes for the year.

If you are a full-time car salesperson who is allowed to use demonstration cars for personal use, you are not taxed on this benefit (it is tax-free income to you), provided there are restrictions on personal use. For example, personal use after normal business hours might be restricted to a 75-mile radius of the dealer's sales office or you might not be allowed to drive family members or use the car for vacation trips.

If you are an employee you can't claim any deduction for business driving of your personal vehicle. Similarly, if your employer provides you with a vehicle and chooses to include all of its use by you (business and personal) as compensation, you cannot deduct the business driving on your return.

Condition

To fully exclude the value of using a company car, your personal use must be restricted or the company vehicle must be one of those listed earlier.

Planning Tip

Your employer is *not* required to withhold income taxes on your personal use of a company car. If there is no withholding for car use and you have not paid enough taxes throughout the year by means of withholding or estimated tax payments, you may wind up owing taxes at the end of the year. You may wish to voluntarily increase your withholding if you know that your employer will not withhold taxes for your car use to avoid the problem. Complete a new Form W-4 and give it to your employer to increase your withholding.

Pitfall

As an employee you cannot deduct any business driving on your personal tax return.

Where to Claim the Benefit

If you are not taxed on using the company car (i.e., your employer does not report it on your Form W-2), you do not have to report anything on your return.

If your employer reports only the actual value of your personal use of a company car, again you do not have to do anything on your return. This income is included in your compensation and reported as such on your return.

Vehicle Registration Fees

One way in which states raise revenues is through the fees they charge for certain activities, including registering cars and other vehicles. The cost of registration may be deductible under certain conditions.

Benefit 🌐

The state registration fees you pay for your vehicle may be deductible. If your car is used only for personal purposes and you itemize deductions, you can deduct auto registration fees based on the value of the car as a state personal property tax if certain conditions are met. You must itemize your deductions to be able to deduct this expense and your overall deduction for state and local taxes (SALT) is subject in 2025 to a $40,000 overall cap ($20,000 if you're married filing separately) (see Chapter 4 under "Real Estate Taxes").

Conditions

To deduct auto registration fees as a state personal property tax, you must meet all 3 requirements:

1. The fee is an ad valorem tax. This means the fee is based on a percentage of the car's value, for example, 1% of the value. Table 7.4 lists the states that satisfy this requirement. Some of these states don't impose the tax, but counties within them do.

2. The fee is imposed on an annual basis, even though it is collected more or less frequently.

3. The fee is imposed on personal property.

4. The fee, plus your other state and local taxes, does not exceed the SALT cap.

If the tax or fee is based on weight, model, year, or horsepower, it is not deductible. But if the tax is based on *both* value and another factor, the portion based on value is deductible.

TABLE 7.4 **States with Ad Valorem Taxes***

Alabama	Michigan
Arizona	Minnesota
Arkansas	Mississippi
California	Missouri
Colorado	Montana
Connecticut	Nebraska
Georgia**	Nevada
Indiana	New Hampshire
Iowa	North Carolina
Kansas	Rhode Island
Kentucky	South Carolina
Louisiana	Virginia
Maine	West Virginia
Massachusetts	Wyoming

*In some states there may be county-imposed ad valorem taxes instead of or in addition to state taxes.
**One-time title ad valorem tax.

Example

Your vehicle registration fee is 1% of the car's value, plus 40¢ per hundredweight. You can deduct the 1% portion as a personal property tax.

Planning Tips

Check with your state to learn if you are exempt from this tax because of your status (e.g., a discharged veteran; a disabled first responder).

If you have questions about whether your state's registration fee is deductible in whole or in part, contact your state tax authority.

If you pay a fee for a vanity license plate, you can deduct the cost in excess of the regular fee as a charitable contribution provided the state gives the funds to a charity and you itemize deductions (see Chapter 5).

Pitfall

There is no downside to deducting auto registration fees as a personal property tax if you are eligible to do so. But the fees are subject in 2025 to the SALT cap.

Where to Claim the Benefit

If you are deducting auto registration fees on your personal car as a state personal property tax, you must file Schedule A of Form 1040 or 1040-SR.

Car Accidents and Other Car-Related Problems

On average, there are over 6 million car accidents in the United States each year. Whether a car is partially damaged or totaled, an owner may have out-of-pocket costs. These may be limited to the insurance deductible or may be a greater amount. The tax law may allow for a write-off, even if the car is used exclusively for personal reasons and not at all for business.

You cannot deduct any property loss from a car accident or as a result of a basic casualty event, such as a fire or storm. But if your car is damaged or destroyed in a federally-declared disaster, such as the California wildfires in January 2025, you may have a deductible loss (see Chapter 12).

Donating Your Car

If you donate your car to a tax-exempt organization, you may be entitled to claim a deduction for the car's fair market value. For more details, see Chapter 6.

Deduction for Car Loans

The average new-vehicle interest rate for a car loan in the first quarter of 2025 was 7.1%, and 20% of buyers took 7-year loans. About 85% of new car purchases and 53% of used car purchases are financed. If you buy a vehicle in 2025 and finance the purchase, you may be able to deduct the interest you pay on the car loan.

Benefit

The deduction for interest on car loans can be claimed whether or not you itemize. The annual limit on the interest deduction is the amount of interest paid up $10,000.

Conditions

The deduction applies to interest on loans taken after December 31, 2024, to purchase a passenger vehicle. There are 3 conditions:

1. *Income.* The full deduction is limited to individuals with modified adjusted gross income up to $100,000, or $200,000 on a joint return. If MAGI exceeds these limits, the deduction phases out. The deduction is reduced by $200 for every $1,000 of excess MAGI. No deduction can be claimed if MAGI is $149,001 or higher for singles, or $249,001 for joint filers.

2. *Type of vehicle.* The deduction applies to any new passenger vehicle made for street or highway use, including cars, vans, minivans, SUVs, pickup trucks, or motorcycles. It also applies to all-terrain vehicles (ATVs) and recreational vehicles (RV)s. The vehicle must have its final assembly in the United States Vehicles can be powered by fossil fuel, hybrid, electric, or other fuel source.

3. *Date of loan.* The deduction applies only to loans obtained in 2025, 2026, 2027, or 2028. Interest on pre-2025 loans doesn't count.

Planning Tips

How do you know how much interest you paid during the year? For a 2025 loan, the lender is required to provide you with an information return no later than February 2, 2026, containing all of the information needed to complete your return. This includes the loan origination date, the amount of interest paid during the year, the outstanding principal of the loan, and the year, make, and model of the vehicle securing the loan.

If you were planning to pay cash for a vehicle purchase, should you instead finance it if you can deduct some or all of the interest? Look closely at the numbers to see if it makes financial sense. If you qualify for the maximum deduction of $10,000, it would save you $2,200 (this assumes you're in the 22% tax bracket).

Pitfall

The deduction is set to run only through 2028.

Where to Claim the Deduction

The deduction is claimed on Schedule 1-A of Form 1040 or 1040-SR.

Credits for Clean Vehicles

The Inflation Reduction Act of 2022 dramatically changed the incentives for buying a clean vehicle—a plug-in electric vehicle (EV), a fuel cell vehicle (FCV), or a hybrid plug-in or hybrid fuel cell vehicle. There is a tax credit for buying a new vehicle and a different credit for buying a used clean vehicle. There is also a credit for buying a commercial clean vehicle. But these credits only apply to vehicles acquired by September 30, 2025. This means that by this date there was a written binding contract and payment has been made. A payment includes a nominal downpayment or a vehicle trade-in.

Benefit ⊕

You can reduce your tax bill by claiming a tax credit for buying a clean vehicle. The maximum credit for a *new* clean vehicle is $7,500. The credit for a *used* clean vehicle is 30% of the sales price, for a top credit of $4,000.

You may have been able to sell the credit to the dealer to reduce the effective purchase price.

Conditions

Different conditions apply, depending on whether the vehicle is new or pre-owned.

NEW CLEAN VEHICLES

There are 6 conditions for claiming the tax credit for buying a new clean vehicle.

1. *Purchase price limit*. Only a vehicle having a manufacturers' suggested retail price (MSRP) of no more than an applicable limit can qualify for the credit. The applicable limit is $80,000 for vans, sports utility vehicles, and pickup trucks, and $55,000 for other vehicles (e.g., sedans).

2. *Income limit*. Modified adjusted gross income (MAGI) cannot exceed $300,000 for joint filers and surviving spouses, $225,000 for heads

of households, and $150,000 for singles and married persons filing separately. There is no phase-out.

3. *Qualified manufacturer*. The vehicle must have a battery capacity of at least 7 kilowatt hours and a gross vehicle weight rating of less than 14,000 pounds. EVs must be made by a qualified manufacturer. FCVs don't need to be made by a qualified manufacturer to be eligible for the credit.

4. *Final assembly requirement*. The final assembly of the vehicle must occur in North America. The Department of Energy has a vehicle identification number tool at https://afdc.energy.gov/laws/electric-vehicles-for-tax-credit; enter the VIN and see whether the vehicle meets the final assembly requirement.

5. *Critical minerals and battery component requirements*. For 2025, the value of critical minerals extracted in the U.S. must be 60%. For 2025, the value of battery components manufactured in the U.S. or assembled in North America must be 60%. No credit can be claimed for vehicles with battery minerals or components from a foreign entity of concern. These include China, Iran, North Korea, and Russia.

6. *Reporting*. The seller must furnish a report to you and the IRS containing your name and your taxpayer identification number (e.g., Social Security number), the 17-character vehicle identification number (VIN), battery capacity, date of sale and sales price of the vehicle, and the maximum credit allowable for the vehicle. The seller must sign a statement under penalty of perjury. You must include the VIN on your tax return when claiming the credit. You can "sell" the credit to the dealer as a way of reducing the purchase price. This effectively lowers the down payment. The dealer must be registered with the IRS for this purpose. The IRS has made it clear that if a buyer eligible for the credit does not have sufficient taxable income to have fully used it if he or she waited to claim the credit when filing the return, there is no clawback—not from the taxpayer and not from the dealer. When selling the credit to the dealer, there is a lot of paperwork; be prepared.

USED CLEAN VEHICLES

There are 5 conditions for claiming the tax credit for buying a previously-owned clean vehicle.

1. *Purchase price*. The cost of the vehicle cannot exceed $25,000.

2. *Qualified vehicle*. The model year of the vehicle must be at least 2 years earlier than the calendar year in which you buy the vehicle. The vehicle must have a gross vehicle weight rating of less than 14,000 pounds and be made by a qualified manufacturer as explained earlier for new clean vehicles.

3. ***Income limit.*** A buyer is eligible for the credit only if modified adjusted gross income does not exceed $150,000 for joint filers and surviving spouses, $112,500 for heads of households, and $75,000 for singles and married persons filing separately. There is no phase-out.

4. ***Qualified sale.*** The used clean vehicle must be purchased from a dealer. It must be the vehicle's first sale to a qualified buyer since August 16, 2022, other than to the original owner.

5. ***Reporting.*** The dealer must furnish a report to you and the IRS containing your name and taxpayer identification number (e.g., Social Security number), the dealer's name and taxpayer identification number (e.g., employer identification number, or EIN), the 17-character vehicle identification number (VIN), battery capacity, date of sale and sales price of the vehicle, and the maximum credit allowable for the vehicle. The dealer must sign the statement under penalty of perjury. You must include the VIN on your tax return when claiming the credit. Just like in the case of a purchase of a new clean vehicle, you can "sell" the credit for a used clean vehicle to the dealer as a way of reducing the purchase price. This effectively lowers the down payment. The dealer must be registered with the IRS for this purpose. The IRS has made it clear that if a buyer eligible for the credit does not have sufficient taxable income to have fully used it if he or she waited to claim the credit when filing the return, there is no clawback—not from the taxpayer and not from the dealer. When selling the credit to the dealer, there is a lot of paperwork; be prepared.

CREDIT FOR COMMERCIAL CLEAN VEHICLES

The credits for new clean vehicles and used clean vehicles discussed above are designed for consumers. If you are in business and it buys a clean vehicle that is subject to depreciation, there is a separate credit. The credit is the lesser of 15% of the vehicle's basis (30% if not powered by gas or diesel) or the incremental cost of the vehicle. The maximum credit is $7,500 for a vehicle with a gross vehicle weight rating (GVWR) of under 14,000 pounds and $40,000 for heavier vehicles. The credit is part of the general business credit explained in Chapter 15.

SELLING A CREDIT TO THE DEALER

If you bought a new or previously-owned EV before October 1, 2025, the dealer could have essentially given you the credit upfront (e.g., reduce the purchase price or the amount of the down payment required). The transfer of the credit to the dealer does not lower the vehicle's MSRP. What you need to know:

- Only individuals could sell the credit. This includes grantor trusts and single-member LLCs where the taxpayer's name (plus tax identification number) is listed as the owner of the trust or the taxable owner of the disregarded entity (the single-member LLC).

- You had to attest to the dealer that you're eligible for the credit (that your 2024 modified adjusted gross income [MAGI] or your estimated 2025 MAGI is below threshold amounts listed earlier in this chapter). If it turns out that your MAGI is too high, some or all of the credit may be recaptured when you file the return for the year of the purchase. But if your tax liability for that year is insufficient to have used the credit, there is no recapture—from you or the dealer.

- This option was available only for the purchase from a registered dealer, who is a seller that registered with the IRS to buy credits.

- If you failed to transfer the credit at the point of sale, you can still benefit from it by claiming it on your return if you're eligible to do so.

- You were not able to sell the commercial clean vehicle credit to a dealer.

Planning Tips

If you use a vehicle for both personal and business driving, the credit for a new or previously-owned EV is available only if the vehicle is used *predominantly* for personal use.

The tax credits are limited to *buying* a clean vehicle, but you may realize savings from leasing a clean vehicle. This results when the dealer claims a credit and passes it on to you. There is no requirement that the dealer do so, but don't hesitate to ask about it.

You may also be eligible for tax breaks on the state or local level, even for vehicles acquired after September 30, 2025. These breaks are in the form of tax credits, sales tax exemptions, and rebates. Find tax breaks in your location from the Department of Energy at https://afdc.energy.gov/laws/search and DSIRE at https://www.dsireusa.org/.

Pitfalls

You can only claim the credit in the year it is placed in service (i.e., when you take delivery). If you order a vehicle in May 2025 but don't take delivery until October 2025, you can't claim the credit on your 2025 return.

You cannot claim the credit if you are a dependent of another taxpayer.

You cannot claim the credit for a pre-owned clean vehicle if you did so within the 3-year period prior to the date the most recent pre-owned vehicle was purchased or you bought it from someone who is not a dealer.

Depending on where you live, you may pay additional registration fees for an EV.

Where to Claim the Credit

The credits for new, used, and commercial clean vehicles is claimed on Form 8936, *Clean Vehicle Credits*, and Form 8936 Schedule A, *Clean Vehicle Credit Amount*, and entered on Schedule 3 of Form 1040 or 1040-SR.

If the vehicle is used for business driving, then the credit is part of the general business credit and subject to limitations. The same form used for personal driving is used to figure the credit and then the business portion is entered on Form 3800, *General Business Credit*; the net general business credit is then entered on Schedule 3 of Form 1040 or 1040-SR.

Credit for an EV Charging Station

Having an EV requires you to charge the battery—at a public charging station, your place of business, or at home with your own charging station. The cost of a charging station for your home ranges from $300 to $1,300 or more, depending the level of the unit, its features (e.g., weather protection, Wi-Fi), length of cable, and other variables. And, depending on the amperage of the unit, you may need additional work for your electrical panel to handle the increased capacity. The good news is you may be able to claim a tax credit for the cost of the purchase and installation of the unit in your home.

Benefit

The credit amount is the lesser of 30% of the cost of hardware and installation, up to a maximum credit of $1,000 for a charging station in a residence. The credit is nonrefundable, so if it exceeds your tax liability for the year, you don't get any tax benefit.

Conditions

To claim the credit, you must be located in an eligible census tract. This means low-income or rural areas explained in Notice 2024-64.

Bidirectional charging equipment may qualify. This is refueling property that charges a motor vehicle but also returns energy to the grid or sends it to your home, appliances, or other vehicle.

Planning Pointers

The U.S. Department of Energy has a mapping tool at https://tinyurl.com/24rv86sh to help you determine if your location is within the required census tract.

Whether or not you qualify to claim a federal tax credit for installing a charging station, you may be eligible for tax breaks on the state or local level. These breaks are in the form of tax credits, sales tax exemptions, and rebates. Find tax breaks in your location from the Department of Energy at https://afdc.energy .gov/laws/search and DSIRE at https://www.dsireusa.org/.

Pitfalls

The credit applies only for charging stations installed by June 30, 2026.

The basis of your home is reduced by the amount of the credit claimed. This means that when you sell your home, your gain will be bigger. But this may not matter if all of the resulting gain is shielded by the home sale exclusion (see Chapter 4).

Where to Claim the Credit

The credit is figured on Form 8911, *Alternative Fuel Vehicle Refueling Property Credit,* and entered on Schedule 3 of Form 1040 or 1040-SR.

Investing

Putting money aside for that proverbial rainy day is an admirable and necessary goal but it can be a difficult proposition, especially when your paycheck doesn't seem to stretch far enough. Still, savings and investing are essential to your financial well-being. According to Federal Reserve Bank, the personal savings rate (the ratio of personal savings to disposable personal income) in the United States was only about 4.6% as of the second quarter of 2025. Fortunately, the tax laws can help you to make the most of your efforts. It also provides tax breaks if your investments don't work out.

Most investment-related expenses that were previously deductible as miscellaneous itemized deductions are **not** deductible. These include safe deposit box rental fees; subscriptions to investment newsletters, online services, and apps; computers and tables used for investments; and fees for financial advice.

This chapter deals with tax breaks for so-called *taxable accounts* and other investments that are not held in tax-favored retirement accounts. The tax breaks for IRAs and qualified retirement accounts, which are tax-deferred or tax-free accounts, can be found in Chapter 5. For more information, see IRS Publication 514, *Foreign Tax Credit for Individuals*; IRS Publication 525, *Taxable and Nontaxable Income*; IRS Publication 544, *Sales and Other Dispositions of Assets*; IRS Publication 550, *Investment Income and Expenses*; IRS Publication 551, *Basis of Assets*; and IRS Publication 575, *Pension and Annuity Income*.

Penalty on Early Withdrawal of Savings

Time deposit accounts and certificates of deposit are fixed for a set term. These savings vehicles, which had been paying very low interest rates in recent years but are higher now due to inflation, generally pay a higher rate of interest than money-market and passbook accounts. But if they are cashed in before maturity, a bank penalty is imposed. The penalty usually is forfeiture of some interest and, in some cases, even principal. The penalty is tax deductible.

Benefit ⬆

If you cash in a certificate of deposit (CD) or savings account before its fixed maturity date for any reason (such as you need the money to pay personal expenses or you can obtain a higher interest rate if you move the money), you may be forced to pay a penalty. The penalty is subtracted from the funds you receive.

You can deduct this penalty, which may be a forfeiture of interest and/or principal (if the penalty exceeds the interest), even though you do not itemize your other deductions. In the case of savings certificates with fixed maturities of longer than one year, your deduction is based on the forfeiture of original issue discount (which is nothing more than a way of figuring interest). Regardless of the maturity involved, this deduction is called a penalty on early withdrawal of savings. There is no dollar limit on this deduction.

Condition

There are no conditions or requirements to meet. As long as you take money out of a savings certificate before the specified maturity date and are subject to a penalty, you can deduct the penalty in full.

Planning Tip

When putting money into time-savings vehicles, such as certificates of deposit, don't extend the investment period beyond the time you *may* need the funds so that you can avoid early withdrawal penalties if you *do* need the money then. Consider splitting your savings into multiple savings certificates with different maturity dates so that you can readily have access to some funds penalty free.

> **Example**
>
> You have $10,000 for savings. Instead of putting $10,000 into a single CD for 5 years, consider putting only $5,000 in for 5 years and putting the other $5,000 into a renewable 12-month CD. Each year you know that you can obtain at least $5,000 penalty free. This will also allow some of the funds to be reinvested for higher interest rates should rates rise (but, conversely, you may lose out on your interest rate if rates decline).

Pitfalls

You cannot net the penalty against the interest you receive and eliminate the need to separately deduct the penalty. You must report all of the interest on the savings certificate and then separately deduct the early withdrawal penalty.

The 10% early distribution penalty usually imposed on withdrawals from qualified retirement plans and IRAs before age 59 ½ does not apply to early withdrawals from savings accounts.

Where to Claim the Benefit

The forfeited amount is reported to you (and the IRS) on Form 1099-INT if the certificate of deposit is for one year or less, or on Form 1099-OID if the certificate of deposit is for longer than one year. You deduct this amount on Schedule 1 of Form 1040 or 1040-SR.

Loss on Bank Deposits

During the Great Depression, there was a run on the banks; depositors rushed to withdraw their money, forcing many banks to go under. Today, there are many protections in place (such as state-mandated funding requirements and

Dodd-Frank, a federal law) to ensure the integrity of banks. But despite these protections, some banks still fail. Losses suffered by depositors of failed banks that are not insured by the Federal Deposit Insurance Corporation (FDIC) or funds not covered by FDIC protection may be tax deductible under certain conditions.

Benefit

If your bank goes under and your account is not covered in whole or in part by FDIC insurance, you can deduct your loss as a non-business bad debt. This means you can deduct your loss against capital gains. If you do not have capital gains or if these losses are greater than your capital gains, you can only deduct up to $3,000 against your ordinary income. Any unused amount of the loss can be carried forward and used in a future year. The rules for bad debts are explained more fully in Chapter 11.

Conditions

The conditions for deducting your loss on bank deposits are simple: The bank must be insolvent or bankrupt so that there is no reasonable prospect of recovering your money, and your deposits must not be covered by FDIC or state insurance.

Planning Tip

Why rely on tax write-offs to make you whole? The best option is to make sure that your deposits are adequately covered by FDIC insurance. Understand your FDIC limits so you don't expose your savings to potential loss, especially when you have accounts in separate institutions that have merged or been taken over.

The rules on FDIC coverage and a listing of the banks with this insurance protection may be found at www.fdic.gov. You can also use the Electronic Deposit Insurance Estimator (EDIE) at www.fdic.gov/edie/ to see where you stand in terms of FDIC coverage for your checking and savings accounts, money market accounts, and certificates of deposit.

Pitfall

The biggest problem with bank losses is knowing exactly what your losses really are. You may recover something when the bank's finances are settled, even if it is only pennies on the dollar. Generally the trustees of a troubled bank will give you an estimate of your expected recovery and loss.

Where to Claim the Benefit

A bad debt is reported on Form 8949, *Sales and Other Dispositions of Capital Assets*. Be sure that your loss is entered in parentheses to indicate a loss amount.

This is then entered on Schedule D, the amount of which is then reported on page 1 of Form 1040 or 1040-SR.

Capital Losses

Wouldn't it be great if every investment turned out to be profitable? Unfortunately, this isn't the way things work—despite your best efforts, investments may decline in value. A mere drop in an asset's value isn't a tax loss; there must be an actual transaction that fixes the loss. If a sale produces a loss, it may be tax deductible.

Benefit

In today's volatile stock market, as well as trading in cryptocurrencies, it's not uncommon to have losses. Capital losses are deductible in full (there is no dollar limit) as an offset to your capital gains for the year. If your capital losses exceed your gains for the year, up to $3,000 of capital losses can be used to offset ordinary income, such as salary and interest income. If your capital losses are more than this $3,000 limit ($1,500 if married filing separately), you can carry the excess forward indefinitely to be used in a future year. The $3,000 limit has not been increased since 1978.

Understand what capital losses are so that you can plan wisely to get the greatest tax benefit from your losses. Capital losses generally arise on the sale or other disposition of capital assets, such as stocks, collectibles, or real estate. Your loss is the difference between what you receive on the sale and your adjusted basis in the property (usually what you paid for it).

Example

In 2022, you bought 100 shares of X Corporation for $10,000. In December 2025, you sell those shares for $6,000. You have a $4,000 capital loss ($10,000 basis − $6,000 proceeds on the sale). If this is your only capital transaction for the year, you can deduct $3,000 in the current year as an offset to ordinary income and carry forward $1,000 ($4,000 − $3,000) to the next year.

There are 2 classes of capital losses: short-term losses resulting from assets held one year or less and long-term losses resulting from assets held more than one year. As a practical matter, while complex rules govern the order in which capital losses are used to offset different categories of capital gains, in the end capital losses can be used to fully offset capital gains.

Conditions

You usually must sell or otherwise dispose of an asset to have a deductible loss. A mere decline in the value of an asset you continue to hold does not entitle you to claim a loss. There are exceptions to the disposition requirement (e.g., a bad debt is treated as a short-term capital loss even though the debt is not sold or otherwise disposed of).

As mentioned earlier, the loss must be with respect to a capital asset. And this asset must be held for investment or business purposes. You cannot deduct a capital loss on an asset held primarily for personal purposes, such as your home, personal car, or boat.

Planning Tips

Don't overlook basis adjustments that may increase your loss by increasing your basis. Take into account:

- Stock dividends you reinvested in the same company
- Brokers' commissions
- Acquisition costs (e.g., attorney's fees to handle the purchase of real estate)
- Selling costs (e.g., real estate broker's fees)

At year-end, review your investment portfolio to see if there are capital losses you want to harvest for tax advantage. But always temper your tax planning with investment considerations. Don't sell only to generate losses; let your investment decisions be driven primarily by economics (e.g., you think the investment will never recover or there are better places to put your investment dollars).

Pitfalls

While you may have an economic loss on a transaction, do not automatically assume it qualifies for capital loss treatment for tax purposes. Certain pitfalls may trip you up.

WASH SALE RULE

You cannot claim a loss if you acquire substantially identical securities within 30 days before or after the date of sale. Under this *wash sale rule*, you do not lose the loss entirely. Instead, you adjust the basis of the newly acquired securities to reflect the loss you could not take. This will enable you to claim the loss when you later sell the newly acquired securities in a transaction that is not subject to the wash sale rule.

What is a substantially identical security? If you sold shares in Nvidia at a loss on March 14, 2025, and purchase shares in Nvidia on April 10, 2025, you are subject to the wash sale rule. But if you sold shares in Lululemon Athletica at a loss on March 14 and bought shares in Tesla on April 10, the wash sale rule does not apply because these are different companies and their stocks are not substantially identical securities.

If you sell a Netflix bond at a loss on March 14, 2025, bearing an interest rate of 4.875% payable in 2029, and purchase a Netflix bond on April 10, 2025, bearing an interest rate of 3.625% payable in 2031, you are *not* subject to the wash sale rule. The differences in the coupon rates and maturities of these bonds make them different securities.

Also, if you sell stock at a loss in your personal investment account and then you cause your IRA or other tax-advantaged account to buy the identical stock within the wash sale period, you cannot take the loss.

To date, the wash sale rule does not apply to sales of digital assets (although one court indicated that hedge funds were subject to the rule for their holdings). There is sentiment in Congress to extend the wash sale rule to Bitcoin and other digital assets for all taxpayers; check the Supplement for any update.

OTHER PITFALLS

You cannot claim a capital loss on the sale or other disposition of all property. Some types of property are not classified as capital assets so they do not qualify for capital loss treatment:

- Business inventory and property held for sale to customers
- Depreciable business property and rental property
- Copyrights, literary compositions, letters, or other such property that you created, that you acquired by gifts from the persons who created them, or that were created for you
- Government publications

If a spouse incurs the capital loss and dies, the loss can be used only in the year of death. Excess capital losses cannot be carried forward and used by a surviving spouse in a later year.

As mentioned earlier, you may not claim a loss on personal-use property, such as on the sale of your residence, vacation property, or personal car. You can claim a loss only on assets held for investment and which are not otherwise excluded from capital loss treatment. While you may view your home as an investment (perhaps your greatest investment), the tax law does not.

INHERITED PROPERTY

As explained earlier, the capital losses you can deduct are the difference between what you receive on the sale or other disposition and your tax basis (usually what you paid for the items). In the case of inherited property that was part of an estate that filed a federal estate tax return, your tax basis for an item of property is reported to you on Form 8971. If you don't receive this form (e.g., the estate is too small to be required to file a federal estate tax return), your tax basis is the value of the property on the date of the decedent's death (or 6 months later if the estate makes an election).

Where to Claim the Loss

To claim capital losses, you must file Form 8949, *Sales and Other Dispositions of Capital Assets*, and Schedule D to figure the deductible amount. Short-term transactions are entered in Part I of Form 8949; long-term transactions are entered in Part II of Form 8949. The form has 3 different ways to determine basis: transactions listed on Form 1099-B with basis included, transactions listed on Form 1099-B without basis included, and transactions not reported on Form 1099-B. You must use a separate Form 8949 for each type of basis determination. Gains and losses are netted in each of these parts and then short-term gains or losses are carried over to Parts I and II of Schedule D and then netted against long-term gains or losses in Part III of Schedule D. Make sure that the amount of any loss entered in column (f) of Schedule D is within parentheses to indicate a loss amount.

You enter the amount of your net capital loss from Part III of Schedule D onto Form 1040 or 1040-SR.

Capital Gains and Qualified Dividends

Normally, net capital gains, capital gains distributions, and qualified dividends are taxed at a top rate of 15%. Those with taxable income below a threshold amount that depends on filing status have a *zero* capital gains tax rate. And those with taxable income above a threshold amount that depends on filing status have a 20% capital gains tax rate.

Benefit

If you qualify, you pay *no* tax on net capital gains (net long-term capital gains in excess of net short-term capital losses), capital gain distributions from certain mutual funds, and qualified dividends.

Conditions

To qualify for the zero tax rate, your taxable income must be below a set amount. Table 8.1 shows the upper limit for taxable income (defined later) that you can receive and still have zero tax on capital gains. The potential zero-tax income (e.g., qualified dividends) is taken into account in determining whether you fall within this threshold.

TABLE 8.1 2025 Ceiling on Taxable Income for Zero Tax Rate

Filing Status	Taxable Income Limit
Single	$48,350
Head of household	64,750
Married filing jointly and surviving spouse	96,900
Married filing separately	48,350

Taxable income is adjusted gross income reduced by the standard deduction or itemized deductions, the qualified disaster loss deduction for non-itemizers, 4 new personal deductions from Schedule 1-A, and the 20% qualified business income (QBI) deduction for owners of pass-through entities; it does not take tax credits into account.

The gains must be from property held long term (usually more than one year). Capital gains distributions and qualified dividends are identified as such on Form 1099-DIV.

Planning Tips

Just because taxable income is above the threshold amount for your filing status does not mean you lose out entirely on the zero tax rate. Depending on your filing status, taxable income, and qualified dividends and capital gains, you may be able to use the zero rate for some of your dividends and capital gains.

If you receive at least one payment for the sale after the year of sale, you have transacted an ***installment sale***. As such, you automatically report the gain as you receive payments. But you can elect out of installment reporting to recognize the entire gain in the year of the sale. Not all property qualifies for installment reporting treatment.

Pitfalls

Receiving too much income in capital gains can push you into a higher tax bracket and void the use of the zero tax rate. For example, say you are single and you estimate that your taxable income for the year will be $42,000. You then sell property you've held for years at a profit of $10,000. This gain will put you over the $48,350 threshold for your filing status, preventing your gain from being fully tax free.

If your taxable income exceeds the threshold in Table 8.1, you pay a tax rate of 15% on your capital gains. But if your income exceeds the threshold in Table 8.2, the applicable tax rate is 20%.

TABLE 8.2 2025 Taxable Income Triggering 20% Tax Rate

Filing Status	Taxable Income Limit
Single	Over $533,400
Head of household	Over $566,700
Married filing jointly and surviving spouse	Over $600,050
Married filing separately	Over $300,000

Where to Claim the Benefit

Dividends and capital gains must be reported on the return, even though they may be tax free because of the zero tax rate. Dividends are reported directly on Form 1040 or 1040-SR, or first on Schedule B if qualified interest and ordinary dividends for the year exceed $1,500. Capital gains distributions and capital gains must be reported on Schedule D and then on Form 1040 or 1040-SR.

Worthless Securities

Investments in a corporation—stocks or bonds—are made with the intention of collecting income and/or making a profit. But some corporations go under and investors are left holding the bag. The tax law allows a deduction for worthless securities. Special rules for losses resulting from Ponzi schemes are discussed later in this chapter.

Benefit 🔾

If you hold stocks or bonds issued with coupons or in registered form that become worthless, you can deduct your investment. Worthless securities are treated as becoming worthless on the last day of the year in which they actually become worthless. This date governs whether the loss is treated as a short-term loss (if you held the security no more than one year prior to December 31) or a long-term loss (if you held the security more than one year prior to December 31).

The loss is treated as a capital loss (discussed earlier in this chapter), even though there is no sale involved. But if the loss relates to Section 1244 stock (discussed later in this chapter), the loss is treated as an ordinary loss up to $50,000 ($100,000 on a joint return).

Conditions

There are 2 conditions you must meet to write off your investment in worthless securities:

1. The security must have had some value at the end of the prior year.
2. The security must have become *totally* worthless.

VALUE IN THE PRIOR YEAR

To claim a loss in 2025, you must show that the stock or bond had some value on December 31, 2024. Generally, you can learn whether the stock has any value by checking your year-end statements from brokerage firms holding your investment. If you hold publicly traded stock in your own name rather than in the brokerage firm's name ("street name"), check newspapers for December 31 to see if the stock is listed in the financial section (only stock with a value is listed in the papers). For example, Enron stock officially became worthless on November 17, 2004 (so the loss was claimed on December 31, 2004), even though the corporation filed for Chapter 7 bankruptcy in 2001. (Chapter 7 bankruptcy is a liquidation process used to go out of business forever.) In early 2025, it was reported that bankruptcy filings were up 14.2% during 2024, but most of them as Chapter 11 reorganizations, which do not make their securities worthless. But there were some Chapter 7 filings in 2025, such as Brueprint Brewing Co. (a brewery that sold beer through Whole Foods and others) and Polished.com (Goedeker's) (a furniture/appliance store).

TOTALLY WORTHLESS

The stock or bond must have *no* value by the end of the year in which you claim the loss. Just because a bond has stopped paying interest or a stock has been delisted from an exchange does not mean it is totally worthless. If you claim a loss, be prepared to present facts showing your security is worthless. You can assume that it is worthless if the company issuing it:

- Goes into bankruptcy that results in a liquidation of the company
- Ceases to do business
- Becomes insolvent

Don't assume that a security is worthless if the company has plans to reorganize in bankruptcy. Companies can emerge from bankruptcy and the stock has value.

Planning Tips

If you hold a security that is partially but not wholly worthless, sell it to nail down your loss. For example, if you think a company is on the brink of bankruptcy, try to sell the security so that you can fix the loss. Typically, your brokerage firm will buy it for a nominal amount, enabling you to claim a loss for the difference between your basis (usually what you paid for it) and what you received for it. Or you can abandon the security, which means that you permanently surrender and relinquish all rights in the security and receive no consideration in exchange for the security.

Bonds not issued with interest coupons or in registered form that become worthless result in a bad debt deduction (discussed earlier under "Loss on Bank Deposits").

You can claim a loss only in the year in which the security becomes totally worthless, but you have 7 years to discover that a security has become worthless. This is because the statute of limitations on amending your return to claim the loss for a worthless security is 7 years rather than the usual 3 years from the due date of your return.

Example

In 2025, you discover that a stock you held became completely worthless in 2018. You have until April 15, 2026, to file an amended return for 2018 (which was due on April 17, 2019) to report the loss.

If you are unsure in which year to claim the loss, it is generally advisable to report it in the earliest year you suspect that the worthlessness occurred and then to renew your claim in each subsequent year when the earliest year proves to be incorrect. This requires that you file amended returns to eliminate the loss from the earliest return and report it on a subsequent return.

Pitfalls

Don't let time pass you by. Once the 7-year period for filing an amended return has passed, your loss can never be claimed. Each year, make sure to check on the status of any questionable securities to make sure you don't overlook a loss write-off you are entitled to claim.

The amount you can write off for worthless securities is limited to your basis in the stocks or bonds. Even though you may have witnessed soaring prices only to be followed by the wipeout, you cannot benefit in any way from those record highs; your tax loss is limited to your basis, which is usually what you paid for the securities.

Where to Claim the Loss

You report worthless securities on Form 8949, *Sales and Other Distributions of Capital Assets* (in Part I if the securities were held for no more than one year; Part II if they were held more than one year). In columns (c) and (d) write "Worthless." Then, in column (f), be sure to enter the amount of your loss in parentheses. Amounts from Form 8949 are then carried over to Schedule D and then Form 1040 or 1040-SR.

Loss on Section 1244 Stock

Typically, losses on stock are treated as capital losses, which are deductible to the extent of capital gains for the year, plus up to $3,000 of ordinary income. But losses on a special type of stock, called Section 1244 stock after the section in the Internal Revenue Code defining it, can be treated as ordinary losses within set limits.

Benefit

If you own stock that qualifies as Section 1244 stock, you can claim an ordinary loss on the sale or worthlessness of the stock. The ordinary loss is limited to $50,000 ($100,000 on a joint return).

Conditions

To be able to treat your loss as an ordinary loss, you must meet the following 2 conditions:

1. The stock must qualify as Section 1244 stock.
2. The amount of your loss cannot exceed the dollar limit.

SECTION 1244 REQUIREMENTS

The issuing corporation can be a C or an S corporation. The stock can be common or preferred (provided the preferred stock was issued after July 18, 1984). But all 4 of these conditions must be met:

1. The corporation's equity cannot be greater than $1 million at the time the stock is issued (including amounts received for the stock).
2. The stock must be issued for money or property (other than securities). If you inherited the stock or acquired it for services rendered to the corporation, you cannot treat your loss as an ordinary loss.
3. The corporation must have derived more than half of its gross receipts during the 5-year period before your loss from business operations (and not

from passive income such as investments, rents, or royalties). If the corporation is in business less than 5 years, then it must have derived more than half of its gross receipts from business operations in all of its years in existence.

4. You must be the original owner of the stock (you cannot have purchased it from the original owner or someone else).

DOLLAR LIMIT

You can treat only the first $50,000 of the loss as an ordinary loss. The limit on a joint return is $100,000, even if one spouse owned the stock in his or her sole name. Losses in excess of this dollar limit may be treated as capital losses (discussed earlier in this chapter).

Planning Tip

You can claim a Section 1244 loss regardless of how you suffer the loss. Whether you sell your stock at a loss or the company goes under, ordinary loss treatment applies if you meet the conditions discussed earlier.

You (and the corporation) must keep certain records and make them available for IRS inspection, if requested. The records should show that the corporation met the qualifications for the stock to be classified as Section 1244 stock. The corporation should keep records on its gross receipts data for 5 years, and you should keep records on what you paid for the stock. If you don't keep these records, you risk losing your ordinary loss deduction.

Pitfall

If you own stock in an S corporation that holds small business stock, the portion of any loss on such stock passed through to you does *not* qualify as an ordinary loss on Section 1244 stock. Under the technical language of the tax law, only individuals and partnerships can claim Section 1244 losses. Even though S corporations are pass-through entities like partnerships, they are not eligible to claim Section 1244 losses.

Where to Claim the Loss

An ordinary loss on Section 1244 stock is reported on Form 4797, *Sales of Business Property*, which you attach to Form 1040 or 1040-SR. This form is used whether the loss arises from the sale of the stock or from its becoming worthless so that no sale takes place. The amount from Form 4797 is entered on Schedule 1 of Form 1040 or 1040-SR.

If the amount of the loss exceeds your dollar limit, you treat the excess loss as a capital loss (discussed earlier). On Form 8949, use code "S" to indicate that the loss is from Section 1244 stock and is more than the amount that is treated as an ordinary loss on Form 4797.

Margin Interest and Other Investment-Related Borrowing

Interest paid to borrow money for the purpose of making investments is viewed as "investment interest." The tax law sets strict limits on when and the extent to which investment interest may be deductible.

Benefit

You can deduct interest on borrowing from a brokerage firm that uses your brokerage account as collateral if the money is used for investment purposes and you itemize deductions. This is called *margin interest*, and the brokerage firm sets the limits on borrowing, interest rate, and other terms of the loan. You can also deduct interest on other loans used to make investments as an itemized deduction to the extent of your net investment income. If your investment interest is more than your net investment income for the year, you can carry the excess interest forward indefinitely and use it in a future year.

Conditions

There are 2 important conditions:

1. The funds borrowed must be used for investment purposes.
2. For full deductibility of the interest, you must have net investment income to offset it.

BORROWING FOR INVESTMENT PURPOSES

It is not the source of the borrowing that determines the treatment of the interest but the purpose for which you use the proceeds from the loan. For example, margin interest is not automatically deductible. If you use the loan to take a vacation, you cannot deduct the margin interest even though the loan arises from your investment account.

If you borrow money to buy stock in a business, interest on the loan is treated as investment interest, not business interest. In contrast, if you buy the assets of a business, the interest is treated as a fully deductible business interest, not investment interest limited to the extent of net investment income.

NET INVESTMENT INCOME

Your investment interest is deductible only to the extent of your net investment income for the year. Investment income includes:

- Interest income
- Annuities
- Royalties

Interest from passive activities that is not classified by the activities as "portfolio income" is not treated as investment income. This includes interest on rental real estate or interest passed through to you from investments in limited partnerships or other pass-through entities in which you do not materially participate. Property subject to a net lease is not treated as investment property (it is treated as a passive activity). As a practical matter, you simply look at the Schedule K-1 (and Schedule K-3 if applicable) sent to you by the entity to see how to classify the passed-through interest.

You must reduce investment income by investment expenses for the year to arrive at your net investment income. Investment expenses are expenses directly connected with the production of investment income. Examples of other investment expenses are found throughout this chapter.

Planning Tips

You can opt to treat capital gains and/or qualified dividends as investment income. If you make this election, your capital gains and/or dividends are not eligible for preferential tax rates and are instead included as ordinary income.

Generally it is *not* advisable to make this election because doing so effectively converts income that would otherwise be taxed at no more than 15% or 20% to income taxed at up to 37% (the taxable income thresholds for the 20% rate are listed in Table 8.2 earlier in this chapter). But the election can make sense in some situations; only running the numbers can determine when this is so.

The amount of investment interest is taken into account in figuring the net investment income (NII) tax. This interest reduces the amount of investment income subject to the tax.

Example

You are in the 32% tax bracket and have $3,000 of capital losses for the year and $6,000 of capital gains. You also have investment interest of $3,000 and no other investment income. If you don't make the election, $3,000 of your capital gains is taxed at 15%, but you can't deduct any of your investment interest this year. If you do make the election, then your capital losses become deductible against ordinary income so that only $3,000 of your capital gains is exposed to ordinary income, while all of your investment interest becomes deductible.

Pitfall

You cannot deduct interest, regardless of the source of the loan, if you use the money to buy or carry municipal bonds (for example, you need to raise cash and you sell your taxable investments while holding on to your municipal bonds).

Where to Claim the Deduction

You figure your investment interest limitation on Form 4952, *Investment Interest Expense Deduction*. You then enter the deductible amount on Schedule A, which is filed with Form 1040 or 1040-SR.

Amortization of Bond Premium

If you buy a bond at a price greater than its stated principal (or face) amount, the excess is called bond premium. You may opt to amortize the premium on taxable bonds; in some cases you *must* amortize bond premium (you don't have any choice).

Benefit ⬤

If you buy a taxable bond, such as a corporate bond, you can elect in the year of the purchase to begin amortizing the bond premium. This means that each year you own the bond, you can offset the taxable interest received on the bond by the amortizable premium amount.

Example

In 2025, you buy a $5,000 corporate bond for $5,500. Your bond premium is $500. Assuming the bond has 5 years left to maturity, you can amortize the $500 premium over 5 years. This means you can use $100 ($500 ÷ 5 years) to offset interest from the bond.

If you opt to amortize bond premium, reduce the bond's basis by the amount of amortization.

If you buy a tax-exempt bond, such as a municipal bond, at a premium, you *must* amortize the bond premium. But you cannot deduct the amortized premium amount. Instead, you reduce the basis of the bond by the amortization for the year.

Example

Same as the preceding example except the bond is a tax-free municipal bond. If you sell the bond at the end of the third year, the basis in the bond is $5,200 ($5,500 − $300). If the sale price of the bond is $5,200, you have no gain or loss on the transaction. If the price is higher than $5,200, you have a taxable gain; if the price is lower, you have a taxable loss.

Conditions

To amortize the bond premium on a taxable bond, you must meet the following 2 conditions:

1. You elect amortization.
2. You figure amortization using the constant yield method. This is a 3-step process under which you determine your yield, the accrual periods to use in figuring amortization, and the bond premium. The computation is rather complicated. For more details, see Chapter 3 of IRS Publication 550, *Investment Income and Expenses*.

Planning Tips

It is usually advisable to elect amortization so you can offset current interest income from the bond. If you do not make the election, you will probably realize a capital loss when the bond is redeemed at par or you sell it for less than you paid for it.

You do not have to elect amortization for taxable bonds held in IRAs or qualified retirement plans. Since the interest is not currently deductible, no offset is necessary.

Pitfall

If you want to amortize bond premiums on taxable bonds, you generally must elect to do so by attaching your own statement to the return indicating this choice. The election applies to all taxable bonds you own and to those you buy in later years.

Once you have made your choice, you can't change it unless you receive the written approval of the IRS. To request a change, you must file Form 3115, *Application for Change in Accounting Method*.

Where to Claim the Deduction

The amortizable amount of a premium is not a separate deduction. Instead, it is an adjustment to the interest reported on Schedule B of Form 1040 or 1040-SR. Report the bond's interest and then subtract the amortization, noting "ABP Adjustment" next to it.

Municipal Bonds

States, local governments, and their agencies raise money to operate through the sale of bonds. They pay interest on the bonds as inducements to investors to buy the bonds (i.e., lend them money). The federal government generally exempts this interest from taxes; there may or may not be any state income tax breaks as well.

Benefit ⊗

Interest on municipal bonds is not subject to federal income tax. You may fully exclude this interest from income. There is no dollar limit.

The exclusion applies to both interest on individual bonds and interest from mutual funds holding municipal bonds.

Conditions

Interest is classified as municipal bond interest only if the bond is issued by a state or local government or government agency.

Planning Tips

Interest from municipal bond funds and municipal exchange traded funds (ETFs) is tax free if the funds hold only tax-exempt bonds.

Interest on municipal bonds may also be exempt from state income taxes. Some states with an income tax do not tax interest on municipal bonds regardless of the state in which they are issued. Others exempt interest only on bonds issued within their state. Check with your state's tax, revenue, or financial department to learn the tax treatment of interest on municipal bonds in your location. The U.S. Supreme Court has decided that it is permissible for a state to tax the interest earned on out-of-state bonds while exempting the interest from in-state bonds.

Pitfalls

Municipal bond interest can affect the amount of taxes you pay on your Social Security benefits. Municipal bond interest, while exempt from federal income tax, is taken into account in determining your provisional income, the figure used to fix the taxable portion of Social Security benefits at 85%, 50%, or zero. If you are a Medicare beneficiary, the tax-free municipal bond interest may also impact whether you are subject to additional premiums for Parts B and D, as well as Part C.

Interest on private activity bonds issued after August 6, 1986, while excluded from income for regular tax purposes, is subject to the alternative minimum tax (AMT) (the interest on such bonds issued in 2009 and 2010 continues to be exempt from AMT). These bonds generally pay a slightly higher interest rate than other municipal bonds. But if you know you will be subject to AMT, it is advisable when making bond investments to forgo the additional interest in favor of municipal bonds not subject to AMT.

Even though interest on municipal bonds is tax free, gain on the sale of the bonds is taxable. For instance, you purchase a bond at par value and sell it 2 years later for $2,000 more than you paid. You have a $2,000 gain that is taxable.

Where to Claim the Exclusion

Even though the interest is fully excludable, you are required to report tax-exempt interest on your return. You report this interest on line 2a of Form 1040 or 1040-SR.

Savings Bonds

United States savings bonds were first sold by the federal government in World War I and again in World War II as a way to raise money. Today, these bonds have become a permanent savings vehicle for the millions of Americans who own them. They can be purchased only online at www.treasurydirect.gov.

Benefits

Tax on the interest on series EE and I bonds can be deferred until the bonds are cashed in or reach their final maturity dates. The interest on these savings bonds may be partially or wholly tax free if used to pay higher education costs. This benefit is explained in Chapter 3 and is not covered in this chapter.

Conditions

Deferral is automatic; you don't have to take any action to receive this tax treatment. You simply do not report the interest annually on your return.

Planning Tips

You can opt to report interest on these savings bonds annually instead of using deferral. This option may make sense when the bondholder has little or no other income so that the interest is taxed at a low rate, if at all.

Example

A child receives a series EE bond at her birth with a face value of $1,000. Since these bonds are sold at a 50% discount (the $1,000 bond costs only $500), any increase in the bond's value over $500 is treated as interest. If the child has no other income, the interest is effectively tax free provided that an election is made to report the interest annually. This election is made simply by including the interest on a tax return filed for the child. File a return to establish this reporting even though the child is otherwise not required to file because his or her income is below the filing threshold.

The U.S. Treasury changed the way in which interest on series EE bonds is computed. Rather than adjusting the interest semiannually, bonds sold on or after May 1, 2005, pay a fixed rate until redemption or maturity (e.g., 2.70% for bonds purchased from May 1, 2025, to October 31, 2025). As a result, Series I bonds may be a better option because their interest rate still adjusts semiannually for inflation. For example, I bonds purchased from May 1, 2025, through October 31, 2025, pay a variable rate of 2.86% plus a fixed rate of 1.10%, for a composite rate of 3.98%.

Interest *may* be tax free if bonds are redeemed to pay certain higher education costs and other conditions are met (see Chapter 3).

Interest is *never* subject to state and local income taxes.

Pitfalls

Do not continue to hold a bond beyond its final maturity date. No interest is paid after this date. As of May 2025, there were 99 million matured unredeemed bonds. Bonds reach final maturity in 30 years for series EE and I bonds.

You cannot redeem an EE or I bond until 12 months after its purchase *unless* your county has been declared a disaster area. There is a 3-month interest penalty for bonds redeemed before 5 years.

Where to Claim the Benefit

You do not have to report interest if you want to defer it; no special form or schedule needs to be filed.

Gain on the Sale of Small Business Stock

The government wants to encourage investments in small businesses. To do so, it has created certain tax breaks should these investments turn out to be profitable. The One Big Beautiful Bill Act enhanced the treatment for gain on the sale of small business stock.

Benefit

If you have a gain on the sale of small business stock—qualified small business stock or QSBS—you can exclude a percentage of the gain from income (called a Section 1202 exclusion and sometimes noted as QSBS). The portion of the gain that is not excluded is subject to a 28% capital gain rate (unless your tax bracket is below this rate so that the tax rate is limited to your bracket, which is what you would pay on ordinary income). The amount of the exclusion depends on when the stock was acquired and how long the stock has been held:

- Before February 18, 2009 (unless it is an empowerment zone business below) and held more than 5 years: 50%
- After December 21, 2000, and before February 18, 2009, in an empowerment zone business and held more than 5 years: 60%
- After February 17, 2009, and before September 28, 2010, and held more than 5 years: 75%
- After September 27, 2010, and held more than 5 years: 100%
- After July 4, 2025, and held at least 3 years but less than 4 years: 50%
- After July 4, 2025, and held at least 4 years but less than 5 years: 75%
- After July 4, 2025, and held at least 5 years: 100%

The maximum exclusion is the greater of 10 times the basis of the stock or $10 million ($15 million for stock acquired after July 4, 2025). The dollar limit is halved for married persons filing separately.

If you don't qualify for the 100% exclusion, you can defer tax on the gain from the sale of QSB stock by reinvesting in other QSB stock and meeting certain conditions.

Conditions for Exclusion

To qualify to exclude a percentage of the gain from income, the stock must qualify as small business stock and you must meet a holding period requirement.

SMALL BUSINESS STOCK

There are 5 conditions for qualifying as a small business stock:

1. The issuing corporation must be a C corporation (an S corporation cannot issue small business stock for purposes of rollover or exclusion treatment).
2. The stock must have been originally issued after August 10, 1993.
3. The gross assets of the business cannot be more than $50 million when the stock is issued, or $75 million after July 4, 2025. The $75,000 million gross asset limit will be indexed for inflation after 2025.

4. The corporation must be an active business (and not a holding or investment company). This requires that at least 80% of the corporation's assets are used in the active conduct of a qualified business. A qualified business is one involved in other than the practice of law, medicine, architecture, engineering, health, performing arts, consulting, actuarial science, financial services, brokerage services, banking, insurance, leasing, farming, hotel or motel management, restaurants, or similar businesses. This means that eligible businesses are in such fields as technology, manufacturing, retail, and wholesale.

5. You must have acquired the stock for cash or other property or as pay for services. You cannot treat inherited or gifted stock as small business stock.

HOLDING PERIOD FOR EXCLUSION

For the special exclusion, you must have held the stock more than the applicable holding before the date of sale. The applicable holding period is listed earlier.

Conditions for Deferral

Instead of using the exclusion, which may not be an option, you can defer gain on the sale of QSB stock if you meet the following 4 conditions:

1. The stock is QSB stock. The requirements for this are listed earlier in this chapter.
2. You held the stock for at least 6 months at the time that gain is realized.
3. You reinvest proceeds in other QSB stock within 60 days of the sale.
4. You make an election for deferral.

Planning Tips

If you acquired qualified small business stock from a C corporation at different times, be sure to track your holding period for each as well as your cost basis in the stock. Then when selling qualified small business stock, you can identify which shares you are selling to optimize your tax position in the year of the sale.

If you are deferring gain, it's not an all or nothing option. The deferred amount depends on how much you reinvest in QSB stock.

You can combine the exclusion with deferral to optimize tax savings. For example, if you have a $20 million gain from a sale made in December 2025, you can exclude $15 million and defer tax on $5 million.

Pitfall

If you deferred gain on the sale of qualified small business stock, understand that eventually you may pay tax on the gain. You have to reduce the basis in the small business stock acquired during the 60-day period by the amount of the deferred gain. When you sell this stock, the reduction will effectively increase your gain.

Example

In 2023, you sell QSB stock that you've held for at least 6 months and acquire new stock within 60 days. The gain from the sale is $10,000, which is deferred. You pay $25,000 for the new stock. Your basis in the new stock is $15,000 ($25,000 – $10,000 deferred gain). In 2025, when the value of the new stock has increased to $35,000, you sell and keep the proceeds. You have a taxable gain of $20,000 ($35,000 – $15,000).

Where to Claim the Benefit

To exclude a portion or all of your gain, report the sale or exchange on Form 8949, *Sales and Other Dispositions of Capital Assets*, as you would if you weren't taking the exclusion and enter the amount of the exclusion as a negative number (in parentheses) in column (g). Use code "Q" in column (f) to indicate you are using the exclusion.

If you are electing to defer some or all of your gain, report the sale or exchange on Form 8949 as you would if you weren't making the election. Then enter the amount of postponed gain as a negative number (in parentheses) in column (g). Enter code "R" in column (f).

Gain on DC Zone Assets

In the past, there were about 180 empowerment zones (EZs) in the United States; urban EZs fall under the jurisdiction of the U.S. Department of Housing and Urban Development (HUD). While these zones continue to apply for certain tax breaks (e.g., a special employment tax credit), they no longer entitle those who invested in these zones to defer gain on the sale of their assets by rolling them over. But certain prior investments in DC Zones may result in tax-free treatment upon a sale in 2025.

Benefit

If you have a gain on the sale of DC Zone assets, you can exclude all of the gain from the sale of assets held more than 5 years in the District of Columbia Enterprise Zone for assets if they were acquired after 1997 and before January 1, 2012. In effect, you are not taxed when you sell these qualified assets.

Conditions

There are 3 conditions for excluding gain on property acquired before January 1, 2012 and sold in 2025:

1. The property must be a District of Columbia Enterprise Zone (DC Zone) asset, which includes DC Zone business stock, DC Zone partnership interest, and DC Zone business property (including real or other property integral to a DC Zone business).
2. You must have acquired the DC Zone assets before January 1, 2012, and held them for more than 5 years before the sale. Obviously, any sale in 2025 meets this time condition.
3. The gain may not be otherwise treated as recapture income or gain from a sale to a related party.

Planning Tips

To determine whether you own property in a DC Zone, see IRS Publication 954, *Tax Incentives for Distressed Communities*.

If you own a business that employs people in a qualified empowerment zone, you may be eligible for a special employment tax credit (see Chapter 14).

Pitfall

The election to postpone gain from empowerment zone assets by making a rollover no longer applies; it expired at the end of 2020.

Where to Claim the Benefit

Report the sale of DC zone stock in Part II of Form 8949 as if you weren't electing the exclusion. Enter "X" in column (f), with the amount of the exclusion reported as a negative number in column (g). Report the sale of DC Zone business property on Form 4797, *Sales of Business Property*.

Gain on Reinvestments in Opportunity Zones

The U.S. Treasury, on states' recommendations, has designated low-income communities as qualified opportunity zones. If you sell property and reinvest your gain in one of these zones within 180 days of the sale, you can opt to defer the gain from your income. Eventually, the deferred gain is recognized, but further gains on your investment can grow to eventually receive tax-free treatment.

Benefit

You can postpone gain on the sale of any property as long as you reinvest it in a qualified opportunity zone through an investment fund. There is no dollar limit on how much gain your can defer; in effect it is limited only by your reinvestment.

Conditions

There are 2 conditions:

1. You usually must make the reinvestment within 180 days of the sale that produces your gain.
2. The sale must be to an unrelated party.

Planning Tips

There are now more than 8,500 qualified opportunity zone funds (called QOFs or "O Funds") for investors. Starting July 1, 2026, and every 10 years thereafter, there will be new designations of Opportunity Zones lasting 10 years, and additional QOFs are sure to arise. As with any investment, check on fund managers, investment fees, and the location in which the funds are invested.

Gain deferred by investments in a QOF before 2027 must be recognized on December 31, 2026. For investments in a QOF made after 2026, there is a 5-year deferral period, after which the gain that was deferred must be recognized. But there is a 10% step-up in the basis of the QOF investment if it's held 5 years (30% for Rural Opportunity Funds, or QROFs after 2026). If you hold it for another 2 years (at least 7 years in total), your basis is increased by another 5% of the gain originally deferred. After 10 years, an election can be made to step up the basis at the time of sale or other disposition. Different rules apply for investments after 2026 (deferral is explained in "Pitfall").

Pitfall

Investing in an investment fund in a qualified opportunity zone presents an investment risk and a tax risk. While you get to defer your gain, you must settle up with the government when selling your investment in a qualified opportunity zone fund, or December 31, 2026, whichever is earlier. (For investments after 2026, there is a rolling 5-year deferral period.) Your basis in the investment in the fund going in is deemed to be zero, so all of your resulting gain attributable to the deferral is taxable.

Example

On March 1, 2022, you sold property to an unrelated party for a gain of $100,000 and on July 1, 2022, you reinvested it in an investment fund. You opted to defer $100,000 gain. If you sell your shares in the fund on March 1, 2025 (3 years after investing), your basis in the shares is zero, so all of the gain the sale attributable to the deferral is taxable gain.

Where to Elect Deferral

The election to defer gain is reported on Form 8949, *Sales and Other Dispositions of Capital Assets*. Enter code "Z" in column (f).

Form 8997, *Initial and Annual Statement of Qualified Opportunity Fund (QOF) Investments*, must be filed each year you hold any investment in a qualified opportunity fund.

Foreign Taxes on Investments

Investors in foreign companies may pay taxes overseas to other governments. To provide a break so that these investors aren't taxed twice, for federal income tax purposes a deduction or tax credit can be claimed if certain conditions are met.

Benefit

If you hold investments in foreign countries, including stocks or mutual funds, you may pay taxes abroad. You can write off foreign taxes you pay in one of 2 ways:

1. Deduct the taxes as an itemized deduction.
2. Claim a tax credit for the foreign taxes.

Either way, there is no dollar limit to the benefit you can claim.

Conditions

The foreign tax must be a tax on income similar to U.S. tax. You cannot write off any tax imposed by a country designated by the U.S. government as engaging in terrorist activities. These countries are listed in IRS Publication 514, *Foreign Tax Credit for Individuals*.

Planning Tips

Generally, claiming the credit is more valuable than deducting the foreign taxes. The credit reduces your tax liability dollar for dollar. You do not have to be an itemizer if you claim the credit.

If you opt to claim the credit and the amount of the credit you can use in the current year is limited because of your tax liability, you can carry the excess credit back to the 2 preceding years and then forward for up to 5 succeeding years until it is used up. You can only use a carryback or carryover in a year in which you have income from foreign sources.

You have 10 years in which to change your choice from deduction to credit or credit to deduction. You can file an amended return for a period of up to 10 years to change the treatment of the write-off on your return.

Example

For the past 15 years, you have been claiming a deduction for foreign taxes you paid with respect to a mutual fund. In March 2025, you discover that it would have been preferable to claim the credit. You can amend returns from 2015 onward. The 10-year period for the 2015 return.

Pitfalls

You cannot elect to treat some foreign taxes as a deduction while treating others as a credit within the same year. You must opt to use one write-off method for all your foreign taxes. But you can change your choice from year to year.

You get no benefit for foreign taxes paid on investments held by an IRA. Since the IRA is not a taxpayer, it cannot claim a deduction or credit for the foreign taxes paid by it. This means the funds in your IRA are reduced by these taxes with no offsetting benefit. You may wish to reconsider investments subject to foreign taxes being held in an IRA.

If you are subject to the alternative minimum tax (a shadow tax system to ensure that taxpayers who successfully reduce their regular tax will at least pay some income tax), you lose the benefit of an itemized deduction for foreign taxes, which are not deductible for AMT purposes.

If in 2025 you have an ownership interest in a foreign corporation with earnings from intangibles (patents, trademarks, copyrights), you may have global intangible low-taxed income (GILTI), which is included in the corporation's income for the year. As an individual, if you make a special election (called a Section 250 election), you are treated as a corporation for purposes of the tax and can claim a foreign tax credit (subject to an 80% limitation). These rules are highly complex and should be discussed with a tax expert.

You may have to complete Form 8938, *Statement of Specified Foreign Financial Assets*, and file it with your personal tax return if the value of foreign accounts exceeds certain thresholds (e.g., more than $50,000 at the end of the year if you're single). This is referred to as FATCA because the reporting obligation was created by the Foreign Account Tax Compliance Act. Check the instructions to this form and IRS guidance at www.irs.gov/Businesses/Corporations/Basic-Questions-and-Answers-on-Form-8938 for more details about the foreign assets to which the form applies.

If you own or have authority over a foreign financial account, including a bank account, brokerage account, mutual fund, unit trust, or other type of financial account, with a value exceeding $10,000 at any time during the year, you may be required to file a Report of Foreign Bank and Financial Accounts (FBAR) annually. FinCEN Form 114 is used for this purpose and is due for 2025 by April 15, 2026 (the same deadline as the one for your federal income tax return) with a 6-month filing extension (this extension is automatic). Filing Form 8938 does not relieve you of the obligation to file the FBAR form. Civil penalties for non-willful FBAR violations are capped at $10,000. The U.S. Supreme Court decided in 2023 that the non-willful penalty applies per form and not per account. There has been no decision on whether this same per-form rule applies in the case of a willful penalty.

Where to Claim the Deduction or Credit

Foreign taxes you pay on investments are reported to you (and the IRS) on Form 1099-INT or Form 1099-DIV. Use this figure for claiming your deduction or credit.

If you are claiming a deduction for foreign taxes, you must file Schedule A. Your deduction is part of your itemized deductions entered on Form 1040 or 1040-SR.

If you are claiming the foreign tax credit related to your investments, you may qualify to report it on Schedule 3 on Form 1040 or 1040-SR (without having to complete Form 1116). This simplified filing option applies if the amount of the foreign tax credit is not more than $300 ($600 on a joint return).

If your foreign tax credit is more than this limit, you must complete Form 1116, *Foreign Tax Credit (Individual, Estate, or Trust)*, and then follow the filing instructions given earlier.

Exercise of Incentive Stock Options

Employees may receive special options, called incentive stock options (ISOs), to buy company stock at attractive prices. The exercise of ISOs is not taxable for regular tax purposes, although the spread between the exercise price and stock price is an adjustment for the alternative minimum tax (AMT) and can result in AMT liability.

Benefit

There is no regular tax on the exercise of incentive stock options.

Conditions

Incentive stock options (ISOs) are a type of compensation that must be granted in connection with employment. An ISO gives an employee the right to buy employer stock at a set price (called the strike price) within a set time period, after the ISO vests (i.e., cannot be taken from the employee unless he or she leaves employment). If the strike price is less than the market price, an employee exercising the option buys the stock at a bargain; the spread between the strike price and market price at the time the ISO is exercised is not subject to regular income tax if the following 2 conditions are met:

1. You must hold the stock acquired through the ISO for more than 2 years from the date the ISO was granted and more than one year after the ISO was exercised.
2. You must have been continuously employed by the employer granting the ISO from the date of the grant up to 3 months prior to the date on which you exercise the ISO.

If the stock acquired through the ISO is sold prior to the required holding period, then there is taxable compensation and immediate capital gain or loss recognition. The rules are complex; see IRS Publication 525, *Taxable and Nontaxable Income*.

Planning Tip

If you hold ISOs, determine how many to exercise this year, factoring in their expiration date and the impact on alternative minimum tax.

Pitfall

While there is no *regular* tax on the exercise of an ISO if certain conditions are met, the spread between the strike price and market price is treated as an adjustment for the alternative minimum tax (AMT). So, exercising ISOs can generate or increase AMT liability. In fact, exercising ISOs is the number one reason why individuals are currently impacted by the AMT.

Where to Claim the Benefit

The exercise of the ISO is not reported on Form 1040 or 1040-SR, except to the extent it is included on Form 6251, *Alternative Minimum Tax—Individuals*.

Losses from Investment Ponzi Schemes

During the financial meltdown in 2008 and 2009, some investors discovered that their money had been lost through Ponzi schemes. Unscrupulous financiers collected funds from investors and used new investments to pay off old investors; this worked until they were unable to bring in new investors and the scheme was exposed. While Bernard Madoff, a Ponzi scheme king, was sentenced to a 150-year prison sentence for these crimes, new schemes continue to come to light (there were about 100 ponzi schemes reported in 2024).

NOTE

Theft losses from romance or kidnapping scams are personal theft losses and not investment losses deductible under the Ponzi scheme safe harbor.

Under a safe harbor deduction, an investor in a Ponzi scheme can deduct 95% of the "qualified investment" if he or she isn't pursuing any third-party recovery, or 75% if pursuing or intending to pursue a third-party recovery. The "qualified investment" is the sum of cash and the basis of property invested in the arrangement over the years, plus income (even so-called phantom income) derived from the arrangement that was included for federal tax purposes in the investor's income, minus any cash or property withdrawn by the investor from the arrange-

ment. After applying the 95%/75%, the deductible amount is then reduced by any actual or potential insurance or SIPC recovery. The deduction is claimed as a miscellaneous itemized deduction. Find more details in Revenue Procedure 2009-20.

Deferral of Income in Commercial Annuities

Annuities are contracts with insurance companies to pay income for life or a term of years. They may be used to ensure you never run out of money during your lifetime. According to LIMRA Annuity Research, total annuity sales in 2024 were $432.4 billion, up 12% over the previous year.

There are 2 basic types of annuities: fixed and variable. Fixed annuities guarantee a set payout at regular intervals (e.g., monthly) based on a minimum interest rate and the company's projections for its returns. Variable annuities allow you to put your funds in certain types of investment, with the payout dependent on investment performance and, in some cases, cost-of-living adjustments. Annuities can be immediate—investing your after-tax dollars and commencing distributions—or deferred—waiting to receive distributions at some time in the future (e.g., when you retire). Generally, annuities end upon the death of the owner or last joint owner, but some may have a guaranteed payout that will be distributed to heirs if the owner(s) dies before this payout has been made.

Benefit

Income that builds up in the annuity over the years is not currently taxed; earnings are deferred until distributions are taken. Usually this occurs when you "annuitize" at a certain age to commence regular distributions for the remainder of the contract. This may be a set number of years or over your life ("single life annuity") or joint life with a named beneficiary such as a spouse ("joint and survivor annuity").

Conditions

To defer tax on the investment earnings in the contract, you must adhere to the terms of the contract imposed by the insurance company.

Planning Tips

If you need money before you want to start annuity payouts, you may be able to take a loan from your contract; this is tax free. Such borrowing is limited of course by the value of the annuity. You must pay interest on the loan and meet repayment terms to avoid taxation.

Once annuity payments commence, only the earnings portion is taxable. Amounts representing a return of your investment cost in the contract (your total investment as of the annuity starting date) are not taxed. The information needed to report the taxable amount of payments is provided to you on Form 1099-R, *Distributions from Pensions, Annuities, Retirement or Profit-Sharing Plans, IRAs, Insurance Contracts, Etc.*

Usually, there is automatic federal income tax withholding on annuity payments, but you may choose not to have withholding or to have additional withholding by completing Form W-4P, *Withholding Certificate for Pension or Annuity Payments,* and submitting it to the insurance company.

Pitfalls

If you take distributions (not loans) from an annuity before age 59 ½ or surrender the contract, you may be subject to a 10% early distribution penalty. What's more, there may be surrender charges imposed by the insurance company for canceling the contract.

If the annuity guarantees a certain payout and you die before receiving it, your heirs must report the income portion of the payout as income in respect of decedent.

Where to Claim the Benefit

While you are deferring earnings, you do not have to report anything on your tax return. Once distributions commence, earnings are reported directly on Form 1040 or 1040-SR.

Losses on Digital Assets

Cryptocurrencies and non-fungible tokens (NFTs) are digital assets that have value just like property you can see and touch. Losses on digital assets are treated the same as losses on other property.

The IRS says that cryptocurrency is not treated as a security like stocks and bonds that are publicly traded, and so no deduction for a worthless security can be claimed if the digital asset has no value. The fact that the cryptocurrency is traded on a cryptocurrency exchange does not change this fact. The IRS also said that a drastic decline in the value of cryptocurrency does not trigger a loss.

If you hold digital assets for investment, then losses on the sale of your holdings may be used to offset gains from other digital asset sales as well as sales of other property. The wash sale rule (discussed earlier in this chapter) does not currently apply to digital assets; check the Supplement for any update.

Determining basis. You can't know if you have a loss without knowing your basis. Generally, the first-in-first-out (FIFO) method is the default method used to determine basis when less than your entire holdings are sold. You may use the specific identification method to specify which digital assets are sold so that you can effectively select the basis that best works for you when assets have been acquired at different prices. To use the specific identification method, you must be able to adequately identify which digital asset unit is sold. This is done by keeping a record of each transaction and giving standing instructions to the broker about using the specific identification method. Each account is treated separately (before 2025 you could essentially lump the basis from different accounts).

You can use apps and software to track basis and determine gain or loss.

Broker reporting. Special rules apply to brokers required to report digital asset transactions. Brokers for this purpose include those that take possession of digital assets (e.g., digital-asset hosted wallet providers, digital asset kiosks, and certain digital asset payment processors). Form 1099-DA, *Digital Asset Proceeds From Broker Transactions,* is used by brokers to report transactions in 2025. Tokenized securities that are settled or cleared on a limited access regulated network (LARN) are reported on Form 1099-B and not on Form 1099-DA. DeFi platforms are not brokers; they are exempt from Form 1099-DA reporting.

Looking Ahead

For transactions in 2026 and beyond, brokers must begin reporting basis for certain transactions. Similarly, real estate professionals treated as brokers must report the fair market value of digital assets paid by buyers in real estate transactions beginning in 2026.

If you acquired digital assets at different times and are selling less than your entire holding, you probably have to treat the items sold as the first ones you acquired (first in, first out). But if you have detailed records, you may opt to designate the items sold as those with the highest tax basis (the ones that cost you the most)—referred to by some tax pros as highest in, first out—as a way to minimize your tax gains. The IRS has yet to rule on determining which tax basis to use for the sale of digital assets.

Digital asset reporting. If you engaged in any transaction involving a digital asset (e.g., cryptocurrency, nonfungible tokens) in 2025, you must answer "yes" to the question on page 1 of Form 1040 or 1040-SR. A transaction includes buying or selling cryptocurrency, receiving it in exchange for goods, services, or any other property, or transferring it for free (including from an airdrop or hard fork). Merely owning digital assets without any transactions means a "no" on the return. Instructions to the income tax return say you must answer the question; don't leave it blank.

On your return. Your digital asset investment transactions—whether or not subject to broker reporting—are reported just like other capital assets, so losses are entered on Form 8949 (see Capital Losses earlier in this chapter).

Trump Accounts

The One Big Beautiful Bill Act created a new type of savings vehicles for newborns in the U.S. This break begins January 1, 2026, but is included here as a heads up. It does not impact 2025 income tax returns.

Benefit

An account established automatically for an eligible child receives a $1,000 contribution from the U.S. Treasury; the receipt of the contribution is not taxable to the child or the child's parent. Additional contributions are permitted by individuals, employers, and exempt organizations. No distributions from the account are allowed until the child attains age 18. Thereafter, distributions are treated like distributions from IRAs (see Chapter 5). This means that earnings in the account are tax deferred and distributions are treated as ordinary income.

Conditions

There are only 2 conditions:

- Child must be born on or after January 1, 2025, and no later than December 31, 2028.
- Both the child and at least one parent must have a Social Security number.

Planning tips

While the federal government seeds the account with $1,000, additional contributions are permitted:

- Individuals can add up to $5,000 per child in tax-free contributions. The dollar limit is indexed for inflation after 2027.
- Employers can contribute up to $2,500 per year (also indexed for inflation) as a tax-free fringe benefit to employees.
- Nonprofit organizations and states can contribute to a qualified class of beneficiary.

Investments can only be made in a U.S. equity index mutual fund or EFT with an annual expense ratio capped at 0.1%.

Parent can opt out of having an account for an eligible child.

Pitfall

There can be only one account per child. If there is more, there is a 100% excise tax on income from any additional account.

Travel

We live in a highly mobile age—we are always on the go for work, play, or other activities. We travel by car, airplane, train, ship, bus, ride share, and taxi. We spend a lot of money annually on getting around. The tax laws can help to defray some of your travel costs in certain situations.

This chapter explains the types of travel expenses you can deduct. You will find an explanation of recordkeeping rules for travel expenses as well as some forms you can use to comply with these rules.

For more information, see IRS Publication 463, *Travel, Gift, and Car Expenses*; and IRS Publication 1542, *Per Diem Rates*.

Business Travel

Americans travel quite a lot for business. The average business trip in 2025 costs $1,400–$1,800 in travel fees (higher for international business travel). The costs of travel, including transportation, lodging, and meals, that are related to business may be fully or partially tax deductible if certain conditions are met.

Benefit

If you are self-employed, business travel is a deductible expense. There is no overall dollar limit on what you can deduct. As an employee, you cannot deduct the business travel that you pay for. But if your employer reimburses you under an accountable plan, you aren't taxed on the reimbursements. An accountable plan is a reimbursement arrangement under which you are required to account for your expenses to your employer within a set time and refund to your employer any excess advances or reimbursements.

Conditions

Business travel costs are deductible if they are ordinary and necessary business expenses. In other words, the travel costs must be business-related and not for personal reasons.

Also, as a condition for claiming a deduction, you must maintain good records (discussed later).

EXAMPLES OF BUSINESS TRAVEL EXPENSES

- Airfare
- Bus fare
- Car expenses (explained in Chapter 7)
- Cab fare
- Convention costs (explained later in this chapter)
- Educational travel, if work-related (explained later in this chapter)
- Fax and Internet charges
- Job-hunting travel costs in the same line of work
- Laundry and dry cleaning during trips
- Lodging
- Lodging taxes
- Meals away from home
- Out-of-town expenses while working on a temporary job assignment (explained later in this chapter)
- Ride share fees plus tips
- Subway and train fare
- Telephone calls

LOCAL OVERNIGHT STAYS

If you paid the cost and you are self-employed, you can deduct it. As long as this is not a compensatory benefit but done for a business purpose, you are not taxed on the overnight stay(s) paid by your employer. For example, your company requires you to stay at a local hotel for the bona fide purpose of facilitating training or team building directly connected with the employer's trade or business.

PART-BUSINESS TRIPS WITHIN THE UNITED STATES

If you combine business with pleasure, as a self-employed person you can deduct your travel costs, such as airfare, as a business expense if the *primary* purpose of the trip is for business. But you can deduct hotel costs only for the business portion of the trip.

Example

You live and work in New Haven and fly to San Francisco for a 5-day business trip. You extend your stay for 2 extra days to sightsee. You can fully deduct your airfare as a business expense since the primary purpose of your trip is business. Your lodging is deductible only for the 5 days on business (the cost of lodging for your 2 personal days are nondeductible).

If you extend your stay over the weekend to obtain more favorable airfare that requires a Saturday night stay-over, this time is treated as business time, not personal time, even if you spend the weekend on personal activities.

If the primary purpose of your trip is for personal activities, you can deduct only local transportation costs to and from business locations as a business expense.

Example

You live and work in New Haven and fly to San Francisco to attend your niece's wedding. Family activities take up 4 days of your trip. On the 5th day you see a client and then fly home. Only local transportation costs from your hotel to the client and from the client to the airport are deductible.

PART-BUSINESS TRIPS ABROAD

If you combine business with pleasure on a trip outside the United States, different rules apply to determine if and the extent to which airfare can be treated as a deductible business expense.

If you control scheduling, you can deduct airfare, lodging, and 50% of meal costs only if you fall within one of these categories:

- The trip lasts a week or less (not counting the day you left the United States but counting the day of your return).
- The trip lasts more than one week, but less than 25% of time (counting both the day of departure and arrival) is spent on personal activities.
- In planning the trip, major emphasis was not placed on personal activities.

If a trip lasts more than one week and you spend 25% or more on personal activities (and cannot show that major emphasis was not placed on these activities), then you can deduct only the portion of expenses related to business. This requires that you allocate costs between business and personal time. Divide the total number of days of the trip by the days spent on business activities to find the deductible portion of your costs.

Example

On Sunday you fly from New York to London for a 10-day stay. You spend Monday through Friday on business and the balance of the trip sightseeing. You can deduct ½ of your airfare, lodging, and meal costs as a business expense (5 ÷ 10).

If you have business meetings scheduled before or after a weekend or holiday, you can treat the days in between the meetings as business days, even though you spend the time on personal activities.

PER DIEM RATES

Instead of keeping track of your actual costs for lodging, meals, and incidental expenses away from home on business, you can rely on government-set standard rates. Incidental expenses include tips for porters, baggage carriers, bellhops, and hotel maids. Self-employed individuals can only use per diem rates for meals and incidental expenses. But if they pay for the travel expenses of their employees, they can apply either of the per diem options:

1. *Maximum federal per diem rate*—an allowance for lodging and for meals and incidental expenses (M&IE) for travel within the continental United

States (CONUS). The rate you use depends on the location you are in and the time of travel. Federal per diem rates may be found at www.gsa.gov (click on Per Diem Rates).

2. *High-low substantiation rate*—an IRS-set rate for lodging and for meals and incidental expenses for business travel within CONUS. One rate applies for IRS-designated high-cost areas while the other rate applies to all other areas in CONUS. The rates for October 1, 2024, through September 30, 2025, may be found in IRS Notice 2024-68. The rates starting October 1, 2025, may be found in the Supplement.

Even though you use a standard per diem rate, you must still apply a 50% limitation to the M&IE portion of the allowance.

If you incur incidental expenses on any travel day for which you do not have deductible meals, you can deduct these expenses at a flat $5 per day.

Planning Tips

If you plan a business trip that is canceled, you can deduct the costs you can't recoup. These costs may include a hotel charge that is nonrefundable or an airline fee to reschedule a flight.

You *must* keep good records of your business travel in order to claim a deduction. The tax law requires substantiation of business travel expenses as a condition of claiming the deduction. You generally need 2 types of records: written information and documentary evidence such as receipts or credit card statements.

You must note certain information in a diary, logbook, account statement, app, or other record keeper. The type of information to record and a sample weekly travel expense form that you can use for this purpose are included at the end of this chapter.

If you are an employee whose employer has an accountable plan, you are required to provide recordkeeping information to your employer.

You do not have to retain receipts for travel costs (other than lodging) of less than $75. For example, you do not need receipts for taxi fares or ride shares under $75.

If you fail to maintain the necessary records or if they are destroyed by events beyond your control, such as a flood or fire, you *may* be able to prove your entitlement to a deduction through your own written or oral statement and other supporting evidence. But it may be difficult to establish the full amount of expenses, and you can lose out on a deduction you are otherwise entitled to claim.

In some situations, especially when records are destroyed through no fault of the taxpayer, courts have allowed taxpayers to estimate their expenses. This is called the *Cohan rule*, named after the famous entertainer George M. Cohan, who convinced a court of his entitlement to a business deduction despite the lack of records.

Pitfalls

Generally the cost of commuting to and from work is not deductible; it is a personal expense. There are certain situations in which commuting costs can be treated as deductible business expenses by self-employed individuals.

- If you incur additional costs to transport tools to and from work you can treat the added cost as a deductible expense.
- You commute to a temporary work location.
- You work from home and claim a home office deduction. The cost of travel between your home and any business location, such as customers' offices, is deductible.
- You work at temporary locations. For example, if you are an accountant or other professional who travels to client work sites for a few days or a week or 2, you can deduct the costs of travel between home and these sites as business travel, *provided* you have a regular work office.

If you are an employee, you cannot deduct your business travel. No deduction for unreimbursed employee business expenses can be claimed. There is an exception for reservists, performing artists, and fee-based government officials.

Where to Claim the Deduction

If you are an employee whose job-related travel costs are covered by an employer's accountable plan, you do not have to do anything on your return; you do have to account for expenses to your employer. Reimbursements for this travel are *not* included on your Form W-2.

If you are self-employed, you deduct your business travel costs on Schedule C.

Temporary Work Assignments

Not everyone who works does so from a fixed location. Some people are stationed at various work locations for a few days, a few months, or even longer. Living away from home means paying for additional housing and travel expenses between home and work. In recognition of the burden these additional costs can place on workers, the tax law allows what might be viewed as personal expenses to become deductible if certain conditions are met.

Benefit

If you are self-employed and work at a temporary location, your travel costs between home and this location are deductible.

If the temporary location is out of town, you can deduct not only your travel costs but also your living expenses, including lodging and 50% of meals. There is no dollar limit on what you can deduct.

Conditions

There are 2 conditions for deducting expenses related to temporary work assignments:

1. The assignment must be temporary.
2. You must have a regular place of business to deduct travel costs between home and work or be away from home on business to deduct travel and living costs.

DEFINITION OF TEMPORARY WORK ASSIGNMENTS

For travel expenses to be deductible, the work assignment must be temporary. This means that the assignment is expected to last no more than one year and does in fact end within this time. A work assignment is *not* considered temporary if it is expected to last:

- For more than one year even if it in fact ends within the year
- For no more than one year but runs beyond this time (although expenses for the period up to one year are deductible in this case)

REGULAR PLACE OF BUSINESS

You must maintain a regular place of business outside of your home, or have a home office that is your principal place of business.

If all of your work takes place at temporary assignments outside of the metropolitan area in which you live, you do not have a regular place of business and cannot deduct your travel costs.

AWAY FROM HOME

You must maintain a tax home from which you are away on business to deduct travel and living costs. Your tax home is your place of business, regardless of where you or your family live. It may be one and the same place if you live and work in the same area.

Example

You live and work in Trenton, New Jersey. You travel to Boston for 2 weeks of business. You can deduct your travel and living expenses on this trip.

Example

You live in Trenton, New Jersey, and work in Washington, D.C. Washington, D.C., not Trenton, is your tax home. You cannot deduct your travel costs between Trenton and D.C. But if you travel for 2 weeks to Dallas, Texas, you can deduct your travel costs between D.C. and Dallas, as well as your living costs in Dallas.

If you are constantly on the road, moving from job to job so that you do not work within any particular locality, you may not deduct your living costs. The reason: You are not away from home on business.

Your residence can be treated as your tax home so that if you travel away from home on business your costs are deductible if you meet 3 conditions:

1. You do *some* work in the vicinity of your residence.
2. You have mortgage expenses or pay rent for the residence while you are on the road.
3. You or a member of your immediate family has lived in the area of your residence for a long time.

If you meet 2 of the 3 conditions, you *may* be able to use your residence as your tax home, but if you meet only one condition, you cannot do so.

If you regularly work in 2 or more locations, your tax home is the area of your *principal* work location. This is usually determined by the time spent in each location, the degree of business activity in each place, what income you receive from each place, where you have your home, and whether either location is temporary. You can't use any single factor to decide which of the 2 locations is your tax home.

Planning Tip

When you travel away from home, be sure to keep accurate and complete records of your travel and living expenses.

Pitfalls

Spouses who live and work in different cities can have different tax homes. Just because they are treated as domiciled within the same place and may vote or file their taxes together, they may be restricted in deducting travel expenses between these locations.

Example

A couple maintains a home in Baltimore, where the husband resides. One spouse has a business in New York City during the week and travels to Baltimore each weekend. Even though Baltimore is the city she considers home, she cannot deduct her travel costs between Baltimore and New York City, nor her living expenses in New York City. Her tax home is New York City, not Baltimore, and she is not traveling on business when she returns to Baltimore each weekend.

Pitfall

If you work in another state, you may be responsible for paying state income taxes there. Check the rules in the state in which you temporarily work.

Where to Claim the Benefit

As a self-employed individual, you deduct your business travel costs on temporary work assignments on Schedule C.

Conventions

Conventions and trade shows are a key way in which businesses can show off their wares, make new connections, and learn about industry developments. To find the best shows to market your products or services, visit https://www.eventseye.com/index.htm. Whether you are an exhibitor or a visitor, your attendance costs may be deductible.

Benefit

You can deduct the cost of attending business conventions, including travel, lodging, 50% of meal costs, and attendance fees, even though there is an element of pleasure associated with such activities. But there are restrictions if you attend a convention held outside the North American area or on a cruise ship.

Conditions

You must be able to show that your attendance at the convention has some benefit to your trade or business. This can be shown by comparing the purpose of the convention as stated in its program or agenda with your official job duties or work.

The fact that you are appointed or elected as a delegate to the convention does not, by itself, establish a business benefit.

FOREIGN CONVENTIONS

If the convention is held outside the North American area, you must show that:

- The meeting is directly related to your trade or business.
- It is as reasonable to hold the meeting outside the North American area as in it. Reasonableness is based on the purpose of the meeting and activities taking place, the sponsoring group or organization, and the homes of active members. The North American area includes all of the locations detailed in Table 9.1.

TABLE 9.1 North American Area for Convention Deduction

American Samoa	Jarvis Island
Antigua and Barbados	Johnston Island
Aruba	Kingman Reef
Bahamas	Marshall Islands
Baker Island	Mexico
Barbados	Micronesia
Bermuda	Midway Islands
Canada	Netherlands Antilles
Costa Rica	Northern Mariana Islands
Curacao	Palau
Dominica	Palmyra
Dominican Republic	Panama
Grenada	Puerto Rico
Guam	Saint Lucia
Guyana	Trinidad and Tobago
Honduras	United States
Howland Island	U.S. Virgin Islands
Jamaica	Wake Island

CONVENTIONS ON CRUISE SHIPS

If you attend a business convention held on a cruise ship, your business deduction is limited to $2,000 per year (a limit in place since the Tax Reform Act of 1986 and not adjusted annually), regardless of the cost of the cruise or the number of convention cruises you take. And even this limited deduction can *only* be claimed if all 5 of these conditions are met:

1. The convention is directly related to your business.
2. The ship is a vessel registered in the United States.
3. All of the ports of call on the trip are in the United States or U.S. possessions.
4. You attach a signed statement to your return that includes the number of days for the cruise, the hours you spent each day devoted to scheduled business activities, and a copy of the program showing the scheduled business activities.
5. You also attach a signed statement by an officer of the organization or group sponsoring the meeting that shows the schedule of business activities each day and the number of hours you attended.

Planning Tip

Keep good records of your expenses at the convention, including a copy of the convention program with notations of the sessions you attended. If the convention has a sign-in book, be sure to sign in at every session. If the convention is held on a cruise ship, follow the recordkeeping requirements discussed earlier.

Pitfall

If your spouse or other person accompanies you to the convention, you cannot deduct the expenses of your companion. This is so even if your companion is helpful to you. As a practical matter, there may be no added cost for a second person in your room, so the only extras for your companion are meals and travel. And if you drive to the convention, even extra travel costs are eliminated.

Where to Claim the Deduction

If you are an employee whose job-related travel costs are covered by an employer's accountable plan, you do not have to do anything, other than account to your employer. Reimbursements for attendance at a business convention are *not* included on your Form W-2. Your employer claims the deduction for your travel costs.

If you are self-employed, you deduct your business convention costs on Schedule C.

Medical Travel

The days of doctors' house calls are largely over. Unless you use telehealth, to obtain medical assistance you must go to the providers' sites—doctors' offices, hospitals, clinics, and other facilities. The tax law lets you treat your travel costs for medical purposes as a deductible medical expense.

Benefit

Medical insurance typically does not cover your expenses for getting to and from the doctor or pharmacy or other travel for other medical purposes. These costs are deductible as an itemized medical deduction. This means that the costs of medical travel are added to your other medical expenses, the total of which is deductible to the extent they exceed 7.5% of your adjusted gross income.

Conditions

To be treated as qualified medical expenses, the costs of travel must be related to obtaining a diagnosis, cure, mitigation, treatment, or prevention of disease or any treatment that affects a part or function of your body.

Deductible expenses include those paid not only for yourself, but also for a spouse and dependents. Who qualifies as a dependent is explained in Chapter 1.

EXAMPLES OF MEDICAL TRAVEL COSTS

- Ambulance hire
- Autoette (auto device for a handicapped person)
- Bus, cab, or train fare to see doctors, obtain treatment (including attendance at AA meetings, or to the gym if you are obese), or pick up prescriptions
- Car use to see doctors, obtain treatment (including attendance at AA meetings or to the gym if you are obese), or pick up prescriptions at 21¢ per mile in 2025
- Medical conferences (travel costs and admission fees) on an illness or condition suffered by you, your spouse, or a dependent
- Lodging to receive outpatient care at a licensed hospital, clinic, or hospital-equivalent facility, up to $50 per night ($100 per night if you accompany a sick child)

Planning Tips

Keep good records of your expenditures for medical-related travel.

- For use of your car, note the date, purpose, and odometer reading at the start and end of each trip, as well as related parking and tolls
- For other travel costs, retain receipts of all expenses

Pitfalls

You cannot deduct the costs of trips taken for general good health. For example, your car mileage to and from the gym is not deductible if you are there to improve your appearance or maintain general good health rather than to treat a condition such as obesity or high blood pressure.

Similarly, if you fly to Florida each winter to escape the cold of New Hampshire, you cannot deduct your travel costs, even though the warm climate or other factors may be beneficial to your health. You are not traveling for the purpose of obtaining treatment or for some other deductible medical purpose.

Medical tourism is a growing practice for those who want to obtain treatment at greatly reduced cost in another country. The cost of travel to a foreign country for medical treatment generally is deductible only if primarily for medical care and there is no equivalent treatment reasonably available within the U.S. The care must be performed by a licensed medical professional.

Where to Claim the Deduction

Medical travel costs, which are part of itemized medical expenses, are reported in the "Medical and Dental Expenses" section of Schedule A of Form 1040 or 1040-SR.

Charitable Travel

Volunteering for your favorite cause may cost you money; just getting to and from your volunteer activity can be an expense. The tax law lets you deduct your out-of-pocket travel costs incurred for charitable pursuits if you itemize deductions rather than taking the standard deduction.

Benefit ⊜

If you use your car or truck for charitable purposes, including attending meetings of organizations you serve, you can deduct either your actual expenses for gas and oil, charging, and other operational costs or mileage at the rate of 14¢ per mile (unchanged since 1998). Whichever method you select, you can also write off parking and tolls.

You can also deduct travel expenses, plus meals and lodging, for overnight trips away from home to serve as an official delegate to a convention of a church, charitable, veteran, or other similar organization.

Conditions

You qualify to deduct your vehicle expenses to the extent that the use of your vehicle is for a tax-exempt organization or governmental unit. To see whether the charity you work for is tax exempt, see Chapter 6.

You qualify for convention-related expenses that you are not reimbursed for if you serve as an official delegate on behalf of a religious, charitable, veteran, or other similar organization.

Planning Tip

Keep track of your mileage and out-of-pocket expenses on behalf of the charity. In a diary, logbook, or app, note the odometer readings for every charity-related trip for which your vehicle is used, as well as any related parking and tolls.

Pitfalls

You cannot deduct travel costs to work on a project for a nonprofit organization if there is a significant element of personal pleasure, recreation, or vacation involved.

You cannot deduct travel costs to attend a charity-related convention if you do not serve as an official delegate.

Where to Claim the Benefit

To claim a charitable deduction for your charity-related travel expenses, you must complete Schedule A of Form 1040 or 1040-SR. Enter your deduction for charity-related expenses in the "Gifts to Charity" section of Schedule A.

Education-Related Travel

Unless you're taking classes online from home or listening to teleconferences, you must travel to a classroom to learn. If the education is work-related and you are self-employed, your travel costs may be deductible.

Benefit

Whether you drive across town to take college credits or fly across the country for a continuing education course, you can deduct your travel costs as a business expense. For example, if you go to night school to take a computer course to keep you up-to-date for your business, which is working with computers, your travel from work to school and from school to home is deductible.

Conditions

For educational travel to be treated as a deductible expense, the education you are traveling for must be work-related. This means that:

- You are self-employed. For example, you cannot deduct as work-related expenses the cost of an undergraduate education because you are not already working at your business.

- You already meet the minimum requirements for your position, based on the laws and regulations of your state.
- The courses maintain or improve your current business skills.
- The courses do not lead to qualification for a new profession.

EXAMPLES OF EDUCATIONAL TRAVEL COSTS

- Car expenses from work to school. You can deduct your actual costs or use the standard mileage rate for business travel (70¢ per mile in 2025), plus parking and tolls.
- Car expenses or local transportation expenses (bus, subway, cab, train, ridesharing, or other fare) of going from your place of business to school and from school to home, *provided* you are regularly employed and going to school is a temporary endeavor (courses are expected to last no more than one year and do, in fact, end within this time).
- Travel costs away from home to attend a course (transportation to and from the course, lodging, and 50% of meals).

Example

Your business is in New York City, and every night for 6 weeks you take a refresher course. Since the course is temporary, you may deduct your travel expenses between work and school and school and home. It does not matter whether you go directly from work to school; your travel costs from home to school, in either or both directions, are deductible. The same is true if you take the refresher course on Saturday or Sunday.

Planning Tip

If you are taking a course out of town and spend some time on personal activities, be prepared to prove that the primary purpose of the out-of-town travel was business-related education. This can be done by showing that you spend most of your time attending the course and only a relatively small amount of time on sightseeing or other personal activities.

Example

You travel from Boston, your place of business, to Las Vegas for a 2-day continuing education program. If your total travel is 3 days, you can confidently show that the primary purpose of your trip is for the education so that your airfare to and from Boston is a deductible travel expense.

Example

Same facts except your trip to Las Vegas lasts 7 days. In this case, it may be difficult to show that the primary reason for the trip was work-related education since you spend 5 of the 7 days on personal activities. But even if the airfare is not deductible, local transportation costs to and from the 2-day course are deductible.

Pitfalls

You cannot deduct travel that is merely educational in nature, even though it may be beneficial to your work. For example, an architect may not deduct the cost of travel to a foreign country to look at the architecture. But if the architect takes courses abroad, then the travel costs become deductible even if the courses are not taken for credit. Decide whether it will save you money to pay for and take a course in order to deduct your travel costs.

If you are away from home for education purposes, you may not deduct travel costs for sightseeing, social visiting, or entertaining while taking the course.

You cannot deduct the cost of traveling to and attending investment seminars, despite how educational and beneficial they may be. The tax law specifically bans this deduction.

You cannot deduct education expenses if you are an employee.

Where to Claim the Benefit

As a self-employed individual, you enter your education-related travel on Schedule C.

National Guard and Military Reservist Travel

There are over 1.3 million members of the National Guard and the Reserves. If you're one of them, you likely have service-related costs and you may be able to deduct them.

Benefit

You can deduct your overnight travel costs as an adjustment to gross income.

Conditions

To claim the deduction, besides the obvious requirement of being a member of the National Guard or in the reserves, you must meet the following 3 conditions:

1. You must incur the costs to attend a meeting more than 100 miles away from home. You are considered to be away from home if you are away from the permanent duty station long enough to require rest or sleep in order to

complete your duties. For naval personnel of a drydocked submarine, your tax home is the area or vicinity of your principal place of employment or shore assignment (not the submarine itself).

2. The costs must relate to overnight transportation, meals, and lodging.

3. The amount of the deductible expenses cannot exceed the general federal per diem rate applicable to the locality to which you travel. You can find these per diem rates at www.gsa.gov (click on Per Diem Rates).

Planning Tips

Keep good records of your travel mileage and expenses to be able to substantiate the deduction you claim.

If you drive your vehicle to attend a meeting that's more than 100 miles away from your home, you can figure the deductible cost of driving using your actual expenses or the IRS standard mileage rate (70¢ per mile in 2025).

Pitfalls

Only 50% of the cost of meals is deductible. Service-related travel expenses that cannot be deducted as an adjustment to gross income are nondeductible.

Where to Claim the Deduction

The deduction for travel expenses that meet these qualifications is figured on Form 2106, *Employee Business Expenses*, and is then claimed on Schedule 1 of Form 1040 or 1040-SR.

Frequent Flier Miles

Whether you travel on business or for pleasure, you can build up frequent flier miles that can be cashed in for fares or upgrades. You can also earn frequent flier miles by charging goods and services to special credit cards that award mileage. Fortunately, there may be no tax cost to you for using frequent flier miles.

Benefit ⊗

You are not taxed on the value of frequent flier miles you earn on business travel and use for personal travel. For example, you earn enough points on your business travel throughout the year to receive free tickets for your summer vacation. You are not taxed on the frequent flier miles as they accrue, and you are not taxed when you use them for travel benefits—business or personal. The IRS, for the moment, has given up trying to tax this benefit because it is too difficult to assign a value to it. There is no dollar limit to the amount of this benefit that you can exclude from income.

Condition

To be excludable from income, frequent flier miles can be used only for in-kind benefits, which include free airline tickets or seat upgrades.

Planning Tips

Check on the expiration date of frequent flier miles you have earned so that you can use them up before it is too late.

Consider donating your frequent flier miles to charity. While you can't claim a tax deduction (there is no way to value the miles, and the donation is viewed as having been made to the user of the miles rather than to the organization), you'll benefit someone. For instance, Make-A-Wish Foundation needs nearly 3 billion miles annually to grant wishes to children with life-threatening medical conditions.

Pitfalls

If you convert frequent flier miles to cash, the cash value of the benefits must be reported as income in this case.

Where to Claim the Exclusion

Since this is excluded from income, you do not have to report anything on your tax return. Frequent flier miles earned as an employee are not reported on your Form W-2.

Recordkeeping for Travel Expenses

The tax law requires you to keep records of your travel expenses as a condition for claiming a deduction. Your travel expense records must include the following information:

- *Amount.* The cost of each separate expense for travel, lodging, and meals. Incidental expenses can be totaled in any reasonable category (such as taxi fares). If you rely on a per diem rate for lodging, meals, and incidental expenses, you need not record these expenses nor retain receipts for them.
- *Time.* Record the dates you leave and return for each trip and the number of days spent on business.
- *Place or destination.* Note the area of your travel (the name of the city, town, or other destination).
- *Business purpose.* Record the reason for the expense or the benefit to be gained, or expected to be gained, from the trip.

You can use the recordkeeper in Table 9.2 to record the amount of your travel expenses each week. You can also use a variety of apps for your smartphone or tablet to keep required records for deductible travel expenses.

In addition to your diary or logbook (created on paper or electronically), you also need documentary proof of your expenses. This usually means retaining receipts, canceled checks, or other proof of what you paid for your travel expenses. But you do not need receipts for expenses under $75 (except in the case of lodging, where proof is required regardless of the amount).

TABLE 9.2 Sample Weekly Travel Expense Record Keeper

Date: From:_____   To:_____

Expense	Sunday	Monday	Tuesday	Wednesday	Thursday	Friday	Saturday	Total
Airlines								
Excess baggage								
Bus								
Train								
Cab/limo/ rideshare								
Tips								
Other costs								
Hotel: Name City								
Breakfast								
Lunch								
Dinner								

Real Estate

The vast majority of Americans own real estate, with 65% owning their own homes as of the second quarter of 2025. (Tax write-offs for your main home are discussed in Chapter 4.) But owning a principal residence isn't the only way to invest in real estate. Many individuals also own second homes or invest in rental properties to generate income. These investments produce important tax breaks. If real estate activities are your business, see Chapter 14.

This chapter covers tax breaks related to real estate investments other than your principal residence. For more information, see IRS Publication 527, *Residential Rental Property (Including Rental of Vacation Homes)*; IRS Publication 587, *Business Use of Your Home (Including Use by Day-Care Providers)*; and IRS Publication 946, *How to Depreciate Property*.

Vacation Home

The rich have traditionally maintained more than one residence, summering in Newport, skiing in Aspen, escaping winters in Palm Beach. But today, second homes aren't limited to the very rich; they are increasingly common among an ever-broadening populace. The tax law offers some tax breaks that help to make ownership of vacation homes more affordable.

Benefit

If you use your vacation home solely for your own personal enjoyment (you don't rent it out at any time during the year), you can deduct your real estate taxes and home mortgage interest (if the vacation home is designated as your second home under the home mortgage interest rules in Chapter 4). But, like your personal residence, there are limits on deducting real estate taxes and mortage interest and you can't write off any of the costs of utilities, insurance, or upkeep.

If you rent out a home that you use for part of the year yourself, you may be entitled to certain tax benefits over and above those allowed for pure personal use of the home. The rules that apply to you depend on your rental period and the time that you use the home.

Conditions for Vacation Home with No Rentals

The conditions for deducting real estate taxes and home mortgage interest are explained in Chapter 4.

Conditions for Vacation Home with Rentals

The conditions you must meet and the benefits you are entitled to depend on how long you rent out the home and how long you use it for yourself during the year. There are 3 categories into which you can fall.

1. Rental of no more than 14 days during the year.
2. Rental of 15 days or more but personal use is for less than 14 days or 10% of the days of rental.
3. Personal use is more than 14 days or 10% of the total days the home was rented for a fair rental price.

TAX-FREE RENTAL INCOME

In the 1970s, residents of Augusta, Georgia, lobbied Congress to get a tax break for renting their homes to visitors of the annual Augusta National Golf Tournament, and the 14-day rule was enacted. Now it also benefits residents of Super Bowl cities and other events. If you rent out your home for no more than 14 days during the year, you do not have to report the rental income. There's no dollar limit on this exclusion and the rental doesn't have to relate to any special event.

In February 2025, because of your proximity to Super Bowl LIX, you rented your home in San Francisco, California, for 3 days. You received a rental payment of $1,900 per night, for a total of $5,700. None of the $5,700 is taxable.

You cannot deduct any expenses related to maintaining the home, depreciation, or any rent you pay. Of course, if you itemize your deductions, you can deduct your mortgage interest provided you designate the home as your second residence, and your real estate taxes (there is no limit on the number of homes for which you can deduct real estate taxes, but the SALT cap applies).

BUSINESS DEDUCTIONS

If you rent out your home for 15 days or more but you personally use the home for less than 14 days or 10% of the days of rental, your rental activities are viewed as a business.

You rent out your home for 3 months and use it for only 1 week during the year. Since the rental period is more than 15 days (it is actually 92 days) and your personal use is less than 14 days or 10% of the days of rental (9 days), you fall within this rule for figuring your deductions from the rental activity.

You must report all of the rental income, but you can deduct from rental income only the mortgage interest, real estate taxes, operating expenses, and depreciation prorated for rental use. If your prorated expenses, including depreciation on a home you own, exceed your rents for the year, you can use the loss to offset your income from other purposes (subject to the passive loss limitations discussed further on).

Personal use of your home includes any day the home is used by:

- You or any member of your family (unless a family member pays a fair rental price)
- Anyone else who pays less than a fair rental price
- Anyone under a reciprocal agreement who lets you use his or her home
- Any other person who owns a part of the home (unless it is rented to that person under a shared equity agreement)

You do not have to count your personal use during the year if your home is rented for at least 12 consecutive months.

Example

You move from your home in March 2025 and start renting it in April 2026. Assuming your rental lasts at least until through March 2026, you do not have to count your personal use in 2025.

Your actual write-offs for the year may be limited by the passive activity loss rules discussed later.

LIMITED BUSINESS DEDUCTIONS

If your personal use is more than 14 days or 10% of the total days the home was rented for a fair rental price, you must report all of the rental income. Your deductions are limited to the amount of rents you receive. And the order in which you claim your deductions is carefully orchestrated:

1. Mortgage interest, real estate taxes, and casualty losses are fully deductible. You can claim them even if they exceed your rental income. But you must apply them first against your rental income to determine how much of your other deductions to claim.

2. Operating expenses, such as utilities and maintenance costs, are deductible only to the extent of your rental income after reduction for mortgage interest and so on.

3. Depreciation and other basis adjustments are deductible only to the extent that rental income has not yet been fully offset by the aforementioned deductions.

Example

You own a condo at the shore. You rent it out for June and July. You use it for August. Since your rental is 61 days and your personal use is 31 days, you must figure your deductions using this ordering rule. Assume you receive $6,000 for the 2 months of rental, and your deductions for the year are $2,000 for interest and $3,000 for taxes. In this case, you can deduct up to $1,000 of operating expenses. Assuming you have at least $1,000 of operating expenses, then you cannot claim any depreciation. Your deductions, in effect, fully offset your rental income so you have no taxable income from your rental activity.

PASSIVE LOSS LIMITATIONS

If the rental of your vacation home is treated as a rental activity (your personal use is fewer than 15 days but the rental period is more than 2 weeks), you are subject to the passive loss rules. Generally, your deductions related to the rental of your home cannot exceed all of your passive activity income from the year (income from this rental activity plus any other passive activities). The law calls them passive "losses" but really means deductions in excess of rental income.

> ### Example
>
> The rental of a vacation home is your only passive activity. Rental income for the year is $6,000, while deductions are $8,000. You can deduct only $6,000 this year.

Carryforward. Passive activity losses in excess of passive activity income can be carried forward and used in a future year when there is passive activity income to offset it. There is no limit on the carryforward period.

Exceptions to the loss limit. There are 3 key exceptions to the ban on deducting passive losses in excess of passive activity income.

1. You can deduct all carryover losses from a passive activity in the year in which you dispose of your passive activity (e.g., sell your vacation home).

2. You can deduct up to $25,000 of passive activity losses in excess of passive activity income from a rental activity in which you actively participate (e.g., approve new tenants, decide on rental terms, and authorize capital expenditures and repairs). The $25,000 limit is phased out when your modified adjusted gross income exceeds $100,000 and is completely phased out when MAGI reaches $150,000. MAGI for this purpose means AGI without taxable Social Security benefits, the exclusion for interest from U.S. savings bonds used for higher education, the exclusion for employer-paid adoption expenses, and the deductions for IRA contributions and student loan interest. If you're married, filing a separate return, and lived apart from your spouse for the entire tax year, the special allowance is up to $12,500. If you lived with your spouse at any time during the year and are filing a separate return, you can't use the special allowance.

> **Example**
>
> You are single with MAGI of $135,000. You actively participate in the rental of your condo at a ski resort. Your rental loss in excess of passive activity income is limited to $7,500: $25,000 – 50% of ($135,000 – $100,000).

3. You are a "real estate professional" who meets certain tests in the tax law. In this case, your losses from rental realty are not subject to the passive activity loss rules (see Planning Tip) that follows.

Planning Tip

If you rent out your vacation home for more than 15 days and use it for less than 14 days or 10% of the days of rental, you are *not* subject to the passive activity loss limitations on your deductions if you are considered a "real estate professional." This means:

- More than 50% of your personal services during the year are performed in real estate trades or businesses in which you materially participate (e.g., work more than 500 hours for the year, which is 10 hours a week for 50 weeks, or your participation is substantially all of the participation for the activity during the year and this is more than the time you spend in a job or on a non-real estate business).
- You perform more than 750 hours of service in real estate trades or businesses in which you materially participate.

Pitfalls

Getting help with home renovations through an HGTV show may be taxable even if the show uses the home for fewer than 15 days. The value of the home improvements is not tax-free rental, but rather taxable income.

If you rent your home to a movie studio or other business for use for fewer than 15 days, you may still receive Form 1099-MISC reporting the rental payment to you (and to the IRS). Because IRS computers match tax returns to these information returns, you must report the income on Schedule E of Form 1040 or 1040-SR and then subtract it as an expense—show the same amount with the caption of "under 14-day rule."

If you rent out your home for more than 15 days but use it for less than 14 days or 10% of the rental days, you cannot deduct the portion of home mortgage interest disallowed under the rental loss rules discussed earlier. In this case, since your home ceases to be treated as a personal residence, you cannot itemize any portion of the mortgage interest.

When you sell your vacation home, don't be surprised by the tax impact that can result. Your gain probably does not qualify for the home sale exclusion (see Chapter 4) because the vacation home is not your principal residence. As long as you own the home for more than one year, your gain is a long-term capital gain.

If you rented the home at any time and claimed depreciation on it, you must recapture the depreciation on the sale. This means that gain to the extent of your depreciation is taxed at 25% (assuming you are in a tax bracket above this rate).

Example

In 2025, you sell your vacation home for a profit of $100,000. You had bought the home in 2017 and claimed depreciation deductions for the rental of the home totaling $2,800. Of the $100,000 gain, $2,800 is taxed at a rate up to 25%, while $97,200 is taxed at 15% (20% if your taxable income exceeds a certain threshold for your filing status).

If you realize a loss on the sale of your vacation home, your ability to claim the loss depends on whether or not the home was used for rental.

- If the home was used solely for personal purposes, no loss can be claimed on the sale.
- If the home was used some of the time for rental activities, you cannot claim a loss on the sale.
- If the home was converted solely to rental, you can then claim a capital loss on the sale. The loss is limited to the decline in value after the conversion.

Example

If the home was purchased for $150,000 and has declined in value to $125,000 when you decide to sell it, you can convert it to rental at this time and figure your deductible loss with reference to the $125,000 value. Assume you sell the home after a year on the market for $100,000. Your actual loss is $50,000 ($150,000 − $100,000), but your deductible loss is $25,000 ($125,000 − $100,000). Converting the home to rental means holding the property out for rental, even if you are unsuccessful in your efforts.

Where to Claim the Benefit

If you use your vacation home solely for personal purposes, you deduct your mortgage interest and real estate taxes on Schedule A of Form 1040 or 1040-SR (as explained in Chapter 4).

If you rent out your vacation home, you report your rents and expenses in Part I of Schedule E of Form 1040 or 1040-SR (unless rental income from your vacation home is tax free).

If you are subject to the passive activity loss limitations, you must complete Form 8582, *Passive Activity Loss Limitations*, to determine your deduction limit for the year.

If you have income from rental activities and you are not a real estate professional, this income is taken into account in determining the net investment income (NII) tax figured on Form 8960, *Net Investment Income Tax—Individuals, Estates, and Trusts*.

Home Office

The president of the United States works from home, but since he doesn't pay for the costs of the Oval Office, he can't claim any deduction for his home office. Neither can the millions of employees with remote work arrangements. This is because employee business expenses are not deductible (with minor exceptions). But if you work from your home and are self-employed, you may qualify for write-offs if certain conditions are met. This is so whether your business is full time or you have a side hack.

Benefit

If you use a part of your home for business, you may qualify to deduct costs related to the home office, including rent (if you lease your residence) or depreciation (if you own your home), maintenance and utilities, and other expenses. In effect, the personal expenses you are already paying become deductible business expenses, so the home office deduction is a write-off that doesn't require you to pay anything other than what you are already paying. Alternatively, you can opt to use an IRS-set standard amount for your home office deduction.

Generally, you figure your home office deduction by apportioning expenses to that space. The IRS generally wants you to make the apportionment based on square footage. If you use the IRS-set simplified method, you can take into account your square footage up to 300 square feet to figure your deduction.

> **Example**
>
> If your home is 2,500 square feet and you use 250 square feet of it for a home office, then generally 10% of your home's expenses are part of your home office deduction if you figure your deduction based on your actual expenses.

If all your rooms are about the same size, you can opt to make your allocation based on the number of rooms. For example, if you have 8 rooms in your home and one is used for business, then one-eighth of your home's expenses are part of your home office deduction.

Once you know the home office space, then decide on the method to use for figuring the deduction. If you use the IRS's simplified method, your deduction is $5 per square foot of up to 300 of square feet, for a maximum deduction of $1,500. If you base your deduction on your actual costs, the computation is more complex. There are 2 general categories of deductible expenses—those directly related to the home office and those indirectly related to the home office. The first category includes only costs for the office itself, and these costs are fully deductible; the second category includes costs related to the home in general, and these are deductible to the extent of your allocation.

> **Example**
>
> If you paint the office, it is a direct expense and is fully deductible. If you paint the outside of your home, it is an indirect expense and is deductible to the extent of your allocation. For example, if your allocation to the home office is 10%, then 10% of the outside paint job is part of your home office deduction.

If you own the home, you claim depreciation on the portion of the house or other unit (not the land) used as a home office (see later in this chapter under Rentals). Usually, depreciation is figured using a 39-year recovery period on a straight line basis. But if the office is within property qualifying as residential rental property (e.g., you use one room in your apartment within an 8-unit building you own), then depreciation is figured using a 27.5-year recovery period.

Conditions

To be eligible to treat costs related to a home office as a deductible business expense (regardless of how you figure the deduction), you must first show that the office is one of the following:

- Your principal place of business
- A place to meet or deal with patients, clients, or customers in the normal course of your business
- A separate structure (not attached to your residence) that is used in connection with your business

Then you must show that you use the home office *regularly and exclusively* for business. Assuming you meet this condition, you must have sufficient income from your home office activity.

PRINCIPAL PLACE OF BUSINESS

The home office must be the prime location for running your business. The business itself need not be your prime activity; you can claim a home office deduction for a sideline or moonlighting business. Usually, prime location means the place where you earn your money. For example, a freelance writer's prime location is the individual's home office.

Your home office is treated as your prime location if it is used for substantial managerial or administrative activities and there is no other fixed location for these activities. For example, an electrician's prime location is the customers' homes where fees are earned. But if the electrician uses a home office to keep books, schedule appointments, and order supplies, and does not have another office, then the home office is treated as the electrician's prime location.

PLACE TO MEET OR DEAL WITH CUSTOMERS

You don't have to use your home office as your prime location. You merely have to use it on a regular basis to meet or deal with customers, clients, or patients. For example, an attorney with a downtown office who uses a home office several times each month to meet with clients qualifies as having a deductible home office. Merely using a telephone or zooming from a home office to talk with clients or customers is *not* considered meeting or dealing with them on a regular basis.

SEPARATE STRUCTURE

If you have a freestanding garage, barn, greenhouse, or studio that you use in connection with your business, it qualifies as a deductible home office. It does not have to be used as an office or qualify as a principal place of business or a place to meet or deal with customers. For example, a florist with a store in the city who uses a greenhouse on her property to grow orchids can treat the greenhouse as her home office.

EXCLUSIVE USE TEST

Whether you figure the deduction based on actual expenses or the IRS-set rate, you must show that you use the home office space regularly and exclusively for business. There is no minimum amount of time that the office must be used to show regular use. Regular use means more than just occasional use.

For purposes of showing exclusive use, you can't, for example, use the family den as an office by day and a family room by night. In one case, a piano teacher was able to show that her living room containing her baby grand piano was her home office; her family never used the room for personal reasons. Incidental use, such as walking through the office to get to personal space because of necessity does not violate the exclusive use test.

You do not have to use an entire room as your office; a portion of a room can qualify. You don't even need to make a physical partition for the space. Just be sure it is used only for business. Furnish it appropriately for your business activity (e.g., a desk, and so on if you run a travel agency business from home).

There is a special rule if you run a day-care business from home. There is another special rule for storing inventory and samples if you have a retail or wholesale business and no other fixed location for the business. These special rules are explained in IRS Publication 587, *Business Use of Your Home*.

GROSS INCOME LIMITATION

Your home office deduction cannot be more than your gross income from the home office activity whether you use the actual expense method or the IRS's simplified method. If you use your home office for a profitable business, this limitation should pose no problem. But if your business is merely a sideline generating modest income or a struggling business, you must check whether this limitation applies to you.

Gross income for purposes of the home office deduction means income from the business activity you run from home, reduced by business deductions unrelated to the qualified use of the home.

If you find that gross income is less than your home office deduction, the deduction becomes limited. Under the actual expense method, your deduction for expenses that would otherwise be nondeductible (such as depreciation and utilities) cannot exceed gross income from the home office activity, reduced by the business portion of otherwise deductible expenses. Some expenses (real estate taxes, mortgage interest, and casualty losses) may or may not be subject to the gross income limitation. It's very complicated and depends on whether you claim the standard deduction, or if you itemize, whether other limitations apply for personal itemized deduction purposes.

If, after going through the computation, you have an unused home office deduction, you can carry it forward indefinitely. (There is no carryover if you use the IRS's simplified method.) The carryforward can be used in any future year in which there is gross income from the same home office activity to offset it. Using the carryforward is permissible even if you are no longer in the same home office.

Example

At the end of 2025 you relocate to a larger home. You have a carryover from 2024. You continue to conduct your sideline business from your new home but cannot use the 2024 carryover in 2025 because you don't have sufficient gross income. In 2026, you can use the carryover from 2024 (assuming your sideline business has sufficient gross income).

Planning Tips

Claiming a home office deduction has often been called a red flag, a signal to the IRS to look closely at the deduction. But if you are entitled to claim the deduction, then by all means do so; just be prepared to back up the position you take on your tax return.

If you were unable to claim the full home office deduction in a prior year due to income limitations, be sure to include any carryover of the home office deduction in your computations for the current year.

If you qualify for a home office, there is an ancillary benefit to consider. Travel to and from your home on business is deductible business travel. In effect, there is no such thing as nondeductible commuting when you have a home office.

Pitfalls

If you are an employee who works from home, whether full-time or some days through a remote work arrangement, you cannot claim a home office deduction. You cannot claim a home office deduction if you are an employee who leases the space to your corporation. The tax law specifically bars a home office deduction in this case. But, like any homeowner, you can continue to claim your regular deductions, such as mortgage interest, real estate taxes, and casualty and theft losses.

If you use the IRS's simplified method and cannot claim a current deduction because of the gross income limitation, you *cannot* carry over the unused deduction to a future year. And, the year you use the simplified method, you cannot claim any carryover of an unused home office deduction from a year in which the actual expense method was used.

When figuring the deduction using actual expenses, all expenses related to your home office are deductible. The cost of landscaping is not part of a home office deduction. Similarly the expenses of a landline to a home office are not part of your home office deduction. You cannot deduct the basic service charge for the first line to your home. But the cost of a second phone line or even extra charges on the first line are separately deductible as a business expense that is not part of your home office deduction.

If you own your home, then any depreciation claimed with respect to a home office after May 6, 1997, must be recaptured when your home is sold. Recapture means that this portion of your gain is taxed at a 25% rate (assuming you are in a tax bracket at or above this level). You must report your depreciation even if you qualify to exclude gain on the sale of your home; you cannot use the exclusion to offset depreciation recapture.

Where to Claim the Deduction

As a self-employed individual, you figure your home office deduction using actual expenses on Form 8829, *Expenses for Business Use of Your Home*. The deduction using the IRS's simplified method is figured on the Simplified Method Worksheet in the instructions to Schedule C.

Timeshares

Owning a timeshare entitles you to use your furnished unit in a resort location for a set period of time each year. In many cases, you can exchange yours for one in another resort or change your fixed time for another. According to the American Resort Development Association, about 10 million households in the U.S. owned one or more timeshares.

Owned for personal use. Timeshares owned for personal reasons are treated in the same way as vacation homes. The tax breaks available for such ownership include:

- Deducting mortgage interest as long as the debt is secured by the property.
- Deducting real estate taxes. The taxes are deductible whether you are billed directly (as is the case in California) or the tax is separately identified on the timeshare maintenance bills (as is the case in Florida).

As in the case of other realty owned for personal use, you cannot deduct homeowners insurance, maintenance fees, or special assessments. Gain cannot qualify for the home sale exclusion (see Chapter 4) because the timeshare can never be your principal residence. Gain on the sale of your timeshare is taxed as capital gain; any loss is not deductible.

Owned for investment purposes. The rules for timeshares owned for investment purposes are explained under the topic of Rentals, which follows.

Rentals

Becoming a landlord by acquiring real estate and renting it out can be a sound financial activity. There is the possibility of making money both from rental income as well as property appreciation upon an eventual sale. The tax law helps to underwrite the cost of being a landlord, allowing for certain tax deductions. But there are limits on and special rules for write-offs associated with rental properties.

Benefit

If you rent out property, directly to tenants or through an online platform such as airbnb, you can deduct your expenses against the rental income. Net income from rentals may entitle you to claim a qualified business income (QBI) deduction. Any loss resulting from having expenses in excess of rental income can effectively be used to offset your other income, such as salary or dividends.

But losses from rental activities are subject to the passive loss rules that may restrict your deductions for the current year.

Conditions

If you own realty—a single-family home, a condo unit, a multifamily home in which you live and rent out a portion, an office building, a strip mall, or any other property—you can deduct expenses related to the property.

EXAMPLES OF DEDUCTIBLE RENTAL EXPENSES
- Advertising to find tenants
- Car expenses to and from the property
- Cleaning and maintenance
- Commissions to real estate brokers when finding tenants
- Depreciation
- Insurance
- Legal and professional fees (but not attorney's fees to buy the property)
- Management fees
- Mortgage interest on rental property
- Repairs
- Security system monitoring fees
- Supplies
- Taxes
- Utilities

PASSIVE LOSS LIMITATIONS

When you rent out property, you usually fall within the passive loss rules (exceptions to these rules are discussed later). Then, generally, your deductions cannot exceed all of your passive activity income from the year (income from this rental activity plus any other passive activities). The law calls them "losses" but really means deductions in excess of rental income.

Example

The rental of a single-family home in which you do not live during the year is your only passive activity. Rental income for the year is $6,000, while deductions are $8,000. You can deduct only $6,000 this year (unless you meet any of the 3 key exceptions in the list following).

Passive activity losses in excess of passive activity income can be carried forward and used in a future year when there is passive activity income to offset them. There is no limit on the carryforward period.

There are 3 exceptions to the ban on deducting passive losses in excess of passive activity income.

1. You can deduct all carryover losses from a passive activity in the year in which you dispose of your interest in the realty in a taxable disposition (e.g., sell your rental property).

2. You can deduct up to $25,000 of passive activity losses in excess of passive activity income from a rental activity in which you actively participate (e.g., approve new tenants, decide on rental terms, and authorize capital expenditures and repairs). The $25,000 limit begins to phase out when your modified adjusted gross income exceeds $100,000 and is completely phased out when MAGI reaches $150,000. MAGI for this purpose means AGI without taxable Social Security benefits, the exclusion for interest from U.S. savings bonds used for higher education, the exclusion for employer-paid adoption expenses, deductions for IRA contributions, the deduction for one-half of self-employment tax, and student loan interest. If you are married filing separately, see the limitation discussed earlier in this chapter.

Example

You are single with MAGI of $135,000. You actively participate in the rental of your beachfront condo. Your rental loss in excess of passive activity income is limited to $7,500: $25,000 − 50% of ($135,000 − $100,000).

3. You are a real estate professional exempt from the passive loss rules. If you are in the real estate business and want to check whether you are treated as a real estate professional exempt from the passive loss rules, see the instructions to IRS Form 8582. Just know that if you have a full-time job in addition to your real estate activities, it's highly unlikely that you'll qualify as a real estate professional.

QUALIFIED BUSINESS INCOME DEDUCTION

Regardless of whether you are actively or passively involved with your real estate rentals, if you show a profit you may be eligible for a deduction of up to 20% of your qualified business income (QBI). The QBI deduction, which is a personal deduction based on your rental income and can be taken whether you itemize or claim the standard deduction, is discussed in more detail in Chapter 14.

The IRS has provided a safe harbor under which a rental real estate enterprise is treated as a trade or business for purposes of the QBI deduction. All of the following conditions must be met:

1. You must keep separate books and records to reflect income and expenses for each rental real estate enterprise.

2. For rental real estate enterprises that have been in existence less than 4 years, 250 or more hours of rental services are performed per year with respect to the rental real estate enterprise. For rental real estate enterprises that have been in existence for at least 4 years, in any 3 of the 5 consecutive taxable years that end with the taxable year, 250 or more hours of rental services are performed per year with respect to the rental real estate enterprise.

3. You must maintain contemporaneous records, including time reports, logs, or similar documents, regarding the following: (i) hours of all services performed; (ii) description of all services performed; (iii) dates on which such services were performed; and (iv) who performed the services. If services with respect to the rental real estate enterprise are performed by employees or independent contractors, you can provide a description of the rental services performed by such employee or independent contractor, the amount of time such employee or independent contractor generally spends performing such services for the enterprise, and time, wage, or payment records for such employee or independent contractor. These records are to be made available for inspection at the request of the IRS.

4. You or the relevant pass-through entity (RPE), such as a limited liability company in which you have an interest, attaches a statement to a timely filed original return for each taxable year in which you or RPE relies on the safe harbor. An individual or RPE with more than one rental real estate enterprise relying on this safe harbor may submit a single statement but the statement must list the required information separately for each rental real estate enterprise.

Planning Tips

Depreciation is a no-cost deduction (you don't spend any dollars to claim the write-off, other than buying the property). How do you figure this valuable write-off called depreciation? It is a deduction *only* for the building (you can't depreciate land), so you must allocate the cost of the property between the building and the land.

> **Example**
>
> You buy a single-family home for rental, paying $280,000. According to your county assessor's assessment for improvements (buildings), you allocate $230,000 to the house. This is your basis for depreciation.

If you convert personal property to rental property (for example, you move from your home and rent it out), your basis for depreciation purposes is your basis (as figured earlier) or the fair market value of the home at the time of conversion, whichever is less (exclusive of the land).

> **Example**
>
> You bought your home (exclusive of the land) for $200,000 in 2012. In 2025, you move from it and rent it out indefinitely. The value of the home in 2025 is $300,000. Your basis for depreciation is $200,000, which is the lower of basis or fair market value at the time of conversion. This basis (plus any capital improvements) is used to figure depreciation in 2025 and beyond.

The amount you claim for depreciation is based on the month in which you place the property into service as a rental and the type of realty involved:

- Residential rental property is depreciated over a period of 27.5 years using the straight-line method and a midmonth depreciation convention. Residential rental property is a building for which 80% or more of the gross rental income for the year is rental income from dwelling units. So, if you own an apartment building with stores at street level, you must see whether the property meets the 80% test.

- Nonresidential property is depreciated over a period of 39 years.

Depreciation is simply your basis in the home or building (but not the land) multiplied by the depreciation rate from the IRS table. Table 10.1 shows depreciation rates for residential property. Table 10.2 shows depreciation rates for nonresidential property.

If you sublease property—you are a tenant who leases the property to someone else—you cannot claim a depreciation deduction. Depreciation for the cost of the building can only be claimed by the owner of the property.

If your landlord activities rise to the level of being a business, you may be eligible for the qualified business income deduction (see Chapter 14).

Pitfall

Depreciation claimed on your rental realty is subject to a special capital gain rate for recaptured depreciation. This means that the gain you realize on the sale is taxed at 25% to the extent of depreciation deductions you have claimed. Gain in excess of this amount is taxed at no more than 20%, or 15% for most taxpayers (assuming you owned the property for more than one year).

Example

On July 5, 2020, you bought an office building for $250,000 (exclusive of the land). You sell it on July 5, 2025, for $350,000. Depreciation deductions total $31,665. Your gain is $131,665 ($350,000 − $218,335). Of this gain, $31,665 is taxed at the 25% rate; $100,000 is taxed at 15% (assuming your taxable income does not exceed a threshold amount triggering a 20% rate). Your total tax is $22,916 ($7,916 + $15,000).

Where to Claim the Deduction

You report your rents and expenses in Part I of Schedule E of Form 1040 or 1040-SR. If you own a multifamily home in which you live, the portion of mortgage interest and real estate taxes is allocated between Schedule E (for the rental portion) and Schedule A of Form 1040 or 1040-SR (for the personal portion of the home, assuming you itemize deductions).

TABLE 10.1 Depreciation Rates for Residential Rental Property

Year	Month											
	1	2	3	4	5	6	7	8	9	10	11	12
1	3.485%	3.182%	2.879%	2.576%	2.273%	1.970%	1.667%	1.364%	1.061%	0.758%	0.455%	0.152%
2–9	3.636	3.636	3.636	3.636	3.636	3.636	3.636	3.636	3.636	3.636	3.636	3.636
10	3.637	3.637	3.637	3.637	3.637	3.637	3.636	3.636	3.636	3.636	3.636	3.636

For years 13–28, see IRS Publication 946, *How to Depreciate Property*.

TABLE 10.2 Depreciation Rates for Nonresidential Rental Property (Placed in Service after May 13, 1993)

Year	Month											
	1	2	3	4	5	6	7	8	9	10	11	12
1	2.461%	2.247%	2.033%	1.819%	1.605%	1.391%	1.177%	0.963%	0.749%	0.535%	0.321%	0.107%
2–39	2.564	2.564	2.564	2.564	2.564	2.564	2.564	2.564	2.564	2.564	2.564	2.564

If you own an interest in rental realty through a partnership or limited liability company that files a partnership return, you report your share of rental income or losses on Schedule E. You'll see the amount you must report on a Schedule K-1 that is given to you by the entity.

You must also complete Form 8582, *Passive Activity Loss Limitations*, to determine your deduction limit for the year under the passive activity rules.

Low-Income Housing Credit

The federal government wants to encourage investments in housing to accommodate low-income individuals. To make such investments attractive to investors, a special tax credit has been made available. The credit effectively operates to replace the rental income investors do not receive because of the rent reductions or breaks provided to certain renters because of their income levels.

Benefit

If you invest in low-income housing—to build it or substantially renovate existing structures—you may be eligible for a tax credit each year for a period of 10 years, generally starting with the year the building is placed in service. The amount of the credit depends on whether the building is new and whether any federal subsidies were used for construction or rehabilitation purposes.

The credit is based on 70% of the qualified basis of each new low-income housing building or 30% of the qualified basis in the case of federally subsidized new or existing buildings. The credit itself is the present value of the 10 annual credit amounts determined as of the last day of the first year of the credit period. There is a minimum 9% for newly constructed nonfederally subsidized buildings.

Conditions

You can invest in low-income housing directly, by building the units or rehabilitating existing ones, or by putting money into a limited partnership or limited liability company that does the building or rehabilitating for you. Either way, to qualify for a credit, the building must be considered a low-income housing building.

LOW-INCOME HOUSING BUILDING

Low-income housing does not mean the property must be located in the slums or that the building itself is a tenement. Rather, the tax law requires only that the building offer a certain percentage of the rental units to tenants with income below fixed levels. For example, the building is considered to be low-income housing if 50% or more of the households have an income which is less than 60% of the area median gross income or which has a poverty rate of at least 25%. How do you know if your building qualifies? You must receive certification from an authorized housing credit agency. The agency allocates the credit to you on Form 8609, *Low-Income Housing Credit Allocation Certificate.*

The building must have been constructed after 1986; older buildings don't qualify.

Planning Tip

Generally, the first year of the credit is the year in which the building is placed in service for low-income housing. But you can elect to start claiming the credit in the following year just by indicating your election on Form 8609. You may wish to do so if you cannot fully benefit from the credit in the year the building is placed in service (see "Pitfall" that follow) or if you will have more income to offset in the following year.

Pitfall

You may have to recapture some of the credit amounts claimed. If you dispose of your interest before the end of a set period, you are subject to recapture. This means that part of the benefit you received from claiming the credit is reported as an additional tax you owe in the year of recapture. The building must continue to meet certain requirements for a 15-year period. If not, then your recapture is figured on Form 8611, *Recapture of the Low-Income Housing Credit.*

Where to Claim the Credit

You figure your credit on Form 8586, *Low-Income Housing Credit.* The credit is part of the general business credit, which is figured on Form 3800, *General Business Credit.*

You may also need to figure whether the passive activity restrictions apply to your claiming the credit in the current year. You do this by completing Form 8582-CR, *Passive Activity Credit Limitations.*

The amount of the credit that can be claimed this year is then entered on Schedule 3 of Form 1040 or 1040-SR.

Rehabilitation Credit

Fix it up or tear it down? The tax law provides a key incentive for restoring certain older properties. The incentive is a tax credit that may be claimed if certain conditions are met.

Benefit

If you spend money fixing up an old building, you may be eligible to claim a tax credit. The credit is 20% for qualified rehabilitation expenditures for a certified historic structure. The credit is taken ratably over 5 years.

There is no overall dollar limit on the credit, but there are certain limitations that may restrict the amount you can claim in the current year.

Conditions

There are 2 conditions:

- The building must be a historic structure
- The costs must be qualified rehabilitation expenditures that exceed a certain amount

HISTORIC STRUCTURES

The credit applies to both residential and nonresidential buildings (such as industrial and commercial buildings). The only criterion is that the building is a historic structure that has been recognized by a national or state registry (placed on the National Register of Historic Places or located in a registered historic district and certified by the Secretary of the Interior as being of historic significance to the district).

The National Park Service must certify that your planned rehabilitation of the building is in keeping with its historic status designation.

MINIMUM REHABILITATION

You can't claim the credit simply for adding a doorbell or making other minor renovations. The credit is limited to expenses of at least a certain amount: $5,000 or your adjusted basis in the building, whichever is greater.

Example

You buy a certified historic structure for a cost of $50,000 (exclusive of the land). To claim the credit, you must spend at least $50,000 on renovations (since your basis of $50,000 is greater than $5,000).

The expenditures must be made within a 24-month period. This period is extended to 60 months if the rehabilitation is undertaken pursuant to a written architectural plan and specifications are completed before the rehabilitation begins.

Planning Tips

When shopping for real estate to purchase for investment or business, consider the impact that claiming the credit may have on your fix-up costs. Also explore any federal or state grants that may be available for restoring historic structures.

Check to see if there are state income tax credits or other incentives (such as property tax abatements) for rehabilitating certified historic structures. The rehabilitation credit can offset both regular tax and the alternative minimum tax.

Pitfalls

The tax credit for rehabilitating an old building falls under the passive loss rules. This means that the credit you are otherwise entitled to claim may be limited by passive activity restrictions. For more details, see the instructions to Form 8582-CR, *Passive Activity Credit Limitations*.

If a façade easement is donated in the same year the rehabilitated building is placed in service, no rehabilitation tax credit can be claimed. If you've previously claimed a rehabilitation tax credit with respect to property and subsequently make a qualified conservation contribution with respect to the façade easement, the charitable contribution is considered a partial disposition of the property. This event triggers recapture of all or part of the credit if the contribution is made within the recapture period (5 years from the placed-in-service date). The deduction for a façade easement is explained in Chapter 5.

Where to Claim the Credit

You figure your credit on Form 3468, *Investment Credit*. You must include the project number assigned by the National Park Service. The credit is part of the general business credit, which is figured on Form 3800, *General Business Credit*.

You may also need to figure whether the passive activity restrictions apply to your claiming the credit in the current year. You do this by completing Form 8582-CR, *Passive Activity Credit Limitations*.

The amount of the credit that can be claimed this year is then entered on Schedule 3 of Form 1040 or 1040-SR.

Like-Kind Exchanges

If you swap real property held in business or for investment purposes and meet certain requirements, gain on the exchange can be deferred. You may see like-kind exchanges being referred to as "tax free," but this is a misnomer; you're merely postponing having to pay tax on your gain.

Benefit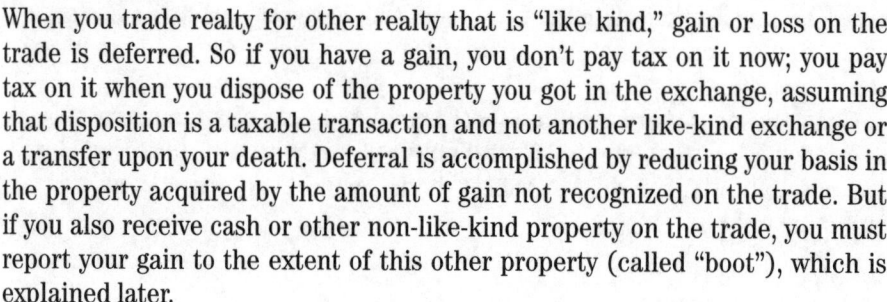

When you trade realty for other realty that is "like kind," gain or loss on the trade is deferred. So if you have a gain, you don't pay tax on it now; you pay tax on it when you dispose of the property you got in the exchange, assuming that disposition is a taxable transaction and not another like-kind exchange or a transfer upon your death. Deferral is accomplished by reducing your basis in the property acquired by the amount of gain not recognized on the trade. But if you also receive cash or other non-like-kind property on the trade, you must report your gain to the extent of this other property (called "boot"), which is explained later.

Conditions

The main condition for deferring gain on a trade of realty is that the property given up and the one acquired in the trade are like kind. If the trade is not simultaneous, you must meet certain time limits.

LIKE-KIND PROPERTY

Most realty held for business or investment purposes is like kind even though one property may be very dissimilar to another. Examples of like-kind realty swaps:

- Commercial property for residential rental property
- A lease that still has at least 30 years to run for an ownership interest in realty
- Improved property for unimproved property
- Lots in urban areas for lots in rural areas

Example

On March 1, 2025, you trade a factory for an apartment building, each worth $1 million. If you'd sold the property, you would have had a $300,000 profit. You don't have to report this profit in 2025, but the basis of the property you acquired becomes $700,000 ($1 million − $300,000). When you sell the apartment building, the gain not recognized on the trade increases the gain reported on this sale.

Not all real property can be exchanged to produce tax deferral. Nonqualifying real property includes:

- Main home
- Real property located outside the United States *cannot* be part of a like-kind exchange. You can't swap a building in Canada for one in the U.S. and defer your gain.
- Vacation homes and second homes unless an IRS-set safe harbor is met (see Rev. Proc. 2008-16).
- Fixer uppers and newly built homes (these are considered "stock in trade" that cannot be exchanged for tax deferral).

You can trade multiple properties, as long as they are all like kind.

Example

You trade a strip mall for 2 office buildings or 5 residential rental properties for 3 vacant lots, all of which are in the United States. These qualify for like-kind exchange treatment. If the trades are not simultaneous, see the time limits that follow.

NON-SIMULTANEOUS EXCHANGES

You don't have to trade properties simultaneously. But if you give up property (the "relinquished property") and receive the replacement later on (a "deferred exchange"), or receive a replacement but don't give up property for a while (a "reverse exchange"), you must watch for certain time limits in order for the trade to enjoy like-kind exchange treatment. And you may use a qualified intermediary, such as an escrow company, to facilitate the trade without you collecting sales proceeds, which is an action that kills like-kind exchange treatment.

There are 2 key time limits:

- You have 45 days from the date you sell the relinquished property to identify potential replacement properties. The identification must be a legal description (e.g., street address or distinguishable name) in writing, signed by you and delivered to a person involved in the exchange, such as the seller of the replacement property or the qualified intermediary. Notice to your attorney, real estate agent, accountant, or similar persons acting as your agent is not sufficient. You can identify up to 3 potential properties of any value or more than 3, but there are value limits on the identified properties.

- The replacement property must be received and the exchange completed no later than 180 days after the sale of the exchanged property or the due date (with extensions) of the income tax return for the tax year in which the relinquished property was sold, whichever is earlier. The replacement property received must be substantially the same as property identified within the 45-day limit.

For reverse exchanges, the IRS has created a safe harbor that essentially uses the same time limits. For more information, see Rev. Proc. 2000-37.

RECEIVING BOOT

If you receive anything over and above the property, such as cash or the payment for you of certain closing costs, the additional property is called "boot." You must report taxable gain to the extent of boot received.

If you pay additional cash on the exchange, it becomes part of your tax basis for the acquired property.

Example

You trade your unimproved land worth $100,000 that you bought for $60,000 for unimproved land worth $85,000 plus $15,000 cash. Of your $40,000 gain, you must report $15,000 as taxable gain in the year of the exchange; you can defer the balance of the gain ($25,000).

Planning Tip

Watch out for tax scams that pitch the use of "tax-free exchanges" for vacation homes or second homes used solely for personal purposes. These do not qualify for tax deferral of gain on the trade.

Pitfalls

If you have a loss, it is advisable to sell the property so you can take the loss for tax purposes. If you exchange the property, you cannot take the loss now; the same deferral rule for gains applies to losses.

Monitor the time limits for non-simultaneous exchanges carefully. You cannot get an extension of time other than if you're delayed by a federally-declared disaster.

Where to Report the Like-Kind Exchange

You report the like-kind exchange on Form 8824, *Like-Kind Exchanges,* and file it with Form 1040 or 1040-SR. If you have to report gain on the exchange (e.g., you receive boot), it is reported on Form 4797, *Sales of Business Property*.

Deduction for Energy-Efficient Commercial Buildings

It has been estimated that commercial buildings use one-quarter of all domestic energy consumption. To encourage owners and lessees of commercial property to make certain energy improvements, there is a special deduction.

Benefit

The cost of energy-efficient property can be deducted up to $5.81 per square foot in 2025.

Conditions

To qualify for a deduction, property must be installed as part of a plan designed to reduce the total annual energy and power costs with respect to the interior lighting systems, heating, cooling, ventilation, and hot water systems of the building by 25% or more, in comparison to a reference building that meets the minimum requirements of the applicable reference standard using certain methods of calculation. The IRS listed the applicable reference standards in Announcement 2023-01.

In 2025, the deduction is $0.58 increased (but not above $1.16) by $0.02 for each percentage point by which the total annual energy and power costs for the buildings are certified to be reduced by a percentage greater than 25%. The applicable dollar value used to determine the increased deduction amount for property is $2.90 increased (but not above $5.81) by $0.11 for each percentage point by which the total annual energy and power costs for the building are certified to be reduced by a percentage greater than 25%. In both instances, the higher dollar limit applies when certain wage and apprenticeship rules for the project are met. The IRS explains wage and apprenticeship rules at https://www.irs.gov/credits-deductions/prevailing-wage-and-apprenticeship-requirements.

The building owner must obtain certification of a plan to reduce overall energy costs before installing the property. There are various ways to satisfy the certification requirement, including use of approved software to calculate energy consumption.

Planning Tip

Check for state tax incentives for making energy improvements. Many states provide deductions and/or tax credits for these improvements. Find state tax incentives at DSIRE at https://www.dsireusa.org/.

Pitfall

The basis of the property must be reduced by the amount of any deduction claimed. This will have the effect of reducing allowable depreciation for the property.

Looking Ahead

The deduction for energy-efficient commercial buildings applies only to projects begun no later than June 30, 2026. They can be completed and placed in service after this date and still qualify for the deduction.

Where to Claim the Deduction

The deduction is a business expense reported by the building's owner or lessee on the proper tax return.

Qualified Improvement Property

If you make capital improvements to the interior of commercial facilities, a deduction for your outlays is not tied to depreciation over 39 years for the cost of the building. Instead, you may be able to take significant write-offs in the year you make the expenditures and put the property into service.

Benefits

Capital improvements (not repairs) made to qualified improvement property can be written off using:

- Section 179 deduction (first-year expensing), up to $2.5 million in 2025.
- Bonus depreciation (another first-year depreciation allowance) of 100% of expenditures after January 19, 2025 (40% if earlier in 2025).

- Regular depreciation. Qualified improvement property has a 15-year recovery period. This comes into play only if costs are not fully written off using first-year expensing and/or bonus depreciation.

Conditions

The deductions apply only to qualified improvement property. Qualified improvement property is an improvement to the interior of a commercial building that has already been placed in service (i.e., not new construction).

Certain improvements are specifically excluded from this definition:

- Improvements that enlarge the building
- Improvements that change the internal structural framework of the building
- An elevator or escalator

The rules for first-year expensing, bonus depreciation, and regular depreciation are covered in Chapter 14 under "Equipment Purchases."

Planning Tips

Capital improvements that cannot be treated as qualified improvement property are nonetheless deductible. The cost may have to be recovered through depreciation or may qualify for more immediate write-offs. It's advisable to conduct a cost segregation study to analyze improvements to a building structure and each key building system to determine maximize write-offs. The IRS has a Cost Segregation Audit Technique Guide at https://www.irs.gov/businesses/cost-segregation-audit-techniques-guide-table-of-contents, which details how such an analysis works. The key building systems are the plumbing system, electrical system, HVAC system, elevator system, escalator system, fire protection and alarm system, gas distribution system, and the security system.

There is a special safe harbor election for small taxpayers that allows improvements to be treated as ordinary repairs, which are currently deductible (i.e., not capitalized and deducted using expensing, bonus depreciation, and regular depreciation). This safe harbor applies if you are in business with average annual gross receipts less than $10 million and you own or lease property with an adjusted basis of $1 million or less. The safe harbor deduction can be claimed if the total amount paid for improvements does not exceed the lesser of 2% of the building's basis or $10,000.

Pitfall

Deductions related to qualified improvement property are limited to those "made by the taxpayer." If the landlord gives the tenant an allowance for improvements, the tenant claims the deduction (various conditions apply).

Where to Claim the Deduction

Deductions for first-year expensing, bonus depreciation, and regular depreciation are reported on Form 4562, *Depreciation and Amortization*. Total deductions from this form are then reported on the applicable business form (e.g., Schedule C for self-employed individuals; Schedule E for landlords).

Conservation Easements

You can benefit from your realty without disposing of it if you're willing to share. You can enjoy a current tax deduction if you donate a conservation easement to a charity, such as a local land trust. Find details in Chapter 6.

Borrowing and Interest

We often choose or are forced to rely on credit to pay for the things we want or need. Whether you are a borrower or a lender, you may be eligible for tax breaks with respect to certain loan activities.

As of the second quarter of 2025, total household debt reached $18.20 trillion, of which $1.18 trillion was credit card debt. While interest on credit cards for consumer purchases is not deductible, interest on certain other borrowing is tax favored, as explained in this chapter. For more information, see IRS Publication 550, *Investment Income and Expenses*, and IRS Publication 4681, *Canceled Debts, Foreclosures, Repossessions, and Abandonments*.

Home Mortgage Interest

If you are a homeowner repaying a mortgage, you can deduct the interest portion of your payments. There is no dollar limit on how much interest you can deduct. The law limits the amount of borrowing you can take into account in figuring your deductible interest on loans taken after October 14, 1987.

- For acquisition indebtedness obtained before December 15, 2017, to buy, build, or substantially renovate your home: $1 million ($500,000 for a married person filing separately)

- For acquisition indebtedness obtained on or after December 15, 2017, to buy, build, or substantially renovate your home: $750,000 ($375,000 for married persons filing separately)

Home mortgage interest is deductible only as an itemized deduction; you cannot deduct the interest if you use the standard deduction.

For more details on deducting home mortgage interest, see Chapter 4.

Student Loan Interest

When you are repaying student loans, you may be able to deduct up to $2,500 of interest annually. The deduction is an adjustment to gross income, so you can claim it even if you do not itemize your other deductions and simply use the standard deduction.

The ability to deduct student loan interest depends on your modified adjusted gross income (MAGI). If your MAGI is too high, you cannot claim this benefit.

If you have student loans forgiven, you probably won't have any income from this debt forgiveness for federal income tax purposes (it depends on the type of loan forgiven), but you may have income for state income tax purposes.

For more details on deducting student loan interest and the cancellation of student loan debt, see Chapter 3.

Car Loan Interest

If you buy a vehicle in 2025 and finance the purchase, you may be able to deduct the interest you pay on the car loan, whether or not you itemize. The annual limit on the interest deduction is the amount of interest paid up to $10,000. There are certain income limits and other conditions that apply for the deduction, which are explained in Chapter 7.

Borrowing from Retirement Plans

A 401(k) or other qualified retirement plan may allow you to borrow from your account. The loan proceeds from a qualified retirement plan are generally not taxable to you. No tax-free borrowing is allowed for IRAs and IRA-based plans, such as SEPs and SIMPLE-IRAs.

Benefit ⊗

Proceeds you receive when borrowing from your 401(k) or other qualified retirement plan are not taxable. The plan must allow for borrowing by participants; a plan is not *required* to offer this option. Assuming your plan does, then the maximum loan is usually limited to 50% of your vested account balance or $50,000, whichever is less. The limits increase to the lesser of $100,000 or 100% of the account balance for disaster victims, and the plan can give an extra year for repayment.

Interest on the loan used for personal purposes (other than acquisition indebtedness explained earlier), such as paying off credit card debt or college tuition, is generally not deductible. Interest on the loan used for investment purposes is deductible under the investment interest rules (discussed later in this chapter), assuming that in 2025 you are not a "key" employee (a more-than-5%-owner, a more-than-1%-owner-employee earning more than $160,000, and a corporate officer with compensation over $230,000). Interest on the loan to buy a first or second residence is deductible if (1) you are not a key employee, (2) the account balance is not used to secure the loan, and (3) the residence is collateral for the loan.

Conditions

The loan can be taken for *any* reason; you don't even have to tell the plan administrator why you want to borrow money. But the reason impacts the repayment term. If you use the loan to buy a principal residence for yourself, the repayment period can be any time frame that is reasonable (e.g., 15 years). If you borrow for any other purpose, you must repay the loan in substantially equal ("level") amounts that include interest and principal within 5 years. Repayment is made at least quarterly, and there may be a processing fee charged for the loan.

For COVID-19-related loans taken in 2020, there was a one-year suspension, so the normal 5-year repayment period was extended to 6 years. Interest continued to accrue during this suspension period. And as mentioned earlier, disaster loans can be extended for up to one year beyond the usual 5-year repayment period.

If you are married, your spouse must consent to the loan.

Planning Tips

If you are on a leave of absence and your salary is reduced so that it's insufficient to repay the loan, your employer may suspend payments for up to one year. If you are in the armed forces, repayment may be suspended during a period of active duty.

The interest rate charged by the plan is usually very low compared with commercial loans. What's more, it is easy to arrange a plan loan. Just ask your plan administrator, complete a short form (you do not have to disclose any personal financial information), and the money is paid to you quickly (usually within days of your request).

If a qualified retirement plan in which you participate allows for a special distribution, you can withdraw up to $1,000 per year for personal or family emergency expenses without the 10% penalty that would otherwise apply if you are under age 59 ½. You self-certify the need; your employer does not check up on your claim. Technically it's a distribution, but you can think of this option as a loan because you can recontribute the distribution within 3 years. No interest is charged on the distribution. But the distribution is reported as taxable income and subject to taxes. If you recontribute some or all of the contribution, you'll need to file an amended return to back out the income and recover the taxes you paid.

You can also effectively "borrow" interest free from your retirement plan or IRA under certain conditions, because distributions can be repaid to your account. A distribution that is repaid within 60 days is not taxed. Also, if you take a penalty-free distribution from your account to buy your first home but the sale falls through, you usually have up to 120 days to recontribute the funds and the distribution is not taxable. If the sale falls through due to a federal disaster, you may have even more time to recontribute the funds. Check with your plan administrator or IRA custodian for details.

Pitfalls

Because retirement plans are designed to build savings for your retirement, borrowing will limit your savings for the future. The money taken as a loan is no longer invested for growth. But the interest you pay on the loan is repaid to your account. You are permitted to continue making contributions to the plan, but most people who borrow in this fashion use their wages for loan repayment and other purposes and effectively suspend making contributions until the loan is repaid, which means another missed opportunity for retirement savings.

If you fail to repay the loan, it is treated as a taxable distribution (called a "deemed distribution") to you, which becomes immediately taxable and, depending on your age, subject to a 10% early distribution penalty. Similarly, if you leave the company before repaying the loan, you usually will have to repay the loan immediately or have a deemed distribution. The amount that is taxable is reported to you on Form 1099-R, *Distributions From Pensions, Annuities, Retirement or Profit-Sharing Plans, IRAs, Insurance Contracts, etc.* For repayments that would otherwise be treated as deemed distributions, you have until the extended due date of your return to deposit the balance to an IRA and avoid taxation. This rule applies if you are terminated or leave the job voluntarily with an outstanding loan balance.

There is a distinction between loans that you take because you have a financial emergency and "hardship distributions." Hardship distributions, which may be allowed for certain severe financial hardships (e.g., facing foreclosure), are always fully taxable and, if you are under age 59 ½, subject to a 10% early distribution penalty (unless there is an exception, such as on account of disability) and they cannot be repaid to the acccount.

Where to Report the Loan

The loan proceeds are not reported on your tax return because a loan does not produce taxable income.

Investment-Related Interest

You can deduct interest paid on loans used to buy or carry investments to the extent of your net investment income received (such as interest income). If your investment interest paid is more than your net investment income for the year, you can carry the excess interest forward indefinitely and use it in a future year. There is no overall dollar limit on this deduction.

You can deduct investment-related interest only if you itemize your deductions. You cannot claim a deduction if you use the standard deduction.

You cannot deduct interest on a loan used to buy tax-exempt securities, such as municipal bonds or muni-bond funds.

For more details on deducting investment-related interest, see Chapter 8.

Business Interest

Business in many cases runs on other people's money. Loans are used to start up a company, buy equipment, and pay operating expenses. Loans used for business come in all sizes—fixed loans for a set term, revolving lines of credit, or even basic credit card charges for purchases made. Fortunately, whatever type of business loan is involved, interest on the loan may be fully deductible. (There is a limit on deducting business interest in 2025 other than for companies with average annual gross receipts in the 3 prior years exceeding $33 million and farming and real property businesses electing to be exempt from the limit; this rule is not discussed here.)

Benefit 🔼

If you borrow money for business—by taking out a loan or charging a business purchase to a credit card on which you finance the payments—you can deduct the interest expense in full against your business income. There is no dollar limit on this deduction.

Condition

The source of the loan does not govern the treatment of the interest. Deductibility depends on what you use the proceeds for. If you use the proceeds for business—for example, to acquire a sole proprietorship—then interest is considered fully deductible business interest.

Interest on a loan used to buy shares in a corporation is viewed as investment interest, not business interest. Interest you pay on tax deficiencies related to your business (for example, a deficiency related to Schedule C of your sole proprietorship) is not deductible. This interest is treated as personal interest, not business interest.

Planning Tip

If you guarantee a loan made to your corporation, you can deduct interest on the loan as business interest, but only when and to the extent you are called upon to do so because the corporation cannot make the payment.

Pitfalls

You cannot deduct business interest that is otherwise required to be capitalized, such as construction period interest. In effect, you cannot deduct interest during the construction period. Construction period interest is added to the basis of the property.

If you borrow money from your corporation, the interest you pay back to the corporation is *not* automatically business interest just because of your relationship to the lender. Again, the treatment of interest depends on what you use the proceeds for. For example, if you borrow money from your corporation to take a vacation, the interest is nondeductible personal interest.

Where to Claim the Deduction

Self-employed individuals who pay business interest deduct these payments on Schedule C of Form 1040 or 1040-SR.

Accrued Interest on Bond Purchases

In the financial world, bonds are bought and sold in the secondary market: After an initial offering, they trade among investors at their current values. But when trades are made between interest payment dates, which is common, bond buyers pay for the interest that is actually received by the bond sellers; the interest is included in the cost of the bond. The tax law allows for a correction of this situation by allowing bond sellers a deduction.

Benefit

If you buy a bond between its interest payment dates, some interest may be included in the purchase price that doesn't belong to you. That interest is payable to the bond seller even though it is reported as payable to you. To correct this inequity, you can effectively deduct the accrued interest. This is not a tax deduction in the true sense of the word. Rather, you are allowed to make a subtraction that amounts to the same thing.

Condition

This subtraction applies only if you are a bond purchaser and there is accrued interest on the bond you buy. This occurs only when the purchase takes place between the bond's interest dates (typically twice a year).

Planning Tips

When purchasing a bond, you can ask your stockbroker or the financial institution selling bonds about interest dates on the security. Knowing the interest dates will apprise you of whether there will be any accrued interest to deal with when you file your return.

If you *sell* a bond with accrued interest, you do not subtract it from interest income. Instead, you reduce the sales proceeds by the amount of accrued interest belonging to the purchaser (which reduces your gain or increases your loss).

Example

If you sell a bond for which you paid $9,500 at $10,000 and have accrued interest of $180, you reduce the proceeds by this amount. As a result, your gain is $320 ([$10,000 proceeds − $180 accrued interest] − $9,500 basis).

Pitfall

Do *not* simply report the net amount of interest figured by subtracting from the interest reported to you on Form 1099-INT the accrued interest you paid when you purchased a bond. Netting the interest in this manner can trigger an examination of your return because your reporting does not match the information sent to the IRS on Form 1099-INT. Instead, follow the reporting instructions that follow.

Where to Claim the Benefit

Accrued interest is subtracted from taxable interest reported on Form 1040 or 1040-SR. In other words, the total interest (regular and accrued) reported to you on Form 1099-INT is reported on the return and then a separate subtraction is made for the accrued interest.

Below-Market Loans

Interest rates continue to be higher than they've been in many years, although business owners may be able to borrow from their companies and children may be able to borrow from parents at little or no interest, realizing a considerable economic benefit. The tax law takes its due through the below-market interest rate rules. Under these rules, phantom interest may be created for lenders and phantom interest deductions for borrowers. While the interest may be phantom, the income from this interest can be very real.

Benefit

If you lend money to or borrow from a relative, friend, or your business at no interest or at highly favorable low interest rates, there may be some tax issues to consider. Depending on who the parties are, the amount of the loan, and the interest rate charged, these results can ensue:

- *Gift loans up to $10,000.* Gift loans, compensation-related loans, and shareholder-corporation loans up to $10,000 have no consequences to the parties. No interest deduction can be claimed with respect to any interest that is not actually paid.

- *Gift loans in the range of $10,000 to $100,000.* No interest deduction can be claimed with respect to any interest that is not actually paid if the borrower's investment income is no more than $1,000.

- *All other loans.* In addition to interest actually paid, a deduction can be claimed for below-market interest (assuming that it is deductible interest). This is the interest that should have been charged, based on the government's applicable federal rate (AFR) for the term of the loan. The lender must report a like amount of income and the lender may be able to offset the income by deducting the forgiven interest in some way.

Example

You borrow $20,000 from your corporation interest free for 5 years. Assuming the AFR for this term is 4.5% at the time the loan originates, your annual interest deduction is $900 for each of the 5 years that the loan is outstanding (4.5% of $20,000). If the corporation treats the forgiven loan as compensation, you must report $900 as compensation each year. From the corporation's standpoint, it picks up $900 interest and deducts $900 compensation.

Keep in mind that even if you have imputed interest from a below-market loan that you've taken, it may not necessarily be deductible. It depends on what you use the loan proceeds for. If you use the funds to buy stocks, for example, you can treat the imputed interest as investment interest (discussed earlier in this chapter). But if you use the funds to pay off your personal credit card debt or take a vacation, you cannot deduct the imputed interest; it is nondeductible personal interest.

Condition

Whether a loan falls within the below-market loan rules depends on the rate of interest, if any, fixed when the loan originates. Loans fall into 3 basic categories:

1. Short-term: 3 years or less.
2. Mid-term: over 3 but not over 9 years.
3. Long-term: over 9 years.

If the loan is payable on demand (there is no fixed term), then the interest rate used for a loan outstanding for the entire year is a blended rate announced by the IRS each July. For 2025, the blended rate is 4.22%.

Each month the IRS publishes AFRs. You can find an index of the AFRs monthly at https://apps.irs.gov/app/picklist/list/federalRates.html.

Planning Tip

When arranging loans between family or other related persons, keep the below-market loan rules in mind. With today's high interest rates, it isn't easy to keep loans from falling subject to the rules. But even if lower or no interest is charged so that income results, the arrangement may still be desirable.

Pitfall

If you are the lender of a below-market loan that does not meet the gift loan or other exemption rules, you have to report interest income even though you do not actually receive any payments.

Where to Claim the Benefit

If you are exempt from the below-market loan rules, do not report anything on your return. If you are a borrower subject to the below-market loan rules, you can deduct your interest payments if such interest is otherwise deductible. For instance, if the interest qualifies as investment interest, deduct it on Schedule A of Form 1040 or 1040-SR (more details about deducting investment interest are discussed earlier in this chapter).

Bad Debts

Lenders never loan money with the expectation they won't be repaid. They expect to collect interest during the term of the loan and recoup the amount of principal in the loan. But reality shows that some borrowers default. Taxwise, lenders may be able to write off these bad loans under certain conditions.

Benefit

If you loan money to someone who fails to repay you, you can claim a loss for the outstanding balance. The conditions for writing off the loss and the manner in which the loss is treated for tax purposes depend on the type of bad debt involved. There are 2 types:

1. **Business bad debts**, which are debts arising in the course of business. For example, your business is on the accrual method of accounting and fails to receive payment on an accounts receivable; this is a business bad debt. Loans made to protect your salary are treated as business bad debts. Business bad debts are fully deductible as ordinary losses against business income.

2. **Nonbusiness bad debts**, which are any other type of debt. For example, you loan money to your friend to buy a car and your friend fails to repay the loan; this is a nonbusiness bad debt. Nonbusiness bad debts also include loans that you make to protect your investments and uninsured bank deposits (explained in Chapter 8). Nonbusiness bad debts are deductible as short-term capital losses.

Condition

You must satisfy 4 conditions in order to deduct a bad debt loss:

1. It is a valid debt.
2. There was a debtor-creditor relationship.
3. The loan was made from your after-tax income or capital.
4. You must show that the debt has become worthless.

VALID DEBT

Your right to repayment must be enforceable and cannot depend on some future occurrence. For example, if the loan violates state usury laws, the debt cannot be deducted when it goes unpaid.

If you own a corporation and make loans to it, be sure that the arrangement is truly a loan and not merely an advance of capital. If the corporation is thinly capitalized (there is just too much debt compared with equity), the IRS may view a supposed loan to the corporation as an advance of capital.

DEBTOR-CREDITOR RELATIONSHIP

You must prove that there was a debtor-creditor relationship. In the context of a business loan, there is usually no issue.

But when you lend money to family or friends, there is the question of whether you are truly lending the money or really making a gift of it.

If you guarantee a loan made to someone else who defaults, you can claim a bad debt deduction when you make the payment *if* it is a business bad debt or a nonbusiness bad debt made to protect an investment. No deduction can be claimed for making good on your guarantee of a loan for personal reasons, such as a favor to a relative or friend.

LOAN FROM AFTER-TAX INCOME OR CAPITAL

If, like most individuals, you are on the cash basis of accounting, you cannot treat nonpayments of salary, rents, or fees owed to you as bad debts. Since you never reported the income (under the cash method you report income only when you receive it), you cannot claim a bad debt deduction for nonpayment.

Example

You are a consultant on the cash method of accounting. You complete a job for which you are owed $2,500. You never recover your fee because the client has gone out of business. You cannot deduct this amount as a bad debt because you never reported the consulting fee as income. While this may seem unfair because of the time and effort you put into the work, the tax law does not view you as having sustained a loss.

WORTHLESSNESS

You must show that the debt will never be repaid. If the debtor has gone out of business or filed for bankruptcy liquidation (not a reorganization), this is a good indication that there is little hope of recovery. Show any steps you have taken to recover on the debt, such as suing for it in court or turning it over to a collection agency. You do not actually have to sue if this action would be futile because you would be unable to collect on a judgment.

In the case of nonbusiness bad debts, you must show that the debt is entirely worthless; a partially worthless bad debt cannot be claimed in this case.

To fix the year of worthlessness, show that the debt had some value on December 31 of the year prior to the year in which you believe the debt became worthless. Then show the identifiable event that leads you to conclude the debt is worthless.

You do not have to wait until the debt is due in order to claim a bad debt deduction if you know that it has already become worthless. You claim the deduction in the year it becomes worthless, not the year in which it is due.

Planning Tips

Whenever you make a loan, be sure to put all of the terms of the loan in writing. This will accomplish a couple of things: It will make the borrower aware of when and how much you expect to be repaid, and, in the case of default, you will have the proof that the arrangement was truly a loan and not a gift.

It's not always easy to tell when a debt has gone bad. You have 7 years in which to file an amended return for the year in which the bad debt became worthless in order to make a claim for a refund. The filing period generally runs 7 years from the due date of the return for the year of worthlessness.

Example

In June 2025, you discover that a loan you made to a friend became totally worthless in 2022. You have until April 15, 2030 (7 years from the original due date of the 2022 return), to file an amended return for 2022 to report the nonbusiness bad debt.

Pitfalls

You cannot claim a bad debt deduction for unpaid child support. For example, if your former spouse owes you $10,000 in back child support, you cannot write this off as a bad debt. The reason: You do not have any basis in the debt so, for tax purposes, you do not have a loss (even though you surely have an economic loss).

Also, you cannot take a nonbusiness bad debt for any debt owed to you by a political party or committee.

If you deducted a bad debt in a prior year and to your amazement you receive repayment now, you must include the amount in income in the year you receive the payment; don't file an amended return. But inclusion is required only to the extent that the deduction in a prior year reduced your tax in that year.

Where to Claim the Benefit

A business bad debt that you make in the course of your business is reported as a deductible item on Schedule C of Form 1040 or 1040-SR. But if you are a shareholder-employee with a loan to your corporation that has gone sour, determine whether it is a business bad debt or a nonbusiness bad debt. A business bad debt in this situation is not deductible by a shareholder-employee.

A nonbusiness bad debt is reported as a short-term capital loss on line 1 of Part 1 of Form 8949. In column (a), enter the name of the debtor and "Statement attached." On your own statement, which you attach to your return, include:

- A description of the debt, including the amount, and the date it became worthless.
- The name of the debtor and any business or family relationship between you.
- The efforts you made to collect the debt.
- Why you believe the debt is now worthless.

Debt Forgiveness

In some situations, lenders may be willing to accept less than the full amount owed in order to get your loan or other obligation off their books. Usually, income from the cancellation of debt (COD) is fully taxable, but there are certain exceptions to this rule that allow you to exclude COD from your income. So a bad economic situation may have a good tax result.

Benefit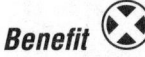

COD income is tax free if you can qualify under any category described next.

Conditions

To be nontaxable, the cancellation of debt must fall within a specific category:

- You are bankrupt.
- You are insolvent at the time the debt is canceled. Insolvency means that your debts exceed the fair market value of your assets immediately before the discharge. The exclusion for COD income is limited to the extent of insolvency.
- The debt is on your main home and you meet certain requirements. Cancellation of mortgage debt is explained in Chapter 4 and is not discussed further in this chapter.
- The debt is qualified farm indebtedness.

- The debt is qualified real property business indebtedness.
- The debt is a student loan made by a qualified lender. Cancellation of these student loans is explained in Chapter 3 and is not discussed further in this chapter.

Planning Tip

If you're excluding COD income because you are insolvent, be sure to retain good records of your assets and liabilities at the time of the debt forgiveness. This will be helpful in case the IRS questions your return.

Pitfalls

If you exclude COD income, you must reduce certain tax attributes (described next) by the amount of the excluded COD income (but not below zero). There is a set order to the reduction of tax attributes, depending upon the reason for the cancellation of debt. When you reduce tax attributes, you effectively increase your income in other ways (e.g., losing deductions or reporting greater gain on the sale or property). The order of reduction is as follows unless a special election (beyond the scope of this book) is made:

- Net operating losses (including carryovers)
- General business credit carryover
- Minimum tax credit
- Net capital losses (including carryovers)
- Basis of property
- Passive activity losses and credits (including carryovers)
- Foreign tax credit

If the cancellation of debt is because of bankruptcy or insolvency and is not because of qualified principal residence indebtedness, the basis of personal-use property (e.g., a home, home furnishings, a car) is made if there is no tax attributes to be reduced.

When you pay less than the full amount of the money owed on a loan or other obligation (e.g., credit card debt), this adversely affects your credit rating (FICO score). So, the sooner you settle up, the sooner you can begin to rebuild a good credit rating.

Where to Claim the Benefit

Forgiven debt is reported to you by the lender on Form 1099-C, *Cancellation of Debt*. If you are excluding cancellation of debt income, you must complete Form 982, *Reduction of Tax Attributes Due to Discharge of Indebtedness*. There is no income to report on your return; just attach the completed Form 982 to the return.

Insurance and Catastrophes

No one likes to think about bad things happening, but happen they do. Natural disasters, wildfires, accidents, building collapses and explosions, rioting and terrorist activities, and war all present serious personal and financial threats that can become reality. When faced with such catastrophes, insurance may carry you just so far, with economic losses outstripping your insurance recoveries. If the losses to personal-use property occur in federally-declared disaster areas, you may be able to deduct them.

This chapter explains the tax rules related to insurance and certain catastrophes. Mortgage insurance is covered in Chapter 4. Losses to your bank deposits and losses in Ponzi schemes are discussed in Chapter 8. Life insurance is discussed in Chapters 13 and 15. For more information, see IRS Publication 547, *Casualties, Disasters, and Thefts (Business and Nonbusiness)*; IRS Publication 584, *Casualty, Disaster, and Theft Loss Workbook (Personal-Use Property)*; and *Disaster Resource Guide for Individuals and Businesses* on the IRS website.

Casualty, Theft, and Disaster Losses

Things happen beyond human control, such as hurricanes, floods, and wildfires, that damage or destroy property. If there is insurance, it may only partially cover the loss. You cannot deduct casualty and theft losses to personal-use property; only losses from *federally-declared disasters* are deductible.

Benefit

If you suffer damage to personal-use property due to a casualty or theft, any insurance proceeds you recover are tax free. If you have a loss in a federally declared disaster area that is not fully covered by insurance or other reimbursements, you may be able to take a deduction for your loss. There is no overall dollar limit on the amount you can deduct, but certain restrictions means that the full out-of-pocket loss is not deductible. The deduction may be claimed whether you itemize deductions or use the standard deduction, but slightly different rules apply.

The amount of your disaster loss is limited to the decrease in the value of property from the casualty or its adjusted basis (usually your cost), whichever amount is smaller.

Rule of thumb: For property that appreciates in value, your loss is usually based on your adjusted basis; for property that declines in value, your loss is usually based on the decrease in value.

Example

You bought a painting several years ago for $2,500 that was valued at $25,000 before it was destroyed in a storm in a federally declared disaster area (you did not have any insurance for it). Your loss is limited to your adjusted basis of $2,500, which is lower than the loss in value of $25,000.

Conditions

To deduct a loss relating to your personal-use property, such as your home or car, you must meet all 4 of these conditions:

1. The loss must result from a federally declared disaster.
2. You must have proof of the loss.
3. You must reduce your loss by any insurance or other reimbursements.
4. The amount of your loss must exceed certain limits if the loss is exclusive to personal items (there are no such limits for business losses).

DEFINITION OF A FEDERAL DISASTER

A federal disaster is "an area in which a major disaster for which the President provides financial assistance under section 408 of the Robert T. Stafford Disaster Relief and Emergency Assistance Act (42 U.S.C. 5174) occurs." In simple terms, a disaster for federal tax purposes means an event that receives a FEMA disaster declaration.

PROOF OF YOUR DISASTER LOSS

You must satisfy all 4 of these conditions for a disaster loss:

1. The damage or destruction of your property occurred in a federally declared disaster area. You can find disaster designations from FEMA at www.fema.gov/disasters.
2. The date of the disaster.
3. The connection between the disaster and your loss (that is, that your loss is the direct result of the disaster).
4. That you are the owner of the property. If you lease property, you cannot claim a loss; this right belongs only to the owner unless you are contractually obligated to return the property in the same condition (in effect, you bear the risk of loss).

INSURANCE REIMBURSEMENTS

If you carry property insurance coverage, you may have little or no loss for tax purposes. You cannot create a tax loss by not submitting an insurance claim to which you are entitled. If you do not submit a claim for a covered loss, you cannot take a deduction, even for the portion of the loss not covered by insurance.

Example

You have insured an item for $10,000 for which you paid $12,000; it is now worth $15,000. If the item is destroyed in a disaster and you do not submit an insurance claim because you do not want the premiums increased on your other property or for any other reason, you cannot deduct any loss. You cannot even deduct the $2,000 that you would have been entitled to had you made the claim and received the full coverage.

What if you have made a claim but have not received any reimbursement from the insurance company by the end of the year? File your return using an estimate of what you expect for reimbursement.

If you receive more in a later year than you had estimated, report the additional insurance recovery as "Other income" on your return for that later year (do not file an amended return for the year of the disaster) to the extent you received a tax benefit from the deduction you should not have claimed. Whether you realized any tax benefit is a difficult determination for which you may need to consult a tax expert.

> ### Example
>
> In 2024, you suffered a casualty in a federally-declared disaster and figured your loss deduction based on the assumption you will receive $10,000 from the insurance company. In 2025, you receive a check from the insurance company for $12,000. On your 2025 return, report $2,000 as "Other income."

If you later receive *less* than you had estimated, you need to file an amended return to increase your loss deduction.

LIMIT FOR ITEMIZED DEDUCTION

If you itemize personal deductions, a disaster loss is subject to 2 limits:

1. *$100 per disaster limit.* You must reduce each loss from a disaster by $100. The dollar reduction applies per event (not per item lost or damaged in the event). You figure your loss separately for each item but then apply only one $100 reduction per event.

    If you are unfortunate enough to suffer losses from 2 different disasters in the same year, you must reduce your loss for each event by $100 (effectively, your total losses are reduced by $200).

2. *Overall threshold.* You deduct disaster losses (other than "qualified disaster losses") only to the extent that the total of all such losses for the year exceeds 10% of your adjusted gross income.

> ### Example
>
> You determine that the unreimbursed damage to your home from a tornado is $8,400, after reducing your loss by the $100 limit (assume you are in a disaster area). If your adjusted gross income for the year is $75,000, you can deduct $900 ($8,400 − 10% of $75,000). If your adjusted gross income is $84,000 or more, you cannot claim any disaster loss deduction.

Losses that cannot be claimed because of the 10% limit are lost forever; you cannot carry forward the unused amount.

LIMITATION FOR NON-ITEMIZERS

If you don't itemize personal deductions, you may still get a write off for unreimbursed losses of personal-use property due to a federal disaster. This is referred to as a *qualified disaster loss*. In effect, you can claim an additional standard deduction amount for the loss. But you must reduce the loss by $500. There is no adjusted gross income threshold for non-itemizers.

But the deduction for qualified disaster losses by non-itemizers is limited to federally-declared disasters beginning no later than December 12, 2024, with the incident ending no later than January 11, 2025. The disaster must have been officially declared by February 10, 2025. Whether Congress will extend the period for federally declared disasters for purposes of this deduction for non-itemizers remains to be seen. See the Supplement for any update.

TIMING OF DISASTER LOSS DEDUCTION

Usually, you claim the loss on the return for the year of the disaster, which gives you plenty of time to amass the information needed to establish your loss when completing your return.

But if you want to claim the loss on a return for the prior year, you must act no later than 6 months after the original due date of the return for the year of the disaster. This 6-month period applies whether or not you obtain a filing extension for your return.

Example

On February 1, 2025, you experience a natural disaster in an area in California declared eligible for federal disaster assistance through FEMA. The due date for the 2025 return is April 15, 2026. You have an additional 6 months from April 15 to make the election to deduct the disaster loss on a 2024 return; this extends the election period through October 15, 2026.

You have 90 days after the due date for making the election to change your mind and revoke your choice by returning to the IRS any refund or credit you received. If you revoke your choice before receiving a refund, you must return the refund within 30 days after receiving it in order for the revocation to be effective.

Planning Tips

How do you determine the decrease in value? There are a few alternatives:

- *Obtain an appraisal.* Use a qualified appraiser to determine the value of the property before and after the casualty (the tax treatment of appraisal fees is discussed later in this chapter).

- *Use the cost of repairs or restoration as the measure of loss.* You can rely on this cost if the repairs are necessary to bring the property back to its precasualty condition, the amount spent is not excessive, and the value of the property after the repairs is not more than it was before the casualty.

- If the loss involves your car, you can *use various online valuation services* to determine the value of your car, including Kelley Blue Book (www.kbb .com) and NADA Appraisal Guides (www.nadaguides.com).

If you are married and one spouse suffers a casualty loss (for example, an expensive uninsured piece of jewelry is lost in a disaster), it may be advisable to file separate returns. This is so where the spouse with the lower AGI suffers the loss. The lower AGI may entitle the spouse to a deduction that would otherwise be blocked because of the couple's combined AGI. Of course, other factors must be taken into account when filing separate returns, such as eligibility to claim other tax benefits that require filing a joint return.

Review your insurance coverage carefully to understand what it does and does not cover. You may be able to expand the coverage under your existing policy; or you may need to obtain other coverage such as flood insurance if you are located within a flood zone. In some cases, you may not be able to obtain coverage because it is just not sold or the premiums are prohibitive. For example, even though federal legislation has provided underwriting guarantees to carriers for claims due to terrorist attacks, many major carriers are simply not covering such events.

Which year should you claim the loss—the year of the disaster or the prior year? Generally, choose the year in which you have a lower adjusted gross income threshold for figuring your loss.

Example

In 2025, you have a $22,800 disaster loss (after the $100 reduction). Your adjusted gross income (AGI) for 2025 is $86,000. Your AGI for 2024 was $75,000. If you take the deduction on your 2024 return, your AGI threshold is $8,600, so only $14,200 of your loss is deductible. If you take the deduction on your 2024 return, your AGI threshold is $7,500, allowing you to deduct $15,300. In this situation, claiming the disaster loss deduction on the prior year's return provides a greater tax benefit.

If your home and its contents are damaged or destroyed in a disaster, figure the loss separately for the home and for the furnishings.

If you are living in a federal disaster area, you may be entitled to certain tax breaks, even if you don't qualify to claim a disaster loss (you might be fully compensated by insurance or might not have had any loss). For example, you may be eligible for various types of disaster assistance, such as disaster relief payments (explained next) or a loan from the SBA.

If you have a loss that isn't from a disaster, you can use it to offset gain from a casualty or theft. Such gain results when insurance proceeds exceed the adjusted basis of the damaged or destroyed property.

If you suffered a disaster loss in earlier years but failed to take a deduction because you didn't itemize, you may be able to file an amended return and claim a net disaster loss—an addition to your standard deduction.

If you are a disaster victim, you may have more time to take certain tax actions. There was an automatic extension for completing various time-sensitive tax actions (e.g., filing returns, completing an IRA rollover) and the IRS has authority to grant additional time (up to one year) for filing returns and certain other tax actions. This automatic period is 120 days for federally- and state-declared disasters after July 24, 2025 (it was 60 days for federal disasters only before July 25, 2025). Check the IRS website at https://www .irs.gov/newsroom/tax-relief-in-disaster-situations for extensions and other disaster relief.

Pitfalls

Not all losses related to a disaster are deductible. You cannot deduct your personal living expenses in temporary housing when a disaster forces you out of your home. You cannot deduct cleanup costs from the disaster.

Your deduction is limited to your economic loss. You cannot recoup anything related to sentimental value.

Example

Your wedding album is ruined during a disaster. The pictures cost a few hundred dollars, which is the limit of your tax loss, even though their value to you is priceless.

Where to Claim the Deduction

You must file Form 4684, *Casualties and Thefts*, to report the loss and figure the amount of the deduction. The deduction is then entered on Schedule A of Form 1040 or 1040-SR.

If you are itemizing deductions, the disaster loss is entered on line 15 of Schedule A. If you do not itemize but have a net qualified disaster loss, you enter the amount on line 16 of Schedule A, with adding on the dotted line "Net Qualified Disaster Loss." Also, on Line 16, list your standard deduction amount (see the Introduction) and add "Standard Deduction Claimed with Qualified Disaster Loss." Combine the 2 amounts (net qualified disaster loss and standard deduction amount), which is then entered on Form 1040 or 1040-SR.

If you are claiming a disaster loss for the prior year for which you have already filed a return, you must file an amended return, Form 1040-X. At the top of the return note "DISASTER LOSS."

Disaster Relief Payments

When disaster strikes, the federal government may provide needed assistance. The Federal Emergency Management Agency (FEMA) steps in to provide grants and other assistance to affected individuals and businesses. (For more information about disaster assistance, check www.fema.gov.) To avoid adding insult to injury, certain government assistance can be received tax free.

Benefit ⊗

You are not taxed on disaster relief payments you receive from federal agencies or charitable organizations to cover personal expenses. There is no dollar limit on the amount you can exclude from income. Your exclusion does not depend on your income or need.

The Federal Disaster Tax Relief Act of 2023, which was signed into law on December 13, 2024, makes it clear that disaster relief payments to victims of the East Palestine, Ohio, train derailment on February 3, 2023, and certain wildfires are tax free. The exclusion of certain wildfire relief payments applies to qualified wildfire relief payments received after December 31, 2019, and before January 1, 2026. The provision relating to the East Palestine train derailment in Ohio applies to amounts received on or after February 3, 2023.

Conditions

Only "qualified disaster relief payments" are excludable. These include payments, regardless of the source, for the following reasonable and necessary expenses:

- Personal, family, living, or funeral expenses incurred as a result of a presidentially declared disaster.

- Expenses incurred for the repair or rehabilitation of a personal residence due to a presidentially declared disaster (whether you own the home or rent it as a tenant).
- Expenses incurred for the repair or replacement of the contents of a personal residence due to a presidentially declared disaster.

Grants under the Disaster Relief and Emergency Assistance Act are excludable from income, but you cannot deduct a disaster loss to the extent you are reimbursed for it by the grants. Cancellation of all or part of a federal disaster loan is also considered reimbursement for a loss (it reduces your casualty loss deduction).

Disaster relief mitigation payments are also excludable from income. These are payments made under the Robert T. Stafford Disaster Relief and Emergency Assistance Act or the National Flood Insurance Act for hazard mitigation of your property, such as to elevate or relocate flood-prone homes.

Planning Tips

If you are the victim of a disaster, be sure to check with your local authorities as well as with FEMA to see whether there are any grants or relief payments you may be entitled to. Other payments may be treated as tax-free disaster relief payments.

If you've suffered a disaster and received relief payments that you previously included in gross income, decide whether to file an amended return and exclude the payments. For instance, victims of the East Palestine train derailment who included relief payments on their 2023 return may want to file an amended return and treat the payments as tax free as a way to receive a tax refund.

Pitfall

Disaster relief payments for business-related expenses, lost wages, or unemployment compensation may not be excluded from income and are fully taxable.

Where to Claim the Benefit

Since qualified disaster relief payments are not taxable, you do not have to report them on your return.

Damages

According to the Institute for the Advancement of the American Legal System, there are more than one million cases filed each year in state courts and about 400,000 in federal courts. Civil actions, such as malpractice claims, may result in financial awards to individuals. The tax law allows only certain types of damages to receive favorable tax treatment.

Benefit ⊗

If you receive compensatory damages for personal *physical* injury or illness, you can exclude your recovery. For example, if you recover damages for a medical malpractice incident that affected your body, the damages are tax free. There is no dollar limit on the amount you can exclude from income.

There is a special exclusion for persons who were persecuted by the Nazis. They can exclude *all* amounts received as restitution payments for their ordeal. The exclusion applies to:

- Heirs or estates of such persons who suffered on the basis of their race, religion, physical or mental disability, or sexual orientation.

- Restitution payments for assets that were lost or stolen before or during World War II.

- Life insurance issued by European insurance companies immediately before and during the war.

- Interest earned on escrow accounts and funds established in settlement of Holocaust victim claims.

- Restitution for victims of human trafficking. Even though the restitution payments are not limited to physical injury, the payments are fully excludable.

- Compensation paid to the wrongfully incarcerated even though the payments do not relate to physical injury. All of the payments received for wrongful incarceration are tax free.

Damages arising out of the purchase of property are treated as a recovery for injury or damage to a capital asset. As such, damages are tax free to the extent of your basis in the property.

Example

You buy land for $100,000. After the sale you learn it is contaminated and sue the seller, who settles with you for $25,000. You are not taxed on these damages. They serve to reduce your basis in the land to $75,000.

If you receive damages for any other reason, including punitive damages for physical injury or any type of damages for personal injury that is not physical, the damages are fully taxable. Nonphysical personal injuries for which damages are taxable include injury to reputation, discrimination, and back pay. Whether payments for sexual harassment are treated as physical or nonphysical personal injury depends on the situation.

Conditions

To claim the exclusion for damages, the award must relate to some physical injury or sickness. Damages for emotional distress are excludable only if they are attributable to a physical injury or sickness. So, if the physical injury causes emotional distress, then damages for emotional distress are tax free.

"Soft injuries," such as headaches, weight loss, and insomnia, arising from a work-related case (e.g., discrimination, sexual harassment) are viewed as emotional distress and not as physical injuries for which damages are tax free. Any awards for these soft injuries are excludable to the extent they compensate for medical costs.

The damages must be compensatory, meaning that they aim to make you whole from your loss (covering medical expenses, etc.). Punitive damages are not tax free, even if they relate to physical injuries.

The damages award can be a negotiated settlement or an award fixed by a court.

Planning Tip

If an action involved both physical and nonphysical injury aspects, be sure that the complaint and/or settlement papers allocate the degree of injury to each part.

Example

Suppose you are injured in a car accident in a state that does not have a no-fault law. You sue for $75,000 for personal injuries and $25,000 for damage to your car. You settle with the other party for $40,000. Of this amount, three-quarters, or $30,000, relates to personal injuries and is tax free; $10,000 relates to property damage and is taxable.

Pitfalls

If you receive interest on an award for physical damages, you are taxed on the interest even though the award itself is tax free.

If you obtain a recovery under a contingent fee agreement with your attorney, you must include the *entire* award in income if such awards are taxable (e.g., defamation actions). How you treat the attorney's fees depends on the nature of the action (see Chapter 15).

Where to Claim the Benefit

Since damages for personal physical injury are excludable from your income, you do not have to report them on your return.

If you receive damages for personal injuries that are not physical (for example, for libel), they are taxable and must be reported as "Other income" on Schedule 1 of Form 1040 or 1040-SR.

Disability Coverage

The statistics about disability are startling. According to the Centers for Disease Control and Prevention (CDC), 28.7% of the adult U.S. population have a disability. Disability can happen at any time during a person's life. To protect against this possibility during your working years, it is advisable to carry disability insurance. The tax law does not treat disability coverage in the same way as medical insurance; special rules apply that *may* allow a deduction for premiums. Benefits from disability coverage may or may not be taxable.

Benefit

Disability benefits you receive under a policy on which you paid the premiums are tax free. There is no dollar limit on the amount of disability benefits you can exclude from income. If your employer paid the premiums on a policy that you are now collecting on, the benefits are taxable to you. If you and your employer shared the cost of premiums, you must allocate the benefits accordingly; you can exclude only the portion that relates to *your* payments.

Disability coverage under Social Security is treated for tax purposes in the same way as Social Security retirement benefits—they may be wholly excludable or included in income in the amount of 50% or 85% of benefits, depending on your filing status and income (see Chapter 15). Generally, the payment of disability benefits under Social Security ends once you attain your full retirement age (for example, 66 years old for someone born in 1943 through 1954; the age increases gradually until it reaches 67 for those born after 1959). At that time you start receiving Social Security retirement benefits.

Condition

Tax-free treatment applies to benefits paid under a policy for which you paid the premiums with after-tax dollars. Tax-free treatment also applies to these types of disability payments:

- Disability pensions from the Department of Veterans Affairs
- Pensions for combat-related injuries or injuries from a terrorist attack
- Disability pensions for anyone who has injuries resulting from terrorist attacks after September 10, 2001

Planning Tips

If your employer gives you the choice between accepting employer-paid disability coverage or paying for such coverage yourself, you may prefer to pay for it so that benefits will be tax free if you become disabled. While your employer's payment of disability insurance premiums may be tax free to you, the price for this benefit is taxability of any disability payments you later receive.

If you are totally and permanently disabled and receive little or no Social Security benefits, you may be eligible for a tax credit called the credit for the elderly and disabled (see the instructions to Schedule R of Form 1040 or 1040-SR).

Pitfall

If you retire on disability and receive a lump-sum payment for accrued annual leave, you cannot exclude this payment; it is fully taxable as additional compensation.

Where to Claim the Benefit

If you are entitled to exclude disability payments you receive, you do not have to report them on your return.

Taxable disability pension payments shown on Form 1099-R are reported on your return as compensation if you have not reached the minimum retirement age set by your employer (use the same line you would for reporting salary, wages, etc.). Once you have attained the minimum retirement age, the disability pension payments are reported on lines 5a and 5b of Form 1040 or 1040-SR.

To determine the portion of Social Security disability payments that are excludable from income, complete the worksheet for Social Security benefits in the instructions to Form 1040 or 1040-SR. Social Security disability payments are reported on lines 6a and 6b of Form 1040 or 1040-SR.

Accelerated Death Benefits

A life insurance policy may provide more than just death benefits. In some cases, it can be used to provide funds during the insured's lifetime. The tax law treats the proceeds during life, called accelerated death benefits, the same as post-death payments (that is, tax free), if certain conditions are met.

Benefit ⊗

Accelerated death benefits are an insurance company's payment of some or all of the death benefits under a life insurance policy on account of terminal or chronic illness of the insured. Viatical settlements involve the selling of a cash-value life insurance policy to a company in the business of buying such policies. Accelerated death benefits and viatical settlement proceeds received by a terminally ill individual are tax free.

Such payments to a person who is chronically ill can be excluded in full to the extent used to pay long-term care costs; per diem payments in excess of care costs are excludable only up to a set dollar limit per day ($420 in 2025).

Conditions

Tax-free treatment of accelerated death benefits and viatical settlement proceeds apply for someone who is terminally ill. This means you have a condition or illness that is expected to result in death within 24 months of certification by a physician. The exclusion applies without regard to the use of the benefits or proceeds.

To qualify for favorable treatment as a chronically ill individual, you must be certified by a licensed health-care practitioner that, within the preceding 12 months, you are unable to perform for a period of at least 90 days 2 or more of the following activities:

- Eating
- Toileting
- Bathing
- Dressing
- Continence
- Transferring (such as getting in and out of bed)

A person also qualifies as chronically ill if certified as requiring substantial supervision for one's own health and safety because of cognitive impairment (for example, the person has Alzheimer's disease).

For a chronically ill individual, excludable amounts must be used to pay long-term care expenses. These are necessary diagnostic, preventive, therapeutic, curing, treating, mitigation, and rehabilitative services, as well as personal care services. The services must be provided under a plan of care prescribed by a licensed health-care practitioner (which includes a doctor, registered nurse, or licensed social worker).

Planning Tip

When shopping for life insurance, inquire about accelerated death benefit options under the policy. You may want to have as many options as possible, even if you never need to use them.

Pitfall

Generally, it is not advisable for someone who is terminally or chronically ill to use life insurance proceeds to cover lifetime care expenses. The purpose for which the policy was originally purchased, such as the care of surviving family members or the payment of funeral expenses and estate taxes, is frustrated by such use. So, using a life insurance policy for lifetime needs is usually a last resort for paying care expenses.

Where to Claim the Benefit

Insurance companies report long-term care insurance benefits on Form 1099-LTC, *Long-Term Care and Accelerated Benefits*. Per diem payments without regard to actual expenses are reported in Box 3. If box 4 is checked, benefits usually are excludable from gross income. Box 5 may be checked to indicate "chronically ill" or "terminally ill." To claim an exclusion for payments made on a per diem or other periodic basis under a long-term care insurance contract, you must file Form 8853, *Archer MSAs and Long-Term Care Insurance Contracts,* with your return.

Legal Fees

In most cases, there is no requirement that a lawyer be used to bring a lawsuit or conduct other types of business. But it is usually advisable to use an expert to protect your rights. Of course, this assistance may not come cheaply. Whether you can deduct legal fees depends on the type of activities involved.

Legal fees are discussed in Chapter 15.

Identity Theft Losses

Identity theft is all too common in the United States today. The FTC reported that consumer losses due to identity theft in 2024 exceeded $12.5 billion. If you become a victim, you can experience damage to your FICO score, delays in tax refunds, and various financial losses.

Unfortunately, identity theft losses for consumers are not deductible. This is so despite the fact that significant dollars are involved, and victims may spend additional dollars and considerable time trying to rectify things.

Identity theft protection services that you receive (as a consumer or an employee) as a result of a company's data breach are not taxable. Such services include credit reporting and monitoring services, identity theft insurance, identity restoration services, and other similar services.

Tax Identity Theft and Relief

The IRS has been working to combat the growing number of identity theft cases where taxpayer information is used to obtain tax refunds, often preventing the legitimate person from receiving his or her refund on a timely basis. The IRS has a landing page for information and assistance on identity theft at https://www.irs.gov/identity-theft-central. Here you'll find a link to the Taxpayer Guide to Identity Theft.

If you think you may be a victim of identity theft, you can protect yourself with respect to your tax return by filing Form 14039, *Identity Theft Affidavit*, with the IRS. This will help to ensure that you receive any tax refund you're entitled to. You must obtain an IP PIN if you receive a notice from the IRS (CP01A) giving you a new IP PIN or because you should have had one because your return was rejected without it. You may choose to get an IP PIN, which may be advisable if you suspect your identity may have been compromised. Find details at www.irs.gov/getanippin.

Your Job

If you're an employee, your job not only is what occupies the majority of your time during the greater part of each week and, hopefully, provides satisfaction; it also gives you a paycheck and perhaps other benefits. You may be eligible for a deduction if you receive overtime pay or tips. And there may be some fringe benefits you receive from your job that are tax free.

In order to earn that paycheck, you may have to expend your own dollars on various things. You cannot deduct most of your unreimbursed employee business expenses (unless you are a performing artist with certain income, a reservist, a state or local government official paid on a fee basis, or have impairment-related work expenses). You may want to talk with your employer about covering some or all of your job-related expenses, such as driving your car on company business. If your employer sets up an "accountable plan" for reimbursing your business expenses, you aren't taxed on the reimbursements (your employer gets to deduct the costs, and the reimbursements aren't subject to employment taxes).

For more information, see IRS Publication 3, *Armed Forces' Tax Guide*; IRS Publication 54, *Tax Guide for U.S. Citizens and Resident Aliens Abroad*; IRS Publication 535, *Business Expenses*; and IRS Publication 587, *Business Use of Your Home*.

Overtime Pay

About 12% of the U.S. workforce receive overtime pay required by the federal Fair Labor Standards Act (FLSA). If you receive time-and-a-half for working more than 40 hours in a work week, you may be able to claim a deduction to offset the reportable income, making your overtime pay tax free.

Benefit

You may claim a deduction for overtime you receive, whether or not you itemize deductions. The deduction is up to $12,500 for singles and $25,000 for joint filers who meet an income limit.

Conditions

There are 3 conditions:

1. **Qualified overtime compensation.** The overtime must be pay under the FLSA in excess of the regular rate of pay. A proposal to expand the definition is pending; check the Supplement for any update.

2. **Income.** You qualify for the full deduction only if your modified adjusted gross income (MAGI) does not exceed a threshold amount of $150,000 for singles or $300,000 for joint filers. The deduction phases out by $100 for every $1,000 of MAGI over the threshold amount.

3. **Social Security number.** You must include a valid Social Security number. If filing jointly, each spouse must include the number.

Planning Tip

If you qualify for the deduction, you may want to adjust withholding or estimated taxes for the year so you don't overpay income taxes.

Pitfalls

The deduction applies only to the portion of pay that is made for overtime.

> **Example**
>
> You receive $20 per hour, it means you get $30 per hour when working overtime. Only $10 per hour for overtime work is taken into account for the deduction.

Overtime pay is still subject to Social Security and Medicare taxes, and the deduction does not change this result.

The deduction does not reduce adjusted gross income, so it does not impact eligibility for other deductions and credits.

The deduction is scheduled to run only through 2028.

Where to Claim the Deduction

The deduction is claimed on Schedule 1-A of Form 1040 or 1040-SR.

Tips

About 4.5% of U.S. employees customarily receive tips as part of their compensation. If you are one of them, you may be able to claim a deduction that offsets taxable tips, effectively making your tips tax free. You claim the deduction whether you itemize or claim the standard deduction.

Benefit

You may claim a deduction for tips you receive, whether or not you itemize deductions. The deduction applies whether the tips are paid in cash, credit, or debit card. The deduction for tips is limited to $25,000.

Conditions

There are 4 conditions:

1. **Eligible tips.** They must be "qualified," meaning they are voluntary amounts received in cash or charged tips received from customers or through tip sharing and reported on Form W-2. Mandatory services charges are not eligible for the deduction.
2. **Income.** You qualify for the full deduction only if modified adjusted gross income (MAGI) does not exceed $150,000 ($300,000 for joint filers). The deduction phases out by $100 for each $1,000 of MAGI over the threshold.
3. **Industry.** You work in an industry in which tipping is standard. The law says "traditionally and customarily." For example, industries include those

in the restaurant and beverage industry (e.g., waiters and bartenders) and those in the beauty services industry (e.g., barbers, hair stylists, nail techs). The IRS released proposed regulations listing nearly 70 occupations in which tips are customary. Check the Supplement for any update.

4. *Social Security number.* You must include a valid Social Security number. If filing jointly, each spouse must include the number.

Planning Tips

If you qualify for the deduction, you may want to adjust withholding or estimated taxes so you don't overpay income taxes.

If you are a tipped independent contractor, see Chapter 14 to learn how the deduction affects independent contractors and the qualified business income (QBI) deduction.

Pitfalls

Tips are still subject to Social Security and Medicare taxes, and the deduction does not change this result.

The deduction is scheduled to run only through 2028.

Where to Claim the Deduction

The deduction is claimed on Schedule 1 of Form 1040 or 1040-SR.

Educator Expenses

There are about 4 million teachers in grades K–12, according to the National Center for Education Statistics. Most teachers spend money from their own pockets to pay for classroom expenses. The tax law lets them deduct their costs, up to a limit, regardless of whether they itemize deductions.

Benefit

If you are an educator, for 2025 you can deduct up to $300 of what you spend out-of-pocket for classroom expenses and professional development courses related to curriculum as an adjustment to gross income; you do not have to itemize deductions to claim this benefit.

Looking Ahead

Starting in 2026, out-of-pocket expenses of educators becomes an itemized deduction. This means there no dollar limit on the amount that can be deducted if teachers itemize their personal deductions. But educators who claim the standard deduction can no longer take a deduction.

Conditions

You must be an educator in grades K–12. This includes not only teachers, but also principals, guidance counselors, and aides. The Tax Court allowed a high school coach to deduct his costs for sports over IRS objections that only classroom expenses counted; the track was his classroom.

You must work at least 900 hours a school year in a school that provides elementary or secondary education.

You must pay qualified expenses. Examples:

- Supplies, books, computer equipment, and other materials used in the classroom (including health and physical education courses).
- Professional development expenses, which are courses related to the curriculum that the educator teaches.
- Personal protective equipment (PPE) and other materials and supplies designed to stem the spread of infection, such as hand sanitizers and disposable gloves.

Planning Tip

Keep receipts to support any claimed deduction for classroom expenses.

Pitfall

If you homeschool your child, you cannot claim this deduction.

Where to Claim the Deduction

Enter the amount of your out-of-pocket expenses up to $300 on Schedule 1 of Form 1040 or 1040-SR.

Prizes and Awards

Recognition for a job well done is always appreciated. When it is accompanied by a monetary item, it may be valued even more. Taxwise, a prize or award may be tax free under very limited circumstances.

Benefit

If you receive certain prizes or awards *other than cash*, you can exclude the amount you receive from income. These include awards of tangible personal property, such as the proverbial gold watch, given as awards for length of service or safety achievements, and your employer is permitted to deduct the cost of those awards. But other prizes and awards are fully taxable.

Conditions

Generally, your ability to exclude employment-related prizes and awards depends on your employer's ability to deduct the payments. But you don't have to be the company's comptroller to determine this; the company will report to you the tax treatment of the award on your Form W-2.

Just to give you some idea of the extent of what you can exclude, your employer's deduction depends on whether the award is part of a qualified award plan. If yes, then up to $1,600 may be given to the same employee during the year. If the award is not part of a qualified award plan, then the annual limit per employee is $400.

Planning Tip

If you receive a valuable prize or award that is *not* tax free, your employer will automatically withhold income taxes on the payment (at your regular rate or a flat rate of 22%). If this withholding is not enough to cover your estimated tax requirements, ask your employer to withhold an additional amount.

Pitfall

If you win a sales or other contest on the job and receive a prize, such as a vacation, you can decline the award to avoid taxation on the benefit. If you accept the prize, you are generally taxed on the value of the benefit.

Where to Claim the Benefit

Prizes and awards that are tax free are reported on your tax return.

Performing Artists

Actors, singers, dancers, comedians, and other performing artists can deduct the same job expenses as any other worker. But the tax law provides a special rule on *how* to claim deductions.

Benefit

If you are a performing artist with income below a set amount, you can deduct your employment-related expenses as an adjustment to gross income (AGI).

Conditions

You must meet all of the following 3 conditions to treat your job-related expenses as an adjustment to gross income rather than as an itemized deduction:

1. You have 2 or more employers in the performing arts during the year with at least $200 of earnings from at least 2 of them.
2. Your expenses from acting or other services are more than 10% of your gross income from such work. For example, you spend $8,000 during the

year on voice lessons and earn $22,000 doing voice-overs and other jobs in the performing arts. Since $8,000 is more than 10% of $22,000, you meet this condition.

3. Your adjusted gross income from all sources (not just performing arts) is no more than $16,000. This fixed dollar amount has not been changed since 1986, although a proposal would increase it considerably; check the Supplement for any update.

SPECIAL RULE FOR MARRIED INDIVIDUALS

You must file a joint return if you are married, unless you live apart from your spouse for the entire year.

If both you and your spouse work in the performing arts, you figure the two-employer requirement and the 10% requirement separately for each of you. Compare your personal employment-related expenses to the money you earn from performing arts jobs.

For purposes of your adjusted gross income, the $16,000 applies to your *combined* AGI. There is a proposal to greatly increase the income limit; check the Supplement for details.

Planning Tip

As with any other type of expense, it is vital to keep good records of your job-related outlays. Retain receipts for lessons you take. Use a diary, app, or other record keeper to note travel expenses and other items.

Pitfall

Even $1 of adjusted gross income over the $16,000 limit means your expenses cannot be deducted. If you anticipate AGI of about this amount, weigh carefully the after-tax cost of accepting work that puts you over the limit.

Example

You earn $15,000 from your work in acting, have expenses of $7,000, and meet the other conditions for treating your expenses as an adjustment to gross income. This means your AGI after the deduction becomes $8,000. But if you have $1,000 more of AGI, your expenses are deductible in excess of $320, so your write-off is limited to $6,680. The $1,000 of additional income nets you only $680 ($1,000 – $320 lost deduction).

Where to Claim the Benefit

You figure your deductible work-related expenses on Form 2106. Your total amount is then entered on Schedule 1 of Form 1040 or 1040-SR.

State or Local Government Officials Paid on a Fee Basis

Not every bureaucrat is a regular employee on the government's payroll. Some government employees are paid under a contract arrangement. Those who are can write off their related employee expenses in a special way.

Benefit

If you are an employee of a state or local government and are paid in whole or in part on a fee basis, you can deduct the business expenses related to these services as an adjustment to gross income rather than as a miscellaneous itemized deduction.

Conditions

The only conditions for treating your business expenses as an adjustment to gross income are:

- You are an employee of a state or local government.
- You are paid in whole or in part on a fee basis.

Planning Tip

If you are a state or local government employee, ask to arrange partial compensation on a fee basis (for example, related to a specific government project) to create an above-the-line deduction for your job expenses.

Pitfall

There is no downside to treating these business expenses as an adjustment to gross income.

Where to Claim the Deduction

You figure your deductible work-related expenses on Form 2106. Your total amount is then entered on Schedule 1 of Form 1040 or 1040-SR.

Repayment of Supplemental Unemployment Benefits

While unemployed, you may receive benefits in addition to regular state unemployment benefits. These "supplemental" benefits may have to be repaid once you obtain employment. If so, you may be able to write them off, either as a deduction or as a tax credit, if certain conditions are met.

Benefit ⊕

If you are required to repay supplemental unemployment benefits in order to qualify for trade readjustment allowances, you can claim a deduction for the repayment as an adjustment to gross income.

In some cases, you may even be eligible for a tax credit (instead of a deduction) for your repayments. The credit is refundable, which means you can receive it even if it's more than your tax liability.

Conditions

To claim the deduction, you must be required to repay supplemental unemployment benefits that you included in income in a prior year. The deduction is designed to wipe the slate clean; you already paid tax on the benefits when you received them and now you are entitled to a deduction to reduce your income, effectively backing out the benefits.

To claim a credit, your repayment must exceed $3,000. Then figure your credit by recomputing the tax you would have paid had you not received the repaid amount in the initial year, and compare the tax with what you actually paid.

Example

In 2024, you received supplemental unemployment benefits and your tax bill was $3,800. In 2025, you repay $5,000. You recompute your 2024 tax, eliminating the $5,000 from income. Without this income, you would have paid $2,774. Therefore, your credit in 2025 is $1,026 ($3,800 – $2,774).

Planning Tip

If you repaid supplemental unemployment benefits in the same year in which they were received, you do not have to do anything; the benefits were never reported as income, so there is no offsetting deduction necessary.

Pitfall

You cannot choose to file an amended return for the year in which the supplemental unemployment benefits were originally paid to subtract your later repayment. Your only choice in handling the repayment is to deduct it or, if eligible, claim a tax credit in the year of repayment if eligible.

Where to Claim the Benefit

If you are claiming the deduction, enter the amount of your repayment on Schedule A of Form 1040 or 1040-SR.

If you opt to treat repayments exceeding $3,000 as a tax credit, enter the credit on 13b of Schedule 3 of Form 1040 or 1040-SR. Note in "IRC 1341" on line 13b of Schedule 3 to indicate the type of credit you are claiming.

Jury Duty Pay Turned Over to Your Employer

Jury duty is a civic duty that is hard to avoid. If you are called to serve, you are paid a nominal amount that is taxable income. But if you also receive your regular wages from your employer and must hand over your jury duty pay, you may claim a deduction for the income you don't get to keep.

Benefit

If you receive your regular pay while serving on jury duty and turn over your jury duty pay to your employer, you may claim a deduction for this action as an adjustment to gross income. This deduction is intended to offset your having to include the jury duty pay in income. There are no dollar limits on this deduction.

Condition

You must be required by your employer to turn over jury duty pay as a condition of receiving your regular compensation.

Planning Tip

Ask your employer whether you can keep your jury duty pay and simply receive your ordinary compensation in excess of this amount so that you reduce your FICA taxes (and your employer saves a like amount in FICA taxes).

Example

Your regular daily pay in 2025 is $180. Assume you serve on a jury for 5 days and receive $50 per day for jury duty in a federal court. If your employer pays you only $130 and allows you to retain the $50, you save $19.13 in taxes ($50 × 5 days × 7.65% rate for Social Security and Medicare taxes).

Pitfall

Don't overlook this deduction for jury duty pay, especially if you receive it early in the year. It's easy to forget about it since payments of less than $600 are usually not reported to you on an information return from the government.

Where to Claim the Deduction

If you are claiming a deduction for jury duty pay turned over to your employer, enter the amount on Schedule 1 of Form 1040 or 1040-SR.

Impairment-Related Expenses

Having a disability may necessitate certain additional expenses in order to work. The tax law recognizes this added cost and allows these work-related expenses to be deductible under a special rule.

Benefit

If you suffer from a physical or mental impairment and you must incur special expenses to enable you to work, you can deduct these impairment-related expenses as an itemized deduction.

There is no dollar limit on this deduction. The deduction may be claimed without regard to the amount of your income.

Conditions

To be eligible for the deduction, you must meet the 3 following conditions:

1. You have a physical or mental disability that results in a functional limitation of employment that substantially limits one or more major life activities.

2. You must pay the expenses in order to work. For example, if you require an attendant at work so you can perform your job, your cost for these services is a qualified expense.

3. You itemize deductions. You cannot use this write-off is you take the standard deduction.

EXAMPLES OF IMPAIRMENTS

Any one of these impairments entitles you to deduct job-related expenses:

- Blindness
- Deafness
- Impairment limiting your ability to perform manual tasks
- Inability to speak or walk

Planning Tip

You may be able to avoid paying some or all of your work-related expenses due to your impairment (no cost to you is better than a deductible one). Under the Americans with Disabilities Act (ADA), your employer must provide reasonable accommodations to enable you to perform your job duties. This may include special equipment or assistance. For more information about benefits to which you may be entitled by the ADA, visit www.usdoj.gov/crt/ada/adahom1.htm.

Pitfall

You cannot claim a double deduction for the same expense, so if you treat some impairment-related costs as a job expense, you cannot also deduct them as a medical expense. For example, Braille books for your work are an impairment-related job expense and also qualify as a deductible medical expense, but if you treat them as a job expense, you cannot also deduct them as a medical expense.

Where to Claim the Deduction

You must complete Form 2106, *Employee Business Expenses* to report your impairment-related expenses along with other unreimbursed employee business expenses. The total amount is then entered as a miscellaneous itemized deduction on Schedule A of Form 1040 or 1040-SR.

Military Benefits

Serving your country in the military won't make you rich, but it may entitle you to a variety of benefits and other assistance. The tax law looks favorably on those in the service by allowing tax-free treatment for a long list of benefits.

Benefit

If you are a member of the armed forces, including the National Guard and the reserves, you may be entitled to certain benefits because of your job status.

EXAMPLES OF TAX-FREE BENEFITS

- Adjustments in pay to compensate for losses resulting from inflated foreign currency
- Benefits under the Servicemembers' Group Life Insurance
- Combat pay
- Death allowance for burial services, gratuity payments to survivors up to $5,000, and travel of dependents to burial sites

- Death benefit payable to family members of those killed in combat
- Defense counseling payments
- Disability pay
- Dislocation allowance (intended to partially reimburse expenses such as lease forfeitures, temporary living costs in hotels, and other expenses incurred in relocating a household)
- Dividends on GI insurance
- Education, training, or subsistence allowances paid under any law administered by the Veterans Administration (VA) (deductible education costs must be reduced by the VA allowance)
- Family allowances for education expenses of dependents, emergencies, evacuation to a place of safety, and separation
- Housing allowances (Basic Allowance for Housing, Variable Housing Allowance, temporary lodging expense allowance, and a moving-in allowance intended to defray costs such as rental agent fees, home security improvements, and supplemental heating equipment associated with occupying leased space outside the United States)
- In-kind moving and storage expenses for relocation pursuant to a military order and incident to a permanent change of station
- Interest on dividends left on deposit with the VA
- Living allowances (Basic Allowance for Subsistence)
- Medical or hospital treatment
- Payments to former prisoners of war
- ROTC educational and subsistence allowances
- State and local payments of bonuses to active or former military personnel or their dependents by reason of such personnel's service in a combat zone
- Survivor and retirement protection plan premium payments
- Travel allowances for annual round-trip for dependent students, leave between consecutive overseas tours, reassignment in a dependent-restricted area, and transportation for you or your dependents during ship overhaul or inactivation
- Uniforms allowance

Condition

There are no specific conditions for claiming these benefits; you are entitled to them if you are a member of the armed forces.

Planning Tips

If you receive a Basic Allowance for Housing (BAH), you can still deduct your mortgage interest and real estate taxes on your home, even though you pay these expenses with your BAH.

Military personnel can treat tax-free combat pay as earned income for purposes of making contributions to a traditional or Roth IRA.

Military personnel can also treat tax-free combat pay as earned income for purposes of the earned income credit (see Chapter 1).

For purposes of the home sale exclusion for gain on the sale of a principal residence, military personnel have a 10-year period (in place of a 5-year period) in which to have owned and used the home as their main home (see Chapter 4).

Pitfall

Nearly half the states partially or fully tax military retirement pay, so check with your state for details.

Where to Claim the Benefit

Benefits that are excludable are not to be reported on your return.

Contributions to State Benefit Programs

You may deduct mandated employee contributions to state unemployment, disability, and family leave programs as an itemized deduction. This deduction is explained in Chapter 15 under State and Local Income Taxes.

Dependent Care Assistance

Your employer may pay for your dependent care costs up to a set amount, or enable you to pay them on a pre-tax basis. The arrangement used to allow you to use your wages for these personal expenses without being taxed on them is called a flexible spending account (FSA).

Benefit

You are not taxed on dependent care assistance—paid by your employer or you through a dependent care FSA for 2025—up to $5,000 ($2,500 for a married person filing separately). Even if both spouses work for an employer offering a dependent care plan, the same dollar limit applies to the couple (i.e., $5,000 per couple).

Looking Ahead

Starting in 2026, dependent care assistance plans can provide up to $7,500 in tax-free benefits ($3,750 for married persons filing separately).

Conditions

Employee salary reduction contributions made on a pre-tax basis and reimbursements of expenses tax free or employer-paid reimbursements have the following conditions:

1. There must be a plan set up by an employer for this purpose.
2. You must have a dependent under age 13, a spouse, or other dependent incapable of self-care.
3. Any reimbursements must be for qualified dependent care expenses. These are the same benefits applicable to the dependent care credit (Chapter 1).
4. No reimbursements may be made for services provided by a child who is under age 19 at the end of the year or any other person who is your dependent.

Planning Tip

If you have 2 or more children, you can use the dependent care FSA to cover costs in 2025 up to $5,000 and then claim the dependent care credit for additional expenses up to $1,000 (total expenses of $6,000 applicable to having 2 or more children).

Pitfall

You must reconcile any dependent care FSA with the dependent care credit (Chapter 1). In effect, you cannot take the credit to the extent you use the dependent care FSA.

Where to Claim the Benefit

Because this is a tax-free opportunity, you do not report the employer payment or the salary amount contributed to the FSA. You can see this amount reflected on Form W-2. For example, the amount for dependent care appears in box 10 of the form.

Fringe Benefits

Wages or salary are only one aspect of remuneration for working. Your job may entitle you to a wide range of benefits, called perquisites ("perks") or fringe benefits, that your employer pays for. (Employer-paid dependent care assistance was discussed earlier in this chapter.) Many of these benefits are fully or partially tax free.

Benefit ⊗

If your employer pays for certain benefits, you may be able to exclude from your income some or all of these items. In many cases, tax-free treatment does not apply if you are an employee of an S corporation in which you own more than 2% of the stock.

There are various limitations and conditions for different fringe benefits, many of which are discussed in other chapters in this book (see Table 13.1).

You may be unaware of certain fringe benefits because you do not have to sign up for them as you would for, say, health coverage or a retirement plan, and they are not reported on your annual Form W-2. These fringe benefits include:

De minimis (minimal) fringe benefits. These are items so modest that accounting for them would be an administrative burden on your employer. For example:

- Birthday cakes
- Doughnuts, coffee, and soda
- Flowers or fruit for special occasions
- Occasional lunch or dinner money
- Photocopying
- Postage on personal items once in a while
- Use of employer's car if not more than once a month
- Work-life referral services

Caution: Some companies have a policy against personal use of company property (e.g., photocopying) and such use can be considered a theft, so ask about your employer's policy on this matter.

Employee discounts. Typically, these are limited to 25% to 30% of the cost of goods such as store merchandise and usually 20% of the cost of services such as dry cleaning.

No-additional-cost services. These are items for which your employer does not incur any additional cost when you use them. For example:

- Flights for airline employees and their families on a standby basis
- Hotel rooms for hotel workers when there is a vacancy

Working condition fringe benefits. These include expenses that would be deductible as an unreimbursed employee business expense on your return if you,

TABLE 13.1 Fringe Benefits in 2025

Type of Benefit	Dollar Limit on Exclusion	Other Limitations	For More Details, See Chapter
Accident and health plans	None (except for long-term care benefits)		2
Achievement awards	Up to $1,600 ($400 for nonqualified awards)		
Adoption assistance	$17,280	Income limitations	1
Athletic facilities	None		
De minimis (minimal) benefits			
Dependent care assistance	$5,000		1
Educational assistance	$5,250		3
Employee discounts			
Employee stock options			8
Free parking	$325/month		
Group term life insurance	$50,000		
Lodging on business premises			
Meals on business premises for convenience of employer			
Meals—*de minimis*			
No-additional-cost services			
Transit passes	$325/month		
Vanpooling	$325/month		
Working condition benefits			

rather than your employer, had paid for them and if the deduction for miscellaneous itemized deductions subject to the 2%-of-AGI floor had not been repealed. For example:

- Clothing and uniforms to wear on the job
- Dues to professional or trade associations
- Subscriptions to work-related publications
- Travel and meals
- Work-related continuing education courses

Transportation fringe benefit. This includes free parking, transit passes, and vanpooling of $325 per month in 2025. You can receive all transportation benefits each month.

Conditions

Different fringe benefits have different conditions and limitations. Table 13.1 on page 381 contains a listing of various fringe benefits that are excludable, including any other limitations that may apply, and references, where appropriate, to the chapter in which you will find an additional explanation.

Planning Tips

Congress may increase the types of tax-free benefits that employers can provide to workers, so check with your employer for benefits for which you may be eligible.

If a fringe benefit is tax free, it may also be exempt from Social Security and Medicare (FICA) taxes. Table 13.2 shows which benefits are exempt from Social Security and Medicare taxes.

TABLE 13.2 Benefits Exempt from Social Security and Medicare (FICA) Taxes

Benefit	FICA Taxes
Accident and health benefits	Exempt (except for S corporation shareholders owning more than 2% of the stock)
Achievement awards	Exempt up to $1,600 ($400 for nonqualified awards)
Adoption assistance	Not exempt
Athletic facilities	Exempt
De minimis benefits	Exempt
Dependent care assistance	Exempt up to $5,000

Pitfalls

Employees in an S corporation who own more than 2% of the stock cannot exclude the following types of fringe benefits from income:

- Accident and health benefits.
- Achievement awards.
- Adoption assistance.
- Lodging on the business premises.
- Meals furnished for the employer's convenience.
- Transportation benefits (free parking and transit passes). Transit passes up to $21 per month can be excluded if the value of the passes is not more than this amount (if more, then all of the benefit is taxable; you cannot exclude the $21 per month).

Certain benefits payable to highly compensated employees (generally executives and other highly paid workers, even those who are not S corporation shareholders) are not excludable. These benefits include:

- Self-insured medical reimbursement plans
- Dependent care assistance if the program favors these employees
- Employee discounts
- No-additional-cost services

Where to Claim the Benefit

Tax-free fringe benefits are not reported on your return. Many fringe benefits are listed on your Form W-2, with any necessary reporting requirements included in the instructions to the form.

Income Earned Abroad

Working abroad does not relieve citizens of their obligation to file U.S. tax returns and pay taxes here. But to make things easier for those working outside the U.S., the tax law lets a limited amount of income be received tax free each year as long as certain conditions are met. The tax breaks for earning income abroad apply to both employees and self-employed individuals.

Benefit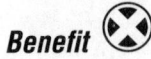

If you live and work abroad, you are not taxed on up to $130,000 of foreign earned income. If you are married and both you and your spouse have foreign income, you may each be eligible for an exclusion. If your foreign earned income is more than $130,000, you are taxable only on amounts in excess of $130,000.

This exclusion is not automatic; you must elect it.

Conditions

To qualify for the foreign earned income exclusion, you must meet 3 conditions:

1. Your tax home is in a foreign country.
2. You meet either a foreign residence test (you live abroad for an uninterrupted period that includes one full year) or a physical presence test (you live abroad for 330 days during a 12-month period). This eligibility requirement is waived for certain countries. For example, in 2024, the eligibility requirement was waived for Ukraine (departure on or after January 18, 2023), Belarus (departure on or after January 26, 2023), Sudan (departure on or after April 20, 2023), Haiti (departure on or after July 27, 2023), Niger (departure on or after August 2, 2023), and Iraq (departure on or after October 20, 2023). Whether these or other countries will be listed by the IRS for 2025 remains to be seen; check the Supplement for any update.
3. You do not work for the U.S. government or a government agency.

You can apply the exclusion only to foreign *earned* income, not to other types of foreign income.

FOREIGN EARNED INCOME

You must have income from the performance of personal services. This includes:

- Allowances from your employer for housing or other expenses
- Bonuses
- Business profits tied to the performance of services
- Commissions
- Professional fees
- Rents and royalties tied to the performance of services
- Salaries
- Tips
- Value of an employer-provided car or housing
- Wages

The earned income must be received no later than the year after the year in which you performed the services.

Once you have established bona fide residence in a foreign country for an uninterrupted period that includes an entire tax year, you are a bona fide resident of that country for the period starting with the date you actually began the residence and ending with the date you abandon the foreign residence.

If you receive payment this year for foreign earned income earned last year, you can exclude this amount this year to the extent that you did not use up your exclusion in the prior year.

Example

In 2024, you earned $95,000 but were paid only $85,000, which you excluded. In 2025, you earn $148,000 and receive the $10,000 for 2024 services. In 2025, you can exclude a total of $140,000 ($10,000 for 2024 pay because you did not use up your 2024 exclusion of $126,500 plus $120,000 exclusion for 2025). You are taxable on $8,000 of your 2025 earnings.

Not all foreign income is eligible for the exclusion. Nonqualified payments include:

- Alimony from a divorce or separation finalized after 2018
- Annuity income
- Capital gains
- Dividends
- Gambling winnings
- Interest income
- Pensions
- Social Security benefits
- U.S. government pay (if you work for the government and are stationed abroad, your pay is not tax free)
- Value of tax-free meals or lodging

If you work in Antarctica, you cannot exclude your income (Antarctica is not considered a foreign country by the IRS).

Planning Tips

What happens if you haven't met the foreign residence or physical presence test by the time your return is due? You cannot claim the exclusion before you have met either test, but you have a choice: You can ask for a filing extension if you expect to meet either test within the extension period.

Example

Your return for 2025 is due June 15, 2026, but you request a filing extension to October 15, 2026, because you expect to satisfy the 330-day test in July 2025, so that you can claim the exclusion on your 2025 return.

Alternatively, you can file your return to report the foreign earned income and then file an amended return to claim the exclusion once you satisfy either test.

Example

Same as the preceding facts except that you won't satisfy the 330-day test until after October 15, 2026. You file your 2025 return and pay tax on the foreign income. Once the test is met, you file an amended return to receive a refund.

Once you make the election to exclude foreign earned income, it remains in effect for subsequent years unless you revoke it. You revoke the election by attaching a statement to your return indicating revocation. You don't need IRS permission to revoke the election.

Weigh carefully whether you want to revoke the election to claim the foreign earned income exclusion. Following a revocation, you may not use the exclusion for 5 years unless the IRS grants you permission to do so. The IRS may grant permission under these circumstances:

- You return to the United States for a period of time.
- You move to a different foreign country that has different tax rates.
- You change employers.
- There is a change in the tax law of the foreign country in which you reside.

Housing exclusion. If you are eligible to exclude foreign earned income, you may also qualify to exclude housing. The basic limit on housing expenses in areas that are not designated as high-cost areas in 2025 is $39,000 (30% of $130,000) ($106.85 per day). The maximum exclusion for areas where the basic limit applies is $18,200 (the basic housing expense minus the basic housing amount, which is $20,800 [16% of the foreign earned income exclusion of $130,000]).

Pitfalls

If you elect to exclude your foreign earned income, you may not deduct any expenses related to such income.

You cannot base a contribution to an IRA or a Roth IRA on excludable foreign earned income.

You cannot claim the foreign tax credit or a deduction for foreign taxes related to excludable foreign earned income. In fact, if you had claimed the foreign earned income exclusion in the past and claim a foreign tax credit this year, you have effectively revoked your election to claim the exclusion. You cannot claim the exclusion for at least 5 years unless the IRS grants you permission to claim the exclusion.

Under a "stacking rule," excluded foreign income is taken into account in figuring the tax rate you pay on income that is taxable.

You cannot claim the foreign earned income exclusion for work in Antarctica, in international waters, or in international airspace.

You cannot claim the foreign earned income exclusion with respect to earnings from any country subject to U.S. government travel restrictions. Countries subject to travel restrictions may be found at www.state.gov/travel and in IRS Publication 54, *Tax Guide for U.S. Citizens and Resident Aliens Abroad*.

Where to Claim the Benefit

To elect the foreign earned income exclusion, file Form 2555, *Foreign Earned Income*, which you attach to Form 1040 or 1040-SR.

Your Business

The United States is an entrepreneurial country—it is the American dream to own your own business, and millions already do. It has been estimated that there are over 34.8 million small businesses, 80% of which have no employees. The U.S. Census Bureau reports that business formation is going strong in 2025.

Most expenses related to running a business are deductible, but timing issues and limitations may come into play. This chapter deals primarily with business deductions for a sole proprietor, independent contractor, or freelancer who files Schedule C (or, for farming, Schedule F). Of course, many rules discussed in this chapter apply to partnerships, limited liability companies (LLCs), and corporations.

This chapter explains the tax rules for various business-related deductions and other tax breaks. These rules apply whether your business is full time or part time (e.g., you do freelance work in the gig economy). If your activity isn't a business but rather a hobby (because you lack a profit motive), then you cannot deduct any expenses for the activity even though all of the income from it must be reported. The rules for claiming a home office deduction are in Chapter 10. Retirement plans for self-employed individuals are discussed in Chapter 5. Health insurance is covered in Chapter 2. Foreign earned income is explained in Chapter 14.

For more information, see IRS Publication 15, *Circular E, Employer's Tax Guide*; IRS Publication 225, *Farmer's Tax Guide*; IRS Publication 334, *Tax Guide for Small Business*; IRS Publication 535, *Business Expenses*; IRS Publication 536, *Net Operating Losses*; IRS Publication 587, *Business Use of Your Home*; and IRS Publication 946, *How to Depreciate Property*. Also see *J.K. Lasser's Small Business Taxes 2026* by Barbara Weltman.

Start-Up Costs

The term "start-up" has a very specific meaning for tax purposes. When you think of the start-up phase of a business, you typically think about the first few years of operation when the business gets going. But for tax purposes, start-up means that period of time just *before* you open for business. It is the period in which you are looking for a business to go into and getting ready to open.

Benefit

When you decide to start a business, you may incur certain costs. Usually, these costs are viewed as capital expenditures that are not currently deductible. But you can deduct up to $5,000 of start-up costs in the year the business begins. If start-up costs exceed $5,000, the balance can be amortized (deducted ratably) over 180 months.

If start-up costs exceed $50,000, the $5,000 deduction limit is reduced dollar for dollar by the excess over $50,000. If start-up costs exceed $55,000, no immediate deduction is allowed; such costs can be amortized over 180 months.

Example

You've been looking into a business to start and have incurred expenses for research, travel, and other related costs of $5,900. You begin business in December of 2025. You can deduct $5,000, plus 1/180 of $900, or $5 for a total of $5,005 in 2025. In 2026 and for the next 13 years, you'll deduct 12 x 1/180 of $900, or $60 each year. In the 15th year, you'll deduct 11 x 1/180 of $900 or

> $55. If your start-up costs had been $54,000, you could have deducted $1,000 ($5,000 – [$54,000 – $50,000]), plus 1/180 of $53,000 in the first year. If your costs had been $55,000 or more, then all of the costs would be deducted ratably over 15 years (1/15 each year).

Conditions

Start-up costs are amounts paid or incurred for creating an active trade or business or investigating the creation or acquisition of an active trade or business. It's a cost that's paid or incurred before the business actually begins, but which would have been deductible if the business had been active.

EXAMPLES OF START-UP COSTS

- A survey of potential markets
- Advertisements for the opening of the business
- An analysis of available facilities, labor, and supplies
- Salaries and wages for employees who are being trained and their instructors
- Salaries and fees for consultants and executives or for similar professional services
- Travel and other expenses incurred to get prospective distributors, suppliers, and customers

Planning Tips

If you do not write off all start-up costs in your first year of business, remember to keep track of your annual deductible amount so you don't overlook the write-off opportunity in the coming years.

If you sell your business before the end of the amortization period (assuming your start-up costs were not initially fully deducted), you can deduct any unamortized amount in the final year of business.

A separate $5,000 deduction limit and 180-month amortization period applies to certain other expenses you may incur in forming a business: incorporation costs and partnership organizational costs. Like start-up costs, make sure that the items fit within the write-off category and then apply the $5,000 deduction limit and 180-month amortization rule.

Pitfalls

Start-up costs are limited to expenses incurred *before* you begin operations. Once you open your doors for business you can no longer include expenses in your pot of start-up expenses.

Start-up costs do not include interest, taxes, or research and experimentation costs.

Where to Claim the Benefit

Report the amortizable amount of your start-up costs on Schedule C (or Schedule F) as "Other expenses." If you have more than one expense, you must list each of them in the space provided for this on Schedule C (or Schedule F).

Qualified Business Income Deduction

As the owner of a pass-through business, there is a qualified business income (QBI) deduction that you can use to reduce taxable income if you're profitable. It is also referred to as the Section 199A deduction, which is the section in the Tax Code that governs it. There is no extra outlay required to enjoy the deduction; you claim it if you are eligible. There are many more rules for this QBI deduction than are covered in this section; see *J.K. Lasser's Small Business Taxes 2026* for more details.

Benefit

The deduction is 20% of qualified business income, to the extent you qualify for it. The deduction is not a business write-off on Schedule C, E, or F; and it is not a reduction of gross income to reduce adjusted gross income. The deduction is taken into account in figuring taxable income on which your applicable tax rate applies. It can be taken whether or not you itemize personal deductions. The 20% deduction is increased by 20% of qualified REIT dividends and income from publicly-traded partnerships (PTP); this is not discussed here.

Looking Ahead

Starting in 2026, there is a new minimum QBI deduction of $400. It applies if you have at least $1,000 in QBI from an active trade or business in which you materially participate.

Conditions

There are various conditions and several limitations on this write-off. The 20% deduction is figured on *qualified business income* (QBI). This is income from a business in the United States, including Puerto Rico. Qualified business income is determined for each of an owner's separate businesses. Only items of income, gain, deduction, and loss allowed in determining taxable income are taken into account for qualified business income.

QBI does not include capital gains (including Section 1231 gains) and losses, certain dividends, and interest not allocable to a trade or business. QBI does not include reasonable compensation to S corporation shareholders or guaranteed payments to partners for services rendered to the business. Any net loss is carried over and treated as a loss generated by the business in a subsequent year.

QBI must be reduced by business-related deductions, including those claimed as adjustments to gross income. These include the self-employed health insurance deduction, the deduction for contributions to owners' qualified retirement plans, and the deduction for one-half of self-employment tax.

Rental real estate activities may amount to a trade or business, making you eligible for the QBI deduction. There's no bright line test for determining whether rental real estate activities are a trade or business. There is a safe harbor for treating a "real estate enterprise" as a trade or business.

Again, there are many more rules for this QBI deduction than are covered in this section; see *J.K. Lasser's Small Business Taxes 2026* for more details.

INCOME THRESHOLD

If your taxable income, not just business income, in 2025 does not exceed $394,600 for joint filers and $197,300 for all other filers, then the deduction is simply 20% of QBI. If your taxable income is over these threshold amounts, then limitations apply

For specified service trades or businesses (discussed later), there is a phase-out of QBI taken into account. The phaseout range for singles is 50,000; it's $100,000 for joint filers. This means that a married person filing jointly who is in a specified service trade or business with taxable income that exceeds the threshold amount by more than $50,000 cannot take any QBI deduction. The phaseout amounts are in Table 14.1. Taxable income for this purpose is figured without regard to the QBI deduction.

Looking Ahead

Starting in 2026, the phaseout ranges for those in specified service trades or businesses is increased: $75,000 for singles and $150,000 for joint filers. These dollar amounts will be adjusted for inflation beginning in 2027.

W-2 LIMITATION

If your taxable income is over the applicable thresholds noted above, the deduction is limited to the *lesser* of (1) 20% of qualified business income, or (2) the greater of (a) 50% of W-2 wages, or (b) 25% of W-2 wages *plus* 2.5% of the unadjusted basis immediately after acquisition of qualified property (there are time

TABLE 14.1 2025 Taxable Income Phaseout for the QBI Deduction

Filing Status	Taxable Income over	Fully Phased Out
Married filing jointly	$394,600	$494,600
Other filers	$197,300	$247,300

limits on what property can be taken into account). This is referred to as the "W-2 limitation."

> ## Example
>
> You are single with taxable income over the applicable amount and are the sole owner of an S corporation in the construction business. You receive wages from the business of $500,000 and QBI of $600,000. The business has W-2 wages (other than what is paid to you) of $300,000 and $1 million unadjusted basis in qualified property. Your QBI deduction is $120,000 because it is the lesser of:
>
> - 20% of QBI (20% of $600,000 = $120,000), or
> - The greater of 50% of W-2 wages ($150,000), or 25% of W-2 wages ($75,000) plus 25% of $1 million unadjusted basis of qualified property ($25,000) = $150,000.

INCOME FROM TIPS

Independent contractors, such as Uber drivers, may receive tips and could qualify for the no-tax-on-tips deduction, whether or not they itemize if the tips are reported on Form 1099-NEC or Form 4137. The IRS has created a list of nearly 70 occupations in which tips are customarily received (e.g., home electricians; tailors), and may qualify for the no-tax-on-tips deduction (see Chapter 14 for conditions for the deduction). But tips related to a specified service trade or business (defined next) do not qualify for the no-tax-on-tips deduction.

SPECIFIED SERVICE TRADES OR BUSINESSES

There's another rule that effectively limits or bars the 20% QBI deduction for specified service trades or businesses (SSTBs), which are those involved in the performance of services in the fields of health, law, consulting, accounting, actuarial science, performing arts, athletics, financial services, brokerage services, or any business where its principal asset is the reputation or skill of one or more of its owners or employees.

If you fall into this category and your taxable income exceeds the applicable threshold, the amount of QBI that can be taken into account phases out over the next $100,000 for joint filers or $50,000 for other filers. In other words, if you are in an SSTB and have taxable income within the phaseout range, only a percentage of qualified business income can be used to figure the W-2 limitation as explained above. If you are in an SSTB and your taxable income in 2025 exceeds $494,600 if married filing jointly or $247,300 if you are any other filer, you cannot take any deduction.

OTHER LIMITATIONS

Even after you jump through all of these hoops, the deduction cannot be more than 20% of taxable income minus net capital gains. And if you have a loss from one or more businesses, it's carried forward to the following year; any 20% deduction allowed in the following year is reduced by the carryover loss.

Planning Tip

While an S corporation owner-employee cannot include compensation in QBI, the compensation is part of W-2 wages for purposes of the W-2 wages limitation.

Usually businesses are treated separately, but you can elect to aggregate them under certain conditions (aggregation isn't allowed for SSTBs).

The IRS has questions and answers on the QBI deduction at https://www.irs.gov/newsroom/tax-cuts-and-jobs-act-provision-11011-section-199a-qualified-business-income-deduction-faqs.

Pitfalls

If your business is a partnership or S corporation, the limitations apply at the owner level. This means that you may or may not be eligible for the qualified business deduction even though your co-owner(s) is or is not.

If you had negative QBI for 2025, it is carried forward to offset positive QBI in 2026. This may mean that even if you become profitable in 2026, you may not be eligible for a QBI deduction because you suffered a loss in 2025. And if you had a loss in 2024, it impacts your 2025 QBI deduction.

If you erroneously claim the qualified business income deduction, you may be subject to a 20% accuracy-related penalty. This penalty applies if the deduction causes an understatement of tax that is greater than 5% of the tax required to be shown on the return for the year, or $5,000.

Where to Claim the Deduction

The deduction is figured on Form 8995, *Qualified Business Income Deduction Simplified Computation* if taxable income is at or below the threshold amounts in Table 14.1, or Form 8995-A, *Qualified Business Income Deduction,* if taxable income is over the threshold amounts. The deduction is then taken on line 13a of Form 1040 or 1040-SR.

Equipment Purchases

It usually takes more than just your brains and hard work to make a business run. You need equipment, from technology-based items (e.g., computers, tablets, and smartphones), to furniture (e.g., desks, file cabinets, and chairs), to industry-specific items (e.g., carpentry tools and heavy machinery). For tax purposes, all of these items are viewed as "equipment" for which special tax treatment may be claimed. Today, the tax law encourages investments in equipment as a means of spurring the economy by allowing an immediate deduction for purchase costs if certain conditions are met.

Benefit ⬆

You can deduct amounts you pay for equipment used in your business as an ordinary business expense. The tax law dictates when and how much of your cost you can deduct. There are 4 sets of rules that come into play:

1. *First-year expensing.* Up to a set dollar limit can be deducted in the year the equipment is placed in service. Higher dollar limits apply for equipment placed in service in certain distressed areas; a lower dollar limit applies for vehicles weighing more than 6,000 pounds. The limit for 2025 is $2.5 million. This is also known as the Section 179 deduction.

2. *Bonus depreciation.* All (100%) of the cost of equipment is allowed to be deducted if purchased and placed in service after January 19, 2025 (40% if placed in service earlier in the year). There is no dollar limit on bonus depreciation.

3. *Regular depreciation.* A percentage of the equipment's basis is deducted over a set term (a recovery period fixed for various types of assets). There is no dollar limit on depreciation.

4. De minimis *safe harbor rule.* If you don't capitalize the cost of an item (i.e., you don't add it to your balance sheet), you can immediately deduct up to $2,500 per item or invoice if you make such an election on your tax return.

Conditions

Equipment purchases are not limited to machinery; the term "equipment" includes just about any type of property other than most real estate.

EXAMPLES OF EQUIPMENT

- Answering machines
- Bookshelves
- Cars (see Chapter 7)
- Computers

- Copiers
- Credit card readers
- Desk accessories
- Desk chairs
- Desks
- Farming equipment (see later in this chapter)
- Fax machines
- File cabinets
- Floor models and displays
- Machinery
- Musical instruments for musicians
- Printers
- Qualified improvement property
- Scanners
- Signs
- Smartphones
- Software purchased off the shelf
- Tablets
- Telephones
- Tools of your trade
- Trucks (see Chapter 7)
- Vacuum cleaners

Slightly different rules apply to the different write-off methods. For example, a particular item may qualify for the Section 179 deduction but not for bonus depreciation.

The rules on depreciation are quite complex, and a complete discussion is well beyond the scope of this chapter. To learn more, see IRS Publication 946, *How to Depreciate Property* or *J.K Lasser's Small Business Taxes 2026*.

Conditions for First-Year Expensing

There are 3 basic conditions for claiming first-year expensing:

1. You must elect it.
2. Your total equipment purchases for the year cannot exceed a set dollar amount.
3. Your taxable income must at least equal your expense deduction.

ELECTION

You must elect to claim first-year expensing (also referred to as a Section 179 deduction because of the section in the Internal Revenue Code governing the deduction).

EQUIPMENT PURCHASES

To qualify for the election, your total equipment purchases for the year cannot exceed a set dollar amount. For 2025, you can claim the expensing deduction only if your total purchases are no more than $6.5 million. The $2.5 million limit phases out on a dollar-for-dollar basis for total purchases over $4 million.

QUALIFIED IMPROVEMENT PROPERTY

Qualified improvement property includes:

- *For residential rental property:* Certain property used to furnish lodging as well as any improvements qualified for nonresidential property (e.g., security system).

- *For nonresidential property:* Improvements to roofs; HVAC (heating, ventilation, air conditioning); fire suppression systems; fire alarm systems and security systems; interior property not considered a structural component.

Qualified improvement property also qualifies for bonus depreciation discussed later. Write-offs for these properties are explained in Chapter 10.

TAXABLE INCOME

Your first-year expensing deduction cannot be more than the taxable income from the active conduct of a business. Taxable income for this purpose means your net income (or loss) from all businesses you actively conduct. If you are married and file a joint return, your spouse's net income (or loss) is added to yours. Taxable income also includes Section 1231 gains and losses (from the sale of certain business property) and salary or wages from being an employee. Taxable income must be reduced by the deduction for the employer portion of self-employment tax and net operating loss carrybacks and carryforwards.

Example

You own a sole proprietorship that shows a $5,000 profit for the year, and your deduction for the employer portion of self-employment tax is $353. Your spouse works as an employee with a salary of $50,000. Your taxable income for purposes of figuring your first-year expensing deduction is $54,647 ($5,000 − $353 + $50,000).

Condition for Bonus Depreciation

The property must qualify for this special deduction. Qualified property includes:

- Tangible property depreciated under the modified accelerated cost recovery system (MACRS) with a recovery period of 20 years or less
- Off-the-shelf computer software
- Qualified improvement property
- Certain plants planted or grafted

Conditions for Regular Depreciation

Depreciation is a method for recovering your investment in property over a period of time fixed by law, called a recovery period. You apply a set percentage (based on the property's recovery period) to the property's basis (generally, its cost) to arrive at your annual deduction. These percentages are found in IRS Publication 946.

Example

In 2025, you place in service a copier machine (5-year property) for which you do not claim any first-year expensing because you are not profitable and you elect out of bonus depreciation. Assume the cost of the machine is $8,000. Your depreciation percentage for the year that 5-year property is placed in service is 20%, so your depreciation deduction is $1,600 ($8,000 × 20%).

Different types of property are classified by their recovery periods:

- 3-year property, such as taxis, tractors, racehorses 3 years and older, and breeding hogs
- 5-year property, such as cars, trucks, copiers, assets used in construction, and breeding and dairy cattle
- 7-year property, such as office fixtures and furniture, fax machines, assets used in printing, assets used in recreation (e.g., billiard tables), and breeding horses and workhorses

There are also 10-year, 15-year (e.g., qualified improvement property), and 20-year types of property as well as realty (27.5 years for residential realty and 39 years for nonresidential realty such as office buildings, strip malls, and factories).

CONVENTIONS

Special depreciation rules, called conventions, come into play to determine your write-offs for the year.

- For property other than realty, a mid-year convention makes a hypothetical assumption that the property has been placed in service in the middle of the year. As a result of the mid-year convention, 5-year property is depreciated over 6 years.

- For property other than realty, a mid-quarter convention applies. If you place in service more than 40% of all your equipment purchases for the year in the final quarter of the year, a special rule dictates the amount of depreciation you can claim for each item placed in service during the year. This special rule is called a mid-quarter convention and generally operates to limit write-offs (although in some cases it may enable you to take greater deductions than under regular depreciation rules).

- For realty, a mid-month convention assumes that the property has been placed in service in the middle of the month it is actually placed in service. The mid-month convention is built into the depreciation rate tables applied to realty.

Conditions for De Minimis Safe Harbor Rule

You must be consistent in your treatment of the items, which means that if you use the *de minimis* rule to treat items as materials and supplies, you can't treat them as an asset on your balance sheet. You must attach your own statement that you are electing to use this safe harbor rule. The statement must make reference to Reg. Sec. 1.263(a)-1(f).

Planning Tips

The amount of your write-offs does not depend on whether you pay cash for the equipment or finance your purchase in whole or in part. If, for example, you finance your purchase, you may wind up deducting more in the first year than you pay out of pocket.

Example

In December 2025, you buy a machine for $25,000, financing it over 5 years at 8% interest, with the first payment due in January 2026. In 2025, you can claim a first-year expensing deduction of $25,000, even though you have not yet paid a penny.

Decide whether to make the first-year expensing election and/or forgo bonus depreciation. Generally, if your current income is modest but you expect it to increase in coming years, it may be preferable to forgo the deduction now in favor of using it against future income that would otherwise be taxed at higher rates.

Bonus depreciation can be used to create or increase a net operating loss (NOL). This means that even if you do not have sufficient current taxable income to use bonus depreciation, the write-off can be taken into account in figuring an NOL.

Pitfalls

Special rules apply to so-called listed property, which includes cars, other property used as means of transportation, and property of a type used for entertainment, recreation, or amusement. You cannot use first-year expensing or accelerated depreciation *unless* business use of a listed property item is more than 50% of total use.

Example

You buy a boat that is used 75% for business and 25% for personal purposes. Since business use exceeds 50%, you can use first-year expensing or accelerated depreciation for the portion of the boat (75% of its purchase price) used for business.

If you sell or cease using property for which first-year expensing has been claimed, you *may* be subject to recapture. This means you're required to report a portion of the previous write-off as income in the year of the disposition of the property. Discuss this rather complicated matter with a tax adviser.

Where to Claim the Deduction

You figure your deduction for equipment purchases on Form 4562, *Depreciation and Amortization.* You enter the amount of your deduction on the line provided for this write-off on Schedule C (or Schedule F).

If you are claiming depreciation this year on an item placed in service in a prior year and you do not have any new items to report, as a sole proprietory you do not have to file Form 4562. Simply attach your own schedule to the return showing the amount of depreciation you are claiming this year.

Expensing of Production Property

If you build a structure used in manufacturing, farming, or refining, you can expense 100% of the cost instead of depreciating it over 39 years. Construction must begin after January 19, 2025, and before January 1, 2029. The deduction is taken in the year the property is placed in service (no later than December 31, 2030).

Payment for Services

You may not be able to do it alone and may therefore need to hire employees to work for your business. The costs of wages, salaries, bonuses, and other payments are deductible if certain conditions are met.

Benefit

Amounts you pay to individuals who provide services to you are deductible as ordinary expenses against your business income. Such payments fall into 2 general categories:

1. Wages and compensation to employees.
2. Fees and payments to independent contractors or to third parties (e.g., temp employment agencies) providing workers to you.

There are no dollar limits on the amount you can deduct for payments for services.

In addition to a deduction for wages and compensation to employees, you may be eligible to claim a tax credit for a portion of these payments.

Conditions

There are several conditions for determining how much to deduct for payments to workers:

- It must be determined whether the worker is an employee or independent contractor.
- Amounts paid must be reasonable.
- Payment must relate to work actually performed.
- Payments must be made in a timely fashion.

WORKER CLASSIFICATION

First, you must determine whether workers are your employees or independent contractors. The key reason for making the distinction is the obligation to pay employment taxes—Social Security and Medicare (FICA) taxes, federal unemployment insurance (FUTA), and state unemployment and other payroll taxes. If you are the employer, you are responsible for the employer's share of taxes as well as withholding income taxes and the employee's share of FICA. If your worker is an independent contractor, then he or she is responsible for taxes.

Generally, for federal tax purposes worker classification as an employee or independent contractor is based on control. If you control when, where, and how work is to be performed, the person is your employee regardless of what label you may attach. If the person is in his or her own business and provides services to you, the person is usually treated as an independent contractor. Worker classification is a perennial "hot" IRS audit issue, so work with a knowledgeable tax adviser to get it right.

REASONABLE PAYMENTS

Compensation paid to your employees must be "reasonable." There's no set dollar amount. Reasonable depends on many factors, including job responsibilities, education level, and location of the business. Payments to yourself as a sole proprietor are not treated as deductible compensation because you are not an employee.

Payments paid to independent contractors must also be reasonable.

PERFORMANCE OF WORK

You can deduct only payments for work actually performed. Generally, this poses no problem for your rank-and-file employees. But if you put family members on the payroll, the IRS may look closely at the relation between their wages and work performed. Keep track of the hours they worked and the tasks they performed as proof that they earned the compensation you paid.

TIMELINESS OF PAYMENT

You may deduct only payments you actually make if you are on the cash method of accounting for your business. If you are on the accrual method (which is unusual for self-employed individuals and most small businesses), payments to rank-and-file employees must be made no later than 2 ½ months after the close of the year (e.g., by March 15, 2026, for compensation earned in 2025) to be deductible in 2025. (Different rules apply to payments to shareholders in C and S corporations.)

Planning Tips

Compensation paid to certain employees may entitle you to claim an income tax credit (more details may be found later in this chapter). These include:

- Work opportunity credit
- Credit for paid family and medical leave if your state does not require it

- Empowerment zone employment credit for workers within designated areas
- Social Security tax credit on certain tips for workers in restaurant and tavern businesses
- Employer wage differential payment credit

Small businesses may also be eligible for an employment tax credit from research activities. The research credit can be used as an offset to the employer's share of Social Security and Medicare taxes up to $500,000 (see instructions to Form 8975, *Qualified Small Business Payroll Tax Credit for Increasing Research Activities*).

Pitfalls

If your workers are employees, you are responsible for employment taxes. This requires you to withhold federal and, if applicable, state income taxes from their wages, as well as the employee share of FICA tax. You must also pay the employer share of FICA as well as FUTA and state employment taxes. If you fail to pay over these taxes in a timely fashion, you may be personally liable for them.

Where to Claim the Deduction

You report the deduction for compensation to employees on the line designated as "Wages" on Schedule C of Form 1040 or 1040-SR. Wages are reduced by employment tax credits you claim (listed earlier in "Planning Tips"). You report payments to independent contractors on the line marked "Commissions and fees" of this schedule.

For farming-related activities, the deduction for wages to employees is reported on the line marked "Labor hired" on Schedule F of Form 1040 or 1040-SR. Wages are reduced by employment tax credits you claim. You report payments to independent contractors on the line marked "Customer hire" of this schedule.

Employment-related income tax credits to which you may be entitled are figured on the following forms (there are more credits that apply if you provide certain benefits to employees and they are not covered here):

- Work opportunity credit: Form 5884
- Credit for paid family and medical leave: Form 8994
- Empowerment zone employment credit: Form 8844
- Social Security tax credit on certain tips: Form 8846
- Credit for employer wage differential payments: Form 5884-A

Supplies

To paraphrase Benjamin Franklin, for want of a paper clip, your business may be lost. Despite predictions of a paperless society, most businesses use reams of paper and other supplies every year. The tax law allows a full write-off for the cost of ordinary supplies as long as certain conditions are met.

Benefit ⬆

Office supplies (including paper, pens, tape, and toner replacements) and cleaning supplies (such as detergent, paper towels, and sponges) are deductible against your business income. There is no dollar limit on this deduction.

Supplies that are part of your inventory are *not* currently deductible; they are part of the cost of goods sold.

Conditions

For supplies to be currently deductible, they must be ordinary and necessary business expenses. They cannot be items with a useful life of more than one year. If they have a longer useful life, they are treated as equipment (discussed earlier in this chapter).

EXAMPLES OF DEDUCTIBLE SUPPLIES

- Binders and presentation material
- Boards and easels
- Business cards
- Cleaning supplies
- DVDs and thumbdrives
- Filing and storage material
- Ink cartridges and toners
- Labels, envelopes, and shipping material
- Paper clips, tape, and staples
- Paper, pads, and notes
- Pens, pencils, and markers
- Replacement parts (which are not part of inventory)
- Rubber stamps
- Small wares of restaurants and taverns (e.g., glassware, paper or plastic cups, dishes, pots and pans, and bar supplies)
- Stationery
- Trash bags

Planning Tips

From a nontax standpoint, it may not make economic sense to load up on supplies even though you can deduct them. You are incurring costs now that could be paid later.

While the cost of supplies is generally deductible, it is a good business practice to economize on purchases. Look for discounts and special business incentives from such office supplies companies as:

- Amazon Business (https://business.amazon.com)
- Office Depot (www.officedepot.com) (OfficeMax is part of Office Depot)
- Staples (www.staples.com)

Pitfalls

Supplies that are part of your inventory are *not* separately deducted. Instead, they are included as part of your cost of goods sold.

Watch the timing of ordering supplies. A current deduction is allowed for supplies expected to be used within the year. A deduction for supplies *not* used within the current year but kept on hand may still be claimed as long as doing so does not distort income, no records are maintained to indicate when supplies are actually used, and no inventory is taken of the amount of supplies on hand at the beginning and end of the year.

Where to Claim the Benefit

Report supplies used in your business on the line provided for this item on Schedule C (or Schedule F) of Form 1040 or 1040-SR. You do not have to complete any additional form or schedule for this purpose.

Gifts

Gifts generally are given because of personal feelings without any expectations or strings attached. But business gifts are usually motivated by gratitude for some business activity or hope for future business activity. In recognition of this fact, the tax law allows a deduction for business gifts, but only in very limited amounts.

Benefit ⬆

You may wish to bestow some gratuitous benefit on employees, customers, dealers, distributors, or other business relations. You can qualify for a deduction for business gifts, but the amount you can deduct is limited. Generally, you cannot deduct more than $25 per gift for any person each year (the same dollar limit in place since 1962). The dollar limit applies even if you attempt to make an indirect gift (for example, you give the gift to a company that is intended for the eventual personal use of a particular person).

Conditions

To claim a deduction for business gifts, you must meet both of the following conditions:

1. Dollar limit
2. Substantiation

DOLLAR LIMIT

The deductible amount of the gift cannot exceed $25 per person per year. The dollar limit does not include incidental costs, such as wrapping, insuring, or shipping the gift.

> **Example**
>
> You give a new vendor a gift that cost you $60. You paid $10 more to insure and ship it. You can deduct $35 ($25 of the $60, plus incidental expenses of $10).

In determining your $25 annual limit, you do not have to count any gifts of nominal value ($4 or less) with your company name imprinted on them that you distribute to a number of clients or customers (e.g., calendars given in December).

SUBSTANTIATION REQUIREMENTS

You must show the cost of the gift, a description of the gift, the date it was given, and to whom. You must also state the reason for the gift (such as the business to be gained from making it). This information should be recorded on an expense log app, or business diary.

In addition, you must have evidentiary proof of the expense, such as a canceled check or receipt for the item.

Planning Tip

Gifts to your employees are *not* subject to this $25 limit because payments to them are usually treated as compensation (discussed earlier in this chapter). As long as regular compensation plus any purported gifts are reasonable, the total is deductible as compensation.

Pitfall

You must substantiate your business gifts in order to support your deduction. If you fail to meet full substantiation requirements, your deduction is lost. For example, merely retaining a receipt for the gift is not sufficient; you need to note all the information listed earlier as full substantiation for the gift.

Where to Claim the Deduction

You report the gifts as "Other expenses" on Schedule C (or Schedule F) of Form 1040 or 1040-SR. If you have more than one such expense (for example, in addition to business gifts, you are deducting environmental cleanup costs), you must list each type of expense in the space provided (or on your own attachment if more space is required).

Self-Employment Tax Deduction

Self-employed individuals pay both the employer and employee share of Social Security and Medicare taxes. But self-employed persons are treated as their own employers to the extent they are permitted to deduct the employer share—one-half—of these taxes.

Benefit 🔼

If you pay self-employment tax on your net earnings from self-employment, you deduct one half of the tax as an adjustment to gross income, whether or not you itemize your other deductions.

Conditions

Self-employment tax is the employer and employee share of Social Security and Medicare taxes figured on your net earnings from self-employment. As long as you show a profit in your self-employment activities of at least $400, you owe self-employment tax and can deduct one half, which represents the employer share. The same is also so if you opt to pay self-employment tax even if you had a loss or a small amount of income.

Planning Tips

To figure your deduction, simply look at Schedule SE, *Self-Employment Tax*, the form used to figure your self-employment tax. The last line in Part I of Schedule SE allows you to figure your deduction. You deduct the employer portion of 7.65% (6.2% of Social Security taxes on 92.35% of net earnings up to $176,100 in 2025, plus 1.45% of Medicare taxes on 92.35% of net earnings from self-employment with no limit).

If you had a loss or a small amount of self-employment income, you may use an optional method for figuring self-employment tax to boost credits for Social Security coverage or increase earned income for purposes of the earned income tax credit or the dependent care credit. There is a farm optional method and a nonfarm optional method. For details about eligibility, see the instructions for Part II of Schedule SE.

Pitfall

The deduction for one-half of your self-employment tax is *not* a business expense, but a personal one. It does not reduce your profits on which you pay income taxes; it merely reduces your gross income to arrive at adjusted gross income. The deduction also reduces qualified business income for purposes of the QBI deduction (explained earlier in this chapter).

Where to Claim the Benefit

You figure self-employment tax, including the maximum deferral amount, on Schedule SE of Form 1040 or 1040-SR. You report the deduction on Schedule 1 of Form 1040 or 1040-SR.

Home Office Deduction

According to the U.S. Small Business Administration, 55% of all firms without employees are home based, as are 23.3% of those with employees. The cost of operating an office from home may be deductible as long as certain conditions are met. The term "home office" isn't limited to clerical space; it can include a workshop, greenhouse, artist studio, or any other area of a home used for business. The rules for claiming a home office deduction are explained in Chapter 10.

Farming-Related Breaks

According to the U.S. Department of Agriculture, there were more than 1.9 million farms in the United States in 2022 based on the census taken that year and released in 2024. The next census won't be taken until 2027 and released in 2029). Farming is considered a type of business and is therefore entitled to deductions available to any other business. But the tax law provides special breaks just for farms.

Benefit

If you operate a farm or farming activity, many of your costs are deductible against your farming income. In addition to any business expense you could claim in a nonfarming business, you may be entitled to special write-offs. Generally, there are no dollar limits on your farming-related deductions.

If you own a farm and sell it, you may be able to spread the gain over 4 years.

Some benefits payable to farmers may be tax free, and some expenses paid by farmers may qualify for a tax credit.

Conditions

Like other business expenses, farming-related deductions must be ordinary and necessary expenses.

EXAMPLES OF FARMING-RELATED DEDUCTIONS

- Chemicals
- Conservation expenses for soil and water
- Custom hire (machine work)
- Enhanced deduction for donations of conservation easements (100% of the contribution base, which is essentially adjusted gross income)
- Feed purchased (there are limits on how much you can deduct for feed to be consumed beyond this year)
- Fertilizers and lime
- Freight and trucking
- Gasoline, oil, and other fuel
- Ginning
- Hired labor (reduced by any employment-related tax credits discussed earlier in this chapter)
- Insect sprays and dusts
- Seeds and plants purchased
- Storage and warehousing
- Tying materials and containers
- Veterinary and breeding fees and medicine

You may also be entitled to the 20% qualified business income deduction discussed earlier in this chapter. Special rules not covered here apply to patrons of cooperatives.

Planning Tips

Some payments to farmers may be tax free. These include:

- Cost-sharing payments under The Conservation Reserve Program (CRP)
- Soil and water conservation assistance payments under a special federal program, which may run as high as $50,000
- Agricultural management assistance program payments

In addition to deductions for farming expenses, you may be eligible for certain tax credits related to farming. These include:

- Credit for federal excise tax paid on kerosene used in your home for heating, lighting, and cooking
- Credit for federal excise tax paid on gasoline, special motor fuels, and compressed natural gas used on a farm for farming purposes
- Credit for federal excise tax on fuels used in running stationary machines, for cleaning purposes, or in other off-highway vehicles

You can claim the credits on your return or claim a refund of the excise taxes you already paid. The credits and your options on claiming them are explained in more detail in IRS Publication 225, *Farmer's Tax Guide*.

Pitfall

Not all farming-related expenses are deductible. You may not deduct your personal living expenses, such as taxes, insurance, and repairs to your home.

Where to Claim the Deduction

Report the deduction on the line provided for it on Schedule F of Form 1040 or 1040-SR. If there is no specific line for the type of deduction you are claiming, list it in the space provided for other expenses (attach your own explanation or description of the expense if not self-explanatory).

Other Business Deductions

Not every expense fits neatly into a business deduction category. The tax law provides a catchall deduction rule, referred to as the ordinary and necessary expense rule, under which an expense can be written off as long as certain conditions are met.

Benefit

A variety of miscellaneous expenses you incur in your business are currently deductible against business income.

Condition

The only condition for deductibility of miscellaneous expenses is that they are ordinary and necessary for your business. "Ordinary" means that they are usual. "Necessary" means they are helpful and appropriate. It doesn't have to be essential.

EXAMPLES OF OTHER BUSINESS DEDUCTIONS

- Advertising costs—promotional costs as well as goodwill advertising to keep your name in the public eye.
- Asbestos removal.
- Banking fees.
- Depletion for certain oil, gas, and mineral as well as timber properties.
- Dues to professional and trade associations.
- Environmental cleanup costs—expenses to restore property to its precontamination condition.
- Insurance (for self-employed health insurance, see Chapter 2).
- Intangibles (e.g., goodwill and covenant not to compete) that are acquired (must be amortized over 15 years).
- Interest on borrowing by small businesses (for example, financing of equipment purchases).
- Leasing costs for equipment.
- Licenses and regulatory fees paid annually to state or local governments.
- Meals with customers, vendors, or other business associates if it is not lavish or extravagant and you or an employee are present at the furnishing of food or beverages and meals while away from home on business (50% of the cost).
- Merchant authorization fees for credit/debit card and electronic payments.
- Moving equipment and machinery.
- Rent for office and other business-related space.
- Repairs to keep property in working order (if repairs add to the value or usefulness of the property, the cost must be capitalized in most cases).
- Repayments of income reported in prior years if over $3,000. *Note:* You may be able to take a tax credit in lieu of a deduction to obtain a greater benefit from the write-off.
- Shipping and postage.
- Storage and warehousing.
- Subscriptions.
- Telephone. If you operate your business from a home office, the basic service charge of the first landline to your home is not deductible. But this ban does not apply to additional charges and the cost of a second business line. The monthly cost of smartphone use is deductible.
- Utilities. Gas, electric, water, and other charges are deductible. If you claim a home office deduction, the treatment of these charges is discussed earlier in this chapter.

Planning Tip

As with all business expenses, keep good records, including receipts, canceled checks, and bills of sale.

Pitfall

Not all expenses you incur in your business are deductible. The tax law specifically prevents you from writing off certain expenses, even though they may be ordinary and necessary to your business.

EXAMPLES OF NONDEDUCTIBLE EXPENSES

- Bribes and kickbacks—even if customary or common business practice, if they are in violation of the law. For example, an insurance broker who pays a referral fee to car dealers who refer customers to him cannot deduct the fee because the car dealers are not licensed to sell insurance.
- Club dues for clubs organized for pleasure, recreation, or any other social purpose (e.g., country club dues).
- Demolition expenses to raze a building. These costs are added to the basis of the land on which the building was demolished.
- Entertainment costs.
- Fines and penalties.
- Interest on a business-related tax deficiency.
- Lobbying expenses to influence legislation.

Where to Claim the Deduction

Deductible miscellaneous business expenses are reported on Schedule C (or Schedule F) either on the line provided for the type of expense (e.g., "Advertising" on Schedule C) or as "Other expenses." If you have more than one such expense, you must list each type of expense in the space provided (or on your own attachment, if more space is required).

Sale of Farm Land

Some farms remain in families for generations. Owners hold on until death to avoid adverse tax results. To promote new farmer access to land, there is a special rule that reduces the tax burden on farmers who sell their land rather than holding it until death.

Benefit ⬤

If you sell farmland after July 4, 2025, you can elect to spread the reporting of capital gains over 4 years instead of reporting it all in the year of the sale. If the sale took place before July 5, 2025, or you do not meet the conditions below, you can still spread the reporting of gain if you receive at least one payment after the year of the sale. See Installment Sales in Chapter 8.

Conditions

To qualify for this option, there are 3 conditions:

1. You must be a qualified farmer. This means you are actively engaged in farming and not a mere investor.
2. You owned the farmland for at least 10 years. Land leased to a qualified farmer for at least 10 years also qualifies.
3. As part of the sale, there is a restrictive covenant that the land will continue to be used as farmland for at least 10 years.

Planning Tip

If you are considering a sale of your farm, watch the 10-year farmland use rule to ensure you have access to the election for spreading the gain from a sale over 4 years.

Pitfall

So-called gentlemen-farmers who own a farm but do not personally work it may not qualify for this 4-year rule.

Where to Report the Gain

The IRS has not yet provided guidance on how to elect to use the 4-year reporting rule for farm sales. See the Supplement for any update.

Business Credits

Not every business expense is treated as a deductible item. Some expenses qualify as tax credits that can be used to reduce tax liability on a dollar-for-dollar basis.

Benefit ⊕

Other expenses you incur in your business may entitle you to a tax credit, which reduces your taxes dollar for dollar. The offset usually is against federal income tax. Those that offset certain payroll taxes are explained under *Planning Tips*. In Table 14.2 on page 414 you will see a listing of tax credits that offset income taxes, the forms you use to figure them, and where the credits are discussed in this book.

TABLE 14.2 Tax Credits

Tax Credit	IRS Form	For More Information, See Chapter
Alcohol fuels credit	6478	14
Alternative fuel vehicle refueling credit	8911	
Alternative motor vehicle credit	8910	
Biodiesel and renewable diesel fuel credit	8864	
Commercial clean vehicle credit	8936	7
Credit for contributions to certain community development corporations	8847	
Credit for employer-paid FICA on certain tips received by employees of food and beverage establishments	8846	14
Disabled access credit	8826	
Distilled spirits credit	8906	
Employer-provided child care facilities and services	8882	
Employer credit for wage differential payments to activated military reservists	8932	
Empowerment zone employment credit	8844	14
Energy efficient home credit	8908	
Investment credit (including rehabilitation property credit)	3468	11
Low-income housing credit	8586	11
Low sulfur diesel fuel production credit	8896	
New clean vehicle credit	8936	7
New markets credit	8874	
Orphan drug credit	8820	
Paid family and medical leave credit	8994	
Previously-owned clean vehicle credit	8936	7
Renewable electricity production credit	8835	
Research credit	6765	
Small employer health credit	8941	
Small employer pension plan start-up costs, auto-enrollment, retirement plan contributions, and military spouse participation credits	8881	
Work opportunity credit	5884	14

Conditions

Each credit has its own conditions. Many of the credits are part of the general business credit, which isn't a separate credit but acts as an overall limitation on these credits. The limit for the general business credit is your regular tax liability (after credits other than those that are part of the general business credit), plus any alternative minimum tax liability, minus whichever of the following is larger:

- Tentative AMT from Form 6251
- 25% of your regular tax liability (after other credits) over $25,000

Planning Tips

Credits in excess of the general business credit limitation are carried back one year and forward for up to 20 years until they are used up. Be sure to keep track of carryfowards so you do not fail to claim credits to which you may be entitled.

There is a special payroll tax offset for research expenses of small businesses. The research credit can offset up to $250,000 of the employer share of Social Security taxes and $250,000 of the employer share of Medicare taxes (both part of FICA).

Pitfall

A special limitation applies to tax credits related to passive activities. See Chapter 10 for more details.

Where to Claim the Credits

Figure the credits on the forms specified for each one. Then, if required, complete Form 3800, *General Business Credit*, to figure the overall limitation on certain credits.

The credits are entered on Schedule 3 of Form 1040 or 1040-SR. Small businesses that claim the research credit as an offset to the employer's Social Security and Medicare taxes check a box on Form 6765, *Credit for Increasing Research Activities* to elect this treatment. The credit is figured on Form 8974, *Qualified Small Business Payroll Tax Credit for Increasing Research Activities*. The credit is then claimed on Form 941, *Employer's Quarterly Federal Tax Return*.

Net Operating Losses

Not every business can be profitable year in and year out. What happens if your business suffers a loss from its operations that effectively wipes out more than your tax liability for the year? You may then have what is called a net operating loss (NOL). You may be able to use this loss to reduce taxes in prior and/or future years.

Benefit

If your business expenses for the year outweigh your income, your loss may give rise to a net operating loss (NOL) that can be used to offset income in certain other years. For NOLs arising in 2025, the loss is carried forward to offset income in future years. NOLs arising in prior years are carried forward to 2025; they offset taxable income for 2025. NOLs claimed in 2025 may offset 80% of taxable income. If the NOL is not used up, it can be carried forward. For farming businesses, there's an option to carry back the loss 2 years and then forward indefinitely.

The net operating loss deduction is not an additional loss deduction. Rather, it is the result of having deductions exceed your business income and applying this excess against income in other years.

Conditions

You must determine whether having a loss in your business for the year results in a net operating loss. You have an NOL if your adjusted gross income is a negative figure. But adjusted gross income for purposes of an NOL does not include certain deductions you are otherwise allowed to take. When figuring your NOL, increase your adjusted gross income by all of the following that apply to you:

- IRA deduction
- Alimony deduction for pre-2019 divorces and separation agreements
- Net capital losses (capital losses in excess of capital gains)
- Self-employed person's contribution to a qualified retirement plan

The qualified business income (QBI) deduction is not taken into account in figuring an NOL.

CARRYBACKS AND CARRYFORWARDS

Net operating losses arising in 2025 may not be carried back (there's an exception for farming businesses, which have a 2-year carryback). NOLs are only carried forward indefinitely until they are used up. Any NOLs carried forward from prior years offset 80% of taxable income in 2025.

Example

In 2024, you have a net operating loss of $100,000 that you carried forward to 2025. If your taxable income in 2025 is $100,000, you may use $80,000 as a net operating loss deduction on your 2025 return.

Planning Tips

Be sure to keep track of NOLs arising in different years, especially since they may be subject to different carryback and carryforward periods not discussed in this book.

Owners of pass-through entities are subject to a limit ("noncorporate loss limitation") on how much losses can be currently deducted. There's an income limit, which varies with filing status. Any loss in excess of this limit is carried forward and becomes part of the NOL.

Pitfall

Be sure to limit your NOL deduction to 80% of taxable income. Because of this 80% limit, the NOL can never bring your tax bill to zero.

Where to Claim the Deduction

Figure your net operating loss on Form 172, *Net Operating Losses (NOLs) For Individuals, Estates, and Trusts*.

A net operating loss is reported as a negative income item; it is not a direct offset to your business income. For example, if your net operating loss carryforward after application of the 80%-of-taxable income limit is $4,400, enter –4,400 on Schedule 1 of Form 1040 or 1040-SR.

Miscellaneous Items

There are some tax benefits that simply defy classification so they cannot be included in any other chapter. You may be entitled to claim them nonetheless.

This chapter explains a variety of miscellaneous tax breaks you may be entitled to claim. The standard deduction amount that can be claimed instead of itemizing personal deductions is explained in the introduction to this book. For more information see IRS Publication 525, *Taxable and Nontaxable Income*, and IRS Publication 529, *Miscellaneous Deductions*.

State and Local Income Taxes

Individuals in all but 8 states (Alaska, Florida, Nevada, South Dakota, Tennessee, Texas, Washington, and Wyoming) and the District of Columbia may be subject to income taxes (those in New Hampshire have an income tax on interest income and dividends only). There may also be income taxes on the local level. These taxes are deductible for federal income tax purposes up to a set limit if you itemize personal deductions.

Benefit

If you pay state and local income tax, through withholding or estimated tax payments, you can deduct the total amount as an itemized deduction up to a dollar limit. The total amount of state and local taxes that is deductible (including state or local income and real estate [SALT] taxes) cannot exceed $40,000 ($20,000 if you are married but file separately). This is referred to as the SALT cap or limitation.

Conditions

There are 3 conditions for claiming a deduction for state and local taxes:

1. You itemize deductions.
2. Your modified adjusted gross income (MAGI) does not exceed a set amount. A full deduction applies if MAGI is no more than $500,000. The deduction phases out so that once it reaches $600,000, the deduction for state and local taxes is limited to $10,000. All of the dollar limits are halved for married persons filing separately.
3. You do not deduct state and local sales taxes.

Looking Ahead

Starting in 2026, the MAGI limits for the SALT cap increases by 1% per year from 2026 through 2029.

Planning Tips

State income tax withholding reported on Form W-2 is deductible, subject to the SALT cap. Withholding includes not only state and local income taxes, but also mandatory contributions you make to state unemployment, disability, or family leave programs. States with one or more of these programs include Alaska, California, New Jersey, New York, Pennsylvania, Rhode Island, and Washington.

You may increase your deduction for state income tax for 2025 by prepaying the fourth installment of state estimated tax. Generally, the fourth installment for 2025 is due on January 15, 2026. This fourth installment would normally be deductible for federal income tax purposes in 2026. But you can pay it before the end of the year to increase the deduction for 2025.

If you deduct state and local income taxes as an itemized deduction, do not forget to add any 2024 state and local estimated taxes that were paid in January 2025 to total payments for 2025.

If, in 2025, you receive a refund of your 2024 state income taxes and you itemized in 2024, all, some, or none of the refund is taxable to you. This is explained later in this chapter under Tax Refunds.

The majority of states as well as New York City have created a way for owners of pass-through entities to get around the SALT cap with respect to state and local income taxes. This move involves having the business—partnership, limited liability company (including a one-member LLC that has elected to be taxed as an S corporation), or S corporation—elect to pay an entity-level tax on the owner's distributive share (a pass-through entity tax, or PTET). The owners then claim an offsetting refundable income tax credit based on the net income passed through to them. This effectively allows such owners to sidestep the SALT cap with respect to taxes on their distributive shares.

Some states allow you to claim a state or local tax credit for a transfer that's treated as a payment of state and local taxes, which is another way to sidestep the SALT cap. The IRS mostly nixed this option. But there is a de minimis exception that allows a deduction if the state credit for state and local taxes is no more than 15% of the amount transferred.

Pitfalls

You may not deduct your state and local income tax if you claim the standard deduction.

If you do not deduct state and local taxes (you do not itemize, or if itemizing, you opt to deduct state and local sales taxes) or your taxes exceed $40,000 ($20,000 if you are married and file separately), you lose any tax benefit from wage or salary contributions you make to state unemployment, disability, or family leave programs. Such amounts are withheld from your pay nonetheless.

Do not prepay state income tax if you are subject to the alternative minimum tax (AMT). State income tax is not deductible for AMT purposes, so prepaying effectively wastes the deduction.

The SALT cap is set to revert to the $10,000 limit applicable after 2028 unless Congress extends the current limit or makes it permanent.

Where to Claim the Deduction

The deduction is claimed on Schedule A of Form 1040 or 1040-SR.

State and Local Sales Taxes

There are more than 12,000 state and local sales tax jurisdictions throughout the United States. The amount of tax you pay depends on how much you buy each year and the state (or states) in which you live. The deduction for state and local sales taxes up to a set limit can be claimed only if you itemize deductions and you do not deduct state and local income taxes.

Benefits

You can deduct state and local sales taxes paid during the year as an itemized deduction. You can claim your actual payments based on receipts for purchases or rely on an IRS table in the instructions to Schedule A of Form 1040 or 1040-SR. The total amount of state and local sales tax (SALT) that is deductible in 2025 (including these sales taxes) cannot exceed $40,000 ($20,000 if you are married but file separately). The SALT limitation applies to these taxes.

Conditions

The conditions for deducting state and local sales taxes under the SALT cap are explained earlier in this chapter under the deduction for state and local income taxes. If you deduct state and local income taxes, you cannot deduct sales taxes, and vice versa.

"Income" for purposes of the IRS optional state sales tax tables is based on total available income for a family. Taxable income for the tables is increased by nontaxable items such as tax-exempt interest; veterans' benefits; nontaxable combat pay; workers' compensation; nontaxable part of Social Security and Railroad Retirement benefits; nontaxable part of IRA, pension, or annuity distributions (but no rollovers); and public assistance payments.

Planning Tips

You can increase the deduction state and local general sales taxes paid on the following items *only*:

- Car
- Motorcycle
- Motor home
- Recreational vehicle
- Sport utility vehicle
- Truck
- Van

- Off-road vehicle
- Leased motor vehicle

You figure the deduction from IRS tables and then add the sales tax on the listed items you bought. If you use the IRS Sales Tax Deduction Calculator at https://apps.irs.gov/app/stdc/, the sales tax on the listed items is taken into account by the calculator based on the information you provide. You can also add in sales taxes paid on an aircraft, a boat, a mobile home, a prefabricated home, or home building materials as long as the tax rate is the same as the general sales tax rate.

If you live in more than one state, you must allocate the deduction found in the IRS tables for the number of days you lived in that state.

Example

If you lived in Arizona for 6 months and New Jersey for the other 6 months, your total deduction for state and local sales taxes is one-half of your amount from the table for Arizona and one-half of your amount from the table for New Jersey.

Just because you live in a state in which you pay income taxes, do not assume that that deduction will be larger than the one for state sales tax. You may have a higher sales tax deduction if you fall into any of the following situations:

- A retiree whose income is primarily from Social Security benefits, certain types of annuities and pensions, and interest on Treasury securities.
- A self-employed individual who had a bad year.
- A person who was laid off from a job.
- A disabled worker who receives nontaxable state disability and workers' compensation payments.

Pitfall

State and local sales taxes that are itemized are not deductible for alternative minimum tax (AMT) purposes, so claiming the deduction in this manner can trigger or increase your AMT liability.

Where to Claim the Deduction

The deduction is claimed on Schedule A of Form 1040 or 1040-SR. Be sure to check the appropriate box on the schedule to indicate that you are claiming a deduction for general sales taxes.

Certain Federal Taxes

Most federal taxes you pay, such as income taxes and the employee share of FICA, are not deductible. But there are some deductible federal taxes:

- Employer equivalent portion (one-half) of self-employment tax (see Chapter 14)
- Employer share of FICA on wages paid to employees
- Estate tax paid on income in respect of a decedent (see later in this chapter)

Tax Refunds

The IRS reported in May 2025 that it had thus far issued nearly 94 million refunds out of the more than 145 million returns for 2024 received, with an average refund of $2,939. Certain refunds, such as refunds of federal income taxes, are fully tax free; state tax refunds may be taxable or tax free in the year in which you receive them, depending on the situation. You don't have to amend any prior year's return if some or all of your refund is taxable.

Benefit

The receipt of a tax refund may be taxable, or partially or fully tax free. Federal tax refunds are *always* tax free (because you are not allowed to deduct your federal income taxes). State and local tax refunds may be partially or fully taxable or tax free, depending on whether you itemized your deductions in the year in which the taxes were paid and certain other factors.

Conditions

If you receive a refund of state (and/or local) income tax for the year in which you claimed the standard deduction, none of the refund amount is taxable to you. For example, suppose you claimed the standard deduction on your 2024 federal income tax return. In 2025, you receive a check for $946 from your state representing a refund of state income tax that you overpaid for 2024. You do not have to report this refund on your 2025 federal income tax return.

If you itemized deductions on your 2024 federal income tax return and receive a refund of 2024 state income taxes in 2025, figure whether none, some, or all of the refund is taxable to you in 2025, based on the tax benefit rule (the benefit that the tax deduction afforded you). If you receive a refund of state income tax, the portion that is taxable and the portion that is tax free depends on the amount of your total itemized deductions as well as what you could have deducted for state and local sales tax instead of deducting state and local income tax after factoring in the SALT cap.

You include in gross income the lesser of:

- The difference between your total itemized deductions taken in the prior year and the amount of itemized deductions you would have taken in the prior year had you paid the proper amount of state and local tax, or
- The difference between your itemized deductions taken in the prior year and the standard deduction amount for the prior year (assuming you were not precluded from taking the standard deduction in the prior year).

Example

You are single and paid state and local taxes in 2024 totaling $19,000 ($5,000 of state income taxes and $14,000 of property taxes). You itemized deductions in 2024. In 2025, you receive a refund of $1,500 of state income taxes due to an overpayment. Because all of the refund in 2025 gave you a tax benefit in 2024 (total state and local taxes were below the SALT cap), all of the refund is includable in gross income in 2025.

Your computations become more complex, if your refund is more than the excess of the deduction you claimed for state and local taxes over what you could have deducted for state and local sales taxes. Generally, the full amount of the refund is taxable if it is less than the excess of the deduction claimed for state income tax in the prior year over what could have been deducted for sales tax, but you'll need to complete a worksheet found in IRS Publication 525.

Planning Tip

Many taxpayers look forward to receiving their federal income tax refunds, but this is poor tax planning. If you are entitled to a refund, then you've made an interest-free loan to the government. A better way is to adjust wage withholding and/or estimated tax payments so you more closely approximate your actual tax bill for the year. Given today's relatively low interest rates, it may make sense to err on the side of underpaying (so you'll owe the government money and some interest), rather than overpaying. The IRS interest rate on underpayments was 7% for each quarter of 2025.

Pitfalls

Whether you actually receive a refund check of state income taxes or apply it to your next year's state income tax bill, you'll have to determine whether none, some, or all of it is taxable, as explained earlier.

If you are owed a federal tax refund or rebate check, the government can apply it to any outstanding federal tax liability, delinquent child support payments, outstanding student loan payments, or certain other payments. The government will inform you by letter of how it applied your refund or rebate amount. If you receive any interest on a federal income tax return, it is includible in gross income.

Where to Claim the Benefit

You do not have to report your federal tax refund and/or rebate check on your federal income tax return. Refunds of state income taxes are reported to you on Form 1099-G, *Certain Government Payments*. If the state income tax refund is tax free, you do not have to report it on your return.

If any portion of a state income tax refund is taxable, it is reported on Schedule 1 of Form 1040 or 1040-SR. Where appropriate, be sure to enter your refund as a *negative* number on Form 6251 so you reduce the income reported for purposes of the alternative minimum tax (AMT).

Legal Fees

William Shakespeare said, "Let's kill all the lawyers." But when a person today wants to right a perceived wrong, he or she usually turns to a lawyer for assistance. The cost of this help, which can be very steep, can be deducted only in certain circumstances.

Benefit

Legal fees you pay for actions that include discrimination are deducted as an adjustment to gross income. Legal fees for certain other personal matters, such as personal injury cases, cannot be deducted.

Legal fees related to your business that meet deductibility conditions are ordinary and necessary business expenses that offset business income. Legal fees to acquire property (e.g., to buy a home) are added to the basis of the property and serve to reduce the amount of gain (or increase loss) when you sell it.

Condition

To be deductible, legal fees must relate to certain discrimination actions in connection with a whistleblower award, or your business. To deduct legal fees as an adjustment to gross income, the claim must be for unlawful discrimination (such as age discrimination on the job), claims against the federal government under Subchapter III of Chapter 27, Title 31, of the U.S. Code, and a private cause of action under the Medicare Secondary Payer statute.

Planning Tips

When engaging an attorney for representation, be sure you fully understand the fee arrangement. For example, even in a contingency fee arrangement (in which you owe no money if you do not recover anything), you may owe the attorney money to cover expenses, such as photocopying and postage, in addition to any portion of the award. And you may have to report the entire award even though you can't deduct the legal fees.

If you incur legal fees in contesting an IRS audit, you may be able to recover reasonable fees for litigation and administrative costs from the government. You must have exhausted available administrative remedies, you must have substantially prevailed in your action, and the government's position was not substantially justified. If you meet all these conditions, usually your recovery is limited to $250 per hour in 2025, although higher fees can be awarded under limited circumstances.

Pitfall

If you pay legal fees to buy property, don't forget to add them to your basis. If you overlook this addition, you'll wind up with a bigger gain than you need to have.

Example

You buy investment property for $100,000 and pay $5,000 in legal fees. You cannot deduct the fees, but you can add them to the basis of the property. Assume that a few years from now you sell the property for $150,000. Your gain is $45,000 ($150,000 − [$100,000 + $5,000]). In effect, you have reduced your gain for tax purposes by the $5,000 in legal fees you added to the property's basis.

Where to Claim the Benefit

You report legal fees related to discrimination claims up to the amount of the award on Schedule 1 of Form 1040 or 1040-SR. You report legal fees paid in connection with an award from the IRS for information provided to help the IRS detect tax law violations ("whistleblower award") up to the amount of the award on Schedule 1 of Form 1040 or 1040-SR.

You report deductible legal fees related to your business or investment properties on the appropriate form: Schedule C, Schedule E, or Schedule F of Form 1040 or 1040-SR.

Gifts You Receive

Whether your birthday gift is a tie, a set of golf clubs, or a check for $25,000, you usually can treat the gift as tax free for income tax purposes. The gift doesn't have to relate to a special occasion, such as Mother's Day or an anniversary, and it doesn't have to come from a relative. All you need is for the transfer to be a true gift and not something else (such as disguised compensation).

Benefit ⊗

Gifts you receive from just about anyone are tax free. Gifts can be in cash or property. There is no dollar limit on the amount of gifts you can exclude from income each year.

Important: Your income tax treatment is separate and distinct from the gift tax rules imposed on the gift's giver (the donor). The fact that a donor can make gifts free from gift tax only up to a set dollar amount per person per year ($19,000 in 2025) does not affect your receipt of the gift. Even if the donor exceeds this limit, your receipt is still entirely tax free for income tax purposes.

Condition

To be treated as a tax-free gift, the transfer must be made with donative intent (a substantive view toward making a gift) and the recipient cannot pay any consideration for receiving it. In most cases, it is entirely clear that a transfer of property is intended as a gift. There are 2 key situations in which the transfer may not be entirely clear and tax-free treatment is not assured:

1. When money is really intended as a loan rather than a gift (see Chapter 11 for rules on distinguishing between a gift and a loan, especially when the parties are related).
2. When money or property is given to employees (see "Pitfalls").

Planning Tip

When you receive a gift of property, be sure to obtain from the donor the following information needed to determine your gain or loss when you later dispose of the property:

- *The donor's basis.* If the basis of the property at the time of the gift was at least equal to its value at that time, then your basis becomes the donor's basis. If the gift's value was less than its basis at the time of the gift (the property had declined in value), then your basis for purposes of determining gain is the donor's basis, but your basis for determining loss is the value of the gift at the time it was made to you. It is possible under the right circumstances that because of these special basis rules, you may realize neither a gain nor a loss when you sell the gift.

- *The donor's holding period.* You can add to the time you own the property all of the donor's holding period. For example, assume the donor purchased stock on July 1, 2021, and gives you the shares on May 1, 2025. If you sell those shares on May 15, 2025, your gain or loss is *long term* gain or loss because the shares are considered to have been held for more than one year (the holding period begins with the donor's holding period).

A donor who is required to file a gift tax return must provide you with the following information within 30 days after the gift tax return's due date (usually April 15 of the year after the year of the gift):

- The name, address, and telephone number of the person required to file the tax return.
- The information specified in the gift tax return (a description of the gift and its value at the time of the gift).

Pitfalls

Money or items received from your employer that are labeled as gifts may, in fact, be nothing more than additional compensation. Small items, such as a holiday turkey or ham, are tax-free gifts to you. But gifts of *any* cash or cash equivalents (such as gift certificates and gift cards) and more expensive items (such as golf clubs) are considered taxable compensation, not tax-free gifts.

Income earned on a gift is taxable (unless such income is also tax-free income).

Example

You receive a gift of $10,000. The receipt of the gift is tax free to you. You use the money to buy a Treasury bill: Interest on the investment is taxable to you. If you use the money to buy a municipal bond, the interest on the investment is tax free because municipal bond interest is tax free.

There is no income tax deduction for *making* a gift. While some gifts may be free from gift tax, there is no break for income tax purposes when you make a gift to an individual. Charitable contributions to IRS-approved organizations are another matter; they are discussed in Chapter 6.

Where to Claim the Benefit

Since gifts are tax free, you do not report them on your return.

Inheritances

Whether you inherit your uncle's gold watch or your mother's entire million-dollar estate, you are not taxed on this inheritance. There are no limits to the amount you can inherit tax free.

While the receipt of an inheritance is always tax free, some inheritances may produce taxable income later on. For example, if you inherit a $100,000 traditional IRA, you are not immediately taxed on the inheritance; there's no tax as long as the funds remain in the IRA. As you start to withdraw funds from the IRA (and you're required to do so in order to satisfy the required minimum distribution rule), you are taxed on this amount. Fortunately, you are entitled to claim a tax deduction for any federal estate tax attributable to this taxable income, called income in respect of a decedent (IRD), which is explained later in this chapter.

Benefit

Inheritances you receive are tax free. There is no dollar limit on the amount of an inheritance you can exclude from income.

Condition

There are no conditions on the tax-free receipt of an inheritance other than the fact you receive the inheritance on account of the death of a person. Inheritances include amounts paid to you under a will, or by the state's rules of intestacy (if the person died without a will), jointly owned property you receive in full when your co-owner dies, and other amounts you receive as a named beneficiary (for example, a person's pension benefits left to you as the designated beneficiary or a bank account you receive because of a transfer-on-death designation).

Planning Tips

When you inherit property, your basis usually becomes the value of the property for estate tax purposes (generally, the property's value on the date of death). This is called a "stepped-up basis." Also, you automatically have a long-term holding period, regardless of how long the decedent owned the property before death or how long you hold it after you inherit it.

Example

On December 20, 2024, you inherit 100 shares of X Company from a decedent who purchased them on November 15, 2018, at $10,000. On the date you inherit them, they are worth $12,000. Two weeks later in 2025, you sell them for $13,000. You have a long-term capital gain in 2025 of $1,000 ($13,000 − $12,000).

For inheritances from certain decedents dying in 2010, there was a modified carryover basis rule (very few estates opted to use this rule). If the estate elected to use the zero estate tax rule, then the basis to an heir is the same as the basis that the decedent had in the property. The stepped-up basis rule continues to apply to the first $1.3 million of an estate, with an additional $3 million passing to a surviving spouse; this amount is allocated by the executor to property passing from the decedent.

Pitfalls

If you inherited property from a person whose estate tax return was required to be filed after July 31, 2015, and received Schedule A of Form 8971 from the estate, you must use the basis specified on this schedule. This is the same amount that the estate used on the decedent's estate tax return. If you use a basis for inherited property that is inconsistent with the amount reported on this schedule, you may be subject to a 20% accuracy-related penalty.

If you anticipate an inheritance and sell your right to receive it, the proceeds you receive are taxable as ordinary income. This is so even though you would have received tax-free income had you waited for the inheritance itself.

If you are named as the executor, administrator, or personal representative of an estate, payment of fiduciary fees to you are *not* tax-free inheritances, even if you are also an heir to the estate.

Income earned on an inheritance is taxable (unless the income is also tax-free income—see the earlier example under "Gifts"). Income includes amounts on assets that previously have gone untaxed, such as traditional IRAs mentioned earlier and annuities.

Example

You are named as the beneficiary of your father's IRA. When he dies, there is $100,000 in the IRA. Your inheritance of this IRA is tax free. Since your father never paid income tax on the funds, you must do so under the required

> minimum distribution (RMD) rules for IRAs (explained in Chapter 5 and in greater detail in IRS Publication 590-B, *Distributions from Individual Retirement Arrangements*). The IRA proceeds are taxable when and to the extent you take withdrawals from the IRA. And you can be penalized if you don't take what you should under the RMD rules.

Where to Claim the Benefit

Since inheritances are tax free, you do not report them on your return.

Life Insurance Proceeds

The beneficiary of a life insurance policy generally can receive the proceeds free from income tax. There is no requirement that the beneficiary be related to the insured (the person on whose life the insurance is based), and there is no limit on the amount of proceeds that can be received tax free.

Benefit

Life insurance proceeds you receive on account of the death of the insured are tax free to you. There is no dollar limit on the amount you can receive tax free.

Condition

To be tax free, life insurance proceeds must be payable on the death of the insured. The insured may be the same person as the owner of the policy or may be someone else.

Planning Tip

Life insurance proceeds can be used during the insured's life on a tax-free basis under certain conditions. The treatment of accelerated death benefits is explained in Chapter 2.

Pitfalls

If you leave insurance proceeds with the insurance company, interest you receive is taxable.

If you paid any consideration for the life insurance policy, then you are taxable on the proceeds. You are treated as having paid consideration if you become the policy owner and there is an outstanding loan on the policy.

> **Example**
>
> A mother has a $100,000 life insurance policy against which she has borrowed $10,000. She gives the policy to her daughter (receipt of the policy is a tax-free gift to the daughter). Shortly thereafter, the mother dies and the daughter collects $90,000 ($100,000 face value of the policy minus the outstanding loan of $10,000). The daughter is taxed on the $90,000.

If you borrow against the policy and then let the policy lapse without repaying the loan, you may have constructive income (income that's taxed to you even though you don't receive the cash). The insurance company will apply the balance of the policy toward outstanding principal and interest on the loan and then issue you Form 1099-R stating the taxable amount.

Where to Claim the Benefit

Where life insurance proceeds received on account of the death of the insured are tax free, you do not have to report them on your return.

Gambling Losses

The National Council on Problem Gambling says Americans spent nearly $150 billion on gambling in 2024. Everyone knows that the odds always favor the house, whether it is a casino, race track, or state lottery. The chances of losing far outweigh those of winning. The tax law allows gambling losses to be deductible within limits under certain conditions.

Benefit

You can deduct gambling losses, plus the costs of wagering (e.g., traveling to a casino) to the extent of your gambling winnings for 2025. The losses do not have to result from the same gaming activities that produce the winnings.

If you are not a professional gambler, then gambling losses are claimed as miscellaneous itemized deductions.

If you are a professional gambler who devotes full time to this activity, you can treat your losses as a business expense. But even in this case gambling losses are limited to the extent of your winnings. And you can't claim the standard deduction.

Looking Ahead

Starting in 2026, the deduction for gambling losses is limited to 90% of losses. This means that the full offset to gambling winnings no longer applies. For example, if a gambler has $100,000 of gambling losses and $100,000 of gambling winnings in 2026, the deduction for losses is limited to $90,000; $10,000 of winnings becomes taxable ("phantom") income even though there is no net gain.

Example

During 2025, you spend $20 every week to play bingo ($1,040 for the year) and you do not win anything. But in December 2025, you win $500 on a state-sponsored scratch-off game. If you itemize deductions rather than claiming the standard deduction in 2025, you can deduct $500 of your bingo losses; the other $540 of your gambling losses is not deductible, and cannot be carried forward to offset winnings in a future year.

Conditions

You must itemize deductions rather than claiming the standard deduction. You report the gambling winnings that equal or exceed your claimed losses for the year for which you have adequate records or receipts to prove your gambling expenses.

The Tax Court says that gambling winnings can include "comps" given to high rollers by a casino, such as a car, jewelry, and tickets to sporting events.

Planning Tips

Keep track of the amount you gamble throughout the year, since you don't know when in the year you will win. For example, retain all losing lottery tickets as proof of your gambling expenses so you can claim these losses when and to the extent you have winnings for the year. If you play the slots, whether you win or lose is calculated with reference to your wager for the day. If you wager $100 in slot tokens, for example, and at the end of the day redeem $60, you have a $40 loss even though you may have had a winning spin of $1,000 during the day.

For the slot machines, determine "losses" carefully. The IRS says your losses are determined as of the end of a calendar day or the casino's gaming day (at the casino's option). Compare what you start the day with against the amount you have at the end to determine your loss (or gain). For example, if you start with $100 and at the end of the day you have only $50, you have a $50 gambling loss even though you may have hit jackpots throughout the day of $200 or $2,000, or had losing spins of more than $50. The casino must report winnings of $1,200 or more on Form W-2G, with no reduction for the amount of the wager.

Pitfalls

Gambling winnings may be reported to you (and the IRS) on Form W-2G, *Certain Gambling Winnings*. The reporting threshold depends on the type of gambling (e.g., horse racing, slot machines, lotteries). If you claim losses in excess of amounts reported to the IRS, be prepared to show you had other winnings and that you reported these other winnings as income on your return.

Be sure to pay sufficient taxes on winnings to avoid estimated tax penalties. Winnings of $5,000 or more are subject to income tax withholding, but this withholding may not adequately cover your liability; you are entirely responsible for estimated taxes on smaller winnings.

Where to Claim the Deduction

If you are not a professional gambler, you claim a deduction for gambling losses in the space provided on Schedule A of Form 1040 or 1040-SR for miscellaneous itemized deductions.

If you are a full-time professional gambler, you can treat your gambling losses as a business expense. The wages must be placed only for your own account. Gambling losses in this case are reported on Schedule C of Form 1040 or 1040-SR.

Estate Tax Deduction on Income in Respect of a Decedent

If you inherit something on which you must pay income taxes because the person who left you the inheritance never did, then you may be eligible for a special deduction related to federal estate taxes paid on certain types of assets left to you. To claim this special deduction, certain conditions must be met. And because there may be no estate tax because of the high estate tax exemption ($13.99 million for a person dying in 2025), this deduction is only for heirs of very wealthy decedents.

Benefit ☰

If you inherit a traditional IRA, annuity, or other income in respect of a decedent (IRD) and must report income from this inheritance, you may be eligible for a miscellaneous itemized deduction for the portion of federal estate tax related to this property. There is no dollar limit on this deduction.

Conditions

To claim this deduction, the IRA, annuity, or other income in respect of a decedent (any income that the decedent earned before death but was not taxable to him or her at that time) must have been part of an estate that was subject to federal estate taxes. State estate or inheritance taxes are not deductible.

Examples of IRD:

- Accounts payable to self-employed business owners on the cash basis
- Benefits from 401(k) and other qualified retirement plans
- Damage awards from lawsuits
- Deferred compensation
- Health Savings Accounts
- Interest on U.S. savings bonds that has been deferred
- Royalties
- Survivor annuities
- Traditional IRAs

Assuming there has been federal estate tax paid on income in respect of a decedent, then figure the portion of the estate tax deductible in the current year. If, for example, you withdraw all of the IRA funds, then all of the estate tax related to this asset is deductible this year.

Example

You inherit a $120,000 IRA from your brother, and your sister inherited an $80,000 IRA from him, so the total IRD from the brother's estate is $200,000. The federal estate tax on your brother's estate is $94,600. The estate determines that without including the IRA and other income in respect of a decedent, the federal estate tax would have been $48,400. The estate tax that qualifies for a deduction is $46,200 ($94,600 − $48,400). This year you empty the inherited IRA, and include $120,000 in your gross income. You can take an itemized deduction of $27,720 for your share of the estate tax, figured as follows:

$$\frac{\text{Value included in your income}}{\text{Total value of IRD}} \times \text{Federal estate tax qualifying deduction}$$

$$\frac{\$120,000}{\$200,000} \times \$46,200 = \$27,720$$

The calculation on the portion of estate tax can become complex when only part of the IRA is withdrawn within the year. A full explanation of how to figure this deduction may be found in IRS Publication 559, *Survivors, Executors, and Administrators*.

Planning Tips

This deduction is often overlooked. If you inherited an IRA from a wealthy individual and have not been claiming the deduction every year in which you report a distribution from the account, consider filing amended returns for all open tax years. You generally have 3 years from the due date of the return to file an amended return. This means you may be able to file for the prior 3 years and obtain tax refunds for each year.

When you receive an inheritance of IRD, be sure to ask the executor for information about estate taxes so you can figure your deduction. Find out about the amount of federal estate tax, the total estate, and what portion of it is the IRD you inherited.

Pitfall

There is no downside to claiming this deduction where allowable. But you must itemize to do it; you can't claim the standard deduction.

Where to Claim the Deduction

Generally, you report this deduction as a miscellaneous itemized deduction on Schedule A of Form 1040 or 1040-SR. When the income in respect of a decedent is long-term capital gain (such as an installment payment on a sale made before the decedent's death), the deduction is not claimed separately but rather treated as an expense of sale. This means you still get the benefit of the deduction, but in the form of a reduction of the gain you report.

Rebates and Discounts

Retailers may offer various rebates or discounts to induce you to buy their products. You may receive an immediate price reduction or, if you submit paperwork, you can get a check in the mail. These rebates and discounts are not taxable to you.

Benefit ⊗

The receipt of a check representing a rebate for purchasing an item is not income. For instance, if you buy a car, you may be able to apply a $1,000 manufacturer's rebate to the purchase price of the car, saving you $1,000 on the spot. Or, if you purchase a computer within a certain time, you may be able to send in a copy of your receipt and proof of purchase to receive a check payable to you (you often have to wait 6 to 12 weeks for this check).

Either way, the IRS says this rebate arrangement doesn't produce any taxable income for you. Instead, it's as if the rebate simply reduced the price of the item you purchased.

Special break for clean vehicle credit bought by dealer. If you acquired a plug-in electric clean vehicle between January 1, and September 30, 2025—new or used—you may be eligible for a clean vehicle credit. At the time of the sale, you had the option of letting the dealer buy the credit from you. This credit transfer had the effect of reducing the purchase price; it does not generate any income to you. The credit is explained in greater detail in Chapter 7.

Planning Tips

While mail-in rebates have declined (and only 40% of these are redeemed correctly), the number of rebates offered through smartphones continues to increase. Check for rebates when you purchase goods.

If your credit card has a rebate program under which you have the option of receiving cash or donating your accrued benefit to charity, the IRS says you are *not* taxed on the benefit, whichever option you choose. What is more, if you itemize and apply your benefit to a charity, you can claim a charitable contribution deduction as long as you meet substantiation requirements (i.e., obtain a written acknowledgment for a donation of $250 or more).

Pitfall

There is no downside to submitting rebate claims, other than the brief time it takes you to do this.

Where to Claim the Benefit

You do not report any rebates or discounts that qualify as tax free to you.

Government Benefits

Individuals may receive payments from the federal and/or state government for a variety of reasons. In many cases, these benefits may be received entirely tax free.

Benefit

Many types of government payments can be received tax free; they are excludable without regard to their amount or your income.

Condition

Most government benefits or payments are fully or partially tax free. Any taxable amounts are usually reported to you on an information return:

- Form RRA-1099, *Payment by the Railroad Retirement Board*
- Form SSA-1099, *Social Security Benefit Statement*
- Form 1099-G, *Certain Government Payments* (for unemployment benefits, RTAA payments, agricultural payments, and taxable grants)

As a practical matter, many types of government benefits are payable to individuals whose incomes are below the level at which a tax return must be filed and taxes are owed. In effect, even taxable benefits become tax free.

EXAMPLES OF FULLY TAX-FREE BENEFITS

- Black lung benefit payments.
- Crime victim payments from a state fund for this purpose.
- Disaster relief and disaster mitigation grants (see Chapter 12).
- East Palestine, Ohio, derailment payments to victims by a common carrier (treated as a tax-free disaster payment)
- Energy conservation subsidies paid by public utilities.
- Federal Employees' Compensation Act (FECA) payments for personal injury or sickness (including death benefits to beneficiaries).
- Federal income tax refunds.
- Foster care provider payments (see Chapter 1).
- Foster Grandparents Program payments for supportive services or reimbursement for out-of-pocket expenses.
- Grants for homes designed for wheelchair living of disabled veterans.
- Grants for motor vehicles for veterans who have lost their sight or the use of their limbs.
- HFA Hardest Hit Fund payments to distressed homeowners.
- Historic preservation grants under the National Historic Preservation Act.
- Holocaust victims restitution (see Chapter 12).
- Interest on insurance dividends left on deposit with the Department of Veterans Affairs.
- Military benefits (see Chapter 13).

- Mortgage assistance payments under Section 235 of the National Housing Act (the homeowner cannot deduct interest paid by this assistance).
- Nutrition Program for the Elderly food benefits.
- Peace Corps payments for housing, food, utilities, and clothing.
- SCORE payments for supportive services or reimbursement for out-of-pocket expenses.
- Senior program payments for supportive services or reimbursement for out-of-pocket expenses.
- Social Security lump-sum death benefit of $255 payable to a surviving spouse.
- State income tax refunds if you did not itemize deductions in the year to which the payments relate.
- Supplemental Security Income (SSI) and Supplemental Security Disability Income (SSDI).
- Survivor benefits of deceased public safety officers (police and law enforcement officers, firefighters, chaplains, and rescue squad and ambulance crew members).
- Volunteer tax counseling for the elderly (TCE) reimbursements for transportation, meals, and other expenses.
- Volunteers in Service to America (VISTA) volunteers, living expense allowances.
- Welfare benefits.
- Winter energy cost reduction payments to qualified individuals.
- Workers' compensation benefits.
- Work-training program payments from state welfare agencies (as long as the payments, exclusive of extra allowances for transportation or other costs, do not exceed public welfare benefits otherwise receivable).
- Wrongful incarceration payments payable to those who were wrongfully incarcerated.

Just because a payment comes from the government does not automatically mean it is tax free. Some government payments are taxable.

EXAMPLES OF TAXABLE BENEFITS

- Alaska Permanent Fund dividend income
- Election precinct officials' payments

NOTE

The One Big Beautiful Bill Act did not change the rules for the taxation of Social Security benefits. It did provide a bonus deduction amount for seniors with income below set limits, effectively eliminating the tax on Social Security benefits for these individuals. The bonus deduction amount is explained in Chapter 1.

- Jury duty pay
- Peace Corps payments for leave allowances, readjustment allowances, and termination payments
- State lottery winnings

Social Security benefits. Social Security benefits may be fully or partially tax free, depending on your filing status, the amount of Social Security benefits, and other income, including tax-exempt interest. The same rules apply to equivalent Railroad Retirement benefits. Table 15.1 below shows the portion of benefits excludable from income. The income threshold includes total income plus tax-exempt interest and one-half of Social Security benefits.

Example

In 2025, you are single with income from wages and taxable interest of $18,000. You also receive $12,000 in Social Security benefits and $1,000 of tax-exempt interest, with no adjustments to gross income. Since total income ($18,000 + 50% of $12,000 + $1,000) does not exceed $25,000, none of your benefits are included in income; they are tax free.

This explanation of the taxation of Social Security benefits is a brief overview that does not include many nuances to be taken into account. For more complete information about excluding Social Security benefits, see IRS Publication 915, *Social Security and Equivalent Railroad Retirement Benefits.*

TABLE 15.1 Income Threshold for the Excludable Portion of Social Security Benefits

	100% Excludable	50% Excludable	15% Excludable
Married filing jointly	Up to $32,000	Over $32,000 but not over $44,000	Over $44,000
Married filing separately	—	—	Automatically applies
Other taxpayers	Up to $25,000	Over $25,000 but not over $34,000	Over $34,000

If Form SSA-1099 shows a negative number (the benefits you are required to repay for any reason exceed your annual benefits), you can't deduct the excess unless it is greater than $3,000. If the negative number exceeds $3,000, you may qualify to figure tax for the year in a special way (see "Repayment of Supplemental Unemployment Benefits" in Chapter 13). Most states with an income tax don't tax Social Security benefits, but some do to some extent.

Planning Tips

If you receive an information return—Form 1099-G—from the government reporting taxable benefits, then know you have to report them as income. Social Security benefits are reported on Form SSA-1099.

If you don't get an information return, check IRS Publication 525 to see which benefits are taxable and which are tax free.

Pitfall

Disability payments from Social Security are taxed in the same way as Social Security retirement benefits.

Where to Claim the Benefit

Those government benefits that are tax free do not have to be reported on your return. Social Security benefits are reported on line 6a of Form 1040 or 1040-SR. The taxable portion is entered on line 6b of Form 1040 or 1040-SR.

Olympic Medals

Americans won more than 100 medals at the Paris Olympics in 2024. Most American Olympians and Paralympians are not taxed on their winnings. The exclusion applies to the cash payments at the Paris Olympics in 2024 ($50,000 for gold, $22,500 for silver, and $15,000 for bronze) as well as the value of the medals (estimated to be about $750 for the gold and $450 for the silver; the bronze has little value). The next Winter Olympics are in 2026 and the next Summer Olympics are in 2028.

Athletes with adjusted gross income exceeding $1 million ($500,000 for married persons filing separately) cannot exclude their winnings.

Alternative Minimum Tax

The alternative minimum tax (AMT) is a parallel tax system that exists to ensure all taxpayers pay at least some tax, even if they can reduce their regular tax through legitimate deductions. You pay AMT to the extent it exceeds your regular tax. Only about 200,000 pay AMT because of changes to the AMT exemption amounts and other rules. Throughout this book, you have seen many examples of items that receive different tax treatment for regular tax and AMT purposes.

Benefit

You can claim an AMT exemption that may eliminate or at least minimize your AMT liability. The 2025 exemption amounts are $137,000 for married filing jointly or a surviving spouse, $88,100 for single taxpayers and heads of households, and $68,500 for married persons filing separately.

Looking Ahead

Starting in 2026, the exemption amounts reset to $500,000 for singles and $1,000,000 for joint filers. Then, starting in 2027, these exemption amounts are adjusted for inflation. Also starting in 2026, the phaseout rate for the exemptions occurs at the rate of 50% (instead of the 25% rate for 2025).

Conditions

There are no conditions for claiming this exemption. Simply apply the correct one for your filing status.

Planning Tip

Even if the exemption amount does not eliminate AMT liability, you can use various personal tax credits to reduce this liability. All nonrefundable personal credits could offset AMT liability.

Pitfall

The AMT exemption is subject to a phaseout for those with alternative minimum taxable income (AMTI) over a set amount. The exemption is reduced by $1 for every $4 over the phaseout threshold (at a 25% phaseout rate). Table 15.2 shows the phaseouts for 2025.

Where to Claim the Exemption

The exemption is claimed on Form 6251, *Alternative Minimum Tax—Individuals*, which is attached to Form 1040 or 1040-SR. If any AMT is owed, it is entered on Schedule 2 of Form 1040 or 1040-SR.

TABLE 15.2 2025 Phaseout Thresholds for the AMT Exemption

Filing Status	AMTI
Married filing jointly and surviving spouse	$1,252,700
Other filers	626,350

Items Adjusted Annually for Inflation

Law changes are one important way in which write-off amounts and restrictions on them change each year. But another, less obvious way is adjustments to certain amounts and limits reflecting cost-of-living changes. Cost of-living adjustments are pegged to the Chained Consumer Price Index for All Urban Consumers (C-CPI-U). Not all items subject to adjustment actually change each year, but the list of the items subject to change continues to grow.

To help you plan your taxes for the future, it's helpful to know that certain limits affecting exclusions, deductions, and credits are raised in step with increases in the cost of living (although some items may be adjusted downward if the times demand it). The following exclusions, deductions, and credits are subject to annual adjustments for inflation. Note that some of the annual adjustments do not begin until after 2025 as indicated.

401(k) 403(b), and 457 plan elective deferrals

accelerated death benefits daily dollar amount that can be paid tax free from a life insurance policy on account of chronic illness

adoption assistance programs the maximum dollar amount and AGI phaseout range

adoption credit the maximum dollar amount and the AGI phaseout range; refundable portion after 2025

affordable health coverage provided by an employer and which prevents eligibility for the premium tax credit

alternative minimum tax (AMT) exemption amount

alternative minimum taxable income for the 26% rate

Archer medical savings accounts the definition of a high-deductible plan (i.e., the range for an annual deductible) and the limit on out-of-pocket costs

attorney's fees recovery from the government

benefits limit for defined benefit plans the dollar limit on benefits under these plans for which contributions are figured on an actuarial basis

charitable distributions to charity the exclusion for transfers from traditional IRAs to a public charity (qualified charitable distributions) by those age 70 ½ and older

child tax credit the value used in determining the refundable credit; basic credit (starting in 2026)

compensation on which qualified retirement plan deductions are based the amount of compensation or self-employment income taken into account in figuring deductions for plan contributions

contribution limit for profit-sharing and other defined contribution plans the dollar limit on deductible contributions to these plans

contribution limit for SEPs the dollar limit on deductible contributions to these plans

dollar limit for depreciation and first-year expensing on luxury cars the maximum deduction for depreciation or first-year expensing for cars and light trucks weighing no more than 6,000 pounds, as well as the dollar limit for heavy SUVs

early distribution penalty exception for victims of domestic abuse

earned income credit the earned income amount, the maximum amount of the credit, the AGI phaseout range, and the disqualifying investment income amount

educational assistance plan dollar limit (starting in 2027)

excepted benefit health reimbursement arrangements the dollar limit on reimbursements

first-year expensing limit dollar limit on amount of equipment that can be expensed as well as the taxable income limit

flexible spending accounts for medical costs the employee salary reduction contribution limit and the carryover limit

foreign earned income exclusion the dollar amount that can be received tax free for performing services abroad

health savings accounts annual deductibles and contributions limits to HSAs for high-deductible health plans

insubstantial benefits from charities dollar limit on what constitutes insubstantial benefits (ignored when figuring charitable contribution deductions)

interest exclusion on savings bonds AGI phaseout range

interest on student loans AGI phaseout range

IRAs contribution limits and MAGI limits for active participants to make deductible IRA contributions

long-term care premiums dollar limit on annual contributions treated as deductible medical expenses

low-income housing credit amounts used to calculate the state housing credit ceiling

parking dollar limit on employer-provided tax-free parking

payments received under long-term care policies or accelerated death benefits daily dollar limit excludable without regard to long-term care expenses or terminal illness

premium tax credit income eligibility threshold

qualified business income deduction taxable income amounts; minimum deduction (adjustment starting in 2027)

qualified charitable distributions the maximum annual limit

qualified longevity annuity contract the maximum contribution

qualified small employer health reimbursement arrangement amounts excludable

retirement savers credit MAGI limit on eligibility to claim a credit for making certain elective deferrals and IRA contributions

Roth IRAs MAGI limit on eligibility to contribute to this retirement savings plan

Social Security wage base for FICA and self-employment tax limit on income taken into account in figuring the Social Security portion of FICA and self-employment tax

standard deduction dollar amount

standard mileage rate for business travel the cents-per-mile rate may be increased or decreased

standard mileage rate for medical driving the cents-per-mile rate may be increased or decreased

transportation fringe benefits dollar limit on excludable free parking, monthly transit passes, and van pooling

Not all of the dollar amounts covered in this book are indexed annually for inflation. There are certain dollar amounts set by law or the IRS that are not adjusted for inflation. In doing tax planning for future years, you can rely on these fixed amounts (unless Congress decides to change them). The following items are *not* adjusted annually:

achievement awards an exclusion for receiving these awards is limited to $1,600 for qualified awards and $400 for nonqualified awards.

business gifts these are deductible only up to $25 per recipient each year.

business travel substantiation no receipts are needed for travel costs under $75 (except for lodging).

capital losses up to $3,000 ($1,500 if married filing separately) of capital losses in excess of capital gains for the year can be used to offset ordinary income.

charitable contribution substantiation rules the dollar thresholds for certain types of substantiation are fixed by law. Donations of $250 or more require a written acknowledgment from the charity. Donations of cars or other vehicles valued over $500 require a special acknowledgment. Appraisals are needed for donations of property valued over $5,000. Additional appraisal rules apply to donations of art valued at $20,000 or more.

Coverdell education savings accounts (ESAs) the maximum annual contribution is capped at $2,000 per year for an eligible beneficiary, and the MAGI limit for making a full contribution is up to $95,000 for singles and $120,000 for joint filers.

cruise ship travel for business the deduction is limited to $2,000.

dependent care assistance employer assistance is tax free up to $5,000 in 2025 ($7,500 in 2026). If your employer offers a dependent care flexible spending account, you can contribute up to the dollar limit annually from your compensation; the amount contributed is not taxed to you.

dependent care credit the maximum amount of eligible expenses taken into account in figuring the credit is $3,000 for one child and $6,000 for two or more children.

disaster losses there is a $100 reduction in the amount of each disaster loss for those who itemize deductions; it applies per event (not per damaged or destroyed).

early distribution penalty exceptions the 10% penalty for taking distributions from qualified retirement plans and IRAs does not apply for birth or adoption ($5,000), disaster recovery distribution ($22,000), and first-time homebuyer (IRAs only) ($10,000).

education credits the income limits on eligibility for the American opportunity credit and lifetime learning credit are fixed.

educational assistance plan dollar on the tax-free benefit (fixed through 2025)

foreign tax credit simplified reporting this is restricted to a foreign tax credit of no more than $300 ($600 on a joint return).

gift loans the below-market loan rules do not apply to gift loans up to $10,000 per recipient.

health savings account additional contribution limit those who are age 55 and older by year-end can add $1,000 to their applicable contribution limit for the year.

home sale exclusion up to $250,000 of gain ($500,000 on a joint return) on the sale of a principal residence can be excluded if certain conditions are met.

loans from qualified retirement plans the maximum loan is 50% of your vested account balance or $50,000, whichever is less (100% of vested benefits or $100,000 for disaster loans).

lodging for medical treatment lodging to receive outpatient care is deductible up to $50 per night ($100 per night if you are accompanying a sick child).

retirement plan reporting the threshold below which annual reporting of qualified retirement plans to the Department of Labor is $250,000.

Olympic medals the adjusted gross income limit for claiming the exclusion for the medals is limited to $1 million ($500,000 for married persons filing separately).

performing artists the conditions for such individuals to deduct their job expenses from gross income rather than as an itemized deduction are fixed. Adjusted gross income from all sources (not just performing) cannot exceed $16,000.

recovering attorney's fees and administrative costs from the government there is a net worth cap on individuals seeking a recovery. The cap is $2 million.

rental losses you can deduct up to $25,000 of rental losses each year if you actively participate in the rental activity and your adjusted gross income is no more than $100,000 (special rules apply to married persons filing separately).

reporting payments to independent contractors only payments of $600 or more in 2025 ($2,000 starting in 2026) to an independent contractor must be reported to the IRS.

section 1244 losses you can treat losses on certain small business stock as ordinary (rather than capital) losses up to $50,000 ($100,000 on a joint return).

standard mileage rate for charitable driving the rate is 14¢ per mile.

student exchange program if you host an exchange student in your home under an agreement with a charitable organization, you can deduct $50 per month as a charitable contribution.

student loan interest the maximum annual deduction is $2,500.

Checklist of Tax-Free Items

When items are not included in income, and in some cases not even reported on the return, there are considerable tax savings. Here is a list of tax-free items for 2025 tax returns.

- 529 plan withdrawals to pay qualified education costs
- ABLE account withdrawals to cover qualified expenses for a disabled beneficiary
- Accelerated death benefits under a life insurance policy
- Adoption costs paid by employer up to $17,280 in 2025
- Awards to certain employees (usually up to $1,600)
- Bequests
- Black lung benefit payments
- Capital gains and capital gain distributions for those with taxable income below a set amount
- Charitable transfers of IRA distributions up to $108,000 in 2025 by those age 70½ and older (reduced by post-70½ IRA contributions)
- Child support payments
- Coverdell education savings account withdrawals to pay education costs
- Crime victim payments from a state fund for this purpose
- Damages received for personal physical injury
- Damages received for wrongful incarceration

- Debt discharged during insolvency or bankruptcy
- Dependent care expenses paid by employer up to $5,000 in 2025 ($7,500 in 2026)
- Designated Roth account distributions (conditions apply)
- Disability payments under a policy in which you paid the premiums
- Disaster relief payments and disaster mitigation grants
- Discounts on purchases you make
- Dividends for those with taxable income below a set amount if the dividends are "qualified"
- Education courses paid by employer (fully excluded if job-related; up to $5,250 if not job-related)
- Federal Employees' Compensation Act (FECA) payments for personal injury or sickness (including death benefits to beneficiaries)
- Federal income tax refunds
- Flexible spending arrangement contributions from salary for health care or dependent care
- Foreign earned income up to $130,000 in 2025
- Foster care payments
- Foster Grandparents Program payments for supportive services or reimbursement for out-of-pocket expenses
- Frequent flyer miles you earn
- Fringe benefits from employers ("perks") if they are *de minimis*, an employee discount, working condition fringe benefits, or transportation fringe benefits
- Gifts
- Grants for homes designed for wheelchair living of disabled veterans
- Grants for motor vehicles for veterans who have lost their sight or the use of their limbs
- Health insurance tax credit for coverage months (the portion of premiums paid by the federal government)
- Health reimbursement arrangement (employer plan)—all reimbursements
- Health savings account distributions to pay for medical costs
- Historic preservation grants under the National Historic Preservation Act
- Home sale gain up to $250,000, or $500,000 on a joint return
- Inheritances

- Interest on insurance dividends left on deposit with the Department of Veterans Affairs
- IRA rollovers
- Life insurance proceeds
- Long-term care benefits under a policy to pay for the care of someone chronically ill ($420 per day limit in 2025 if benefits are paid under a per diem contract)
- Meals and lodging furnished on the employer's premises for the employer's convenience (accepting onsite lodging must also be a condition of employment)
- Military benefits, including combat pay and death benefits
- Minister's housing allowance
- Mortgage assistance payments under Section 235 of the National Housing Act
- Mortgage debt cancellation on a principal residence up to $750,000, or $375,000 for married filing separately (only for 2025)
- Mortgage loan proceeds (including proceeds on refinancing)
- Municipal bond interest
- Nutrition Program for the Elderly food benefits
- Payment for wrongful incarceration
- Peace Corps payments for housing, food, utilities, and clothing
- Prizes to certain employees (usually up to $1,600)
- Public safety officers' survivor benefits
- Rebates on purchases you make
- Restitution payments for Nazi victims and victims of human trafficking
- Retirement planning advice paid for by an employer
- Roth IRA distributions (all contributions, plus earnings in the account for at least 5 years that are withdrawn after age 59 ½, or on account of disability, death, or first-time homebuying)
- Savings bond interest if used to pay qualified higher education costs of certain taxpayers
- Scholarships, fellowships, and grants covering tuition, fees, books, supplies, and equipment for a degree program
- SCORE payments for supportive services or reimbursement for out-of-pocket expenses

- Senior Companion program payments for supportive services or reimbursement for out-of-pocket expenses
- Senior Corps program payments for supportive services or reimbursement for out-of-pocket expenses
- Small business stock gain (percentage of gain excludable depends on when the stock was issued and how long is was held before the sale)
- Social Security benefits if your income is below a threshold amount
- Student loan debt cancellation in some cases
- Supplement Security Income (SSI) and Supplement Security Disability Income (SSDI)
- Transportation fringe benefits up to $325 per month in 2025
- Tuition reduction for employees of educational institutions
- Vacation home rental income if the rental is no more than 14 days during the year

Checklist of Nondeductible Items

Unfortunately, not everything you spend your money on gives rise to a tax deduction or generates another type of tax break. Most of your personal expenses, such as food, clothing, and recreation, are nondeductible items. The same is true for most employee business expenses. The tax law also specifically bans certain write-offs. Of course, in some cases, while a deduction may be banned as a general rule, there may be circumstances under which it becomes deductible (so check throughout the book for exceptions to the general rule).

The IRS has identified a number of scams (the IRS calls them the "Dirty Dozen" because it identifies 12 scams each year) in which sharp promoters incorrectly advise taxpayers to claim certain types of write-offs. Here are some types of situations that the IRS has over the years cautioned taxpayers against:

- *Employee retention credit scams.* Promoters promise that just about every business is eligible for this credit when in reality only businesses that suffered a partial or full suspension of business operations are eligible. *If you think you are eligible and can still file an amended return, check with your CPA or other tax adviser to be sure.*

- *Online account help from third-party scammers.* These scammers pose as legitimate helpers on tax matters to gain access to personal information for identity theft. *Don't give out personal information to anyone you don't know or haven't verified as legitimate.*

- *Spearfishing.* This is phishing targeted to businesses to gain access to customers and clients. *Don't respond to any email or open any attachment if you don't know the sender.*

- *Phishing.* Scammers purporting to be from the IRS send e-mails seeking to obtain personal information used for identity theft. Spear phishing is a more sophisticated version aimed at tax professionals. *The IRS never contacts taxpayers by e-mail without prior notice of the communication; the IRS already has taxpayers' personal information.*

- *Tax advice from social media.* People online through TikTok and other social media platforms share wildly inaccurate tax advice, such as urging the self-creation of a W-2 as a way to fraudulently obtain a tax refund or stating there's a self-employment tax credit when there isn't one. *Don't blindly follow tax advice from social media. If you see something that sounds good, check it out through IRS FAQs or a tax professional before relying on it.*

- *Pervasive telephone scams.* Callers pretend to be from the IRS in order to steal money or identities ("vishing"). If you know you don't owe money (i.e., you never received a bill from the IRS), don't respond. *Instead, call the Treasury Inspector General for Tax Administration at 800-366-4484 to report the call.*

- *Identity theft.* This has topped the list of scams in the past several years, despite considerable IRS efforts to thwart it where taxes are concerned. Thieves are looking for ways to use a legitimate taxpayer's identity and personal information to file a tax return and claim a fraudulent refund. *Avoid problems with obtaining your legitimate refund by safeguarding your tax information; contact the IRS Identity Protection Specialized Unit.*

- *Preparer return fraud.* Dishonest tax return preparers, often promising refunds too good to be true, can leave taxpayers owing taxes and penalties for underpayments. Or they may have client refunds directed to themselves, leaving clients with difficulty obtaining what they are owed. *Taxpayers remain liable for taxes owed on their returns.*

- *Fake charities.* Scam groups masquerading as charitable organizations may lure people into making donations. These donations aren't tax deductible. *Check the IRS's online list of approved organizations at* https://apps.irs.gov/app/eos/ *before making a donation.*

- *Inflated refund claims.* Scam preparers induce taxpayers (usually those with low income or poor English skills) to claim inflated or erroneous write offs (e.g., false claims for education credits or the earned income tax credit), often based on fake Social Security benefits. They may use phony W-2s and 1099s to create the illusion of income. *Only use a reputable return preparer, as explained earlier.*

- *Inflated deductions.* Some may pad deductions, such as charitable contributions and business expenses to which they are not entitled. *Only claim deductions to which you are entitled. If you pad deductions, you may be subject to significant penalties and even criminal prosecution.*

- *Frivolous tax arguments.* Some promoters encourage taxpayers to make unreasonable and outlandish legal claims to avoid paying their taxes. These arguments don't hold up. *Don't be talked into using a frivolous argument. Read the truth about frivolous tax arguments from the IRS at* www.irs.gov/privacy-disclosure/the-truth-about-frivolous-tax-arguments-introduction.

- *Hiding income offshore.* The IRS is working with some offshore banks to learn the identity of depositors who fail to report their offshore income on their U.S. returns. *The IRS continues to develop investigation procedures to catch nonreporters.*

- *Filing false documents to hide income.* This usually involves inflating earned income to maximize the earned income tax credit to which a taxpayer is not eligible (or at least not in the amount claimed). *Taxpayers can be subject to penalties, interest, and even criminal prosecution.*

- *Excessive claims for business tax credits.* Scammers induce taxpayers to claim credits that they aren't eligible for, such as the credit for fuel used in off-highway vehicles (e.g., farm equipment) or the research credit designed for increasing research activities. *Taxpayers who agree to submit these claims may be liable to penalties of $5,000 for frivolous arguments or even criminal prosecution.*

- *Abusive tax shelters, trusts, and conservation easements.* These are investment schemes, which are listed or reportable transactions requiring taxpayers to disclose them on their returns; the schemes promise write-offs greater than amounts invested. *These schemes can result in both civil and criminal penalties.*

- *Trust deductions for personal expenses.* Promoters tell taxpayers to transfer their assets to trusts and have the trusts deduct the cost of food, clothing, and other personal expenses. *Personal expenses, other than those explained throughout the book, are not deductible.*

- *"Abuse of charitable deductions."* These abuses include attempts by donors to maintain control over donated assets or income from donated property. They also include schemes involving the donation of noncash assets, including easements on property, closely held corporate stock, real property, and overvaluations of property donations. *No deductions are allowed for illusory donations, and there are penalties for significant overvaluations.*

- *"No gain realized" deduction*. Like the claim of right doctrine, promoters tell taxpayers to claim a miscellaneous itemized deduction on Schedule A equal to their adjusted gross income. *There is no such deduction*.

- *Zero returns*. Promoters instruct taxpayers to enter all zeros on the return (rather than reporting their actual income items). *Income must be reported unless there is a specific tax rule for exemption or exclusion*.

- *Misuse of CRATs*. Charitable remainder annuity trusts (CRATs) are transactions in which a donor gives property to a charity but retains an annuity interest, usually for life or the life of the donor and spouse. However, the IRS says CRATs funded with property that has a fair market value higher than the tax basis as a way to step-up basis and eliminate potential ordinary income and capital gains to the donor when the trust sells the property is an abusive transaction. *This transaction must be disclosed on Form 8886*, Reportable Transaction Disclosure Statement.

- *Slavery reparations*. Promoters suggest that African Americans can claim a deduction or credit for reparations. *There are no such reparations and no such allowable deduction or credit*.

- *Home-based businesses*. While there is a deduction allowed for legitimate home-based businesses, promoters tell taxpayers to fictitiously create a business run from home so that a deduction will be allowed. *Fake businesses do not support real deductions*.

- *Shared earned income credits*. Promoters tell taxpayers that they can "share" dependents in order for multiple taxpayers to claim the earned income credit with respect to the same dependents. *Only eligible taxpayers can claim the earned income credit and only one credit is allowed for each dependent*.

- *Offer-in-compromise mills*. Companies make outlandish claims, usually in local advertising, about how they can settle a person's tax debt for pennies on the dollar if they pay a fee. They pay the fee whether or not eligible for relief. *Individuals can obtain the same results on their own, if eligible, by working with the IRS*.

Nondeductible Items

Here is a listing of items you may *not* deduct:

- Additional Medicare taxes on earned income and net investment income for high-income taxpayers
- Alimony payments under divorces or agreements executed after 2018
- Attorney's fees on buying a home

- Bank fees, such as monthly checking fees on a personal account
- Bar examination fees
- Blood donations
- Bribes
- Burial fees
- Car expenses (other than limited interest on car loans) for personal use of the car
- Child support payments
- Club dues for recreational, social, and athletic clubs
- Commuting expenses
- Compensation to housekeepers and other domestic employees
- Cosmetic surgery not medically needed
- Country club membership
- Credit card interest incurred for personal expenditures
- Debts belonging to another person that you pay
- Demolition costs
- Disability insurance premiums
- Education costs for your child's primary and secondary school
- Elective deferrals to 401(k) and similar plans
- Employee business expenses
- Entertainment costs
- Estimated tax penalties
- Expenses of earning tax-exempt income
- Federal income tax
- Fifty percent of meal costs for business
- Fines
- Funeral expenses
- Gambling losses in excess of winnings (only 90% of losses beginning in 2026)
- Gift tax
- Gifts you make to family and friends
- Health spa expenses
- Hobby losses
- Interest on loans to buy or carry tax-exempt securities
- Investment advisory fees

- Investment seminars
- IRA contributions by participants with AGI over set limits
- Job-related expenses
- Kickbacks
- Life insurance premiums
- Lobbying expenses (other than in-house expenses up to $2,000)
- Losses from the sale of your home, furniture, car, and other personal items
- Losses in excess of at-risk limits
- Losses on sales to related parties
- Lost or misplaced cash or property
- Lunches with coworkers
- Moving expenses
- Organ donations (e.g., a kidney)
- Over-the-counter medications for purposes of the itemized deduction (unless purchased with a prescription)
- Partially worthless securities
- Passive activity losses in excess of passive activity income
- Penalties
- Personal disability insurance premiums
- Personal interest (such as credit card interest)
- Personal living expenses (such as food, clothing, rent, and utilities)
- Pet food (other than for Seeing Eye dogs or therapy animals, which may be a deductible medical expense)
- Points paid to refinance a home mortgage
- Political contributions
- Professional accreditation fees
- Property settlements when dissolving a marriage
- Reimbursed expenses you receive under an accountable plan
- Repairs to your home or personal car
- Repayment of loans
- Rollover contributions
- Roth IRA contributions
- Sales tax if you deduct state and local income taxes
- Social Security and Medicare (FICA) taxes
- Spousal travel costs

- State and local income tax if you deduct state and local sales tax
- State inheritance taxes
- Stockholder meetings, expenses of attending
- Tax penalties
- Tax return preparation costs
- Title insurance
- Toiletries
- Travel as a form of education
- Uniforms
- Union dues
- Vacations
- Veterinary fees
- Voluntary alimony payments
- Voluntary unemployment benefit fund contributions
- Wash sale losses

Common Mistakes to Avoid

The IRS doesn't give you deductions and credits automatically; you have to claim them. It doesn't send you a refund of a tax overpayment; you have to submit a claim for it. And you may be missing out on tax-saving opportunities. All of these errors are mistakes that can be avoided. The IRS has a list of some common errors that can delay the processing of your return, resulting in having to wait for a refund or even triggering an audit of your return.

Mistake: Not filing electronically. The National Taxpayer Advocate has said that paper is the IRS's kryptonite. Filing electronically ensures your return is processed as quickly as possible, which is important if you are expecting a tax refund. Filing electronically also avoids math errors. You can file electronically with your computer, smartphone, or tablet, or use a tax return preparer who can e-file for you.

Mistake: Not using the correct filing status. You could miss out on tax-saving opportunities. Fortunately, tax software, including IRS Free File, also helps prevent this mistake when selecting a tax return filing status. If you are unsure about your filing status, the Interactive Tax Assistant on IRS .gov can help you choose the correct status, especially if more than one filing status applies.

Mistake: Failing to answer the digital asset question. The processing of your return will be delayed while the IRS sends you a letter asking for a response. If you received, sold, exchanged, or otherwise disposed of any financial interest in any digital asset in the year, you must answer "yes" on page one of your return. If you didn't do any of these things (e.g., you merely held digital assets), answer "no." Don't leave it blank.

Mistake: Failing to report all taxable income. Underreporting income may lead to penalties and interest. Organized tax records help avoid errors that lead to processing delays and may also help to find overlooked deductions or credits. Have all your income documents—W-2s, 1099s, K-1s—on hand before starting your tax return.

Mistake: Omitting unemployment compensation. This income is taxable in 2025 even though there had been a partial exclusion in 2020.

Mistake: Failing to verify the name, birth date, and Social Security number entries of dependents. Dependents affect filing status as well as eligibility for various deductions and tax credits. If you don't enter them correctly, you may lose out, so correctly list the name, Social Security number (SSN), and date of birth for each person claimed as a dependent on your return. Enter each SSN and individual's name on a tax return exactly as printed on the Social Security card. If a dependent or spouse doesn't have and is not eligible to get a SSN, list the Individual Tax Identification Number (ITIN).

Mistake: Failing to attach Form 8962 for the premium tax credit. If you received assistance with paying health insurance premiums for coverage obtained through the government marketplace, you must attach Form 8962. If you file electronically, your form won't be accepted for processing without it.

Mistake: Failing to attach Form 8936 to report the sale of a tax credit to a dealer on the purchase of an electric vehicle. The form must be filed even if you are entitled to the amount of the credit you transferred to the dealer when you acquired the vehicle before October 1, 2025.

Mistake: Having incorrect check routing and account numbers. If you want a tax refund to be directly deposited into a designated account, a wrong number will misdirect your refund. Double check that the financial institution routing and account numbers entered on the return are accurate.

Mistake: Mailing paper returns to the wrong address. Returns sent to the wrong IRS Service Center will delay processing (and the receipt of a tax refund where applicable). Paper filers should confirm the correct address for where to file on IRS.gov or on he form instructions, to avoid processing delays.

Mistake: Not signing and dating the return. Again, returns that aren't signed and dated won't be processed; the returns aren't complete. If filing a joint return, both spouses must sign and date the return. E-filers can sign using a self-selected personal identification number (PIN).

Mistake: Not keeping a copy of the return. When ready to file, make a copy of your signed return and all schedules for your records. Yes, you can obtain copies later on from the IRS, but why go through this hassle? You need copies to help you prepare future returns and you may also use them for other purposes (e.g., obtaining a home mortgage).

Mistake: Using a disreputable tax preparer. It's you, the taxpayer, who is responsible for what's on the return. Using a disreputable preparer may expose you to an audit, interest, and penalties.

Index